'A work of the highest quality about an astonishing man. It is gripping from start to finish, searingly shocking, revelatory and deeply moving – the more so because there is no false note, no striving for effect. The research is prodigious and the complexities deftly woven into the narrative . . . A profoundly troubling and important work'
Jonathan Dimbleby

'Astonishing . . . An indispensable part of Holocaust history'
*Guardian*

'*The Escape Artist* is marvellous. It is original, meticulous and utterly compelling – and ultimately a deeply tragic tale'     Philippe Sands

'Fascinating and gut-wrenching . . . Freedland at once illustrates this true tale of heroism, endurance and survival, while educating us on the reality of the Nazi regime'     *Evening Standard*

'An indispensable, unflinching, bone-hard book. Compelling reading'
Howard Jacobson

'Thought-provoking . . . One of the many important philosophical lessons that Freedland draws from this story is that information is not knowledge if it is not believed'     *New Statesman*

'Powerful, important, compelling and superbly told. This is a book that needs to be read'     Bart van Es

'Riveting . . . *The Escape Artist* includes harrowing details about Auschwitz that still have the power to shock. But the reactions to Vrba's testimony by those in power – ranging from lack of interest to outright antisemitism – are nearly as horrifying'
*New York Times*

'Utterly enraging. Mind-bending. Life-changing. *The Escape Artist* is not just one of the best books I've read about the Holocaust, it is one of the most important books I've ever read. Buy it. Give it to your friends. Give it to your children'     Jamie Susskind

'Raw and gripping . . . [A] compelling portrait of this neglected hero of Holocaust resistance leaves an inescapable imprint of a past now in danger of being minimised or forgotten . . . It's time to honour him for the incredible feat that helped save so many Jewish lives from Nazi extermination'     *Wall Street Journal*

'A masterpiece of page-turning history: an escape story that is also a fearless exploration of some of the most profound questions that face humanity. Rudolf Vrba's extraordinary testimony will deepen your understanding of the Holocaust – and compel you to think afresh about our own times, and the role of truth, denial and fragile memory. Magisterial'     Matthew d'Ancona

'A painstaking and very readable reconstruction . . . A valuable, if depressing, reminder, at a time when veracity is everywhere under threat, of the fragility of the truth'     *Times Literary Supplement*

'I read it with my heart beating fast, full of horror, rage, despair – and admiration for this potent demonstration of the stubborn resilience of the human spirit'     Tracy Chevalier

'An extraordinary story, compellingly told in this gritty account'     *BBC History Magazine*

'[A] nail-biting affair'     *Literary Review*

'This is not only an electrifying work of narrative history, it's a gripping origin story. The command that we "Never Forget" the Holocaust can rightfully be traced to a young man who exposed the horrors of Auschwitz by virtue of his extraordinary memory and tremendous bravery. As told by the gifted writer Jonathan Freedland, *The Escape Artist* is a story I'll always remember'     Mitchell Zuckoff

'Unmissable . . . Freedland tells – with the verve of the bestselling novelist that he is – the story of Rudolf Vrba . . . The narrative is extraordinary. In great and heart-stopping detail it tells of Vrba's plan and how he executed it'     *Jewish Chronicle*

Jonathan Freedland is a *Guardian* columnist and former foreign correspondent. He was named Columnist of the Year in 2002, Commentator of the Year in 2016 and won an Orwell Prize for Journalism in 2014. The presenter of BBC Radio 4's contemporary history series, *The Long View*, Freedland is a long-time contributor to the *New York Review of Books* and co-host of the *Unholy* podcast alongside the Israeli journalist Yonit Levi. He is the author of eleven other books, two of them non-fiction, including his first book, the award-winning *Bring Home the Revolution*. He has written nine thrillers under the name Sam Bourne, among them *The Righteous Men* which was a *Sunday Times* number one bestseller, and has sold over two million copies worldwide.

## Praise for *The Escape Artist*

'A brilliant and heart-wrenching book, with universal and timely lessons about the power of information – and misinformation'

Yuval Noah Harari

'Combining immersive storytelling with unflinching rigour . . . Freedland's unforgettable book is a valiant, clear-eyed bid to set the difficult, determined man at its centre alongside the likes of Anne Frank, Oskar Schindler and Primo Levi as a figure whose story has come to define the Holocaust'

*Mail on Sunday*

'A magnificent book. I could scarcely breathe at some points. What a tribute to its extraordinary hero, and it's such an important and necessary story to read . . . I can't praise it too highly. What an achievement'

Philip Pullman

'A deeply moving biography . . . [Vrba] died almost forgotten, and Freedland's brilliant research and writing rightly resurrect him. His story must be told and read: a brave man who did his best to warn a world which wouldn't listen'

*Financial Times*

'Will rank alongside Anne Frank's diary and Primo Levi'

Tom Holland

'Meticulously researched . . . shocking but thrilling, and ultimately overwhelmingly inspiring'  *Daily Mail*

'An immediate classic of Holocaust literature. Superbly researched and written, it is both a gripping story and deeply moving, I literally could not put it down'  Antony Beevor

'Vivid, compassionate . . . This harrowing and astonishing story is told with pace and verve, and is an important addition to Holocaust historiography'  *The Economist*

'Immersive, shattering and, ultimately, redemptive . . . An epic of terror and endurance . . . Written with Freedland's page-turning, gripping, hard-edged immediacy, *The Escape Artist* is profound in thought, boundless in humanity, an immediate modern classic'  Simon Schama

'Thanks to Freedland's addictively immersive storytelling, [Vrba] finally has the biography he deserves'  *The Times*

'Awe-inspiring, exciting and poignant, this is a thrilling read, a piece of redemptive storytelling and a work of important Holocaust historical research: Freedland has given Rudolf Vrba his rightful place in history – and in the process written a book that I couldn't put down'  Simon Sebag Montefiore

'Excellent . . . thrilling . . . rich in the kind of details that haunt you long after you have turned the last page'  *Sunday Times*

'A must-read standout piece of history . . . This is Freedland at his finest . . . It is both a celebration of the extraordinary will, courage and resilience of the hero – Rudi Vrba – and an all too prescient warning of how hard it is to wake up the world to things it would prefer not to see'  Emily Maitlis

'A compelling piece of work'  *Daily Telegraph*

'Rudi Vrba, a Slovakian teenager, got away from Auschwitz . . . in order to alert the world to the horrors he witnessed there. Most of his intended recipients declined to read his stomach-churning report, didn't believe it, or didn't care. We have it within us to care now. I didn't know Vrba's name previously. I will remember it for the rest of my life'
Melissa Fay Greene

'As compelling as a thriller: first is the excitement of the escape and then comes the desperation to make sure the world knew. But this is the darkest thriller you'll ever read. The book isn't just the story of one man, but it is the story of Auschwitz told in unflinching and painful detail from Rudolf's own words'
*Jewish News*

'The story of Vrba's escape from Auschwitz, exquisitely told by Jonathan Freedland, soars like a thriller. Exhilarating, deeply moving and historically important'
Simon Parkin

'A riveting read and a great achievement, restoring Rudolf Vrba to his rightful place in the pantheon of Holocaust survivors'
*The Tablet*

'The past isn't over, and Jonathan Freedland's well-researched and compelling book is the irrefutable proof of that'
Roxane van Iperen

'A powerful, informational, emotional read'
*Irish Daily Mail*

'The incredible but little-known story of Rudi Vrba, who escaped from Auschwitz and tried to warn the world, but whose warnings fell mostly on deaf ears. It's an astonishing account, both of human brutality and resilience, and although it's non-fiction, it reads like a thriller'
C. J. Carey

'A riveting tale with a fascinating protagonist . . . Freedland delivers a gripping description of Vrba and a companion's planning, breakout, and gruelling walk to Slovakia . . . A powerful story of a true hero who deserves more recognition'
*Kirkus Reviews*

# The Escape Artist

*The Man Who Broke Out of Auschwitz
to Warn the World*

JONATHAN FREEDLAND

JOHN MURRAY

First published in Great Britain in 2022 by John Murray (Publishers)
An Hachette UK company

This paperback edition published in 2023

1

Copyright © Jonathan Freedland 2022, 2023

Maps drawn by Nicky Barneby, Barneby Ltd.

Map of Auschwitz I and labels on map of Auschwitz II adapted from maps by
Nikola Zimring, Rudolf Vrba Archives, LLC 2018, used with permission.

A CIP catalogue record for this title is available from the British Library

Paperback ISBN 9781529369069
eBook ISBN 9781529369076

Typeset in Bembo Std by Palimpsest Book Production Ltd,
Falkirk, Stirlingshire

Printed and bound in Great Britain by Clays Ltd, Elcograf S.p.A.

John Murray policy is to use papers that are natural, renewable and
recyclable products and made from wood grown in sustainable forests.
The logging and manufacturing processes are expected to conform to the
environmental regulations of the country of origin.

John Murray (Publishers)
Carmelite House
50 Victoria Embankment
London EC4Y 0DZ

www.johnmurraypress.co.uk

For my father, Michael Freedland, 1934–2018

His memory is a blessing.

# Contents

# *Author's Note*

WHEN I WAS nineteen years old, I went to the Curzon cinema in Mayfair in London to see the nine-hour epic documentary *Shoah*. It was not a normal movie-going experience. Partly it was the length of the film; partly it was the audience. In the room were survivors of the Holocaust. My friend made the mistake of bringing popcorn, but he did not get very far with it. He had barely begun chomping when a woman from a nearby row leaned over and slapped him, hard, on the thigh. In an accent thick with the sound and memories of pre-war Europe, she said: 'Have you no respect?'

The film left a deep mark, but one of the interviewees stayed with me more than any other. His name was Rudolf Vrba. In the film, he is shown testifying to the greatest horrors in human history, horrors he had witnessed first hand, horrors he had survived. Very briefly he mentions something extraordinary, a fact which made him all but unique among Holocaust survivors. Aged nineteen, no older than I was as I watched the film, he had escaped from Auschwitz.

I never forgot his name or his face, even though, over the decades, I would be struck how few others had ever heard of him. And then, some thirty years after that night in the cinema in 1986, I found myself returning to Rudolf Vrba. We were living in the age of post-truth and fake news, when the truth itself was under assault – and I thought once more of the man who had been ready to risk everything so that the world might know of a terrible truth hidden under a mountain of lies.

I began to look into the life of Rudolf Vrba, finding the handful of people still alive who had known him or worked with him or loved him. It turned out that his teenage sweetheart and first wife, Gerta, was living alone, aged ninety-three, in Muswell Hill in north

London. Over half a dozen summer afternoons in the plague year of 2020, she and I sat in her garden and talked of a young man, then called Walter Rosenberg, and the world they had both known. She handed me a red suitcase packed with Rudi's letters, some telling of almost unbearable personal pain. A matter of days after our last conversation, once Gerta had told me the story in full, I got a phone call from her family, letting me know that she had passed away.

Rudi's second wife and widow, Robin, was in New York. She and I talked for hour after hour too, as she filled in the story of the man Rudolf Vrba became, the memories he had entrusted to her, the love they had shared. What soon became clear as I listened, and as I immersed myself in the official documents, testimonies, memoirs, letters, contemporary reports and historical accounts on which this book is based, was that this was more than the true story of an unprecedented escape. It was also the story of how history can change a life, even down the generations; how the difference between truth and lies can be the difference between life and death; and how people can refuse to believe in the possibility of their own imminent destruction, even, perhaps especially, when that destruction is certain. Those notions were stark and vivid in the Europe of the 1940s. But they seemed to have a new, fearful resonance in our own time.

I also came to realise that this is a story of how human beings can be pushed to the outer limits, and yet still somehow endure; how those who have witnessed so much death can nevertheless retain their capacity, their lust, for life; and how the actions of one individual, even a teenage boy, can bend the arc of history, if not towards justice then towards something like hope.

I left the cinema that night convinced that the name of Rudolf Vrba deserved to stand alongside Anne Frank, Oskar Schindler and Primo Levi, in the first rank of stories that define the Shoah. That day may never come. But maybe, through this book, Rudolf Vrba might perform one last act of escape: perhaps he might escape our forgetfulness, and be remembered.

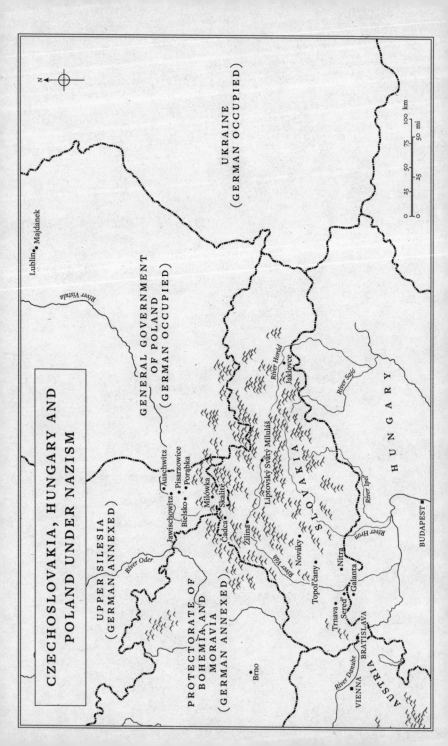

# CZECHOSLOVAKIA, HUNGARY AND POLAND UNDER NAZISM

N

100 km
75
50 mi
50
25
35
0

UKRAINE
(GERMAN OCCUPIED)

Lublin • Majdanek

River Vistula

GENERAL GOVERNMENT
OF POLAND
(GERMAN OCCUPIED)

UPPER SILESIA
(GERMAN ANNEXED)

River Oder

Auschwitz • Pisarzowice
• Porąbka
Miłówka
Bielsko •
Jawischowitz • Skalité
Čadca •
Žilina •

River Horád

River Sajó

Jaklovce •

S L O V A K I A

Liptovský Svätý Mikuláš

Novaky •

Topol'čany •

Nitra •

Galanta •
Trnava •
Sereď •

River Hron

River Ipel'

River Váh

H U N G A R Y

BUDAPEST ■

PROTECTORATE OF
BOHEMIA AND
MORAVIA
(GERMAN ANNEXED)

Brno •

River Danube

VIENNA ■
BRATISLAVA ■

AUSTRIA

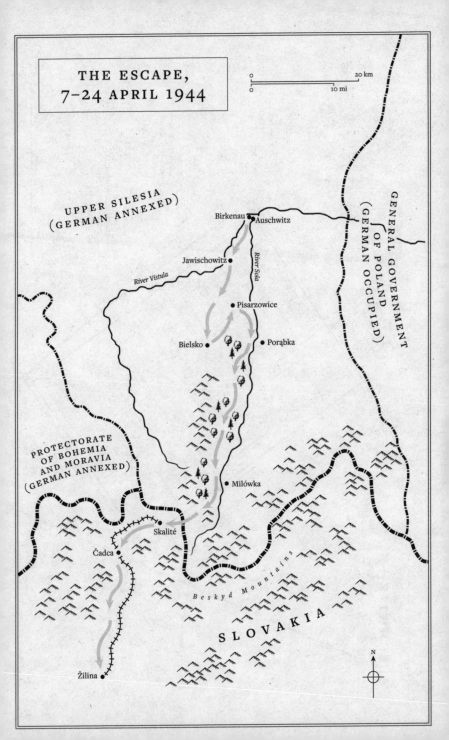

# THE ESCAPE,
## 7–24 APRIL 1944

UPPER SILESIA
(GERMAN ANNEXED)

GENERAL GOVERNMENT
OF POLAND
(GERMAN OCCUPIED)

Birkenau • Auschwitz

Jawischowitz •

*River Soła*

*River Vistula*

• Pisarzowice

Bielsko • • Porąbka

PROTECTORATE
OF BOHEMIA
AND MORAVIA
(GERMAN ANNEXED)

• Milówka

Skalité •

Čadca •

*Beskyd Mountains*

SLOVAKIA

Žilina •

N

0   10   20 km
0         10 mi

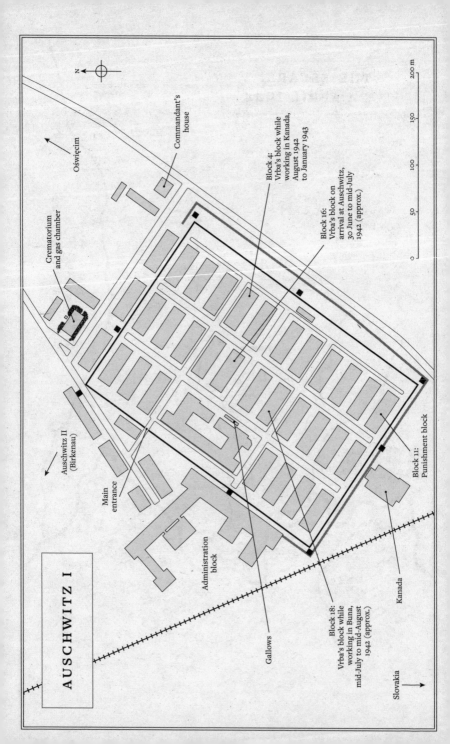

AUSCHWITZ I

N

Oświęcim

Commandant's house

Crematorium and gas chamber

Block 4:
Vrba's block while working in Kanada, August 1942 to January 1943

Block 16:
Vrba's block on arrival at Auschwitz, 30 June to mid-July 1942 (approx.)

Block 11: Punishment block

Main entrance

Administration block

Gallows

Block 18: Vrba's block while working in Buna, mid-July to mid-August 1942 (approx.)

Kanada

Auschwitz II (Birkenau)

Slovakia

200 m
150
100
50
0

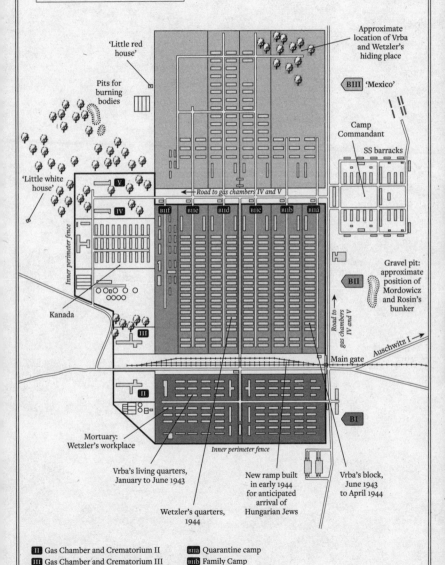

# AUSCHWITZ II (BIRKENAU)

N

'Little red house'

Pits for burning bodies

Approximate location of Vrba and Wetzler's hiding place

BIII 'Mexico'

Camp Commandant

SS barracks

'Little white house'

← *Road to gas chambers IV and V*

Inner perimeter fence

BIIf  BIIe  BIId  BIIc  BIIb  BIIa

BII

Gravel pit: approximate position of Mordowicz and Rosin's bunker

Kanada

III

Road to gas chambers IV and V

Auschwitz I →

Main gate

II

BI

Mortuary: Wetzler's workplace

Vrba's living quarters, January to June 1943

Wetzler's quarters, 1944

*Inner perimeter fence*

New ramp built in early 1944 for anticipated arrival of Hungarian Jews

Vrba's block, June 1943 to April 1944

II  Gas Chamber and Crematorium II
III  Gas Chamber and Crematorium III
IV  Gas Chamber and Crematorium IV
V  Gas Chamber and Crematorium V

BIIa  Quarantine camp
BIIb  Family Camp
BIIc  Men's camp
BIId  Men's camp
BIIe  Gypsy camp
BIIf  Men's infirmary camp

0   100   200   300   400 m

Prologue

# 7 April 1944

AFTER DAYS OF delay, weeks of obsessive preparation, months of watching the failed attempts of others and two years of seeing the depths to which human beings could sink, the moment had finally come. It was time to escape.

The two other prisoners were already there, at the designated spot. Wordlessly, they gave the nod: *do it now*. Walter and Fred did not hesitate. They climbed on top of the timbers, found the opening and, one after the other, they dropped inside. A second later, their comrades moved the planks into place above their heads. One of them whispered, 'Bon voyage.' And then all was dark and silent.

Without delay, Walter set to work. He pulled out the *machorka*, the cheap, Soviet tobacco he had been told about, a batch that had been prepared as instructed: soaked in petrol and dried. Slowly, he began to wedge it into the cracks between the wooden boards, sometimes blowing on it gently, puffing it into place, hoping against hope that the Soviet prisoner of war who had taught him the trick was right, that the scent would be repellent to dogs. Not that they were relying solely on Walter's handiwork. They had already made sure that the ground around the hideout was liberally sprinkled with the treated tobacco, so that the canine SS would not even draw near. If the Red Army man's confidence was well-founded, Walter and Fred should be able to crouch in this hole beneath the woodpile, silent and undisturbed, for exactly as long as they needed: three days and three nights.

Walter stared at the phosphorescent hands of his watch. Time was crawling. He wanted to stand up, to stretch, but he could do no such thing. His arms and legs were cramping up, but he knew he would have to endure that and endure it in silence. It was too risky to talk. At one point, Walter felt Fred, who was six years older than him, take his hand and squeeze it. Walter was nineteen years old.

What was that? The sound of footsteps – and they were getting closer. Was this the end for Walter and Fred, so soon after they had begun? Reflexively, each man reached for his razor blade. They were clear on this point: they might be caught, but they would not let themselves be interrogated. They would end it in this hole in the ground; they would turn this hideout into a burial pit.

Not that the SS would leave them here. They would drag their dead bodies back to the camp. They would prop them up on spades or hang them from the gallows, a sign of warning placed around their necks, the same performance that followed every other failed escape. They would make trophies of their corpses.

Walter's nerves seemed to be tightening with each passing second. This pit they were in was so small. But then the footsteps, if that was what they were, faded away.

At 6 p.m. that Friday night it came, the shriek of the siren. It was a howl to make the air vibrate and the blood freeze in your veins, a thousand wolf packs baying in unison. The pair had heard it enough times, a sound so piercing even the SS men would put their fingers in their ears. The noise was appalling, but every inmate welcomed it: it meant that at least one of their number had been found missing from the evening roll call – and that, perhaps, a prisoner had escaped Auschwitz.

That was their cue. Fred and Walter moved out of the main space, which had been built to hold four, and wriggled into the side branch, a kind of passageway, that could accommodate only two. It was intended to be an extra layer of protection: a hiding place within the hiding place. The pair squeezed in and lay dead still, side by side. For Walter, it was almost a relief. Now at last the waiting was over; battle was joined. Each man had tied a strip of flannel across his mouth, so that he would not betray himself – and the other – with a cough. The only movement came from the luminous hands of the watch.

They would not see it, but they knew what the siren would bring.

And soon enough they could hear it: the manhunt under way. The pounding of close on 2,000 pairs of jackboots, tramping across the ground, the senior men alternately swearing and barking orders – *screaming* them, because, given what had happened a couple of days earlier, another escape was a humiliation – the dogs slavering as they rooted out any sign of frail, quivering human life, 200 of them, trained and primed for this very purpose. The SS would search every ridge and every hollow; they would comb every bush, examine every ditch and shine a light into every trench of the sprawling metropolis of death that was Auschwitz. The search had begun and it would not let up for three days.

Fred and Walter could be precise about that because the Nazis had a security protocol from which they never deviated. This outer part of the camp, where prisoners laboured as slaves, was guarded only during the daylight hours when the inmates were working. No need to watch over it at night, when every last prisoner was herded back inside the inner camp, with its double lines of electrified wire fences. There was only one exception to that rule. If an inmate was missing, presumed to have attempted an escape, the SS kept up the outer ring of armed sentry posts, every watchtower occupied by a man with a machine gun.

It would stay like that for seventy-two hours, while the SS searched. After that, they would conclude that the escapee, or escapees, had got away: from then on, it would be the responsibility of the Gestapo to scour the wider region and find them. Those guarding the outer cordon would be ordered to withdraw, leaving it unmanned. Which meant there was a gap in the Nazi defences. Not a literal gap, but a loophole. If a prisoner could somehow hide in the outer area during those three days and nights after the alarm had been sounded, even as the SS and their dogs strove to sniff them out, then he would emerge on the fourth night into an outer camp that was unguarded. He could escape.

Walter heard a familiar voice. That murderous drunk, Unterscharführer Buntrock, was close by, giving orders to some luckless underlings. 'Look behind those planks,' he was saying. 'Use your heads!'

Fred and Walter braced themselves. The SS men got nearer. Now they could hear boots climbing on to the boards overhead, sending a fine sprinkling of dirt down into the cavity beneath. The pursuers were so close, Walter could hear the heaviness of their breath.

Next came the dogs, scratching at the wood, snuffling and sniffing, shifting from plank to plank, their panting audible through the timber walls and ceiling. Had the Soviet prisoner been wrong about his special brew of tobacco? Or had Walter misunderstood his instructions? Why had these animals not been driven away by the smell?

This time Walter reached for his knife rather than his razor; he wanted a weapon to use against others rather than himself. He felt the throb of his heart.

But, miraculously, the moment passed. The SS men and their dogs grew more distant. Inside their tiny double coffin of a hiding place, Fred and Walter allowed themselves the comfort of a smile.

The relief never lasted long. All through the evening and into that first night, the sounds of footsteps and barking dogs would come nearer, then grow distant; rising and falling, louder then softer, then louder again, as the searchers kept returning to this same corner of the camp. Walter liked to think he could sense frustration in the voices of the SS men as they probed the same ground, again and again. He would hear them cursing as they gave a second and then a third poke to a pile of timbers or roof tiles, sweeping an area they had already swept twice before.

Both of them were desperate to flex or stretch, but hardly dared. Walter longed to warm his ice-cold hands and feet, but even the slightest movement saw his whole body gripped with searing cramp. If one of them dozed, the other would remain taut with tension, listening for any hint of movement nearby. Even sleep brought no rest, just nightmares of an endless present, stuck in this subterranean box: hellish below ground, worse still above.

They heard the morning shift begin, the familiar sounds of forced labour. This area was a construction site, and it soon echoed to the banging of timber, the clanking of metal, the barking of dogs and the shouting of the SS and their henchmen. Fred and Walter reckoned that the risk that their woodpile would be disturbed by slave workers was minimal – these planks were not earmarked for use any time soon – but they could hardly relax. Perhaps ten hours passed before the noise quieted and the *Kommando* marched back to barracks.

Throughout, the two men kept still, knowing that back in the inner camp the SS would be searching every hut, store, washroom, latrine and shed, turning every barrack building upside down. Naturally there was a system: the method was to search in a series of ever decreasing circles, with the sniffer dogs in the middle of the pack, closing in on their prey. And once they got to the centre of the smallest circle, they would start all over again.

The Nazis came so close, so often, Walter considered it a wonder he and Fred had not been discovered hours ago. Fred saw it differently. 'Stupid bastards!' he said when it was safe to break the silence. Perhaps it was bravado. Twenty-four hours in, Fred was no more able to eat or drink than Walter. They had stashed some provisions in this narrow passage: several pounds of bread, carefully rationed into chunks, as well as some margarine and a bottle filled with cold coffee. But, such were their nerves, neither had the stomach to touch a thing.

Somehow the hours dragged their way through Saturday to reach Sunday. Now the pair decided to take a chance. For the first time since the sirens sounded, they emerged from the side cavity into the relative expanse of the bunker itself. Even though Walter had tried to fill the gaps in the wall and the ceiling with the treated tobacco, he had not plugged them all: some of the frosty morning mist seeped through.

They were so stiff from lying still. Fred could not move his right arm and he had lost all feeling in his fingers. Walter massaged his companion's shoulder to get the blood circulating. They did not linger in the larger space for long.

The SS kept up the search. Fred and Walter froze as they heard two men, Germans, a matter of yards away. It was in the early afternoon, and they could pick up every word.

'They can't have got away,' said one. 'They must be still in the camp.'

The Germans began speculating about Fred and Walter's likely hiding places. One was clearly pointing to something. 'How about that pile of wood?'

Walter and Fred did not move.

'Do you think they might be hiding under there?' the second voice said. 'Maybe they built themselves a little alcove.'

The first one thought it unlikely. After all, he mused out loud, and not inaccurately: 'The dogs have been over it a dozen times.' Unless, that is, the missing Jews had found some ingenious way to put the dogs off the scent.

Then some words of resolve, a declaration that it was 'worth trying' and the sound of two men scrambling to get nearer.

Once more, Walter grabbed his knife. Fred did the same.

The two Germans climbed on top of the woodpile, which they proceeded to dismantle, board by board. They took off the first layer, then the second, then, with some effort, the third and fourth.

If it had come ten seconds later, it would have been too late. Not for the first time, indeed this may have been the eighth or ninth time, Walter's life was saved by a random moment of good luck, in this case one that could not have been more perfectly timed.

Far off there was a sudden commotion, the voices distant but excited. Fred and Walter could hear the men just above them pause, their ears seemingly cocked to pick up what was happening. A second passed. Then another. Finally, one of the pair said, 'They've got them! C'mon . . . Hurry.' And, down below, Fred and Walter heard their would-be discoverers scramble away.

Sunday night passed into Monday morning. Now it was a count-down, Walter staring at the hands of his watch, knowing that if they could hold out just a little longer . . .

The morning shift returned, bringing with it the same din, the same barking, both human and animal, for another ten hours, each minute passing at the same agonising pace.

Eventually the *Kommando* returned to barracks. The three days were nearly up.

At 6.30 p.m., Walter and Fred finally heard the sound they had longed for. Announced loudly, it rang out: *Postenkette abziehen! Postenkette abziehen!* It was the order to take down the *grosse Postenkette*, the outer chain of sentry posts, shouted from one watchtower to the next and then the next, circling the entire perimeter, becoming louder when it got nearer, fading as it shifted further away, before it finally completed a full circuit. To Fred and Walter, those words, bellowed out by the men who had enslaved them and murdered hundreds of thousands of their people, sounded like the sweetest music. It was an admission of defeat by the SS, recognition that they had failed to recapture the two prisoners they had lost.

As SS protocol demanded, the outer ring of watchtowers was vacated, the cordon shrunk to lock in only the inner camp. Walter could hear the SS guards returning to the smaller loop of sentry towers. This was the great flaw in the Auschwitz system, the gap through which he and Fred had long planned to make their escape.

They were sorely tempted to rush, but they restrained themselves. First they had to emerge from the side cavity. For Walter, even inching forward sent a sharp pain shooting through his arms, legs, trunk and neck. His muscles were stiff and cold, his first movements jerky and uncertain, as if his body needed to relearn basic motor function. It took time for both of them, but finally they were in the main pit. They squatted and stretched, rotating their wrists and feet; they hugged each other in the darkness.

Now they took a deep breath and pressed their palms against the roof, trying to give the bottom board a push. But it would not move. They tried another spot on the ceiling. Still it would not budge. Was this to be the fatal flaw in their plan? Had they accidentally sealed themselves into their own tomb? It was the one thing they had not practised or even thought about. They had assumed that, if you could pile a plank on, you could take it off. But lifting boards is easy from above, when you can remove one at a time. Not so from below, when the weight of the entire stack is pressing down.

Shoving in tandem, grunting with pain, they managed to lift one of the bottom planks no more than an inch. But it was enough to give them purchase. Now they could get hold of it, just enough to shove it sideways. Fred turned to Walter with a smile. Thank God for those Germans who nearly found us, he whispered. 'If they hadn't moved those planks, we'd have been trapped.'

It had taken longer than either man had imagined, but finally there was an opening in what had been the roof of their home since Friday. There was a glimpse of the moonlit sky.

They summoned their strength again, shifting and shoving the boards until they could, with excruciating effort, haul themselves up and out. At last, they had done it. They were out of that hole in the ground.

But they were not yet out of the camp. There was still so much ground to cover if they were to become two of the first Jews ever to break out of Auschwitz and stay out. Even so, for the teenage Walter Rosenberg, it was an exhilarating feeling – but not a wholly new one. Because this was not his first escape. And it would not be his last.

# PART I

The Preparations

# I

## Star

FROM THE START he knew he was special. He was not yet Rudolf Vrba, that would come later. His name was Walter Rosenberg and he had only to look into his mother's eyes to know he was a one-off. Ilona Rosenberg had waited so long for him, desperate for his arrival. She was already a stepmother – her husband, Elias, came with three children from a previous marriage – but that was not the same as holding a baby of her own. For ten years, she had yearned for a child; the doctors told her she should stop hoping. So when Walter arrived on 11 September 1924, she greeted him like a miracle.

She doted on him, as did his half-siblings, two brothers and a sister, all of them more than a decade older, with Sammy and Fanci in particular more like an uncle and aunt than a brother and sister. The object of the kind of attention usually reserved for an only child, little Walter was precociously clever. He was four or five when Fanci, keen to meet up with her boyfriend, would drop Walter off at the one-room schoolhouse where her friend worked, so that someone other than her could keep an eye on him. He was meant to play or crayon in a corner, but she would return to find the teacher pointing to Walter Rosenberg as an example to be followed by the other children, some of them twice his age.

'Look how well Walter is doing his work,' she would say. He was not much older when his family would find him quietly turning the pages of a newspaper.

He was born in Topol'čany in the west of Slovakia, but close to the middle of the new land of Czechoslovakia that had been created just six years earlier. Before long, the family had sold up and headed to the far east of the country, edging close to Ukraine – to Jaklovce, a speck on the map so forgettable trains would pass through without ever stopping. They could not stop: there was no station, not even a platform. So Walter's father, the owner of a local sawmill, took it into his head to build a platform and modest waiting area – a structure which, to Walter's delight, doubled as the family's *sukkah* during the autumn week when Jews are commanded to demonstrate their faith in the Almighty by eating their meals in temporary huts, exposed to the heavens.

The young Walter enjoyed life in the country. The family kept chickens, with pride of place given to an egg-laying hen. When the parents noticed that eggs were going missing, Fanci was ordered to keep watch: perhaps a fox was raiding the henhouse. One morning Fanci discovered the culprit and it was an unlikely predator: her little brother was breaking into the coop, stealing the eggs and eating them raw.

The Rosenbergs did not stay in the village long. Elias died when Walter was four years old, so Ilona headed back west, where the family had roots. Now she needed to make her own living. She went out on the road, a travelling saleswoman, supplying or altering the lingerie and underwear she made herself. But it was hardly the ideal set-up for raising a young child. She once left Walter with a friend, what Ilona would have called 'a kept woman'. Angry with a patron who had discarded her, the woman bribed Walter to pretend that he was the couple's love child, as she paraded around town loudly complaining about, and naming, the terrible man who had abandoned her and this darling little boy. Walter was rewarded for his performance with a trip to the bakery and whatever cake he fancied.

After that, Ilona decided that her son should live with his grandparents in Nitra. It worked out well. Walter soon formed a strong bond with his grandfather, who raised him in the customs of strictly orthodox Judaism. Occasionally, he might run an errand that took him to the home of the town's much respected rabbi, and on Fridays Walter would follow his grandpa as he and all the other men headed to the river, using it as a *mikva*: submerging their bodies in the water, making of it a ritual bath where Jews cleanse themselves in preparation for the sabbath.

Walter liked tradition and he loved his grandparents: he was happy.

The only cloud in the sky was a variant of sibling rivalry with his Viennese cousin Max, who was a couple of years older than him. Walter knew his grandfather took pride in his achievements in school, but he suspected that the old man liked Max more.

After his grandmother had a fall, and Walter's grandfather decided he could no longer bring up the young boy alone, Walter was despatched to a Jewish orphanage in Bratislava. There, he impressed his teachers once more with his studiousness – asked to name his hobbies, he would say languages and reading, though he did make time to play football – and the headmaster suggested to Ilona that she should enrol her son in one of the city's elite high schools. It would mean establishing a permanent residence in Bratislava, and hiring a young woman to act as Walter's guardian while she remained on the road, but if the best was available to her boy, Ilona was determined he should have it.

When the time came to pose for a class photograph in the autumn of 1935, the outline of the man to come was visible. Just eleven years old, he may have looked a little nervous but he already had presence. His dark hair swept over to one side, and with the thick, dark eyebrows that would accompany him for life, he sat straight-backed, regarding the lens with intensity. The other boys did as they were told and posed with their arms folded. But not Walter.

He was still wearing *tzitzit*, the traditional fringed vest of the devout Jewish male, but his mother had made a cummerbund for him, to keep the tassels hidden. The *payos*, or sidecurls, which Walter would have worn in Nitra, were gone. For the first time, he was free to make his own religious decisions, without the influence of either his grandfather or the orphanage. One afternoon, strolling the streets of Bratislava with some lunch money in his pocket, he decided to put God to the test: he went into a restaurant and ordered pork. He took the first bite and waited for the bolt of lightning to strike. When it did not come, he made up his mind – and made the break.

Pupils at the gymnasium were given a choice of religious instruction: Catholic, Lutheran, Jewish or none. Walter chose none. On his identity papers, in the space set aside for nationality, he could have entered the word 'Jewish' but instead chose 'Czechoslovak'.

At school, he was now learning not only German but High German. (He had struck a deal with an émigré pupil: each boy would give the other advanced lessons in his native tongue.) In the class picture for 1936, his gaze is confident, even cocky. He is staring straight ahead, into the future.

But in the photograph for the academic year 1938–9 there was no sign of fourteen-year-old Walter Rosenberg. Everything had changed, including the shape of the country. After the Munich agreement of 1938, Adolf Hitler and his Hungarian allies had broken off chunks of Czechoslovakia, parcelling them out between them and, by the spring of 1939, what was left was sliced up. Slovakia announced itself as an independent republic. In reality it was a creature of the Third Reich, conceived with the blessing and protection of Berlin, which saw in the ruling ultra-nationalist Hlinka, or Slovak People's Party, a mirror of itself. A day later the Nazis annexed and invaded the remaining Czech lands, marching in to declare a Protectorate of Bohemia and Moravia, while Hungary seized one last chunk for itself. Once the carve-up was done, the people who lived in what used to be Czechoslovakia were all, to varying degrees, at the mercy of Adolf Hitler.

In Slovakia, the teenage Walter Rosenberg felt the difference immediately. He was told that, no matter the choice he had made for religious studies classes and the word he had put in the 'nationality' box on those forms, he met the legal definition of a Jew and was older than thirteen; therefore, his place at the Bratislava high school was no longer available. His education was terminated.

All across the country, Jews like Walter were coming to understand that although the new head of government was a Catholic priest – Father Jozef Tiso – the state religion of the infant republic was Nazism, albeit in a Slovak denomination. The antisemites' enduring creed held that Jews were not merely unreliable, untrustworthy and irreversibly foreign, but also endowed with almost supernatural powers, allowing them to wield social and economic influence out of all proportion to their numbers. So naturally the authorities in Bratislava moved fast to blame the country's tiny Jewish community – 89,000 in a population of two and a half million – for the fate that had befallen the nation, including the loss of cherished territory to Hungary. Propaganda posters appeared, pasted on brick walls; one showed a proud young Slovak, clad in the black uniform of the Hlinka Guard, kicking the backside of a hook-nosed, side-curled Jew – the Jew's purse of coins falling to the ground. In his first radio address as leader of the newly independent republic, Tiso made only one firm policy commitment: 'to solve the Jewish question'.

After Walter's expulsion from school, Ilona abandoned her work as a travelling saleswoman and the pair moved to Trnava, a small town thirty miles east of Bratislava. It was a shock after the capital: here all life, and multiple narrow lanes, converged on a central square named for the Holy Trinity and dominated by not one but two churches. In summer, Trnava was a cloud of heat and dust, the marketplace reeking of manure, hay and human sweat, the whole town overwhelmed with the stench emanating from the nearby sugar plant as it processed beet. Escape could be found in the countryside, with its flat fields of ripe corn and fresh breezes only a cycle ride away.

But if the Rosenbergs, mother and son, were hoping for refuge, they had come to the wrong place. The government's determination to tackle the so-called Jewish question reached even here, touching small-town Trnava with its community of fewer than 3,000 Jews whose two synagogues stood a matter of yards apart. Not that the good people of Trnava needed much prompting: they had set fire to both synagogues a matter of weeks after Slovakia had gained its autonomy, in December 1938.

Walter soon joined up with a group of Jewish teenagers, who, like him, had been banished from the realm of learning. On the first day of term, the schools had hung signs on their gates announcing that Jews and Czechs were excluded, while their former friends chanted, 'Jews out, Czechs out.' After that, Walter and the other young Jews of Trnava, those in the eighth grade and above, were left to their own devices, wandering around town with no classes to attend and no place to be. Under the new rules, they were barred even from learning alone. Which is why Walter and his friend Erwin Eisler went one day to the local council building to hand in their text-books, obeying an order introduced to guard against the threat of Jewish children studying in their own homes. Walter had complied dutifully, surrendering his books, but Erwin surprised him. Normally, Erwin was bashful, blushing at the mere mention of girls and ducking invitations to join the gang as they headed to a neighbourhood café. But on this day he showed unexpected pluck.

'Don't worry,' he whispered. 'I've still got that chemistry book.'

He had held on to one of the two volumes on inorganic and organic chemistry by the Czech scientist Emil Votoček. Thereafter Walter and Erwin would pore over that single text, teaching themselves in secret the knowledge their country was determined to deny them.

The self-teaching continued wherever the teenagers got together. Sometimes they gathered in a meadow known after its previous incarnation as 'the pond', sitting around, trying to make sense of the world that seemed to have turned upside down. Walter soon established himself as a dominant presence, his intelligence setting him apart. One girl, thirteen-year-old Gerta Sidonová, became steadily more enraptured by him, hanging on his every word. Her parents took him on as a personal tutor, though she doubtless found it hard to concentrate on what he was saying. She hoped he considered her his girlfriend, though the signals could be mixed. One time, they had agreed to meet for a date but he stood her up. Afterwards, Gerta confronted him. He had gone to meet her, he told her. But as he approached he had seen that she was wearing a hat with pom-poms. That had prompted him to turn straight around and head in the opposite direction. She looked like a nine-year-old in that hat, he said. He was fifteen: he could not be seen with a child.

And yet the Jewish teenagers of Trnava had few options beyond each other. They, along with their families, were steadily excluded from the life of the town they had called home. It was the same story across the country. The Tiso regime was determined to impoverish and isolate Jews, first banning them from government jobs, then imposing a quota on the numbers allowed to work in the professions. Later Jews were banned from owning cars, radios or even sports equipment. Each new ordinance would be posted on a bulletin board in the centre of town: the Jews would check it every day, to see what new humiliation awaited them.

Walter and his mother had no assets to speak of, but those Jews who did were stripped of them, bit by bit: first their land was seized, then their businesses expropriated. Aryanisation, the authorities called it. Gerta's father tried to keep his butcher shop alive by handing it over to an assistant who had been shrewd enough to join the Hlinka Party. They called that 'voluntary Aryanisation', by which Jewish-owned businesses would surrender a stake worth at least 51 per cent of the company to a 'qualified Christian candidate'. The name of the programme was a stretch, because the Nazis did not regard the Slovaks as Aryans, but rather as a category of Slav. As such, they were firmly *Untermenschen*, an inferior people. Still, they were deemed superior to the Jews, and that was what mattered.

Beatings became commonplace, mainly of Jews but sometimes of those non-Jews who showed insufficient zeal in tormenting their Jewish neighbours. The national socialist paramilitaries pressured the people of Trnava and every other Slovak town or city to boycott Jewish businesses and Jews in general.

There was no hiding place, not even once your front door was closed and you were in your own home. From 1940, as Londoners were enduring the nightly air raids they would soon call the Blitz, Slovak gendarmes took the policy of expropriating Jewish property to a more direct, more literal level. They would enter Jewish homes and loot them, while the children could only stand and watch. They might grab a tennis racket or a coat, a camera or a treasured family heirloom or even, as in at least one case, a full-sized piano. Sometimes they would venture out of town, finding a Jewish-owned family farm and taking away the animals. It was open season. If a Jew had it, a Slovak could take it.

But the new republic had barely got started. As Walter turned seventeen, in September 1941, Tiso's government introduced its own version of the Nuremberg laws, the Jewish Codex. Now, Jews were barred from public events, clubs and social organisations of any kind. They were allowed to venture out or shop only within prescribed hours. They could travel for only limited distances. If they wanted to buy property, they were subject to a 20 per cent surcharge: a Jew levy. There were limits on where they could live; they were to be confined to a few streets, an early step towards the ghetto. The head-line on a pro-government news sheet bragged that, in the undeclared contest among fascist states, 'The strictest laws against Jews are Slovakia's'.

But the change which had the most immediate, most visible effect on Walter was also the crudest. From now on, any Jew in Slovakia over the age of six had to identify themselves by means of a yellow Star of David, six inches across and attached to their outer clothes. If Walter and the other Jewish kids pitched up at Trnava's skating rink or cinema, one glimpse of the yellow star and they would be turned away. While the friends they once knew were out late on the high street, the Jews were bound by a curfew. They had to be out of sight by 9 p.m.

Walter did not rebel against any of these rules. He was not even that shocked by them. Perhaps it was because the ratchet had tightened slowly, over time, so that each new turn did not seem so extraordinary considering what had come before. Whatever the explanation, Walter wore the yellow star, just as he accepted that, with his education terminated, he needed to find work. He picked up what he could as a manual labourer, but employers only hired Jews if there was no one else available. Any Jew lucky enough to get a day's shift would be paid at the lower rate: there were two wage scales, a lower one for Jews, a higher one for everyone else.

This was life for the teenage Walter Rosenberg. Eating Wiener schnitzel and fried potatoes in the cramped kitchen of the home he shared with his mother; attempting to teach himself new languages – in addition to the German, Czech and Slovak he already spoke, along with some rudimentary Hungarian – usually from a dog-eared textbook; meeting with his friends at the pond, debating the competing merits of the -isms of the age, arguing over whether it was socialism or communism, liberalism or Zionism, that would come to their rescue. On the one hand, Zionism's message of Jewish pride and possibility was balm to young Jews bruised by daily humiliation and exclusion. On the other, surely Zionism was another nationalism doomed to fail in a world that could be healed only by universal brotherhood, and was it not the socialists who were leading the fight against Nazism?

They thrashed it out in the long hours they spent huddled together, shunned by their neighbours, branded by the yellow stars on their chests.

And yet, despite it all, they were still teenagers. There was time for laughing and flirting, for boys to chase girls, girls to chase boys and for both to break each other's hearts. Walter was not tall – not much more than five foot six inches – but he carried himself as if he were. Those dark eyebrows, his thick head of hair and wide, mischievous smile, meant he was never short of attention.

Then, in February 1942, the letter arrived. It looked like a court summons or military draft notice, instructing Walter to present himself on this day at this time and at this place, bringing with him baggage no heavier than twenty-five kilograms and containing no gold. The message was clear enough. Walter's country was no longer content merely to corral him and his fellow Jews in ever shrinking spaces, with no work and no opportunities. Now it wanted to banish them altogether. Jews were to be stripped of their citizenship, despatched across the border to Poland to live in what Walter and the others imagined were 'reservations', like those fenced-in lands they had heard about in America, set aside for 'Indians'.

The order came wrapped in gentle, even genteel, language. Jews were not to be *deported*, still less expelled. No, they were to be *resettled*. And not all the Jews. Only the men, only the able-bodied, only those aged between sixteen and thirty. If they would agree to go voluntarily, quietly and without fuss, then nothing would happen to their families, who would be allowed to stay behind and follow later. As for the prohibition on gold, why surely that was obvious: gold could only have been acquired through Jewish knavery and deviousness, not through hard work, and therefore any gold that Jews might have in their possession was the rightful property of the Slovak nation, to which, no matter their place of birth or erstwhile citizenship, Jews no longer belonged.

It was all part of the plan, cooked up with the approval of an SS official, Hauptsturmführer Dieter Wisliceny, who had been despatched to Bratislava from Berlin nearly two years earlier. The strategy was simple enough: starve the Jews of funds by confiscating their property, seizing their assets and denying them the ability to earn a living – and then denounce them as an economic burden on the hard-working, long-suffering Slovak nation. It had been easy to cast Jews as parasites when they had wealth; it was easier still now they had nothing. The Hlinka government, their German patrons at their side – brothers in national socialism – had calculated that, once the Jews were beggared, the Slovak public would be only too glad to see them dumped over the border. And of course it made sense to start with young men like Walter. If the Hlinka government were to rid the nation of an entire minority, better to remove first the fit and strong, those who would form the heart of any future resistance.

Walter stared at the letter that had come through his door, telling him when and where he should present himself. The one thing he knew, as the winter of 1942 gave way to the first intimations of spring, was that he would refuse to be removed from his own country. It struck him as a stupid instruction. No, he would not allow himself to be packed off in a train, destination unknown. Of course, he would do no such thing. He had been born in Slovakia; Slovak was his native tongue. He was a Slovak. He would not be picked up and thrown out like a piece of garbage, leaving his mother defenceless. While she cooked her perennial evening meal of Wiener schnitzel and apple strudel, Walter told her of his decision.

'I'm going to England,' he said. 'To join the Czechoslovak army in exile.'

She looked at him as if he were mad. They argued about it for an hour, him in one room, she in the kitchen next door. At intervals, over the din of clanking pots and pans, she would let out a new expression of derision at the very idea.

'Why not slip up to the moon and cut yourself a slice of green cheese? But be back in time for supper!'

For Ilona, this was typical of her son and his hare-brained schemes, on a par with that crazy business of teaching himself English and Russian.

'*Russian!* Why can't you settle down like everyone else and learn a decent trade?'

These days there was a man in Ilona's life and he was a locksmith.

Surely, she said, that was a perfectly respectable occupation. But no, Walter had to do it his way.

'I don't know where we got you. You're certainly not like any of my side of the family.'

Besides, she wanted to know how, exactly, he proposed to reach England.

'Through Hungary,' he said. True, the government in Budapest was allied to the Nazis, but at least Hungary was not deporting its Jews. 'Then to Yugoslavia.'

That sparked another round of argument, with Walter unable to specify precisely how he would criss-cross occupied Europe, whether by land or sea, and how he would finally reach England. But if he could not get beyond Yugoslavia, he had a contingency plan. He would sign up with the partisans led by Josip Tito and become a resistance fighter.

More crashing of saucepans. Round and round they went, Ilona convinced that this was madness, as lunatic a mission as heading to the stars, and just as doomed. But Walter would not back down. Finally, he faced her and said in a calm, steady voice: 'Momma, I'm not going to be deported like a calf in a wagon.'

The crashing and shouting stopped. Ilona Rosenberg understood that her son's mind was made up.

After that, she became his co-conspirator, assembling the clothes he would need and scrabbling together what little money she had. And coming up with a solution to his most immediate problem: how to get out of Trnava and to Sered', the town that five years before would have been deep in the Slovak interior but which now hugged the Hungarian border.

'You'll have to take a taxi,' she said.

Now it was Walter's turn to point out the absurdity. Who ever heard of someone hailing a cab to freedom?

And yet he could see there was no other way. There was a driver they knew who might just do it, despite the risk to himself: ferrying a Jew that kind of distance was strictly forbidden. Still, there were some in Trnava who had not forgotten those they once regarded as neighbours, some who still remembered the debts of friendship.

Which is how, one night in early March 1942, the young Walter

Rosenberg came to be crouched on the worn leather seats of one of the few cars in Trnava, a town where a horse-drawn wagon was the norm, heading for the Hungarian border. He did not look back. He was not thinking of the past, nor imagining the future, but rather attending to a task that had to be completed right now, in the present.

He looked down and ripped the yellow star from his coat.

# 2

## Five Hundred Reichsmarks

O N THAT NIGHT in March 1942, the future consisted only of the empty darkness that stood between him and the frontier separating Slovakia from Hungary. After half an hour, the taxi driver had dropped him off; it was not safe to get any closer. Walter would do the rest on foot. He checked his pockets: a map and compass, a box of matches and some money. Two hundred crowns, given to him by the mother he had left behind.

He walked through the night, down narrow lanes and across flat, empty fields. He was excited. True, he was leaving one fascist-ruled country for another; he was hardly taking a short walk to freedom. But this was the first step. And at least in Hungary they were not loading Jews on to trains sending them who knew where.

As he walked, what had been a gentle snowfall grew heavier. He kept marching, but the cold was gnawing into his bones. The adrenaline had insulated him at first, but it only lasted so long. The teenage bravado was fading too. Now he felt alone and frightened; he was a boy in the dark.

The hours of night passed, punctuated by the crunch of his boots on the freshly settled snow. At around five o'clock in the morning, with sunrise still an hour away, he saw another cluster of lights. Fewer than he had seen in Sered', because this was the slightly smaller town of Galanta. That's when he knew he had done it. There had been no formal frontier, no sentried fence, but he had crossed the border. He was in Hungary.

From there, he had an address: relatives of a schoolfriend. They were shocked to see a boy on their doorstep at dawn, his clothes covered in mud. But they took him in, gave him a bath and breakfast and explained that he had to leave right away: for a Hungarian to be caught helping a Slovak refugee was to risk a prison sentence for harbouring a spy.

They got him to the station, armed him with a ticket and a conspicuous copy of a nationalist, antisemitic newspaper – just to be on the safe side – and put him on a train to Budapest. He had an address there too, given to him by resistance-minded friends in Trnava. It was for a contact in Hungary's socialist underground, who let Walter stay with him as Walter tried, and failed, to secure false documents and, with those, a job. Without them, he could not stay in Budapest for long; eventually someone would turn him in to the police.

After ten days, the comrades of the underground came to an unlikely decision. The best bet, they concluded, was for Walter to retrace his steps and head back to Trnava where contacts would be standing by with false Aryan papers. Once armed with those, he could resume his original escape plan.

And so he re-enacted his escape backwards. Except now, as he attempted to cross the border to go back into Slovakia, he was stopped by two Hungarian border guards, aiming their rifles directly at him. Instinct made him run – until he heard the sound of gunfire and a different instinct made him stop.

The guards approached, only for one to hit his head with the butt of his gun while the other greeted him with a hard kick in the crotch. They frogmarched him to the nearest border post, where he was punched in the mouth and propelled into a wall. A corporal arrived, eager to join the fun: he hit Walter repeatedly with his pistol.

The Hungarians were insistent that Walter was a spy, a charge they accompanied with a punch or a kick each time they made it. Walter denied it, insisting that he was a Jew from neighbouring Slovakia who had crossed the border into Hungary, looking to find refuge in the capital. He was on his way to, not from, Budapest. But he had not reckoned on the piece of paper the men found in his pocket. It did not contain the names or addresses of the contacts who had harboured him: he had relied on his memory for those. Nor did they find his money: while in Hungary, this son of an expert maker of women's underwear had sewn the banknotes into the flies of his trousers. What they found was less valuable, but much more incriminating. It was a tram ticket. From Budapest.

The man in charge was now clear that, since Walter had lied, he must obviously be a spy. And so the man wanted to know: who were Walter's accomplices?

The interrogation moved to a table, where it lasted for three brutal hours. But the seventeen-year-old Walter did not crack. Perhaps that convinced the Hungarian officer that he was, after all, no more than a Jewish refugee looking to escape deportation. He allowed two soldiers to take Walter away.

As the men dragged him into no man's land, Walter was convinced they would kill him and ditch his body here. He took out the money he had hidden and gave it to them, but it made no difference. They kept dragging him to what was surely a certain death. And then, suddenly, they panicked. They realised they had messed up. They had inadvertently crossed the border. They were now in Slovakia. If they shot this boy, that would alert the Slovak border guards – along with their dogs and machine guns. For a second, they threatened to cut Walter's throat with a bayonet, but fear seemed to get the better of them: they turned him loose.

He ran as fast as he could, but his body was too battered to get very far. He stumbled and fell. He had wanted so badly to escape but now, he knew, it was over. He lost consciousness.

When he came round, it was to the sound of someone speaking. The voice was not familiar, but the language was. 'Jesus, he's still alive,' were the words he heard. And he heard them in Slovak.

Those Hungarians had been right. They had crossed the border into Slovakia and now these men, shining a torch into his face, were Slovak border guards coming across a body that they had assumed was a corpse.

They took him to an inn, where he was given brandy and a chance to wash away the blood and clean up his wounds. But the respite would not last long. He was back in the country of his birth, the only country of which he had ever been a citizen – but he was also in the country he had tried to flee, a land now run by fascists who bragged that they were world leaders in the business of hounding Jews.

So, inevitably, his welcome home included a trip to the local police station, where he was branded a 'dirty, bloody Yid' who had sought to escape resettlement solely because he was too lazy to work, like all those other Yids – and then shoved into a cell and locked up for the night.

The next morning, Walter's jailers transferred him to a camp in the small town of Nováky, some sixty miles away. Walter could comfort himself that he had avoided deportation: he was still in Slovakia. On the other hand, he was a prisoner, as far away from London and from freedom as ever.

He was shoved into a huge barracks, along with several hundred other men and soon got the lie of the land. This place, he learned, had two functions. It was a transit camp, a holding facility where Jews were held before they boarded trains for the unknown, initially filled up by people just like Walter – young, single men and women who had received the summons and were selected for deportation – later taking in entire families from the surrounding mountains and villages. They had been brought there not by German SS men, but by Slovaks who had assigned themselves the task of rooting out their Jewish neighbours from their hiding places and arresting them. It turned out that, in their eagerness to be rid of the Jews, the Slovaks were paying the Germans for their work – and paying quite generously. For every Jew deported, Bratislava handed Berlin 500 Reichsmarks, officially to cover the costs of food, shelter and supposed retraining. There was an extra charge for transport, payable to Deutsche Reichsbahn, the German state railway company. It was expensive, but the Nazi deportation service came with a lifetime guarantee, a promise that in return for those 500 Reichsmarks the Jew in question would never return. Better still, the Nazis allowed Slovakia to keep any and all property confiscated from the Jews who had been expelled. If the Rosenbergs' neighbours, or the Sidonovás' or those of any other exiled Jew, liked the look of the home that had been left behind, they could take it.

The transit-camp section of Nováky did brisk business. From 25 March 1942, around the time Walter pitched up there, until 20 October that same year, precisely 57,628 Jews were deported from

Nováky and the camps like it dotted around Slovakia. Their destination was either the Lublin region of Poland or a camp much closer to the Slovak border, constructed near the town of Oświęcim.

But Nováky served another purpose too. It also contained a labour camp, where 1,200 or more Jews were kept against their will and used as slave workers. It did not take long for Walter to see that they were not slaves for Germany, but for the country of which they had, until now, been citizens. Some 350 Jews worked at Nováky as tailors, seamstresses and needleworkers, making uniforms for the Slovak police among other things. The products were supplied, doubtless at ultra-competitive prices thanks to the absence of labour costs, to the domestic Slovak market.

The labour at Nováky was forced and the inmates were held behind barbed wire. But the work was indoors and it was not back-breaking. The food was basic – bread and jam, pea soup and potatoes – but there was food. There was a nursery school, kindergarten and elementary school as well as a library and, every now and then, a musical recital or a show. Families were allowed to live together, in barracks sub-divided into tiny, hutch-like rooms.

All this was eyed enviously by the men in the transit camp alongside Walter who, cooped up for days, traded slivers of rumour and crumbs of uninformed speculation, asking each other questions none of them could answer. They talked about transports and dates, wondering if a train was coming to take them away today, tomorrow or never. Having failed to win a coveted place in the labour camp, they were kept here, in these barracks, two Hlinka Guards outside the door and only one thing certain: that worse was to come.

Waiting to know his fate did not suit Walter. One day, as casually as he could, he tried to chip into the barracks chatter by asking the question that had nagged at him the instant he arrived.

'Tell me,' he said. 'What are the chances of getting out of here?'

The room fell silent. Eventually one detainee laughed, as if taking pity on a young child. 'He wants to go home!'

'Jesus,' said another. 'That's all we need. A bloody troublemaker!'

Walter kept his plans to himself after that. Nevertheless, and though he was the newest arrival in this place thanks to his failed effort to make it across the border, he retained full confidence in his ability to pull off what none of these men had apparently even considered. He was convinced he could escape.

There were advantages to being poor, alone and seventeen. One of them was that when the Hlinka Guards on the door demanded someone from the barracks go to the labour camp and help bring back food, Walter was the obvious choice. He was young and fit and, even the grumpiest of his fellow inmates recognised, he needed a break: he had no one to look out for him.

He used his very first trip across the divide for reconnaissance. He was struck by how open the labour camp was, open to the daylight and the sunshine, with a clear view of the surrounding wheatfields. More important, Walter spotted immediately that the perimeter of this part of the camp was marked out by a barbed-wire fence that was, at least to his teenage eye, pathetically inadequate. Better still, he could see only a single guard tasked with patrolling it. One man, guarding a boundary that was a thousand yards long. Within the closed universe of Nováky, there was a perverse logic to it. Everyone wanted to get out of the transit camp so they could make it into the labour camp. Once they had, why would they want to escape?

Walter was tempted to make a run for it there and then. He reckoned he was capable of it, and he knew there was no time to waste: he could be pushed on to a deportation train at any hour of any day. Still, he had learned from his previous, abortive efforts at escape: preparation was all. He would need a plan. And he would need an ally.

In the cramped, crowded transit barracks he had run into Josef Knapp, a young man from Walter's own birthplace of Topol'čany who, like him, had dreamed of freedom in Britain, and who, like him, had tried to find it by fleeing through Hungary, and who, like him, had failed. Young Josef, tall and good-looking, was pining for the girlfriend he had left behind in Topol'čany. In one conversation, he let slip that he had money. He had evaded the initial body-search on arrival at Nováky; he had managed to hide some cash. For Walter, he was the ideal co-conspirator.

Now a plan began to take shape. Walter would persuade the guard that the food run he had been doing between the transit and labour camps had become a two-person job, what with all the new arrivals. The guard, seeing no threat to what mattered to him most – his own daily access to the kitchen and all its wares – nodded the proposal through. Now Walter and Josef would be able to cross into the Nováky labour camp together and unhindered.

Once they had, it was easy. The solo guard on the perimeter fence was nowhere to be seen, which meant the pair could simply duck under the wire and run as fast as they could. After three minutes, they reached a stream bringing fresh water from the forest. They slid down its banks, crossed and kept on running. No more than ten minutes after that, they were plunged deep into the woods, the light of the sun dappled by the trees and the only noise the sound of their own laughter. They had done it. They had broken free.

They kept walking. Eventually, and following their plan, they split up: Josef would go to a village where he had friends who would hide him, Walter would catch a train to Topol'čany, to find Zuzka, Josef's girlfriend. Josef himself did not dare show his face there: too likely that someone would recognise him and turn him in. Walter would then sit tight in Topol'čany and before long Josef would send word – and money. With that, Walter could then complete the journey he had tried and failed to make weeks ago: he would go back to Trnava, and pick up the false Aryan papers arranged by his socialist contacts in Budapest.

Walter did as he was told, finding Zuzka's home and knocking on her door. She went off to see her boyfriend, while Walter waited patiently, dependent on the goodwill of her parents – both non-Jews who were taking a great risk harbouring him.

He waited and waited. But Josef never did send word or money. Walter soon understood that he had been betrayed. He said goodbye to the girl's parents, and the shed where they had hidden him, and decided to fend for himself in the town where he had been born.

He managed a few hours before making a big mistake. He went into a milk bar to refresh himself. Except a Slovak gendarme was there at the same time. Walter tried to leave as inconspicuously as he could, but it was no good. The policeman followed him out, demanding to see Walter's papers.

Walter ran for it, but it was an uneven contest. The gendarme had a bike and soon caught up with him, taking him to the station and into custody. Before handing him over, he asked Walter if he knew what had given him away. Walter shook his head. It turned out that the policeman had noticed that he was wearing two pairs of socks on a warm, summer's day. Why would anyone do such a thing, unless they were on the run?

Inside the police station, they seemed to know all about him. There had been a warrant out for his arrest, including a full description of the escapee Walter Rosenberg. It had been circulated throughout the country the instant he had slipped under the barbed wire of Nováky. His escape had made him a wanted man.

That night they locked him in a cell, then locked the police station and left him unwatched and unguarded. Their parting gift was a few cigarettes for company, and a warning not to take his own life.

The following day they handed Walter Rosenberg over to the Hlinka Guards. The journey was brief, the train accomplishing in minutes what had taken him and Josef many long hours. For all the ingenuity of his escape, he was back behind that wire fence, back in Nováky. He was a prisoner once more.

# 3

# Deported

WALTER TOOK IT as a compliment. His return to Nováky was greeted with a bespoke beating from the Hlinka guardsmen whose reputation had been dented by his escape. They avenged their humiliation by punching and kicking him, taking it in turns, whacking him with the butt of their rifles, stopping only with the arrival of a commanding officer who seemed anxious that they not pummel their captive to death. Word of a murdered prisoner would spread through Nováky, among those held in the transit camp in particular, and that could cause panic which, for reasons Walter would come to understand, was the last thing those overseeing the deportation wanted. And so the beating concluded, with orders that Walter be held in a special cell – just him and one other man – and that he be put on the next transport.

Sure enough, when the next train pulled in, collecting Jews to be shipped off, his name was on the list. His captors were determined that Walter Rosenberg would not make fools of them a second time. On the railway platform, while every other Jew on the transport lined up to be processed and have their papers examined, Walter was assigned his own personal Hlinka Guard who, armed with a sub-machine gun, stood watch over him and him alone. When the moment of departure came, the Hlinka Guards had a final word of advice, tailored just for him.

'Try to escape again and you're a dead duck,' they said. Once more, Walter chose to be flattered by the degree of attention.

It would be wrong to talk of passengers 'boarding' that train. The Jews of Nováky were cargo and they were loaded as such. They did not sit in carriages, but were packed in wagons. Walter's rough estimate – and he was good at guessing numbers – was that there were eighty of them jammed into that single wagon, along with all their luggage. They were cheek by jowl, head to armpit.

Most of those surrounding him were either much older or much younger than he was: the wagon was full of children, their parents and the elderly. Slovak Jews his own age had been deported in the initial wave, when Walter had made his first attempt at escape. The presence of children changed things. All it had taken at the station was for the guards to hit one of the adults; after that, stillness reigned. The sight of that single blow had so distressed the children that from then on, instinctively and collectively, the adults had understood that they needed to restrain themselves, obey whatever instructions they were given and maintain the illusion of calm. They needed to reassure the children that what had happened was an aberration, that it would not happen again.

At first, those jammed in the wagon tried to adjust to their new situation. There was co-operation, even camaraderie. The deportees shared what food they had, Walter passing around the salami that had been a parting gift from his overnight cellmate. There was even an attempt at a wedding toast for a newly married couple who, like many young sweethearts, had married in a hurry, prompted by Father Tiso's pledge that no families would be separated by deportation. And, as the train jerked along for hour after hour, the human cargo tried to observe human decencies. An unspoken convention demanded that they look away from, and give a pretence of privacy to, whoever took their turn at the single bucket.

This, Walter realised, was the fate he had tried so hard to escape. He had crossed borders, waded through water and hiked through forests to avoid being packed like a calf in a crate. And yet here he was.

In those first hours, there was conversation, mostly about the new lives that awaited them. Where exactly were they going? What would this new place be like? Children asked their parents if there would be schools and playgrounds. Others guessed that their destination would prove to be a glorified labour camp or else a ghetto. Life would be hard but it would be endurable. Besides, this resettlement would surely prove to be temporary, a strange and unwanted consequence of a war that would not last much longer.

A key exhibit in these deliberations, conducted by people who were standing for hours on end, barely able to turn to those who might be speaking on their left or right, were the letters home sent by those who had been deported first. Several in the wagon had heard from a son or daughter, cousin or niece, who had been deported early and had written to say all was well. These letters were consistently positive, praising the food the deportees had to eat and the housing they had been allocated, assuring those who had been left back in Slovakia that resettlement was not so bad after all.

And yet there was a recurring motif to these letters, besides the comforting note of good cheer. Not all of them, by any means, but several included an oddity, a detail that did not fit. One woman described a note from a cousin that signed off with a chirpy insistence that the cousin's mother sent her love. And yet the mother in question had died three years earlier. Another woman said she had been similarly puzzled by a reference to an old neighbour apparently thriving in his new home, even though both letter writer and recipient knew the old man had been in the ground for years.

Walter listened, but had little to add. He had received no letters, let alone any with unexplained errors. Besides, he was preoccupied, staring out of the opening that passed for a window, watching the landscape as it went by. He was trying to memorise the route, so that he would be able to work his way back. He was thinking, as always, of escape. The thought did not leave him even when, in the late afternoon of that first day, towards 5 p.m., the train pulled into Zwardoń on the frontier that separated Slovakia from Poland, the wagons were emptied and the Jews were forced to line up and be counted. The Hlinka Guards now gave way to the Nazi SS, the Germans taking charge of the train, replacing the driver with one of their own. Even then, Walter was trying to plot a way out.

Except the route after that point made no sense that Walter could divine. The train was going so slowly, then making long stops when it seemed to be stuck in the middle of nowhere. The wagon remained shut so they had no way of looking around. Were they in Kraków? Or was this Katowice? Perhaps it was neither; perhaps they had reached Częstochowa. It was so hard to tell. The train seemed to be taking a roundabout route, long and winding, perhaps even doubling back on itself. Walter looked for the logic in it, but could find none.

Time seemed to stretch. Unbelievably, his wristwatch said he had been rammed into that wagon for twenty-four hours. Plenty of the deportees, Walter included, had come with food, which they had eaten, but few had thought to bring enough water. So now, after one full day in the cattle truck, the children complained of a terrible thirst. Their lips were parched, they were becoming light-headed. Before too long, the need had become desperate. They craved water. A mere glimpse of a river, or of a billboard promoting beer, through the slats of the cattle truck became a torment.

The camaraderie of the first hours, of the wedding toast and the shared food, was long gone. There were fights, including over access to the bucket in the corner that was now spilling over. The thirst drove people to distraction, stripping them of the layers of courtesy or charm they had worn when they had left Nováky. With the water supply dried up, the recriminations and accusations grew.

And still Walter could see no logic to this journey. They were heading east, then he would glimpse the sign of a station they had already passed and realise they were now heading west. Sometimes the train would be shunted into a siding, to make way, Walter presumed, for a military transport deemed a higher priority. The delay in that siding might last twenty minutes or it could last sixteen hours, you never knew how long until it was over. But, every time, water was out of reach. Or, if it were within reach, there was no system for fetching it, no person who was allowed to get off and collect it: the cattle truck would remain shut.

One of those times, Walter could see through the slats of the wagon that their train had pulled up alongside a locomotive which was, at that moment, having its water tanks refilled. He could see the hose, gushing with water, gallons of it, some of it going into the train engine, the rest splashing on to the tracks. The sight of it was too tantalising. Walter stuck an arm through the gap, held out his mug and asked the locomotive driver for some.

The man ignored him, so Walter asked again. The engine driver did not even make eye contact as he replied, 'I'm not going to get myself shot for you bastards.'

They had been on the train for twenty-four or forty-eight hours by then, maybe longer, and yet it was that moment that perhaps shook Walter most. The Jews in the wagon were not only being degraded in front of each other, they were being rejected by the outside world. That driver could see and hear sick children begging to drink and he could not even look in their direction. Bastards, he had called them, while he stared into the middle distance.

Walter cursed him as a selfish, heartless swine. Only later did he understand that the SS had issued an edict that anyone caught helping deportees would be shot on sight. Only later did he appreciate that, before their train had crawled its way across the Polish countryside, another would have come and another; perhaps a man had given water to the people on those transports, only to pay with his life or with the life of his wife and children, as the Nazi SS mowed them down with machine-gun fire. Maybe the engine driver had witnessed the meting out of such instant punishment and had learned that, if he wanted to stay alive, it would be best not to see the human hands poking out of the cattle trucks holding out empty cups, best not to hear the cries of children gasping for water.

The journey went on, in fits and starts, in thirst and in stink, for three days. Maybe more, it was hard to tell. It meant that when the train finally stopped, when the wagon door was finally pulled open, those stacked inside felt relief and, strange to say it, gratitude. They felt sure the worst of their ordeal was over. They felt sure that, wherever they had arrived, it had to be better than what they had just endured.

This was their expectation as the train inched through the central station in the city of Lublin, juddering to a halt just past it. It may even have lasted for a second or two as the doors of the cattle truck were pulled open to reveal the welcoming party: a phalanx of SS men, armed with rifles, machine guns, sticks and whips.

But then the order came.

'Men fit for work aged between fifteen and fifty are to leave the cars. Children and old people remain.'

SS officers were marching up and down the length of the train, barking out a version of that instruction, always in German, though sometimes more concisely put:

'All men between fifteen and fifty, out!'

What? That made no sense. They had been told over and over that families would not be separated, that they would be resettled in these new villages *together*. They had had the word of the Slovak president, Father Tiso, himself. That's why those newly-weds had rushed their marriage.

Perhaps it was not an actual separation; maybe it was just a matter of sequencing: the men between fifteen and fifty would get off the train first, and the women, the children and the elderly would follow. Could that be it?

The answer came swiftly. No sooner had the younger men hauled themselves out of the wagons, clambering down as best as their legs, stiff with immobility, would allow, forming a line by the railway tracks as instructed, than the doors of the cattle trucks were pulled shut. Once he had got his bearings, Walter could see that the station was surrounded, chiefly by guards in distinctive uniforms who turned out to be Lithuanians, armed with automatic weapons.

A reflex made those left behind in the wagons reach towards their husbands, their sons, their brothers, poking their hands through the gaps in the timbers of the cattle trucks. It was not a gesture of fare-well so much as a plea, a desperate grasping for the consolation of touch. The SS men saw it too and responded with great efficiency, moving along the length of the train with their whips and sticks, striking those outstretched hands, whether they belonged to a bereft grandmother, bewildered toddler or new bride. Eventually, and with effort, the train wheezed away. The men watched it recede. Their families were gone.

The men comforted themselves by speculating that perhaps those they loved were being resettled after all. At the very least, they were not here, being herded into line by the SS, who used their sticks and whips as prods as they warned the men that they were about to march and that they had a long trek ahead of them.

If it would be easier, the men were told, they were welcome to put their suitcases on a truck; they would receive them later. Many took advantage of that offer, but not Walter. He was travel-ling light, with only a knapsack on his back. Besides, he had something the other men lacked. Younger than almost all of them, he had experience. Enough of it to have taught him that trust was a fool's game. Had he not learned that lesson when he made the mistake of trusting Josef, after their shared escape from Nováky? The bag would stay in the hands of the only person Walter could trust: himself.

The march was into the city of Lublin, though Walter noticed that their captors did not take main roads. The SS preferred to stick to back streets, as if they did not want this procession – like an ancient parade of slave drivers and their captives – to be seen. But once they had passed through Lublin, once they were on the open road, heading south-east of the city, any restraint was dropped. One SS man saw Walter's wristwatch. At gunpoint, he demanded it. Walter gave it to him.

After a while they passed a clothing factory. In the courtyard, lined up, were hundreds of prisoners, perhaps a thousand of them, obviously Jews. They all wore the same thing, a uniform of dirty stripes, and they were queuing for food. Walter stared at the men and felt his spirits sink.

The arrivals' destination was a site originally designated as a prisoner-of-war camp, known locally as the 'little Majdan' thanks to its proximity to the Lublin suburb of Majdan Tatarski. In Polish: Majdanek. But its official designation was as a *Konzentrationslager*, a concentration camp. Though that, as Walter would eventually discover, was an understatement.

# 4

# Majdanek

H<small>E CAUGHT HIS</small> first glimpse of it as they approached from a small hill, spotting the watchtowers, barracks and barbed-wire fence. But it was only once the gates of Majdanek opened before them that Walter and his fellow deportees saw those who were already imprisoned there. They looked like ghouls rather than men. Their heads were shaved and their bone-thin bodies were covered with threadbare uniforms, in those same macabre stripes. Their feet were in wooden clogs or else bare and visibly swollen. Walter did not know who they were or what had happened to them.

They never made eye contact with Walter or any of the newcomers. But they did speak to them. One came towards Walter straightaway, to deliver a warning that he and all the others would soon be deprived of their personal belongings. The rest carried on working – fetching, carrying, sweeping or digging – but out of the corner of their mouths, they would ask 'Any food? Anything in the pocket?' It was a practised routine, the words fired out automatically. And when someone tossed a morsel of food in their direction – it was too risky to hand food over directly – the reaction told Walter all he needed to know about life in Majdanek. The prisoners pounced on those tiny crumbs, fighting over them. They seemed to snarl, like starved dogs. And when guards stepped forward, to beat the prisoners with clubs, striking them on their backs as they hunched over the scraps, the captives ignored it, as if even the chance of a tiny bit of cheese or bread was worth the pain.

But Walter and the other new arrivals were not to be tourists in Majdanek for long. They were moved at speed through the camp's rigidly demarcated sections: one for the SS, one for 'administration' and a third for prisoners, which was itself further divided by barbed

wire into five sub-sections or 'fields' – Walter would be in Working
Section No. 2, along with plenty of other Czech and Slovak Jews
– with a watchtower in the corner of each, and two further rows
of electrified barbed-wire fencing surrounding the entire area. Walter
noticed that in this outdoor prison made up solely of drab, wooden
barracks, nothing grew. He could not see a single tree. It was as if
the earth had been scorched.

Induction was immediate. First, despite Walter's resolve to trust
no one, he was parted from his backpack. He was ordered to hand
it in at a barracks which styled itself as the Left Luggage counter.
The absurdity of that designation – more than that, the smirk it
contained, the mockery of those who saw it – would soon be obvious
even to a Majdanek novice. True, when Walter surrendered his bag
he received a ticket for it. But that only added to the black-is-white
dishonesty of the whole exercise: once left, this luggage would never
be reclaimed.

Next came the 'baths', though that too was misleading. It was
another barracks, except it was equipped with troughs and reeked
of disinfectant. The new prisoners were ordered to strip and then
immerse themselves in fetid water, like sheep in a dip. Those who
hesitated were hit with sticks.

Then they were to be sheared. The hair was taken off their heads
in seconds. After that, they were stood on stools so that all the hair
could be shaved from their bodies, including their armpits and
private parts. The stated purpose was pest control, getting rid of
lice, but for the SS there was an added benefit: draining the prisoners of a portion of their humanity. Finally, the men were handed
clothes: the striped jacket and trousers, wooden clogs and cap of a
concentration-camp prisoner.

At each stage, Walter looked less and less like himself. Now he
and all those who had arrived in the wagon a few hours earlier
looked the same as each other and more like those already here.
Still, and strangely, at the very moment the newcomers were losing
their individuality, the veteran prisoners began to gain theirs, at least
in Walter's eyes. Slowly he started to differentiate the striped spectres,
one from the other. He began to recognise some of their faces. These
were not shadows from the underworld, but rather fellow Jews from

Slovakia: the son of a rabbi Walter had known, a schoolteacher, the owner of a garage, a librarian, the son of a blacksmith whose party trick had been to bend a coin with his teeth. They were all here.

At the gate of one field, he spotted Erwin Eisler, his old study partner from Trnava, the boy who had defied the rules and illicitly held on to a chemistry textbook. Now, emaciated, he was pushing a wheelbarrow and scavenging for food.

Walter could see that there was a category of prisoner that inhabited a grey zone between captives and captors. These inmates might be dressed slightly differently, with a jacket or trousers that deviated from the regulation stripes, and often wore a green triangle over the heart, which he soon learned was the symbol across the concentration-camp universe for those inmates who were not Jews – whose triangles were yellow – but men banished to a camp following a conviction as a common criminal. A red triangle marked out a political prisoner, pink a homosexual, purple a Jehovah's Witness, but among these men the colour was almost always green. They were *Kapos*, deployed by the SS to do the brute work of enforcement, meting out violent discipline to their fellow inmates at the slightest provocation and sometimes for no reason at all. The men who had started clubbing those prisoners fighting for scraps of food from the new arrivals? They had been *Kapos*. As far as Walter could tell, what they lacked in Nazi rank they made up for in cruelty.

There was one last familiar face Walter would see in Majdanek. It belonged to his elder brother, Sammy.

Walter had not been in the camp long when a friend whose job involved carrying wood between sections told him that he had seen him, that indeed Sammy was in the next field.

Walter could hardly believe it. He knew both his brothers were in the same situation as he was, that they had been earmarked for deportation and supposed resettlement. But here, in the very same camp? Walter had to fight the urge to run that very moment to the barbed-wire barrier that separated one field from the other. But he had learned already that that was to take a lethal risk. Early on, he saw a man, working close by and apparently driven mad in his despair, make a sudden dash for the barbed-wire fence. He could only have gone a few paces when the shot rang out. Walter did not need to be taught twice: he understood that anyone seen near those fences could be killed in an instant. If he was to meet Sammy, there was a protocol to follow, one that demanded patience.

To talk to someone in a different section, you had to wait till dusk, when there were fewer *Kapos* around. There could be no congregating by the fence, because that too would get noticed. Instead, you had to wait your turn, queuing up away from the wire, out of sight.

The same system applied on both sides of the fence, so that Walter could see a small group forming on the other side of the line, as far away from the wire as he was, waiting in the shadows. But then, in the failing light, he saw it: the tall outline of his brother. A mutual reflex of recognition kicked in. At the same instant, they raised their arms in greeting.

But it was not yet their turn. Walter and Sammy had to watch as two others gingerly approached the boundary for their own moment of snatched conversation. Walter stood ready, a coiled spring. He watched the two already at the wire, waiting for the first sign that their conversation was coming to a conclusion.

At last, the man closest to him, on Walter's side of the fence, began to turn away. That was Walter's cue. He strode forward, watching as Sammy did the same. Soon they would be talking to each other, brother to brother. Who would have believed it, here in Majdanek.

But then, in an instant, the quiet of this twilight rendezvous point was broken. From nowhere came a gang of *Kapos*, clubs aloft. They began hitting the man who had just finished talking to his friend, truncheoning him in the head until he was out cold. Like birds scattering at a sudden sound, all those who had been waiting their turn disappeared into the dusk.

Walter was told the following day that Sammy had been moved to another field. There would be no night-time meet-up. In fact, Walter would never see his brother again. But the memory of that brief salute in the evening light, each raising their arm to the other, brother to brother – that memory would stay with him for ever.

The seventeen-year-old Walter was a quick student, a necessary quality in a concentration camp where the orientation period was measured in seconds. Training had been next to non-existent, beyond a few barked words of instruction on that first day from the *Oberkapo*, a chieftain among the *Kapos* but still a nothing in the eyes of the true masters of Majdanek. The *Oberkapo* had told Walter and the other new arrivals about the ritual of the *Appell*, the twice-daily roll call, morning and evening. How they were to gather in a square at the centre of the prisoner area, surrounded by the different fields, and line up in rows of ten. Caps off when an SS man approached, caps on when he moved away. They practised in the pouring rain for several hours. They were otherwise not to move a muscle, on pain of death. Any mistake or lapse in order would be punished with a beating.

So now Walter had had an education in two of the several ways people could die in Majdanek. You might be shot or you might be beaten to death. Other methods were also available. The barracks were so badly built, flimsy and cold, and so overcrowded – with sometimes up to a thousand people in a glorified hut meant to house 200 or fewer – that it was easy to get sick. Some barracks had no glass in the windows; many had no bunks at all: inmates had to sleep on the floor. The bunks consisted of nothing more than three long tables, stretching the length of the entire hut, placed one on top of the other. Supposedly that created a set of three-storey bunk beds.

There was a shortage of clothes and of medicine. Even the most basic sanitation was missing: there was no place to wash yourself or your clothes. There was no sewage system. During the day, wholly exposed sewage pits served as latrines. At night, there were large wooden containers in each barracks which functioned as communal toilets. Walter would soon discover that dysentery stalked the camp. Even if the disease did not kill you outright, getting it was a death sentence. Dysentery meant you were deemed unfit for work. And if you could not work, you were dead.

Some would try to defy the disease, lining up for work as if they were fit, only to empty their bowels where they stood. Walter remembered the fate of one fellow prisoner, Eckstein, a rabbi from the Slovak town of Sered', who caught the disease. It meant that one day he came to roll call a few minutes late. Their captors could not tolerate that. The SS officer in charge ordered his men to seize the rabbi and dip him head first in one of the latrines, submerging his face in sewage. Then he poured cold water over him, as if cleaning him off. Once that was done, the SS man drew his revolver and shot the rabbi dead.

Illness was rife and there was hardly any food to eat or water to drink. In the morning, before roll call and after a 5 or 6 a.m. wake-up, it might be black chicory coffee or an infusion brewed from weeds. In the evening, perhaps ten ounces of bread, accompanied by marmalade or a pale imitation of butter, artificial fat of the worst quality, washed down with the same brew they had drunk at the start of the day. Twice a week there might be a slice of horsemeat sausage or beetroot. No wonder Erwin had looked so skeletally thin.

Given all this, Walter should not have been surprised by one aspect of the morning roll call that had been overlooked in the *Oberkapo's* briefing. But he was, all the same. While he and the others did their best to line up in neat, regimented lines of ten, as instructed, there was a category of prisoner that did nothing of the sort. It consisted of the dead, heaped in a pile just behind the living, and counted just as methodically, their bodies taken to the crematorium and burned. These were the men who had died in the night, whether from hunger, violence or something less visible – the light going out, as they lost the will to live. Walter did his best to count the dead and then remember the number, keeping a mental tally in his head. It became a habit.

After roll call, it was work, much of it back-breaking. Work, Walter understood rapidly, was life. The message was rammed home in the camp song, in which they were drilled during their first days at Majdanek and which they were forced to stand and sing, again and again, for hours on end, even after a full day's grinding toil, which took an enormous physical effort. Once memorised, the words stayed with Walter long afterwards. He could not shake them:

> *Aus ganz Europa kamen, wir Juden nach Lublin.*
> *Viel Arbeit gibt's zu leisten, und dies ist der Beginn.*

> From the whole of Europe came we Jews to Lublin
> Much work has to be done, and this is just the beginning.

For some, the work that had to be done meant being marched by the *Kapos* away from Majdanek itself, to nearby industrial sites and factories. Walter watched as the men left the camp, that hymn to the nobility of labour ringing in his ears, and a thought planted itself, one that would not grow and ripen until much later.

For him, there was to be no such offsite trip. He was to work in the camp itself, in construction, carting around bricks and wood at speed, under pressure from *Kapos* who would hit anyone who did not keep running.

And so on that day in the summer of 1942 Walter Rosenberg became one of the 13,000 Slovak Jewish men who were shipped to Majdanek to work as slaves. Quite what he and his fellow prisoners were building was not clear. Nobody told them.

Of course, he never stopped thinking about escape. He was as determined as ever to do it, but it was clear that there was a right way and a wrong way to go about it. The fate of the man who had rushed at the fence confirmed that merely to be suspected of trying to escape was a capital crime. After that, Walter would not even allow himself to get close to the barrier, lest it look like an attempted escape. No, breaking free from Majdanek would require a much greater act of imagination than his escape from Nováky.

Opportunity came sooner than he would ever have expected. He heard a *Kapo* patrolling the barracks, bellowing out an appeal for 400 volunteers to do farm work.

Walter did not hesitate. Farm work was rich in possibility. It would be away from the camp; most likely, there would be transport involved, probably a train. That created options. The work would be out in the open, away from this tightly policed prison camp. That made escape at least imaginable. Among the thousand men who eagerly offered themselves as volunteers, Walter was one of the first.

'I'm leaving the camp soon,' he told one of the more seasoned prisoners, with something like pride. 'The train's due to leave in a few days.'

His fellow inmate, a Czech political prisoner, gave him a kick. 'Are you crazy? Do you know where that train's going?'

'No,' Walter replied, ditching the load he had been carrying.

'Look, you fool. I've been in Dachau. That was bad enough.' Back there, he explained, when the SS truly wanted to punish someone, this new place was where they sent them. The Czech was adamant: Walter was making a huge mistake.

'Go there and you'll die,' he said.

But Walter's mind was made up. For him, the destination was irrelevant. The exit from Majdanek and the chance of escape that came with it, that was the point. Or as he put it to his older comrade: 'Anywhere's better than this dump.'

When the day came for the volunteers to leave, Walter sought out the Czech to say goodbye. The man did not wish him luck. He told him simply, 'You'll be sorry.'

After that, Walter lined up with the rest of the volunteers as they were told to strip out of and discard their striped uniforms and put on regular clothes instead. They were handed trousers, jacket, shirt and cap, all ill-fitting and mismatched. Walter looked at the clothes and wondered who had worn them before. They might belong to any one of them, the prisoners gathered in this gang of 400 or the inmates they were about to leave behind. They might be the garments of the dead, those whose bodies were stacked and counted each morning at roll call.

Walter understood immediately why this change of costume was necessary. They were about to be marched to Lublin station, back through the streets of the city. The SS men clearly did not want the locals to see the way they kept their slaves. Hence the caps, to cover up their shaven heads.

Still, real clothes were real clothes and Walter and the others were glad to be wearing them. It took the edge off the long delay, as they stood around for hours waiting to be checked and processed. Eventually they were formed into a column, SS men took up their positions on either side of them, and they began to march. After just twelve days in Majdanek, Walter was leaving. It was a fine morning in late June and he was focused on what he thought lay ahead: the chance of something different, above all the chance of escape.

As if reading his mind, the SS officer in charge addressed Walter and his fellow would-be farm workers once they had arrived at Lublin station. He explained that they would be given food for the journey, which they should save because he had no idea how long it would last.

'And remember,' he said. 'It is useless trying to escape.'

Naturally, that only made Walter think about it more. No sooner had the heavy doors of the cattle truck been locked and bolted and the train got under way than he was looking for gaps in the enemy's defences. Even before that, when the captives were herded inside, he was looking for a potential co-conspirator.

As luck would have it, he saw a familiar face, a fellow veteran of Nováky. His name was Josef Erdelyi and there was another connection too: Walter had been at school with Josef's girlfriend.

Walter had learned to make swift assessments and he soon determined that Josef was made of the right stuff, that he could be trusted: after his experience with the other, love-struck Josef in Topol'čany, Walter knew that that was the one indispensable quality. Soon he had whispered the word 'escape'. Josef was receptive and both now began to examine the wagon closely. The window was barred, but the floor offered possibilities. If they could only punch a hole in it, they could wait for the train to slow down, then drop through it and out. They agreed to do nothing till after nightfall. In the dark, a getaway would be easier.

It did not take long for that hope to fade. At their first stop, twenty-four hours into the journey, when the doors were opened for the first time, the SS man in charge barked out another briefing. There was to be a headcount, here and at every stop to come. If any man was found missing, 'ten men in his wagon will be shot'.

That put an end to it. It was one thing to risk his own life. But to take the lives of ten others? No. And if there was one thing Walter had learned these last few months, the SS did not make empty threats.

They travelled another thirty-six hours in that cattle truck. It followed the same pattern as the voyage that had taken Walter from Nováky to Majdanek less than a fortnight earlier. The initial food ration – in this case, some bread, marmalade and salami – ran out along with the little water they had been given. The thirst was as intense as it was before, perhaps even more so given the suffocating heat of a wagon packed with eighty adult men. Once again, there would be no relief: the train stopped outside, rather than at, the stations where there might be a chance to fill up. When those breaks came, Walter and his fellow captives had to watch the SS men drinking from canteens that seemed to overflow with fresh, cold water.

Eventually, the train slowed down for the last time as it arrived at its destination. Walter peeked through a gap in the wagon doors. He saw watchtowers, which were familiar enough, but also buildings made of brick, so different from the primitive wooden shacks of Majdanek.

The doors were opened and the SS corralled the prisoners off the train and into line. Once their masters were satisfied, they were ordered to march.

Walter noticed another difference. He was walking on a proper, paved road, not one of the dirt tracks of Majdanek. Most striking of all, he saw bushes and trees – such a welcome sight after the desolate blankness of the camp outside Lublin.

Something like optimism entered his heart that summer evening, as he approached this mysterious place. It endured even as he saw the beam of the searchlight on the camp entrance, illuminating the posse of SS men who stood there, gun in one hand, the leash of an Alsatian dog in the other. It drew strength from the clean, well-kept courtyard and from the tall, double gates that guarded this place, bearing a simple three-word slogan: *Arbeit Macht Frei*, Work Makes You Free. If work was what this place was about, that was all to the good. He was young and fit; he could certainly work. Thank heavens he had rejected the advice that would have kept him in Majdanek and away from here. Because fortune really did seem to have smiled upon him.

It was 9 p.m. on 30 June 1942. And Walter Rosenberg was in Auschwitz.

# PART II
## The Camp

# 5

## We Were Slaves

WALTER ROSENBERG SAW the twin rows of white concrete posts, each one equipped with porcelain insulators and linked by what looked to be high-voltage wires, and concluded that an electrified double fence enveloped the camp. He saw the watchtowers, on each of which was posted an SS man, his hands on a mounted machine gun; he saw the searchlight that constantly swept the camp after dark; and he saw the highly disciplined dogs that accompanied their SS masters. He looked closely at it all and wondered what secret was being guarded at this place that made it so imperative that no one ever be allowed to break out.

That first late evening he still had reason to believe that he had taken a step up from the filth and chaos of Majdanek. The barracks were not just solid – brick built, on several floors and as big as a secondary school – but each one had its own number, marked on both a painted sign and an electric lantern by the doorway.

It was dark when they were marched towards Block 16, then sent down to the basement. There they had a briefing of sorts from the block senior, a *Kapo*, wearing the distinct green triangle of the criminal (a convicted murderer, as it happened). This man warned the new arrivals that, no matter how thirsty they got, they were not to drink the water from the tap on the wall: that was a fast track to dysentery. Walter committed the advice to memory. He slept that night on the floor.

The next morning brought a 5 a.m. start for *Appell* at 6 a.m. As he had already learned at Majdanek, roll call was to count both the living and the dead, the latter category understood also to include the dying. If the figures all tallied, and no one was missing or presumed escaped, then the roll call would be declared over and the corpses could be taken away – each body carried by a single prisoner on his back, with the lifeless head lolling over one of his shoulders. As the pairs staggered off, they looked to Walter like double-headed monsters, prisoner and corpse joined together shuffling slowly towards the mortuary: it was hard to tell which one was dead and which alive, because they were both skin and bone.

It was strange for him and the other new arrivals, lined up in their civilian clothes, watching the inmates march off to hard labour while they were to stay behind. They were left to amble around the camp, around its open areas at any rate, trying to make sense of it. It was only on the following day that they were plunged into the ritual of induction, a re-run of the process Walter had undergone two weeks earlier in Majdanek.

It began with a forced trip to the showers. The *Kapos* beat them in there with clubs, herding 400 into a room built to contain thirty at most, then beat them back out again, kicking and clubbing them until they were standing naked in the cold. After that, still naked and shivering, came something new. They lined up to be tattooed with their Auschwitz number. Two fellow prisoners acted as clerks, taking down the inmates' names and places of birth: Walter was entered into the ledger as having been born in Pressburg, the old Austro-Hungarian name for Bratislava. He gave his occupation as 'locksmith', adopting the trade of the man who was not quite his stepfather but regularly at his mother's side. That done, it was time to be marked. Previously, the tattooing process had meant being leaned against a wall by a prisoner who then pressed a special stipple, resembling a stamp with metal numbers, into the left side of the chest, just under the collarbone. Often it was done with such brutality that many deportees fainted. But on this day, Walter was offered a choice. He could be branded on the left or right arm, on the outside or the underside. Walter nominated the top of his left forearm, where the mark would be immediately visible, and so it was done. For the next two and a half years, he would not use his name officially again. From that day on, he was 44070. Before long he would learn the importance of numbers in Auschwitz, how a low, 'old number' marked you out as a veteran, putting you closer to the top of the camp hierarchy whose strictures and privileges inmates strictly observed.

Eventually, they were given clothes. Their old ones were taken away, never to be returned and they were handed the familiar uniform made of coarse cloth, patterned with dull grey-blue and white stripes. So Walter would be a human zebra like all the others. Yet as he pulled on the tunic-cum-shirt – his number sewn on to it alongside the standard symbol for Jewish inmates, a star formed from two triangles, one the red of a political prisoner, the other yellow – as well as the trousers, baggy cap and wooden clogs, he took comfort, and not only from the fact that he was no longer exposed to the elements. He also liked that he was now indistinguishable, at a glance at least, from the rest of the pack, that he could, if he worked at it, melt unnoticed into the crowd. To disappear was, in its own way, a kind of escape.

And yet he could not escape death. He saw it in the faces of those who marched off for work, in neat rows of five and columns of one hundred, straight after roll call. There was something strange about the way many of them walked, more marionette than human, their movements jerky and angular as they struggled to keep up. They were inspected as they left, watched by a man whom Walter would come to fear as an especially vicious brute among brutes, SS-Oberscharführer Jakob Fries. He was improbably tall, a mountain of a man, his face broad, his eyes pitiless, forever armed with a club almost as big as he was. His task was to weed out those too weak to work. His favoured method was to test their strength with his stick or his boot. If they could withstand the blow or the kick, then they might be allowed to carry on to work. If they could not, their fate was sealed.

There was a term for such men and Walter soon learned it. The living dead, walking skeletons with bowed heads and sunken, hollow eyes, were known in the camp as *Muselmänner*: non-men whose muscle and flesh had wasted away, who were expiring in plain sight, the breath of life leaving them slowly but inexorably. And yet, in some, the will to survive still flickered. Before an inspection, it was not uncommon to see two *Muselmänner* slapping each other in the face, to redden their cheeks and feign vitality. Walter watched those Fries deemed unfit staggering back into the camp where, if they were lucky, they might be given some manageable task, perhaps in the timber yard. If not, they would be sent to the camp hospital. That, Walter soon understood, was a death sentence.

Death was all around. On that first day, Walter saw a team of prisoners loading a cart with what he estimated were 200 corpses, piling them up like so many carcasses on a butcher's wagon. Close by were a couple of prisoners he recognised from Trnava.

'What's going on here?' he asked one of the pair, gesturing towards the dead. The reply was delivered without emotion.

'They're today's harvest.'

They were looking at the corpses of men who had died the previous evening, whether through a beating or starvation or illness. Their bodies would be taken away and burned. Walter was left in no doubt that what he had seen was utterly routine.

He learned something else from those two prisoners, something important that would stay with him. It was about the fate of the rest of the men who had made up the pair's original transport from Trnava. There had been 600 of them at the start and now only ten remained, including these two, Otto and Ariel. It turned out that the rest had been given an horrific task: burning the bodies of Soviet prisoners of war killed by the SS. Those who survived that ordeal were then put to death, Otto explained, 'because they knew too much'.

Walter would hear of such things in snatched fragments, piecing them together slowly and over time. All he knew on those first days in Auschwitz was that staying fit and strong was essential – he was glad of those days in the orphanage, playing football – and that work was a prerequisite for survival.

Walter was assigned initially to the SS food store but that did not last long. He and Josef would be bounced around multiple labour details. Their first transfer was to Buna.

Buna was to be a mammoth *Industriekomplex*, a planned network of factories and plants that would sprawl across an expanse of land bigger than the main Auschwitz camp and the much larger neighbouring site at Birkenau, known as Auschwitz II, put together. 'Buna' was the product that would be made there, a form of synthetic rubber deemed necessary for the war effort. But first these factories had to be built, work that would be done by slave labour. Which is where Walter and Josef came in.

Wake-up came at 3 a.m., too early for roll call. A green-triangled German *Kapo* issued the advice that from now on the men should eat only half of their nightly bread allocation, saving the rest for the following morning because there would be no food till noon and they would need it. 'You're going to work harder than you've ever worked in your lives,' he said. Before that, there was a heavy march to be completed. Walter, Josef and the others headed off in the now familiar fashion: rows of five, columns of one hundred, past the scrutinising eye of Oberscharführer Fries, and through the gate.

The very first time Walter walked out through that gate, when the second black-and-white barrier lifted, he had allowed himself a fleeting thought of escape. Surely, the mere act of leaving the premises like this meant that it was at least theoretically possible. But that consoling thought had dissipated the day he reached one of the higher storeys of the building that housed the SS food store. From that vantage point he saw that the outer reaches of Auschwitz were surrounded by a perimeter of their own, a chain of watchtowers much like the ones that policed the inner camp: structures with windows on three sides, the fourth left open for the SS man behind a mounted machine gun. Walter understood then that the camp had been laid out in such a way that anyone trying to break for the outer fence would be visible instantly from these crows' nests. They would be gunned down before they even got close.

So there was no exhilaration to be felt in the dark as Walter, Josef and the others marched into the unknown, no kernel of hope that they might see a gap in the Nazi defences. There was only dread.

They reached a railway track. There they waited until a long goods train – made up of some seventy or eighty wagons – pulled in. An instant later, the SS men were using clubs and dogs and the threat of automatic weapons to push the men into the wagons. The pressure of it was suffocating. The truck was divided into two, one section for what Walter estimated was about one hundred prisoners, the other for the *Kapo* and three or four henchmen. The last time Walter had been kicked and shoved into a cattle truck like this, his first instinct had been to look for an opening, a hatch, some means of escape. He had no such thoughts now. His only goal was to survive.

The journey was awful. They were crammed so closely together that the smell of blood, sweat and shit made him gag. One man close by was nursing an arm broken by a *Kapo*, another had succumbed to dysentery. Walter was desperate to get off that train.

But exit brought no relief. From the instant the doors of the cattle truck opened, Walter understood that what he had endured so far was mild compared to what was to come. The *Kapos* were already in a fury, whipping and beating the prisoners at a frenetic pace, lashing them as they shouted, 'Faster, you bastards!', watched by SS men who, armed with guns and Alsatian dogs, seemed to be in a similar fever, kicking the *Kapos* for not moving quickly enough.

Walter saw a *Kapo* bludgeon a man just in front of him who had made the mistake of stumbling. The blow made the man stagger, straying out of line, which prompted an SS officer to open fire. But the SS man missed, killing the prisoner next to his target. Now a *Kapo* demanded that the stumbling prisoner pick up the dead body and carry it.

'This is not a graveyard!' he bellowed.

That set the tone. Men, weak from hunger, deprived of sleep and under a hot summer sun, were being lashed like pack animals, pushed to use the strength they did not have to go faster and faster. The walk was a couple of miles, though it felt much longer. It was at around 8 a.m., having had nothing to eat or drink since being woken five hours earlier, that they finally reached the building site.

Walter surveyed a diabolical scene. At first glance, it was as one might expect: cement mixers, iron girders, timber, concrete posts, metal rods standing to attention, half-completed structures waiting to be filled in and finished. But all around men were running from one place to another at an abnormal pace, as if in a film played at double or triple speed.

The prisoners were harried at every turn, slaloming between *Kapos* who would kick them or hit them with a stick or metal pipe if they slackened and SS men who would shoot at the slightest provocation. It never let up, the air crackling with the sound of gunfire or a whip lacerating human skin, prisoners falling dead and still the *Kapos* demanding the living move faster.

Walter was tasked with shifting bags of cement. A sack was thrown on to his back and he had to run as fast as he could with it, dodging his way through an assault course of *Kapos* prodding him to move ever more quickly, whipping or hitting him every ten or fifteen yards. Walter saw fellow prisoners fall, only for a *Kapo* to crush their skull, leaving a corpse Walter had to take care not to trip over. Once he had reached the mixing machine, there was no rest. He had to run back, double time, to get another bag. And then another and another. For hours, it went on, in the heat and the dust, without food or drink or pause.

This was how the men of Buna were worked, tyrannised and brutalised to meet an impossible deadline, men falling to the ground from exhaustion and starvation or else from the bullet or bludgeon of their masters.

Walter barely had time to look up. Still, he could not help but notice a further element to this already deranged picture, one that took it from the cruel to the outright surreal. For the prisoners and their tormentors were not the only players in this drama. Dispersed among them were civilians: besuited men carrying note-books and folding rulers, for all the world like a team of well-heeled architects inspecting the construction of a new office building or concert hall. These men who appeared not to see them – indeed seemed able to look right through them, even as they threaded their way through a minefield of dead bodies – were not SS officers or *Kapos* but the engineers and managers of the site's proprietor, the German industrial conglomerate IG Farben.

After four hours, a whistle blew and Walter could stop. He saw Josef nearby, sunk to the ground, his head between his knees. It was noon, and food appeared. A version of soup, the same as every other day, either potato or turnip, doled out in one bowl containing about a litre, to be shared between five people. There were no spoons. So desperate men, famished from the work and thirsty from the heat, would have to discipline themselves to swallow no more than the two or three mouthfuls that were theirs. Afterwards, the same routine, one bowl between five men, this time containing some ersatz tea.

The thirst built up over the morning was intense. There was a water tap, but once again the prisoners had been warned: it was infected. Anybody who drank from it would die. Even so, there were some who could hold out no longer. They drank from the tainted source, and soon they were dead.

At 1 p.m., the whistle blew again and somehow, from somewhere, they had to find the strength to resume work. Not all of them could do it. Some lay on the ground, where the *Kapos* would give them a good kicking or clubbing to see if they were faking exhaustion. Often it was not mere tiredness; they were unable to move because they were dead.

Walter and Josef, however, got lucky. They were recruited by a French civilian who wanted them for a less onerous task: twisting metal rods to form structures that would soon be encased in concrete. The Frenchman explained that his patch was about forty yards square and that inside it he was in charge. But if Walter or Josef were to step beyond it, there was nothing he could do: they would be at the mercy of the *Kapos* and the SS.

Walter believed it because he had already seen that much of the Buna building site was divided into small sectors, perhaps ten yards by ten yards, each guarded by an armed SS man. Whoever so much as stepped outside their sector during working hours was shot without warning for having 'attempted to escape'. That occasioned much sport for the officers of the SS and their enforcers. A *Kapo* would grab a prisoner's hat, then toss it over the ten-yard perimeter fence, telling him, 'Run for the hat.' If the prisoner refused, he would be clubbed by the *Kapos* for disobeying their orders. But if he did as he was told, he would be shot by the SS.

Thanks to their patron, Walter and his friend were exempt from such treatment. When the whistle blew for day's end at sunset, they only had to look at the state of the returning party to appreciate their luck. For the living were now shoulder to shoulder with the dead and the dying. Auschwitz rules demanded that any working party of one hundred that had left the main camp had to return in the same number. That meant those who had survived the day at Buna had to carry back with them those who had not: one body between two prisoners, carried on their shoulders like a rolled-up rug. Counting had become a habit, and Walter made a quick tally. By his calculation, every group of one hundred included between five and ten corpses.

They too had to be present for the evening roll call which followed a day's work. Those who could not stand up to be counted were stacked on the ground in piles of ten. There was a distinct pattern. The first body down would have its legs spread, so that the second corpse could be laid on top of it, though in the opposite direction, with its head between the first man's legs. The legs of this second man would then be spread, so that a third could be placed on top, facing in the same direction as the first, with its head once again between the legs of the corpse below. That way, each stack would be easy to count: five heads on one side, five on the other. This smoothed the process for the SS considerably. They merely needed to count each stack as a unit of ten. That handily mirrored the pattern for the living, who also lined up in rows of ten in such a way that the SS officer could count them at speed. To count up a barracks that was meant to contain, say, 953 people could be the work of a minute: ninety-two rows of the living with three more in the last row, plus three stacks of the dead. Easy.

With that done, a gong would be sounded signalling that no one was to move. If they did, they would be shot. Now, once the entire camp was perfectly still, a second SS team could check the numbers from each barrack, then bring those figures to the camp commandant who was seated by a table at a central point in a spot by the kitchen block. His team of registrars would add up the numbers and then declare the number of prisoners present in the camp. They did not specify how many were dead and how many were alive. It happened that way every morning and every evening, day after day.

Perhaps because they were young, perhaps because, thanks to their French protector, their work at Buna was lighter than others', Josef and Walter endured a month or more in a place that devoured almost all who entered. They worked out that, of their initial column of one hundred that had marched to Buna on that first day, only the pair of them had survived.

It meant that they were around for the temporary suspension of the Buna shuttle, as the daily transport of workers to and from the site was stopped following an outbreak of typhus, thought to have originated in the women's camp. Those prisoners who had somehow endured the back-breaking labour, the hunger and the brutality of the *Kapos* were now succumbing to disease. The Buna death rate, already high, was climbing; the authorities feared that IG Farben's civilian employees might get infected. Walter, Josef and the others were reassigned. Their new workplace was the gravel pits.

Located just outside the perimeter, these were natural quarries, deep reserves of gravel for which the Auschwitz authorities had found a use. The gravel would help in the manufacture of concrete posts for the camp. Excavating it was not easy, but they had Jewish slaves for that – including Walter.

The pits were so deep that, even when standing in them, the prisoners' heads were below ground level. From there, they were instructed to shovel the gravel on to a horse-drawn wagon that was waiting by the lip of the pit. Everything about it was hard. For prisoners starved into weakness, just lifting the shovel was an ordeal: it was so heavy. But merely lifting it was not enough. The inmates had to raise it above head height if they were to have any chance of getting the gravel on to the bed of the wagon. Except the gravel was full of water, which not only made it even heavier, it also meant every time they pitched a spadeful, they got drenched. The water would trickle from their necks to their shoulders, right down to their toes, soaking them to the skin. Prisoners found their feet, barely protected by a pair of wooden clogs, rapidly became swollen. For all his youth and vigour, it happened to Walter: he soon found he could not move properly.

The problem was so widespread, the overseers ordered an inspection by a medical 'commission'. Walter did not have to be told what would happen to those deemed unfit to work.

When the time came, he lined up with the others, ready to be judged. It took all his strength to stand at full height, keep his back straight and hold the pose. He was desperate to control himself, not to let his expression give him away. Even if he wanted to scream, these men would not see his swollen feet or the intense pain he was in.

Two hundred men failed that test. They were sent immediately to the adjoining camp at Birkenau. But Walter was not one of them. His performance had worked; he had mastered the pain. He was still alive.

Would he have survived even one more day in the pits? He never had to answer that question, because he was – in another stroke of fortune – transferred once more. Now he was detailed for labour at the Deutsche Ausrüstungswerke or DAW, the German Equipment Works, an SS-owned business whose vast premises were right by the main Auschwitz camp, and which were perhaps eight times the size.

The DAW specialised in kitting out the German military, whether with boots, uniforms or military hardware. Among the items its workers made, perhaps destined for use by German troops on the eastern front in midwinter, were skis. Walter's job was to paint them. After what he had seen at Buna and what he had been through in the gravel pits, the prospect must have seemed like a holiday. He would be indoors and, besides, how strenuous could ski-painting be?

But there was nothing casual about this assignment. Each worker had to paint a prescribed minimum number of skis each shift: 110. Failure to paint that number, and paint them properly, would bring a thorough flogging. It meant there was no let-up.

Walter only had to look at a fellow DAW group to see the consequences of missing a production target or falling below the standards set by their captors. Nearby was a group charged with making cases for shells, including, at one point, a batch of 15,000. The order was completed only for an inspection to reveal that the cases were fractionally too small. The SS determined that that was a deliberate act and they shot several Jews for sabotage.

But soon there was a new threat to confront. One August evening, the prisoners returned from a day's labour to find the camp abuzz, lit up not just by the usual searchlights but by portable ones carried by SS men wearing battery packs on their backs. Everyone seemed to be up and about, the workers of both the night and day shifts all gathered in the main square. But they were not lined up for a special roll call. Instead, Walter could hear the sound of wood against stone, of clogs scuffling on the ground at a frenzied tempo: men were running backwards and forwards, as if in some crazed round of late-night exercise.

It took a while for Walter to understand. They were kept standing and in silence for hour after hour, as midnight came and went, waiting and waiting until 3 a.m. when Walter caught a glimpse, in the glare of the searchlight, of the club-wielding human mountain, Jakob Fries, presiding over a macabre nocturnal Olympiad.

As if assessing competing athletes, Fries had each prisoner move past one by one. Once an inmate was directly in front of him, he would inspect the man's legs. If they looked bloated, a jerk of Fries's thumb would send the man to the left. If they did not, Fries would order the prisoner to sprint: twenty yards there, twenty yards back. Those who ran well were pointed to the right. Those who staggered or swayed were sent to join the other rejects on the left.

One after another, they came before Fries. *Run*. To the left. *Run*. To the right. *Run*. To the left. To the left. To the left. *Run*. To the right . . .

Walter looked over at the group on the left, who were now being led away as others took their place. He had been in Auschwitz long enough, he had heard enough stories, to know what happened to those who failed Fries's fitness tests. Meanwhile, the inspection line was getting shorter. Soon it would be him.

He was so tired, the exhaustion eating into his marrow. During the long wait, he had fallen asleep while standing up. And now it was his turn. Despite the fatigue and the hunger, he knew that he was about to run for his life. He would have to mine deep into himself and find, buried somewhere, a pocket of energy. He set off.

He ran the first stretch as hard as he could, his feet pounding on the ground. On the return leg, he could see him, the monstrous Fries, standing there with his club, waiting.

Now would come the verdict.

The Oberscharführer raised his hand, most of it balled into a fist, and jerked his thumb. He had assessed Walter Rosenberg, who prided himself on being a fit and strong lad not yet eighteen years old, and decided to send him not to the right but to the left.

Exhausted as he was, breathless as he was, Walter could feel himself fill up with fear. His friend Josef was running now, stumbling then stumbling again. When Fries despatched him too to the left, to stand with Walter and about forty others, that sealed it. They had both failed the test. Walter looked at his fellow rejects and noticed something that, at last, explained what was happening. These men were shivering, but not from the cold. They had a fever. Which could mean only one thing. Typhus.

So that was why they were examining the prisoners' legs. They were looking for signs of the dark spotty rash or the joint and muscle pain that would count as early symptoms. Now Walter understood. The masters of Auschwitz feared the camp was about to be engulfed by a new wave of the disease. In March, they had responded to an outbreak in the women's camp by dunking those infected in baths of Lysol, but that only made things worse, accelerating the spread. Before long, typhus was claiming 500 lives a month. If it had only been prisoners who were at risk, the SS would not have worried: prisoner lives were dispensable. But the Nazis dreaded this disease for themselves. The lice that carried it had no respect for rank or racial classification: they could transfer the blood of an infected Jew to an Aryan in an instant. What's more, the SS saw that the well-fed found it harder to recover from typhus than did the starving. If they wanted to eradicate the louse, they would have to eradicate all those who carried it. Put another way, they would not attempt to heal the sick. They would kill the sick.

So it was that those who failed Jakob Fries's sprint test that August night were put to death: on 29 August 1942 a total of 746 prisoners were killed. Walter and Josef, wobbly on their feet after so many hours without food or sleep, had been selected to stand among the condemned. They had been chosen to die.

Not more than twenty yards away stood those who had won from Fries the reprieve of a rightward flick of the thumb. Walter eyed the distance between the two groups, his and theirs, wondering if there was a way to make a run for it. But there were SS men all around, armed and vigilant. There was surely no way.

The ranks of the rejects were swelling. With his gift for swift and accurate counting, Walter estimated there were now eighty of them. Judging by what he had seen, the guards would wait till the number had reached a hundred, then march them off. If he waited much

longer, he would be led to his death, he was sure of it. And yet to
break out was to guarantee the same outcome. Those of his fellow
condemned who had similarly worked out their fate had surely
reached the same conclusion: weak and sick and surrounded by
armed SS men, there was nothing they could do. He and Josef
exchanged desperate whispers.

And then, once again, Walter was blessed with good fortune and
an unexpected act of kindness. It came in the form of two sudden,
sharp blows to the shoulders.

'You bastards! What the hell are you doing here?'

The speaker was a *Kapo*, one known to Josef rather than Walter.
He was berating the pair of them for failing to obey orders, for
standing in the wrong group. Loudly, he shoved them out of the
gathering of the dead and towards the living. Once there, he dropped
the performance, gestured towards those now being led towards the
crematorium, those with whom Walter and Josef had stood a matter
of seconds earlier, and said, 'You're lucky, boys.' It was the truth.

After that, the group was marched towards a hole in the fence
that separated the men's section from the women's. Since his arrival,
Walter had done little more than glimpse the inmates there, just
enough to see that they did not look like any women he had ever
seen. They were starved, dressed in old rags of Red Army uniforms,
and were barefoot or wore wooden shoes. Their hair was shorn.

Walter and the others were told to strip and then move through
the hole. First, though, two *Kapos* performed one last inspection of
their legs, then wiped their naked bodies down with a cloth soaked
in disinfectant. Only then were they free to pass through into what
had been the women's camp. It was now vacant. Half the previous
occupants had been deemed too ill to be allowed to live; the other
half had been relocated to the women's camp in Birkenau.

It was quite a cull that night. The Auschwitz grapevine said that
half the prisoner population of the camp had been murdered. But
it did not solve the typhus problem. There would be another weeding-
out of the sick in mid-October, another the following January and
another in February.

For Walter and the others, it meant a new start. Their heads were
shaved to stubble again, they were washed and issued with a new

striped uniform. They would live in the former women's camp and, thanks to the thinning out of the ranks, there would be more space. New work units were organised too. Walter would not return to Buna, the gravel pits or the ski-painting workshop, but would be sent somewhere else: Canada.

# 6

## Kanada

CANADA WAS ANOTHER country and another world. A land of plenty, where stomachs were full, the wine was fine and the menu forever packed with exotic delights. It was a place of sensual pleasures, of crisp sheets, silk stockings and soft, plush furs. There was wealth in every denomination, gold and silver, diamonds and pearls. It might have been the richest, most luxurious place in Europe. And it was in Auschwitz.

Walter had heard tell of Canada, or rather Kanada, the Auschwitz Eldorado where no one ever went hungry, where, on the contrary, the most pressing question was which delicacy to feast on first. Only those blessed with the most improbable luck found their way there. And Walter was to be blessed once more.

It came after the typhus purge, when he was still naked, his skin still glistening with disinfectant. In the throng of men who had survived the cull, he heard someone speaking Slovak. Instinctively, Walter approached. The man turned out to be a dentist from a town not far from Trnava. A prisoner for five months, Laco Fischer counted as a hardened veteran – and he took a shine to Walter and Josef, two fellow Slovak Jews.

He told them that he had once walked the gold-paved ground of Kanada and that he was determined to get back. He had heard they were looking for recruits and he still had some pull with the *Kapos* from there. He used it, recommending himself and both of them into the bargain. Their youth, their strength, their relative fitness made them eminently eligible hires for what Walter would soon discover was an elite unit. With a word from the dentist, and after a brief physical test – another sprint, there and back – the *Kapos* gave the nod: Walter and Josef were in.

Now, after the sweat and struggle of his first few weeks in Auschwitz, where each day entailed a frantic, exhausting effort to survive, everything improved. They were housed in the basement of Block 4, offered actual showers, with water that was neither stone cold nor scalding hot. Each man had his own bunk and blanket. Whatever cruelties the SS and their enforcers maintained outside this building, inside it the *Kapos* spoke to them in an even voice, with no shouting and no snarling. Most notable, there were no beatings. Walter could hardly believe his fortune.

In the morning, the *Appell* revealed how much had changed. It seemed as if there were half as many prisoners assembled in twice the space. The *Muselmänner* were gone; only prisoners capable of holding their heads back and their shoulders straight were present. To Walter, Auschwitz now resembled a body whose diseased limbs had been amputated. It was shameful to admit it, but he found the sight of it almost exhilarating.

Then came the order, summoning the *Aufraumungskommando*, the Clearing Command, to march to work. This was the Kanada group, and Walter was proud to be part of it.

Their destination was close to Walter's last place of work, the DAW. It consisted of six large barracks. Five of them were wooden, each the size of a large stable, while the sixth was built from brick with a veranda from which the SS man in charge could watch proceedings, all arranged around a huge, square yard. Walter estimated it as covering more than two acres. The area was enclosed by barbed wire, with a watchtower in each corner, manned by guards armed with machine guns. What stunned Walter was the mountain formed in the middle, a vast pile of every kind of luggage: suitcases, rucksacks, trunks, parcels and kitbags. Nearby was a similar hill, formed entirely of blankets, thousands upon thousands of them. Close to that was another mound, shaped out of the battered and worn steel of pots and pans.

For this was the place officially known as the *Effektenlager*, the store of personal effects. Here were brought the belongings of all new arrivals to Auschwitz, taken from them as soon as they arrived. It fell to the Clearing Command to open the knapsacks and suitcases and sort the items inside, separating those things that could be used from those that were to be discarded.

Walter barely had a moment to absorb what he was seeing before he was plunged in to work. The prisoners were to attack the mountain of luggage at top speed, grabbing as many bags as they could carry, ideally two suitcases in each hand, then running with their load to one of the stable-sized storerooms, where they were to drop the bags on to a giant blanket laid out on the floor. Warehouse workers would then pounce on the cases or trunks, rip them open and spill out the contents, ready for expert sorters to descend. At lightning pace, they would form new piles: men's clothes, women's clothes, children's clothes and so on, until those heaps were taken away to groups of women prisoners, who would then subject them to a more meticulous sorting. In that mission, they had three key tasks. First, they were ordered to separate what was damaged or broken from what was usable. Second, they were to remove any and all indications of Jewish ownership: usually that meant tearing off the yellow star from a jacket or coat, though a tag bearing a Jewish name was similarly unwanted. Finally, and most importantly, they were under strict orders to search for any hidden valuables. That meant running a careful finger along the seams of all clothing, looking for any jewellery or money that might have been concealed there.

That would explain the initially baffling activity that caught Walter's eye by one of the warehouses. A row of perhaps twenty women were straddling a bench, flanked by rows of zinc buckets. On one side, the buckets were full of tubes of toothpaste, which Walter assumed had been extracted from the trunks and suitcases. The women would squeeze out the paste, then discard the empty tube. It seemed such mindless, pointless work. Until someone explained that every now and again they would find a diamond, stashed in a toothpaste tube by an Auschwitz deportee who had hoped it would serve as an insurance policy. Sometimes it was not a stone they found in the tube but coins or a wad of banknotes rolled up and placed within.

The work of the toothpaste squeezers, or rather the thinking behind their work, was how Kanada got its name, at least according to one theory. It was said that German-speaking members of the clearing squad could often be heard asking, as they sorted items, 'Kann er da nicht was drin' haben?' (Might there be something [of value] inside?). *Kann er da* became Kanada. Alternatively, it was because in the years before the war large numbers of Slovaks, and Poles too, had emigrated to Canada. The legend grew that even a peasant who could not make a living at home could find a plot of land and make a better life for themselves in Canada. In the central European imagination, Canada was a mythic land of untold wealth.

But there was no time to dwell on the improbability of this place, because Walter was to be a mule, spurred to work by the blows and kicks of Kanada's two SS *Unterscharführers*, men whose names he would not forget: Otto Graf and Hans König, the latter known as *der König von Kanada*, the King of Kanada. In the real world, before Auschwitz, both had been actors in Vienna. Here they were forever in character, goading and prodding the human baggage animals before them, administering brutal and summary injustice. Walter had been working for only a few minutes when he saw König flog a prisoner to death for helping himself to something he had found in the suitcase mountain: an apple and a piece of bread.

Soon Walter understood the dead man's mistake. At one point, while shuttling back and forth between the mountain and the storehouses, one of the cases Walter was carrying split open. Among the shoes and shirts that spilled out were sandwiches and a hunk of salami. The sight of them stopped him, partly because he had not eaten for the best part of two days and partly because he remembered the advice the Kanada veteran had given. In Kanada, he had warned, it was best to go easy. Only dry bread for the first day or two; for a stomach shrivelled by two months of Auschwitz rations, anything more would be too much.

So Walter did not pick up the food that had tumbled out of that bag. Even if he had wanted to, there was no time. König and Graf were on him the second the bag broke, thumping him to get on. But in that moment, while the SS men were diverted, the prisoner behind Walter had, like a bird spotting a worm, swooped down, picked up and swallowed the salami without breaking stride. That, then, was how the prisoners of Kanada sated their appetite. Walter learned his lesson. He began to anticipate the beatings of others meted out by the *Unterscharführers*, to prepare for them, almost to look forward to them. Because when they came, he could steal and eat and survive.

Food was all around in Kanada, so long as you knew when and how to take it. That, surely, was why the women of Kanada looked like real women, not the shaved, stick-thin ghouls, the female *Muselmänner*, whose barracks had just been vacated. These were women of conspicuous flesh and warm blood, young and in rude health, the mere sight of whom distracted the adolescent Walter Rosenberg. They were watched over by women *Kapos*, who themselves looked flush and, odder still, elegant.

He was reeling from the strangeness of it all, as well as rushing to do as he was told and keep ahead of the boots and sticks of the SS men. But slowly, as he got used to the work and as he had enough food in his belly to allow something other than hunger and immediate physical survival to enter his thoughts, he began to see what he was actually looking at in Kanada.

Perhaps it was the family photographs that would so often drop out of a trunk or rucksack. Maybe it was the pile of children's shoes. Or perhaps it was the area crammed with babies' prams, hundreds of them, both grand and modest, new and old, shiny and worn. Whatever it was that did it, soon Walter could not help but draw the conclusion which should have been obvious from the start.

He had arrived in Auschwitz on a cattle truck packed only with those deemed fit enough to work as slaves. From then on, those had been the only kind of people he had encountered in the camp: fellow prisoners, male and female, forced into hard labour. To be sure, he had seen many of them beaten and starved to death, or else sent to an infirmary from where they emerged as corpses to be burned. Still, for those who could escape that fate, Auschwitz was a labour camp: brutal and hellish, yes, but a labour camp. Is that what he had told himself? Because now he had to let in a much darker truth.

He had had vague suspicions, of course he had. How could he not, given what was all around? But, if he was honest, he had tried to smother those. Now that he had seen Kanada, he could do so no longer.

Clearly, it was not only the fit and capable, people like him, who had been brought to Auschwitz. Look at those clothes, piled high, the dresses of old women, the trousers of old men. Look at those little shoes. Look at those prams.

Now he understood. The lemons, the tins of sardines, the bars of chocolate, the shawls, the shirts, the leather shoes, the children's toys, the apples, the figs, the sandwiches, the winter coats, the cognac, the underwear, the wristwatches, the faded pictures of family outings, they had all been packed by anxious mothers and worried grand-fathers, embarking on what they believed, or hoped, was resettlement for a new life. Each item had been chosen carefully, for space was limited. They had been able to keep only what they could carry, holding their last worldly goods close as they were squeezed into those airless, filthy cattle trucks. That was why there was a mountain of pots and pans: these people thought they were moving house. They had come with their elderly and with their children. The more pessimistic had taken precautions – sewing a diamond into a hem, hiding cash in the lining of a suitcase, squeezing dollar bills into a condom, then secreting it in one of those tubes of toothpaste – preparing a nest egg for the future, to be spent in the unlikely event all went well or to be used as a bribe if things turned desperate.

These people had never set foot in the Auschwitz that Walter knew, the Auschwitz of *Arbeit Macht Frei*, morning roll call and assorted working *Kommandos*. They had certainly entered the Auschwitz complex; that much was clear now. The proof was right in front of him. But they had disappeared, swallowed up by the night. In Kanada, he was surrounded by the evidence, though the SS were at pains to disguise it. Walter noticed that once the suitcases and knapsacks had been shaken out and emptied in the storehouse, another group of prisoners would rush to take them off to be burned, along with any identifying documents. It seemed important to the Nazis that the people who had come here, whose most intimate property was stacking up in the *Effektenlager*, should leave no trace.

The thought did not form immediately. It took time, perhaps because it was too enormous, too at odds with everything Walter had learned, and wanted to believe, about science and progress and civilisation. But, eventually, he had to conclude that he was not only a prisoner in a concentration camp, a *Lager* of slave labour, but an inmate of something altogether new: a factory of death. Here was a place where women and men classified as being of no value – or rather, deemed by their very existence to pose a mortal threat to the health of the German nation and the Aryan race – were murdered. They were killed, along with their aged parents, along with their children, along with their babies. Walter had seen the piles of shoes with his own eyes. There could be no escaping the reality. The Nazis were bent on eradicating the Jewish people and they were doing it right here, in Auschwitz.

Until now, had he told himself that the smoke from the crematorium in the main camp was generated by the dead who had fallen by the wayside at Buna, or collapsed on the march back to the camp from a day's work in the gravel pit, or withered through hunger, or succumbed to a *Kapo*'s blow, or failed Fries's typhus test, or simply expired in the darkness of the barracks? Had he failed to realise that more bodies were burning than even that grim tally could account for? Had Walter seen the two plus two that was in front of him, but failed to make four, either because he was diverted by pain and hunger and the need to stay alive, or because some truths are too hard to digest?

It cannot have been easy to believe in such a thing as a death factory, a round-the-clock facility designed and operated for the chief purpose of murdering human beings. After all, no place like it had ever existed before. It was outside human experience and, perhaps, outside human imagination.

Walter was eighteen – his mind sharp and quick to adjust. But now he faced things almost impossible to fathom.

# 7

## The Final Solution

THIS WAS WHAT Walter did not know and could not imagine.

Auschwitz was not built to be a byword for murder and death. In the months before Walter Rosenberg arrived on that summer's evening in 1942, its primary purpose was something else, the vaguest outline of which was a project Walter had intuited before he even got there, back when he was in a mere outer circle of hell in Majdanek.

When the Germans invaded Poland in late 1939, the site just outside the town of Oświęcim in Upper Silesia was an empty, derelict barracks originally built for the Polish army: hence those solid brick buildings that had so impressed Walter on arrival. It was an enterprising SS police leader who spotted its suitability as a place to hold and terrify troublesome members of the newly occupied Polish nation. Admittedly, the twenty two-storey buildings, wooden stables and one-time tobacco storehouse were run down, the land around was boggy and both the sewerage and water supply were not up to much. But those faults could not outweigh its singular advantage: its proximity to the railway network. A junction to the main line connecting Kraków to Katowice was nearby. For its intended function, it was perfect. Thanks to the slave labour of 300 Jews from Oświęcim, it did not take too long to knock it into shape.

Early in 1940, Auschwitz, as its new German masters had named it, opened its doors to hordes of Polish political prisoners, and the camp commandant, Rudolf Höss, set to work building new structures, some of them on the erstwhile army parade ground, and repurposing old ones. He wasted no time in converting a former ammunition store into a facility that rapidly became essential: a mortuary. Prisoners had a tendency to die in the camp so the mortuary soon had to be upgraded, equipped with furnaces that allowed inmates' corpses to be burned on-site, thereby saving Höss the laborious and costly task of ferrying them to a local crematorium.

The Germans had ruled Poland for a year when the SS concluded that Auschwitz's potential was being squandered. The place was wasted on mere incarceration of awkward Polish dissenters. There was money to be made.

Tellingly, concentration camps came under the SS-Wirtschafts-und Verwaltungshauptamt, or SS-WVHA, the Main Economic and Administrative Office of the SS. 'Economic' was the operative word. The head of the SS, Heinrich Himmler, was ambitious to match the Third Reich's military might with economic might, and sought to construct nothing less than an industrial empire, anchored in south-east Poland. It would be predicated on a key economic advantage, one enjoyed by the great empires of the past: slave labour. Tens of thousands of imprisoned workers could build the factories and plants that would turn this newly German terrain into an industrial power-house and it would cost the Reich next to nothing. Walter had had an inkling of this grand scheme in Majdanek when he saw the *Kapos* march teams of inmates off to work in assorted factories and workshops around Lublin. But it was Auschwitz, with its excellent transport links and proximity to Silesia's coal mines, that, by October 1940, Himmler had decided should be the engine of the effort, a throbbing generator of wealth for the new Nazi empire, fuelled by the involuntary labour of the people it now ruled. Their work was all. Hence the slogan, borrowed from the concentration camp at Dachau: *Arbeit Macht Frei*.

Himmler ordered a massive expansion of the camp, so that it soon took in the neighbouring village of Brzezinka, now endowed by the Germans with a charming name whose literal translation was 'birch-tree alley': Birkenau. In January 1942, Himmler ordered that 100,000 Jewish men and 50,000 Jewish women be sent to Auschwitz-Birkenau to work.

But within a few months Auschwitz was to acquire a new role. Walter's arrival coincided with the haphazard integration of the camp in July 1942 into what the Nazis were now calling the Final Solution to the Jewish Question. The goal had been formally adopted, the decree sealed, six months earlier in the tree-lined Berlin suburb of Wannsee, where the heads of the multiple German government agencies tasked with handling the Jews gathered at lunchtime on 20 January 1942 in a splendid house by the lake, with Reinhard Heydrich in the chair, and set about organising the ultimate stage of their war against this one, small people: elimination.

By the time Walter was shipped off, the effort had already been under way for nearly a year following Operation Barbarossa, the Nazi invasion of the Soviet Union in June 1941. It happened in the forests of Lithuania and the woods of Poland, in the fields of Belarus or in a ravine by the name of Babyn Yar outside Kyiv, where mobile killing units, *Einsatzgruppen*, would gather Jewish civilians in their hundreds and shoot them from inches away, usually in the backs of their heads or necks, their bodies falling into trenches and pits. By the end of 1941, some 600,000 Jews across the freshly conquered east had been murdered that way.

Those mass shootings never let up. In fact they intensified throughout the Nazi-occupied Soviet Union, as the SS cleared out ghettos, massacring their inhabitants. But after Wannsee the plan was to supplement those efforts with a smoother, more streamlined approach, one that would transport Jewish children, along with their mothers, fathers and grandparents, to dedicated killing centres in occupied Poland. There, Jews would either be murdered straightaway or they would face 'annihilation through labour': put more simply, they would be worked to death.

The first such place was Chełmno, in the west of the country, where they began murdering Jews on 8 December 1941, one day after the Japanese attack on Pearl Harbor that would at last draw the United States into the war. They did it by herding their victims into vans, locking the doors of the vehicle, then feeding the exhaust pipe back in, poisoning all those who were inside. It took just four months to kill more than 50,000 people that way, most of them Jews from the ghetto the Nazis had created in Łódź.

But the Nazis did not want to rely on gas chambers on wheels. They wanted fixed, purpose-built camps. As 1941 turned into 1942, they built Belzec, then Sobibor and finally Treblinka, refining the method of murder by gas. Majdanek joined the endeavour around the time Walter passed through there. As for Belzec, that was where the elderly and the women who had been crammed into that train from Nováky, including the young bride who stretched out her hand towards her groom, were taken and killed.

Auschwitz was not like those first three camps, built for the sole purpose of murdering Jews. From the start it had always had several missions, only adding the destruction of Jewish life to its portfolio relatively late. It acquired that function gradually, incrementally, even erratically. The process was a story familiar to any industrialist: steady expansion, as capacity grew and grew to cope with demand.

It began, after a couple of small-scale trials in August 1941, with the first experiment in mass killing conducted in the basement of Block 11 in the main camp the following month: 250 sick Polish inmates from the infirmary, some 600 Soviet prisoners of war and ten others were gassed on 4 September 1941. The killing worked well enough, but the location was not quite right. To reach the basement, there was a labyrinth of corridors to negotiate, which made removing the corpses and airing out the block cumbersome. Besides, it was not discreet enough. Block 11 was inside the camp perimeter; there were prisoners around. Happily for Auschwitz's rulers, there was an alternative location, tucked out of view.

It was known initially as the 'old crematorium', later designated Crematorium I. They had been burning corpses there since August 1940, but after the test run at Block 11 the SS decided on a change of use for the biggest room in the building. Until then, this long, windowless room had served as a morgue: fifty-five feet long, fifteen feet wide and nine feet high. But now the morgue was to be repurposed into a gas chamber. That meant insulating the doors, and creating several openings in the ceiling through which pellets of Zyklon B might be dropped. The room could easily fit between 700 and 800 people, a thousand at a squeeze. Once again, Soviet prisoners were the guinea pigs. Ordered to undress in an anteroom, they thought they were entering the mortuary for delousing. They filed in quietly, though when the granules of Zyklon B were shaken down through the hole in the roof and exposed to the air below there were cries of 'Gas!' and a great bellowing sound as the trapped prisoners hurled themselves against both doors.

Before long, the gas chamber was ready for Jews. Those chosen to die would be brought to the doors of the crematorium on trucks or, if they had been taken to Auschwitz in freight trains, they might make this last leg of the voyage on foot, marched there in orderly fashion, five abreast. When the group was mostly made up of the elderly, they would walk slowly, their faces worn by the journey that had brought them there, and by all that they had endured up to that moment. The yellow stars looked large on their tatty clothes.

The SS men seemed to be unarmed, though in fact they had pistols hidden in their pockets. They would offer words of encouragement and reassurance, telling the Jews that they would soon be allocated work suitable to their trade or profession. Then the two SS men in charge would stand on the roof of the crematorium, to address the Jews gathered below. One of them was Maximilian Grabner, chief of the Politische Abteilung, the Political Department, tasked with the killing. He spoke in a voice that was warm, even friendly.

'You will now bathe and be disinfected. We don't want any epidemics in the camp. Then you will be brought to your barracks, where you'll get some hot soup. You will be employed in accordance with your professional qualifications. Now undress and put your clothes in front of you on the ground.'

The captives were exhausted; they were desperate to believe their ordeal might be at an end. So they stepped forward, entering the one-time mortuary, children clinging to their mothers and fathers. Some were unnerved by the smell, the strong odour of cleaning products, perhaps bleach. Others looked for water pipes or shower heads in the ceiling, and could see none. A tremor of dread pulsed through the mass that was packed into this hall, and which was still growing. More and more people shoved themselves into the space. And yet the SS men were still there, still among them, ushering them forward, engaging in small talk, cracking the odd joke. Few noticed that these same SS men, smiling and friendly, were keeping a sharp eye on the exit, waiting for their cue.

It came when the last Jew had come in and the room was declared full, at which point the Nazis slipped out. Instantly the door was closed, a door trimmed with rubber that sealed it airtight. Then the sound of a heavy bolt, drawn securely into place.

Now the tremor turned into a wave of the deepest terror; it rippled through those locked inside. Some started banging on the door, demanding to be let out. They hammered with their fists. This time their SS guards offered no word of reassurance. Some of the men laughed. Others taunted their captives: 'Don't get burned while you have your bath!'

Those who were not looking at the sealed doors were instead gazing upward, noticing that the covers had been removed from the six holes in the ceiling. Perhaps the most terrifying sight was that of a head in a gas mask at one of the openings; it prompted a howl from those who saw it.

The head belonged to one of the 'disinfectors' who with chisel and hammer opened the tins whose labels announced: 'Poison Gas! Zyklon.' The cans were full of blue granules, each one no bigger than a pea. It was hydrogen cyanide in solid form; it had only to be exposed to the air for the prussic acid to escape from the pellets and transform into deadly gas. The disinfectors did not risk inhaling any fumes themselves. The instant the tin was open, they poured the crystals down the holes. Once the tin was empty, they covered the vent back up – though one SS man once saw a colleague briefly lift the covering and spit into the hall on those below, to add insult to lethal injury.

Grabner would watch carefully. Once he was satisfied that the Zyklon had been dispensed, he signalled to the driver of a truck, who had parked close by for this exact purpose, to start up his engine. His job was to make enough noise to drown out the cries and screams of the young and the old that would otherwise have filled the sky.

Grabner's eye would stay fixed on the second hand of his watch. He was counting the two minutes it usually took for that animal sound of howling, the desperate weeping and praying, the violent banging and knocking to give way to a pained groaning and finally, two further minutes later, silence.

Then the truck drove away; the guards stood down. The cleaning squad – the men of Kanada command – came for the piles of clothes that had been neatly arranged, just as the SS man had advised. Eventually, once the room was declared sufficiently ventilated to be free of gas, the prisoners of Special Command, the *Sonderkommando*, would go inside to remove the bodies. They tended to be bunched up by the door, the corpses closely packed where the murdered, in their last few moments, had tried to force their way out. The limbs were often intertwined with each other, a tangle of arms and legs that had grown rigid thanks to the gas and which testified to the final chaos and terror. The bodies seemed to be leaning on each other and their mouths, sometimes still foaming, were wide open – as if agape in shock.

That was how it was at the beginning, when the sole gas chamber in use was the improvised one in the Auschwitz main camp. But steadily things changed. As the camp expanded and stretched into Birkenau, it made sense to install gassing facilities there, on the spot, rather than to rely on a single gas chamber some distance away – one that was soon creaking under the strain of overuse. There was another calculation too. Even outside the perimeter, and despite the effort to conceal it, the activity at Crematorium I attracted attention. Too many were noticing what was happening. Even when the truck driver had his engine running, or a motorbike was doing laps of the area, to hide the noise, prisoners close by were able to hear the sound of the heavy coughing and retching as the gassing began; they could hear the screams, of the children especially. The solution was an isolated and empty farmhouse – its owners had been evicted – near the birch forest which gave Birkenau its name.

The SS called the building Bunker 1 or, more charmingly, 'the little red house', and it was not too difficult to adapt. They simply bricked up the windows, reinforced and fitted seals to the doors and drilled holes in the walls through which they would drop the granules of Zyklon B. They covered the floor with wood shavings, to absorb the blood, urine and excrement of the dying. That was up and running by May 1942. A month later there was a sister building in operation a few hundred yards away. It too was a secluded farmhouse, similarly adapted, and it was known as Bunker 2 or 'the little white house'. That came on stream in late June or early July 1942, just as Walter arrived in Auschwitz.

This was the very time that Auschwitz's role in the Final Solution was ratcheting up. In the first part of the year, the gassings were sporadic and regional. They consisted mainly of irregular transports of Jews from surrounding Silesia. But in midsummer, just as Walter was marching off to the construction site in Buna, there was a change.

From July, transports began to arrive from across Europe daily, sometimes twice a day, usually carrying around a thousand people. They included Walter's former neighbours in Slovakia, but also Jews from Croatia, Poland, Holland, Belgium and France: some 60,000 people in July and August alone. Admittedly, these were meagre numbers compared to those racked up by the senior partners in Operation Reinhard: Belzec, Sobibor and Treblinka killed approximately one and a half million people between them in 1942, more than 800,000 in Treblinka alone. Apart from a relatively small number of 'Gypsies', mainly Roma and Sinti, all were Jews. In that same year, the figure at Auschwitz was 190,000, less than an eighth. Even so, by the time Walter was branded as 44070, the mass murder that would come to define Auschwitz was under way.

And yet Walter only really began to know of it that moment in Kanada where, in that pile of tiny shoes, the truth was staring him too hard in the face and he could not look away. Perhaps he could be forgiven for taking so long to understand what would eventually seem obvious, for failing to absorb the evidence that surrounded him, for failing to turn clear facts into knowledge. The SS had taken great pains to keep this operation hidden, even from those who were living at the scene of the crime.

The first killing site, the old crematorium, was already away from the barracks, but the SS went further to conceal it, disguising it with trees and shrubs, so that what was in fact an underground bunker once used as an arsenal would appear to be a natural mound. The second and third sites, the little red house and the little white house, were chosen very deliberately: abandoned farmhouses, safely out of sight.

The transports would arrive at night, under cover of darkness. And the Birkenau of the summer of 1942 was not the Birkenau that would come later, teeming with many thousands of prisoners. At this stage, the population was sparse. There were few witnesses.

Nor yet was there the telltale, near-permanent cloud of smoke, belching out from the chimneys of the crematoria. That would only come the following year, in the spring and summer of 1943, with the construction of the purpose-built killing machines that would be known as Crematorium II and Crematorium III, later joined by the smaller, simpler pair Crematorium IV and Crematorium V. When II and III were working at full throttle, they could burn as many as 1,440 human beings each day. Though they were built to be even more efficient – with both gas chamber and accompanying set of ovens on the same ground-floor level, thereby obviating the need for a service elevator to transport the bodies up from the place of death to the place of burning – IV and V struggled to cope. Little bits of know-how picked up by the stokers and furnace operators of the *Sonderkommando* – sorting corpses according to their combustibility, with the bodies of the well-fed used to speed up the burning of the bone-thin – helped, but not enough. Designed to be the last word in cremation technology, even these ovens and chimneys could scarcely keep up with Auschwitz's phenomenal output of corpses. For all that, the SS could congratulate itself on having constructed a set-up that operated with the seamlessness of a Ford production line, ensuring that the gassing and incineration of Jews ran smoothly in a single, well-designed, properly ventilated site.

In the summer that Walter became an inmate of Auschwitz, however, things were much cruder. The corpses of the gassed were simply buried in the ground, in deep ditches carved into the Birkenau forest. The ground itself seemed to protest, refusing to swallow the dead: in the heat, body parts, rotting and stinking, appeared to emerge from the earth. The stench was nauseating and it pervaded the entire camp. Fluids were leaking from decomposing bodies, a black, foul-smelling mass that oozed out of the soil and polluted the groundwater. Even putting aside the health risk to the wider area, it hardly concealed what the Nazis were doing.

With the new crematoria not yet functioning, and mass burial unpalatable, there had to be an alternative. As it happened, the SS had a secret unit specialising in precisely this question, devising the most efficient system of disposal of human bodies. One method, piloted at Chełmno, seemed to work best. First, dig a deep pit. Next, fill it with the dead. Then set the bodies alight. Once that was done, send in a heavy bone-crushing machine to grind the skeletal remains into powder, which could then be scattered, leaving no trace behind.

That was good enough for Auschwitz commandant Höss, who ordered that the *Sonderkommando* be forced to work on a new task: digging up the bodies already buried in Birkenau. That meant the prisoners pulling the decomposed corpses out of the ground with their bare hands. At gunpoint they were made to stack them in ditches, then set them alight, so that they burned in the open air. Afterwards, thanks to the heavy grinding machine, all that was left was ash and fragments of bone. Those were scooped up and poured into rivers or dumped in the nearby marshes, where they might offer no incriminating clue. The rest were used to fertilise the fields and surrounding farmland. Even when reduced to ash and dust, the Jews would be compelled to serve the Reich.

Understanding of all this reached Walter slowly and in fragments. There would have been rumours, of course, originating with the few prisoners who were privy to Auschwitz's secrets, starting with the *Sonderkommando* themselves. But that talk would have circulated only among those with senior ranking in the hierarchy of inmates; it would not have reached a lad who had only been in the camp a couple of months.

And so Walter's knowledge was confined to what he could see in Kanada: the worldly goods the dead had left behind, a piece of luggage for every soul extinguished by the men who ruled this place. He had to deduce, as a matter of logic, that Kanada flowed with milk and honey only because those who had brought such delights there had been murdered.

Walter was still eighteen when he no longer fought this under-standing, when he began to absorb that he was a prisoner in a site of industrial slaughter, and that the group targeted for eradication was his own.

But he was allowed almost no time to digest it, because there was still more he had to take in – another, related revelation that was, in its own way, just as shocking.

# 8

## Big Business

WHAT WALTER SAW in Kanada was proof that Auschwitz had not lost its founding ambition, the one nurtured by Heinrich Himmler. Even if it were now tasked with the business of mass murder, its Nazi proprietors were clearly determined that Auschwitz should continue to serve as an economic hub, that even in its new mission it should turn a profit.

For Kanada was a commercial enterprise. Every item that was not broken was collected, sorted, stored and repackaged for domestic consumption back in the Fatherland. In one month alone, some 824 freight containers were transported by rail from Auschwitz back to the Old Reich, and those were just the ones carrying textiles and leather goods. Walter could see this traffic for himself, how a goods train would pull up every weekday to be loaded with stolen property. It could be high-quality men's shirts on a Monday, fur coats on a Tuesday, children's wear on a Wednesday. Nothing would be allowed to go to waste. Even the unusable clothes were sorted, then graded: grade one, grade two, grade three, with that last category, the worst, shipped off to paper factories, where the garments would be stripped back to their basic fibres and recycled. If there was even a drop of value, the Nazis would squeeze it out. Murder and robbery went hand in hand.

Some of these goods would be distributed for free to Germans in need, perhaps via the Winterhilfeswerke, the winter relief fund. A mother in Düsseldorf whose husband was off fighting on the eastern front might have her spirits lifted by the arrival of a thick winter coat or new shoes for the children – so long as she did not look too closely at the marks indicating the place where the yellow star had been torn off or think too hard about the children who had worn those shoes before.

Besides the women's clothing and underwear and children's wear, racially pure Germans back home were eligible for featherbeds, quilts, woollen blankets, shawls, umbrellas, walking sticks, Thermos flasks, earmuffs, combs, leather belts, pipes and sunglasses, as well as mirrors, suitcases and prams from the abundant supply that had caught Walter's eye. There were so many prams that just shifting one batch, running into the hundreds, to the freight yard – pushed in the regular Auschwitz fashion, namely in rows of five – took a full hour. Ethnic German settlers in the newly conquered lands might also get a helping hand, in the form of furniture and household items, perhaps pots, pans and utensils. Victims of Allied bombing raids, those who had lost their homes, were also deemed worthy of sharing in the Kanada bounty: they might receive tablecloths or kitchenware. Watches, clocks, pencils, electric razors, scissors, wallets and flashlights: they would be repaired if necessary and despatched to troops on the front line. The fighter pilots of the Luftwaffe were not to miss out: they were given fountain pens that had once inscribed the words and thoughts of Jews.

A few items would find a new owner on the spot. Those SS men who could get away with it, accompanied by their wives, would treat themselves to a trip to Kanada, dipping into the treasure trove for whatever took their fancy, whether it be a smart cigarette case for him or a stylish dress for her. The place was brimming with luxuries for every possible taste.

Still, it was not these delights that gave Kanada its economic value or that took Auschwitz closer to its founding goal of becoming a moneymaking venture. A clue to the greater treasure was in that bench of women squeezing toothpaste tubes, looking for jewels or rolls of banknotes. Even beyond the high-end goods, Kanada was awash with precious stones, precious metals and old-fashioned cash.

Walter saw it with his own eyes, often barely concealed, stashed by victims in their luggage. It might be in dollars or English pounds, the hard currency that deportees had acquired after selling their property: their homes or their businesses, sold at giveaway prices in the hurried hours before their expulsion from the countries where their families had lived for generations. There was a team of clearance workers who specialised in finding money and jewels, but everyone in Kanada had the argot: 'napoleons' were the gold coins that carried the image of the French emperor, 'swines' the ones that bore, even a quarter-century after the Bolshevik revolution, the face of the Russian tsar. There seemed to be cash from every corner of the globe, not only francs and lire, but Cuban pesos, Swedish Croons, Egyptian pounds.

Walter had never seen wealth like it, a colossal fortune tossed note by note and coin by coin into a trunk set aside for the purpose. All the stolen valuables went into that trunk: the gold watches, the diamonds, the rings, as well as the money. By the end of a shift, the case would often be so full that the SS man would be unable to close it. Walter would watch as the Nazi in charge pressed down on the lid with his boot, forcing it to snap shut.

This was big business for the Reich. Every month or so, up to twenty suitcases, bulging with the wealth of the murdered, along with crates crammed with more valuables, would be loaded on to lorries and driven, under armed guard, to SS headquarters in Berlin. The destination was a dedicated account at the Reichsbank, held in the name of a fabulously wealthy – and wholly fictitious – individual: Max Heiliger.

Not all the gold shipped off to enrich the non-existent Herr Heiliger came from wedding rings, bracelets and necklaces, and not all of it passed through Kanada. There was another source too. The Nazis resolved that merely plundering the belongings of those they murdered was not enough: there was wealth to be extracted from their bodies too. The men of the *Sonderkommando*, already tasked with removing the corpses from the gas chambers minutes after death, were given an extra duty. They were to shear the hair off the dead. It had both a commercial value – bales of cloth made from human hair found their way to German factories – and a military one – hair could be used in delayed-action bombs, as part of the detonation mechanism. Ideally, it would be women's hair, which was thicker and longer than men's or children's.

Any artificial limbs found on a corpse were also unscrewed and collected, for reuse or resale. Still, the more lucrative asset was an internal one. It fell to some men of the *Sonderkommando* to prise open the mouths of the dead, often still foaming, and check for gold teeth. If they spotted any, they ripped them out with pliers. It was hard work, interrupted by regular breaks as the 'dentists' paused to vomit. But all those gold teeth added up. Between 1942 and 1944, an estimated six tons of dental gold were deposited in the vaults of the Reichsbank. Overall, an internal and top-secret 'List of Jewish property received for delivery' compiled at the start of February 1943 estimated that over the preceding year the haul from the archipelago of Nazi-operated death camps across Poland had reached 326 million Reichsmarks: in the US currency of the early 2020s, that would be $2 billion.

Walter only knew what he could see, which was a corner of the camp kinetic with sorting, bundling, loading and shipping. To the naked eye, it would have looked like any other trading station, busy and thriving. Nevertheless, even if Walter could not see the full impact of Kanada on the war economy of the Third Reich, he would soon understand how it shaped the bizarre and upside-down world of Auschwitz itself.

At the end of his first day, serving as a glorified mule, dodging the sticks and clubs of the Nazi overseers, ferrying cases and trunks back and forth, he got his first inkling of how things worked. As always, he and the other prisoners lined up in rows of five, ready to march back to the camp. First, though, there would be an inspection.

About fifteen men were picked out and searched thoroughly. If they were found to have stolen so much as a tin of sardines, they were flogged. Perhaps twenty SS lashes for a couple of lemons, twenty-five for a shirt. A stolen hunk of bread would bring lighter punishment: a good kicking and a thump. After that, the Clearing Command were sent on their way, only to face another check once they had reached the gate of the main camp. There Fries and his henchmen awaited, poised to give the men of Kanada another good frisking. They found one man who had taken a shirt, and Fries promptly murdered him on the spot, beating him to death. But he was the only one. The rest of them made it to Block 4 and the chance to assess what the day had brought.

For Walter it was eye-popping wonder and the beginnings of a dark knowledge. For the others, the hours in Kanada had borne more tangible fruit. Somehow these prisoners had defied not one but two searches to bring back all manner of riches. One had come away with a bar of soap, another had hidden several sausages about his person. Out it all tumbled: six cans of sardines delivered by one inmate, two pounds of figs stashed by another. There were lemons, salami, a ham, even a packet of aspirin. And that was before you took a glance at the men's feet. With great discretion, almost every one of them had got rid of the wooden clogs that were standard issue for Auschwitz prisoners and swapped them for real shoes: some of them suede, some of them in a crocodile skin that was comically incongruous. Walter would do the same before long, once he had been reassured by the older hands that stolen footwear would bring no punishment. It was seen as a perk of the job.

Indeed, a place in the Clearing Command allowed a handful of inmates a life of improbable, surreal luxury. Female sorters would find themselves wearing new shoes and clothes, and fresh underwear, every day. They might sleep in silken nightshirts and on cotton bedsheets. They had access to perfume and stockings and, if they were working the night shift, might spend the afternoon bathing in the sun, cooling off with a splash of water, or reading one of the many books that the condemned had packed into their suitcases. They did this even as the air was filled with the odour of burning flesh.

But at this moment in Block 4 the hoard spilling out of the men's sleeves, trousers and tunics was not quite like that. The Kanada prisoners had not taken these items to serve as creature comforts for their own use. Their function was very different. A lemon in Auschwitz was not merely a lemon. It was a unit of currency. And so it was for every one of the spoils of Kanada.

The term of art was 'organising'. If you wanted to survive Auschwitz, you had to 'organise': meaning, you had to take what was not officially yours, either by stealing it yourself or trading with someone who had. The basic coin of the realm was the food ration. Those in charge of ladling out the soup or handing out the bread would hold some back, so that they could 'organise' a favour with an extra dab of margarine or morsel of potato. But thanks to the presence of Kanada, the inmate economy of Auschwitz became much more elaborate than that.

Delicacies and luxury goods could buy whatever was needed, even if the rate of exchange was often perverse. A diamond ring might be swapped for a cup of water; a bottle of champagne traded for quinine tablets; a precious gem for an apple, to be passed to a sick and hungry friend.

The value of cash was different in Auschwitz. Walter was once sorting the goods from a transport of Polish Jews from Grodno which, by the standards of Kanada, were of poor quality, certainly nothing to compare to the treasure that accompanied Jews from France, Holland or Belgium – communities that had not suffered Nazi occupation, and privation, nearly as long. He had picked up a loaf of bread which felt odd in his hand. The consistency of it was not right. He broke off a chunk and saw that it had been partially hollowed out. Inside was what turned out to be $20,000, in hundred-dollar bills.

Walter had to make an instant calculation. He could do as he was supposed to, and deposit the cash in the trunk set aside for money and valuables. Or he could try to keep it. Though what would be the point? The needs of an Auschwitz prisoner were almost infinite, but they had little use for money.

Even so, Walter decided to take a risk. He hid the 200 notes and waited till he had a break to relieve himself. It made no sense, he knew that. If he were caught with the cash, death would be the sanction, he was sure of it. But he took the risk all the same. And this time no one stopped him.

When he reached the lavatory, or the hole in the ground that served that purpose, he did not hesitate. He took the money and threw it away. Was it an act of resistance? Partly. He and the other prisoners in Kanada had already made a habit of using twenty-dollar bills as toilet paper (though for this purpose English pounds were preferable, since they were only printed on one side). Better they be used that way than allow the Nazis to get hold of hard currency. So yes, it was a small act of sabotage. But destroying $20,000 was also an act of spite. He could not keep that money himself. There was no one he could give it to. Still, he could see no good reason why the Germans should have it. Either that money would further enrich the Reich or it would be destroyed. The people who had earned it had been destroyed, so it was right to destroy the money. That was Walter's logic. The lavatory felt like the right place for it.

Which is not to say that he did not find things he valued in

Kanada. Among the most poignant discoveries in the luggage of the victims were textbooks and exercise books: confirmation that the Nazis had successfully tricked the Jews into believing the 'areas of resettlement' would be genuine communities, complete with schools for their children. All papers had to be burned of course, but one day Walter came across a children's atlas. Instinct made him flick through the pages until he found a map of Silesia: he remembered from his own schooldays, which now seemed a lifetime ago, that that was the region that took in the triangle where the borders of Germany, Poland and Czechoslovakia met – or used to meet, at any rate. He ripped out the page and hid it under his shirt.

When the moment came, it was back to the latrine. Except this time, he would wait before destroying what he had taken. As methodically as he could, he studied the map, working out exactly where this camp, and he himself, were. He then got rid of it, but not before he had committed what he had seen – and what it meant for his dream of escape – to memory.

Most of Kanada's bounty was precious in a more direct way, because of what it could buy. For an intricate black market operated in Auschwitz, among the 'old numbers', those veterans who had secured positions as *Kapos* or block elders, especially. They traded goods they could get hold of for privileges, but also for safety and for human lives: their own and those they chose to protect. A block elder would have access to rations intended for the prisoners nominally in their care. A *Kapo* in the kitchen had access to meat. Both could use those goods to buy preferential treatment, for themselves or for others.

In the Auschwitz financial system, Kanada played the role of central bank: it was where the wealth was stored. And yet there was a perverse paradox: Jewish prisoners who worked there had better access than either their *Kapo* overseers or their Nazi masters. Most SS men could not simply stroll in, browse the wares and help themselves to what they fancied. They needed an inmate to pilfer the item for them. In return, the prisoner needed to be sure no SS man would check him on his way out. Precious wares in return for a blind eye. That exchange would form the basis of a set of transactional relationships that developed between members of the

SS and the handful of Auschwitz prisoners who could get anywhere near Kanada.

Those relationships soon created a hierarchy among the prison population. Inmates with access to Kanada's riches could bribe *Kapos* and SS men for better workplaces for themselves or for their relatives or friends. They might buy from the block elder a better position in the barracks or a much needed rest in the infirmary with a promise that they would be protected, rather than left to die.

Officially, the SS did not tolerate such corruption. They would inspect barracks, ostensibly looking for stolen goods: in truth, they were extorting the block elders, demanding to be paid off with Kanada delights. The elder had to give the SS men what they wanted, and so would lean on any inmate who could 'organise'. In return, that inmate would see an improvement in his own conditions.

This was the unique political economy of a death camp where the worldly goods of a doomed people were stolen and piled up, the mountain of wealth growing higher every day. And now that he was working in Kanada, Walter Rosenberg was at the centre of it.

He proved himself a reliable worker. Soon the old hands were calling him by his first name. He was promoted, no longer simply carting trunks and suitcases to the warehouses where they were unpacked, but moved to the next stage of the process: ferrying blankets filled with clothes to the sorting station, staffed by women, many of them fellow Slovaks. Like everyone else in Kanada, he learned to be constantly trading: slipping the girls a bar of chocolate in return for some bread and cheese, a sip of lemonade or just a smile.

Walter's direct overseer, a green-triangle *Kapo* called Bruno, used him as a personal courier, getting him to carry gifts to his lover, a Viennese beauty who served as his counterpart in charge of the Slovak sorting girls. Back and forth Walter would go, carrying a fresh orange on one trip, a fine wine the next. The *Kapo* couple even had a hidden love nest, crafted out of piles of blankets in one of the warehouses.

But during one shift Bruno pushed Walter too far. He loaded him up until Walter looked like an heiress in a department store: a bottle of Chanel, sardines from Portugal, gourmet sausages from Germany, an elegantly wrapped bar of Swiss chocolate, all concealed in a heap of clothes. And that was the moment the SS man in charge of Kanada, Scharführer Richard Wiegleb, did a spot check on Walter, demanding he drop what he was carrying to the ground. Out it all tumbled. Wiegleb saw everything.

'Well, what a strange collection of clothes.' He checked off the items, one by one.

He demanded to know who had put Walter up to this. He knew it was Bruno but he wanted confirmation. And he intended to beat this young Jew until he got it. He ordered Walter to bend over.

'Who gave it to you?' he asked, before bringing the cane down on Walter's backside.

'Who gave it to you?'

He asked the same question again and again, slicing into Walter's flesh. As the stick rose and fell, Walter could feel the eyes of the entire Kanada detail on him: even if they were carrying on with their work, they were watching.

Wiegleb administered forty-seven blows that day. Some of the Kanada veterans said it was a record. And though the agony of it made him fall to the ground unconscious, Walter Rosenberg never answered the SS man's question.

When he came round, the pain was excruciating. Walter could barely move. He knew he was not fit to work, which in Auschwitz meant he would die. The lashing inflicted by Wiegleb had left an open wound which had become infected, his immune system barely capable of mounting a defence given an Auschwitz regimen of insufficient nutrition, hygiene and sleep. His legs and backside swelled like balloons. He developed an abscess in his left buttock, which had to be drained. Left unattended, it would kill him. He needed an operation.

The very idea of it, in Auschwitz, was ridiculous. It would require 'organising' on a huge scale. Doctors, orderlies, block elders: they would all have to be bribed. There were very few people in the camp with the heft to pull that off. Which meant Walter's fate rested on Bruno the *Kapo*: would he acknowledge that he, along with his Viennese lover, owed Walter their lives? There was nothing compelling him to do so. It would be easier to let Walter die, taking his secret with him. But if he did that, no regular inmate, or *Kapo* for that matter, would ever take a risk for Bruno again. Such were the calculations of Auschwitz.

And so Bruno bartered and traded until he had arranged treatment for Walter, as well as a supply of medicine, food and drink, all direct from Kanada. He was owed enough favours by enough people to make it happen. The operation, when it came on 28 September 1942 – just as German forces and the Red Army were locked in deadly combat in the battle of Stalingrad – was traumatic. Walter felt the incision of the blade before he was properly anaesthetised. He tried to shout, but could make no sound. He eventually passed out from the shock.

But the surgery was successful: Walter got himself discharged a week later. Not for the first time, though he had been knocked down, he had got back on his feet. That meant an immediate return to work. The trouble was, he had been marked down for the industrial construction site at Buna. Given the state he was in, that kind of hard labour would kill him.

Walter mentioned Bruno's name to the hospital registrar, and that was enough to get the order revoked: he was sent back to the Clearing Command instead. It was too risky for him to show his face in Kanada itself: Wiegleb would see him and instantly know that he had been defied. But Bruno had a solution. Walter would go to the source. He would work on the ramp.

# 9

## The Ramp

THIS WAS NOT the first unloading ramp, a railway platform really, that had been in use in Auschwitz. Walter was familiar with that first one: it had been the place where he had got on and off the goods train that had shuttled him and the other prisoners back and forth in cattle trucks to the construction site at Buna. No, this was its replacement, only recently pressed into service. It was on the site of the freight station that once served the town of Oświęcim, sandwiched between the so-called mother camp, Auschwitz I, and its soon-to-be much bigger offspring, Birkenau, or Auschwitz II. It was here that the mass transports of Jews arrived. They called it the *Alte Judenrampe*: the old Jewish ramp.

Walter's job would be among the squad of slaves who were the first to see the doomed arrivals off the trains as they came in, removing their luggage and clearing out the cattle trucks that had brought them to Auschwitz.

The work was not sought after by the prisoners of Kanada. It was more physically demanding than labour in the storehouses or at the sorting tables and it was more dangerous. The mortality rate around Wiegleb and his men was high anyway, but on the ramp it was higher still. The SS were liable to lose their patience and lash out. They wanted everything done so fast.

Walter worked on that ramp for ten months straight. In that time, he helped unload about 300 transports, seeing the dazed and frightened faces of perhaps 300,000 people if not more: Jewish children and their parents, the old and the young, the broken and the defiant, from across the continent, in what for almost all of them was the final hour of their lives. As the nights went by, and as the days turned to weeks and then months, and as the tens of thousands of faces passed by, his old dream of escape did not disappear. But it did change. It became something harder and sharper, tempered less by hope than by resolve. It now aimed for something much larger than himself.

This is how the job worked. Transports would usually arrive at night. When the train carrying a new batch of Jews was about a dozen miles away, word would reach Auschwitz, where the officer on duty would blow a whistle and shout, 'Transport is here!' Then everyone involved, SS officers, doctors, *Kapos*, drivers, would take up their positions, the SS men heading over to the *Judenrampe* in trucks or on motorbikes. Meanwhile, the relevant detail of the Clearing Command, some 200 strong and known as *Rollkommando*, or the rolling group, would be told to get ready. It might be the middle of the night, four in the morning, but an SS man would come to Block 4 and wake them, and then they would be marched out, past the electric fences, watchtowers and machine guns of the Auschwitz main camp, escorted by an SS group that had been waiting for them at the main gate.

From there, they would march the twelve or thirteen minutes it took to reach a wooden platform beside a stretch of railway track that branched off the main line. The platform was long and narrow: just three or four yards wide, but perhaps 500 yards long, long enough, at any rate, to accommodate a locomotive pulling fifty cattle trucks. Walter and the *Rollkommando* would take their positions and wait.

Next, a group of SS men would come, perhaps a hundred of them, and take up their own positions, one man every ten yards, along the full length of the wooden platform so that it was completely encircled. They had rifles and dogs. Only then would the escort that had brought Walter and the others stand down, because the men of *Kanadakommando* were now inside a tight, armed cordon. The electric lights would be switched on, so that the ramp was lit as brightly as if it were noon. It might be shivering cold, but the prisoners would wait in their coarse, striped uniforms, in rows of five, as always.

The main track was no more than twenty yards away. It was an important line, connecting Vienna to Kraków, and sometimes regular passenger trains would go by slowly enough that the prisoners could see the travellers inside. Walter would spot the dining car and wonder what the ladies and gentlemen within made of the illuminated spectres lined up on the platform. Or maybe they blinked and missed them. Maybe they just did not see.

Soon a new group arrived, the SS officers, men on a more exalted plane than the guards who formed the ring. Walter thought of them as a gangster elite, neat as mafiosi in their crisp uniforms and polished boots, with the swagger of seniority. The buttons on their uniforms were gold rather than silver. They held nothing so gross as a club, but rather a gentleman's cane; some wore white gloves. There would be between a dozen and twenty of them, including a doctor. This group would be in charge of proceedings.

Finally, the signal would be given and slowly the train would pull in, the locomotive at the front. There would, Walter noticed, be a civilian in the driver's cab.

The guards in the outer ring did not move. Instead there would be a handover, as the commander on the train handed papers and keys to his counterpart on the platform. Those keys would then be distributed by the man in charge to his subordinates, and they would take a position in front of the wagons, usually one SS man for every two or three cattle cars. Then, at a signal, they would step forward and unlock the wagons. Walter and the others would get a first glimpse of the mass of people held within.

*Alles raus! Alles raus!*

To reinforce the instruction, the SS men would sometimes kick or hit the first few people to tumble out of the wagon, whacking them with a walking stick. Close by were *Kapos*, armed with clubs and sticks of their own. Walter knew the condition these new arrivals were in: their thirst, their hunger, their disorientation after being for days on end cramped into that tiny, fetid space with so many others. And now, as their eyes adjusted to the dazzling lights, they were being driven out, and told to get off quick, quick. *Take no luggage with you! Leave everything behind!*

The deportees were herded immediately into columns, one for men, the other for women and young children, each made up of rows of five. In an instant, families were divided, husbands parted from wives, mothers from sons. The night sky began to echo to the din of tears and separation.

All the while, and under the direction of the *Kapos* and their clubs, Walter and his fellow prisoners were set to clearing out the wagons. At speed, Walter would climb into a cattle truck, oblivious to the stench, pick up two heavy bags, jump back down and throw them on to the heap that was forming fast on the ramp. In his first few days, his focus was on mastering the physical requirements of the job and seeing what he could get out of it for himself. Deprived of the more readily accessible largesse of Kanada HQ, he and the other 200 men of *Rollkommando* had to make their own luck.

Walter was a quick study and before long he could tell at a glance whether a case was packed with clothes, kitchenware or food. Soon he got the hang of running with two suitcases while taking a bite of salami, tossing it to another inmate, all without being spotted. He developed a new skill: the ability to open a tin and wolf down its contents in a few, unobserved seconds.

The Kanada boys knew which Jews they were unloading by the provisions that suddenly became available. If they were tasting cheese, they had just received Jews from the Netherlands. If it was sardines, a transport of French Jews had arrived. Halva and olives identified the Greek Jews of Salonica, dressed in colours Walter had never seen before and speaking a language that was new to his Ashkenazi ear: the Sephardic Jewish dialect of Ladino, or Judeo-Spanish. He saw them all, delivered to Auschwitz by the thousand.

Only when every last bag or suitcase was off the train – loaded on to trucks and taken to Kanada – could the *Rollkommando* attend to clearing out the dead. The order of priorities was very clear, and any deviation from it was punished. After all, extracting worldly goods was Kanada's core business. Luggage came first, the dead second.

Corpse removal was an unpredictable business. A transport from the east, in midwinter, that took ten days, might leave as many as a third of the passengers, perhaps 300 people, dead on arrival. But if the train had come from the west, from Prague or Vienna or Paris, where the Nazis had had to maintain at least the appearance of a civilised act of resettlement, and if the journey had taken no more than a couple of days, then there might be only three or four corpses on board. The same was true of the number of dying in each cattle truck, those who were not yet dead but who lacked the strength to stand up and get off the train, even under threat of a blow from the bamboo cane of an SS man. They too had to be dealt with – and *Laufschritt*, at the double. Always at the double.

That meant grabbing all the unmoving bodies, two inmates to each corpse or semi-corpse, one clutching the ankles, the other taking the wrists, and dashing to the end of the platform, spurred on by the club and the cane of the *Kapo* and the SS, where a fleet of trucks would be waiting, sometimes half a dozen of them, ready to ferry the lifeless for disposal. These were dumper trucks, the kind whose back can lift to tip out a load of sand or gravel, but for this operation the cargo box remained flat and open. Walter and his fellow corpse-bearer would have to skip up the rear steps at the back of the vehicle – *Laufschritt, Laufschritt* – where more prisoners were on hand to receive the load. They would take hold of the body and stack it, while Walter and his comrade would turn around and charge back to the empty train, to retrieve any other Jew who had not survived the journey. At no stage did anyone separate the dead from the dying. There was no time and no capacity to distinguish between the two categories. Breathing or not, the bodies were tossed on to the truck and the truck would then make the short drive to the crematorium for burning.

The two columns of deportees now moved forward towards the gangster elite, to the reviewing party that would decide their fate. They did not know it, but the new arrivals were about to face selection. If they were sent to the right, they would be marched off first, registered as prisoners and given the chance to work and therefore to live, if only for a while. If they were directed left, their imminent destiny was death.

The SS man in charge was usually the duty doctor, sometimes Josef Mengele, or sometimes a mere corporal of the sanitation service, charged with picking out those who were unfit to work: the old, the sick, the very young. Walter noticed that good-looking women between the ages of sixteen and thirty would be picked for survival and grouped together in a row of their own. There might be women who were fit and strong, and certainly capable of work, but if they had children in tow the SS finger would point them towards the left: the Nazis did not want the disruption of mothers making a scene on the ramp as they were torn from their young. It was simpler, cleaner, to keep them together and murder them both.

It was all done at speed and sometimes, amid the noise on the platform and the cacophony of different languages, the selector would dispense with the flick of the finger and use the crook of his walking stick to grab the neck of the Jew before him and tug him or her towards the left or right. That was especially useful if, say, a son and father were pleading not to be separated: the SS man would physically pull them apart.

Within the SS, the decision-makers argued over what proportion of deported Jews should be killed instantly and what proportion should be spared or, more accurately, killed at a slower pace, by means of 'annihilation through labour'. Some wanted as many Jews to be enslaved as possible: why squander their value as workers before exploiting it? Even if these Jews were too weak to work more than a week or two, surely a few hours of manpower were better than none. Others thought it foolish to burden the working arms of Auschwitz with anyone but the healthiest and strongest Jews: all the rest should be despatched to the gas chambers without draining even a modicum of the camp's resources.

The argument went back and forth without ever securing a resolution from Heinrich Himmler, the head of the SS and the only man who could have decided it. But the debate was settled in practice if not in theory. Four out of every five Jewish arrivals at Auschwitz were selected for immediate death. If you looked too old or too young to work, if you were conspicuously weak or unwell, you were sent to the left. From there, for most of the period Walter worked the ramp, you were directed to board one of the large SS trucks that were waiting for you, or else to walk the mile and a half from the camp to the little red house or the little white house, and there meet your death.

In this process of selection that played out night after night, there was no role for the *Rollkommando* except to stand and watch. At Buna or the gravel pits, Walter had done work that would break a young man's back. But this was work to break the heart. Under the glaring lights, and amid the chaos and the din, the screams and the tears, he was seeing up close the faces of the doomed, and he was seeing so very many of them. Still in his teens, he had to contemplate the last goodbyes of mothers and sons, fathers and daughters, in the minutes before they were murdered, and from just a few feet away. Starvation rations, filth, hard labour and constant, casual violence: he had learned to endure all those, to let his body absorb the blows. But now it was his soul that was taking a beating.

In the storehouses of Kanada, among the piles of blankets and shoes, he had had an intimation of the victims; he could imagine their lives. But here on the ramp, he could see them. And with each new train, he had to relive a dread most knew only once: the terror of arriving at Auschwitz.

Some would have been destroyed seeing what Walter saw, others driven mad by it. Neither response was unknown in Auschwitz. Walter was indeed brought low, low enough that fellow prisoners noticed a change in him. The brashly confident, even cocky teenager who had arrived at Auschwitz began to show signs of nervousness and depression. Some found him emotionally volatile.

And yet Walter did not succumb and he did not lose his mind. On the contrary, he applied that precocious brain of his – the brain of the boy who had taught himself chemistry from a single forbidden textbook – to what he saw. Perhaps it was his way of coping, a kind of willed detachment, but where others might have tried to avert their gaze, Walter watched all the more acutely.

He noticed the variations: how the SS might play nice one night, wielding the stick or the jackboot the next; how one day might bring a single transport, the next five or six; how sometimes 75 per cent of the new arrivals would be sent to the gas chambers, sometimes 95 per cent. But Walter had learned enough science to know that it was all about spotting patterns, and before long he had found one. Once he had, it was all he could see – and it filled him with a new determination, urgent and fervent, to break out.

There was so much to take in, especially for one still so young: that he was both a witness to and a target of a programme of industrialised, continent-wide murder, and that this project aimed both to eradicate an entire people and to turn a profit for the murderers.

But now he was coming to see another dimension that enabled all the rest. Slowly at first, he realised that the Nazis were engaged in a great and devastating trick, that the crime unfolding before him rested on a single, essential act that made the entire enterprise possible: deception.

The Nazis lied to their victims at every step of their journey towards destruction, step after step after step. Those people falling out of those stinking cattle trucks had boarded them believing they were being taken to new lives in a new place: 'resettlement in the east', they called it. Those Jews had packed up their belongings and held on tight to them because they thought they were building a new home, one that would need pots and pans, clothes for their backs and toys for their children. They believed that because that was what the Nazis had told them and it was what their own friends and families had told them, in the form of those postcards home that they did not realise had been written at gunpoint – those messages of forced cheer that Walter had heard read out on the train on the way to Majdanek – and which were designed to seal the lie.

The lying carried on the instant the SS men unlocked the wagons. If they were in a hurry, if there were to be five or six transports in a single day, they would be brutal. But if there was time, if the weather was good and the air was warm, the SS men might lay on a different show. They would pretend that the dreadful journey the new arrivals had endured had been some kind of aberration, a mistake that was about to be rectified. 'Good God,' they might say, 'in what state did those horrible Slovaks transport you? This is inhuman.' Those transported from Paris or Amsterdam, people raised to expect the best of the civilised Germans, were primed to believe that anyway, to feel relief that, at long last, they were now in the hands of German officers who would, naturally, ensure that food and drink would be available, that their luggage would be looked after and that order was about to be restored.

If time permitted, the pretence would continue as the new arrivals climbed on to the trucks that would take them to the killing sites. SS men, their manners impeccable, might help the sick clamber aboard, offering a helping hand. For those heading to the death chambers on foot, there was more reassurance in the form of enquiries about the Jews' professional qualifications or trades back home. Why would they ask such things if they did not intend to make use of the deportees' skills?

If anyone asked where they were being taken, the answer came back: 'For disinfection.' Given how squalid the journey had been, that made sense. More reassurance came on that trek past the Birkenau camp, and then across the meadow, from the sight of an ambulance – a green military van bright with a Red Cross – driving slowly behind their ragtag column, occasionally picking up those who could not keep walking by themselves. The vehicle did carry a doctor. But his purpose was not healing the sick or saving lives. The medic inside was the SS doctor who would supervise the gassing, and the cargo on board consisted of cans of Zyklon B. Walter knew all about that too: the Red Cross vans originated in Kanada, and one of his occasional jobs was to load them with the deadly canisters.

The scene of the crime itself was disguised, as was the murder weapon. The doomed believed they had been brought to a secluded, bucolic spot, a farmhouse alongside two wooden huts for undressing, enclosed by fruit trees. By Crematoria IV and V, there were flower beds.

Once there, the deception did not let up. These were the Jews' final minutes, but the Nazis encouraged them to believe in a future they did not have. 'What is your trade? A shoemaker?' the officer would ask again. 'We need them urgently, report to me immediately after!' As the victims followed the order to strip off their clothes, the SS would tell them that they were about to bathe, that they should stay calm and that afterwards they would be given 'coffee and something to eat'. That was when the reminder would come to tie all shoes into pairs, so that they would not go astray and so that, 'Afterwards you won't have to waste time finding the other shoe.' In fact, the SS were thinking practically: the shoes of murdered children would only be of use back home if they came in pairs. When the Jews were finally pushed inside the gas chamber, the trickery did not end. The sign on the doors read, 'To the Baths'. In the gas chambers that came later, in Crematorium II, the ceiling was dotted with fake showerheads. (Even the gas itself was part of the deception: the manufacturers of Zyklon B had altered their product, ridding it of the artificial odorant which, previously, had acted as a warning to anyone who got within inhalation distance. Now there was nothing but the faint, bitter almond smell of hydrogen cyanide to give it away.) Walter soon understood that all this was not some cruel and elaborate joke. It had a clear and rational purpose. That much was plain from his own work on the ramp.

He and his fellow slaves of the Kanada command were under the strictest orders not to breathe a word to anybody getting off the trains. There was to be no contact whatsoever. Walter had seen what would happen if that rule were broken.

One night there came a transport from the concentration-camp-cum-ghetto of Theresienstadt in Czechoslovakia. It was one of the western transports, where the Nazis had made an effort to keep up appearances, and where the human cargo arrived in relatively good condition. One of those disembarking was a well-dressed Czech mother, holding the hands of her two small children, and she was clearly relieved to have arrived at last. She said as much to a German officer: 'Thank God we're here.' She was one of those deportees who believed that the nation of Goethe and Kant would at last bring a measure of sanity to proceedings.

That proved too much for one of Walter's young comrades who, as he ran past her, hissed words meant both to scold and warn: 'You'll soon be dead.'

The woman looked not so much scared as affronted by this intrusion from a ghoulish man in pyjama stripes, his breath foul, his head shaved, a prisoner who was surely therefore some kind of criminal. Why else would he be here, looking like that? Instantly, she approached a German officer as if she were the aggrieved patron of a Prague department store, demanding to see the manager. 'Officer, one of the gangsters has told me that I and my children are to be killed,' she complained, in perfect German. The SS man, gloved, his uniform creased in all the right places, gave her his most benign and trustworthy smile and said, 'My dear lady, we are civilised people. Which gangster said this to you? If you would be so kind as to point him out.' She did as she was asked, and the officer took out his notebook and quietly wrote down the number of the prisoner, visible on the man's tunic. Afterwards, when everything was finished and all the people had gone, the officer sought out that prisoner and had him taken behind the wagons and shot. Walter was among those who carried his corpse back to the camp. At around the same time, the woman who had complained was gassed, along with her two young children.

Other prisoners tried to give gentler warnings, and valuable advice, as the selection loomed. *Say you're sixteen*, they might whisper to a young teenager. *Tell them you're thirty-five*, they might urge a man the wrong side of forty. *Look fit. Act healthy. Be strong.* Hardest of all was the counsel blurted out in a second to mothers: *Give up your children, let the old folks take them.* What was any parent to make of such an instruction? How was it possible to understand advice whose premise was: your children will die anyway, so save yourself?

But to give such a warning was to risk the fate of the boy Walter had seen taken off and murdered. Walter witnessed for himself the pains the Nazis took to ensure their intention remained hidden, chiefly by cutting off the information supply. He saw how he and the rest of the *Rollkommando* were under orders to ensure no trace of the previous transport remained, so that there would not be so much as a clue that anyone else had been at this same *Judenrampe* a matter of hours earlier. They had to clean it down to the last speck. He saw too how the SS men moved among the Jews as they lined up on the platform, demanding that nobody speak. 'Silence, everybody!' they would shout. 'This is not a synagogue!' There was purpose to that order. If no one could speak, no one could pass on a rumour or share whatever doubts might be forming, whatever inferences were being made. No one could voice the question: what are they going to do to us?

The SS wanted no hint of the slaughter to leak out. It was one reason why the Nazis developed an elaborate lexicon of euphemism to cover what they were doing. Jewish arrivals were not murdered, but rather subject to 'special handling' or 'special treatment'. The men who had to pull apart their corpses, cutting off their body hair and pulling out their gold teeth, were members of nothing more gruesome than the blandly named 'special squad'. It was for that same reason that the SS tried to drown out the screams of the dying with the sound of an idling engine, the same reason the gas chambers were first sited in locations that were remote and unseen, the same reason Auschwitz itself had been chosen for the work of slaughter – in part because it was isolated. No one was meant to know.

Running back and forth on the ramp for those ten long months, whether carrying corpses or suitcases, Walter gradually understood why the Nazis were so bent on keeping their victims ignorant of their fate, even to the last.

They needed their killing machine to run smoothly and without disruption, and that required their victims to be calm or at least amenable to instruction. Given the time pressure the SS were often under, with another transport coming down the track, there was no room for delay caused by panic or, worse, rebellion. Ideally, the SS liked to keep their victims tranquil by organising a gentle, polite disembarkation. But if time was tight, a swish of the cane would bring quiet by more direct means. Either way, what mattered was ensuring that the Jews coming off those trains did not know what fate awaited them. If they did, they might begin to cry out, they might start pushing and shoving, they might refuse to form columns, in rows of five, and instead rush for the barbed-wire fences or even at their captors. True, they would be overwhelmed and pacified eventually: the SS carried sub-machine guns and their victims had nothing but their own bodies, weakened by hunger and thirst. But still, there were sometimes a thousand or more people on that platform, outnumbering the Nazis by perhaps ten to one. If the Jews knew what was coming, what sand might they be able to throw in the gears of the machine that was poised to devour them? They might not stop it, but surely by even a modest show of defiance they could slow it down.

Walter saw it with new clarity. The factory of death that the Nazis had constructed in this accursed place depended on one cardinal principle: that the people who came to Auschwitz did not know where they were going or for what purpose. That was the premise on which the entire system was built.

It would not need a full-blown revolt to disturb its equilibrium. Even a ripple of panic among the doomed would unsettle the Nazis and their plan. The way Walter saw it, Auschwitz was an abattoir and he had seen enough of those in the Slovak countryside to know that it is much easier to slaughter lambs than it is to hunt deer. If you have to catch animals individually, hunting them down one by one, it is slow, awkward work. It is never as fast or efficient as driving thousands at a time, herded and neatly organised, towards their deaths. The Nazis had devised a method that would operate like a well-run slaughter house rather than a shooting party.

Walter understood it well because he was standing every day and every night on the threshold of the abattoir. The sight of it nearly broke him. In those ten months, there were some fellow prisoners who feared Walter Rosenberg was about to crack. But just at the point when he might have come apart, he was filled instead with a hot and unstoppable urge: he had to act.

It did not take long for him to realise what he had to do. If the Nazi plot to destroy the Jews relied on keeping the intended victims entirely ignorant of their fate – to ensure they were lambs, not scattered deer – then the first step towards thwarting that murderous ambition was to shatter the ignorance, to inform the Jews of the capital sentence that the Nazis had passed on them. It was the only way to stop the killing. Somebody had to escape and sound the alarm, issuing the warning that Auschwitz meant death. Around the time he turned eighteen years old in September 1942, as he watched the SS decide with a flick of a finger who would live and who would die, Walter concluded that person should be him. His first chance came more quickly than he could ever have imagined.

# 10

# The Memory Man

THE OPPORTUNITY CAME without warning and quite by accident. It was night-time on the ramp, and Walter was doing his usual work, running back and forth along the platform, carrying two suitcases at a time, as the SS officers reassured the arrivals on this latest transport that they did not need to bother about their luggage: the 'squad of criminals', referring to the prisoners of the *Rollkommando*, would take care of things and save them the bother of carrying their own bags. The criminals, the SS would add, were kept under the strictest discipline: 'So you don't need to worry about your property. Just leave everything.'

During one dash, with a case in each hand and a rucksack on his back, Walter stumbled and fell. His foot had snagged on a loose plank on the wooden platform. Flat on his face, he saw something he had never spotted before. Looking through the planks, he could see through to the ground about ten feet below. The thought struck him immediately: right here, under the ramp, there was a space. Which meant there was a hiding place.

He finished his shift but an idea was forming. The ramp was getting worn down by continual, heavy use: hundreds, sometimes thousands, of people trampled on that timber surface, night after night. There would be other loose planks. If he could pull up just one, out of sight of the throng, he could slip down below and hide.

The trick would be to wait. The SS's practice with each new transport was, initially, to surround the entire train but, as the Kanada detail worked their way through each cattle truck, from one end to the other, the cordon would shrink: the SS men did not bother encircling those wagons that had been emptied. Which meant that if you could wait underneath the ramp long enough, then creep back to the end of the train, under the platform and out of sight, you would find it empty and unguarded. You would be outside the cordon.

The position was perfect too. The ramp was in the no man's land between the Auschwitz main camp and Birkenau; it stood beyond the outer perimeters of both. If you could wait till that night's selection was over, until the latest batch of deportees had been despatched either as new prisoners to the camp or to the gas chambers, and until the SS had returned to barracks, you could then head out into the Polish countryside.

The next night and the nights that followed, Walter cased the ramp as he worked, sketching out how he would make his escape. He would have to stash food and clothes, purloined from Kanada. He looked hard to see if the SS placed a guard at the deserted end of the platform. If they did, and if it were just one man, Walter reckoned he could take him out with a knife and not make a sound.

Above all, he studied the wooden floor of the platform, searching for the weakest, most pliable plank, the one that could be lifted up and slotted back into place within a second or two. Soon Walter had created a mental map of the entire surface. He would make his move any day – any night – now.

But then the *Rollkommando* returned to the ramp for a new transport and Walter saw that it had changed. The gaps had gone. Perhaps spotting the danger of a complete collapse, the camp commandant had ordered that the platform be reinforced with concrete. It had happened fast. Walter reached his glum conclusion in an instant: there would be no escaping that way.

It meant that he would have to keep on working the ramp, seeing Jews sent to their deaths, taking mental notes of everything he saw, in preparation for the day he would tell the world. Later he would realise that, in some ways, he needed the mission he had given himself. It helped him get through each day, enabling him to endure what he was seeing unfold and, though it was harder to articulate, what he was seeing in himself.

For at eighteen years old Walter would witness events so harrowing they could change the life of the person who glimpsed them. He was witnessing such moments not once or twice, but day after day after day. He was in Auschwitz, a place where moral boundaries had dissolved long ago, where everything was permissible. This was a place where Dr Mengele once punished a Jewish woman by making a dog of her young son, because she had, in self-defence, killed an SS attack dog: he had the boy trained at the point of a whip to run on all fours, bark without pause and attack and bite Jews. Walter was in a place where one inmate might steal bread from another, even when that prisoner was dying and when the bread was covered in faeces. He was in a place where, after an execution by firing squad, prisoners might rush up to the warm corpses and eat what they could of their bodies, one reassuring another that a human brain was so delicate it could be eaten raw, without cooking.

On the ramp, Walter was watching the Nazis wielding bamboo sticks to herd children and anyone over forty to their deaths in gas chambers and he was doing nothing to stop them. He was loading the canisters of Zyklon B himself. Surely he was morally obliged to run at the first SS man in sight, put his hands around that man's neck and throttle him, no matter the cost to himself. Was that not his duty?

After all, he could not claim ignorance. Unlike these families, who had boarded the train to Auschwitz in orderly fashion, having obeyed the instruction to bring their authorised twenty-five kilograms of luggage, he *knew*. The veil of deception had been torn from his eyes long before.

He had wanted to act; it was shaming to keep quiet while seeing all this murder around him. Worse, his work on the ramp made him a collaborator in the big lie: by cleaning out those wagons, by removing every last trace of each transport, he was helping keep the next batch of victims ignorant of their fate, and the next and the next.

But he knew he could do nothing. The reason was not so much that, if he did, it would ensure his instant death, but rather the inevitable Nazi reprisal that would follow. Not against him – he would be dead – but against his fellow inmates, those he would have left behind. Any act of resistance would be met with instant and grossly disproportionate punishment. If Walter had attacked one SS man and killed him, the SS would have killed, what, a hundred prisoners? And killing would be the least of it; death would feel like liberation given the torments their captors would inflict on them first. The SS were inventive in that area; Walter had heard the stories from the hell that was Block 11, the investigation block or, more accurately, the torture block. So no, there would be no heroic act of self-sacrifice on the *Judenrampe*. There could be no such thing, because no man would ever be sacrificing himself alone. The inmates were bound by a sense of responsibility to each other. They were not just prisoners; they were hostages.

And yet, like so many young, intelligent men before him and since, Walter yearned for there to be some meaning to his life, some meaning especially to his own enforced silence and inaction in the face of extreme evil. If he could live long enough to escape and warn the Jews of their fate in this accursed place, might that not justify the fact that he had stood by impotently as mass murder was committed in front of him? If he were able not merely to observe this horror, but eventually to testify to what he had seen, might that not justify his own survival? He did not yet know the phrase survivor guilt, but the teenage Walter intuited it and sought to pre-empt it.

It was around then, and with this new self-instructed mission in mind, that Walter set about a task that would both provide a meaning to his own descent into the underworld and change the course of history. He would record what he was seeing. Not in a diary full of sharp, human observation nor in mental sketches and notes that would one day blossom into great works of art; as it happened, and unbeknown to him, there were others in Auschwitz doing that. No, Walter was a student who had thrived in mathematics and the natural sciences. His language was numbers and hard facts. He would collect the data of industrialised murder.

And then he would memorise it. The number of trains, the number of wagons per train, the approximate number of passengers, the point of origin. He had no idea how he would get this information out, but he knew as a matter of instinct that if it was to be effective – if it was to be *believed* – it would have to be detailed and accurate. He soon devised a method, which worked like a child's memory game. Each day he would say to himself everything he already knew, before adding whatever new nugget of information he had acquired that day. The trick was to keep surveying the mountain of facts that was accumulating in his head, scaling it once more every single day, becoming ever more familiar with each layer of it, adding to it only incrementally. In that effort, the Nazis helped him.

The numbering system they imposed – branding every deportee who survived selection, and became a registered prisoner, with a string of digits inked into their flesh and worn on their striped uniform – that system acted as a precious record, and reminder, of transports past. For the numbers were not random. Instead, they advanced chronologically: the more recent the transport, the higher the number.

As time went on, Walter came to recognise these figures and the stories they told. If he spotted a tunic bearing a number between 27400 and 28600, he knew that he was facing a figure worthy of the highest respect, a survivor of the first convoy of Slovak Jewish men back in April 1942. If the number was between 40150 and 43800, there was a strong chance that the wearer had come to Auschwitz from France, brought there on one of three transports in June 1942. Between 80000 and 85000 revealed that the prisoner was among the few who had been selected for labour from the convoys of trucks, not trains, which arrived without interruption during one thirty-day spell, bringing in Polish Jews from the ghettos of Mława, Maków, Zichenow, Łomza, Grodno and Białystok. Those 5,000 apart, the rest were what Walter and his fellow inmates called 'civilians': women, men and children who would never work as slaves in Auschwitz, those whose sole acquaintance with the camp would be the railway platform, the truck and, finally, the gas chamber.

Walter saw examples of all these numbers around him in the camp, worn by those who had been directed right rather than left at the *Judenrampe*. They served as a living record of the trains and trucks that had come to Auschwitz full of those condemned to die.

Working on that ramp day in and day out, emptying out every transport, Walter had a vantage point that was exceptionally rare. And working in the clearing *Kommando* allowed him to see places others either never saw or saw but never lived to remember. In November 1942, for example, a group of Kanada men were sent to clear out a pile of clothes that had been left at the gas chamber of the Auschwitz main camp. Walter was one of them. From the outside, he was able to note the roof covered with earth, and then, once he had entered the building, he could see the garage-style doors of the gas chamber along with its two side openings. He was able to step inside the room itself. He could stare into the darkness.

Perhaps this project of his, to see and remember, to count the Nazis' victims as they came in, was quixotic and doomed; he could be killed at any moment, and the knowledge methodically building up in his head would die with him. But if such a goal made sense at all, there were few better placed than Walter Rosenberg to attempt it. He was able to see so much, and he had the brainpower to remember it.

As he worked through those months, climbing on to the filthy cattle trucks and removing the luggage that contained valuable goods and sentimental trinkets, food supplies and heirlooms, he only became more convinced that he had understood the Nazis correctly. A smooth process of destruction was what the SS wanted and, for that, absolute, watertight ignorance was a prerequisite. One incident on the ramp confirmed his analysis.

It was a moment so fleeting, it seemed almost to evaporate. But Walter would never forget it. On a cold night in late 1942, and for only a few seconds, the bubble of ignorance in which the Nazis sought to envelop their victims was pierced.

It was around midnight when it happened. Walter and the others had ushered in a transport of French Jews: the kind that usually made for an easy evening for the Nazis. These were western European Jews whose skin had not been thickened by ghettos, pogroms or recent persecution; they had lived largely comfortable lives and their first instinct was to believe what those in authority said to them. Sure enough, on that winter's night, they were doing precisely as they had been told. They were lining up for selection.

Suddenly, out of the darkness came a truck. Walter and the others were used to it; it was a nightly occurrence. It would ferry that day's load of prisoner corpses – those who had been beaten to death, crushed by the weight of work, starvation and disease or else finished off in the infirmary – from the Auschwitz main camp to Birkenau, where the bodies would be burned. Its route involved crossing the railway tracks, just ahead of the platform.

Usually when the vehicle was approaching, there would be a signal and the arc lights that flooded the ramp would be switched off for two or three seconds to allow the truck to cross over. But on this night the switch failed. The lights stayed on.

It meant that the French deportees, neatly lined up in their rows awaiting further instructions, saw – brightly lit up – the vehicle as it came closer and reached the railway line. It tried to push forward, surmounting the tracks. It nudged up against them, but could not progress: it was too heavy, weighed down by its load.

Now, in the white electric light, those on the platform watched as the truck surged forward only to lurch back, the whole vehicle bouncing and swaying as it tried to advance. And as it heaved, its cargo was disturbed; the bodies on board started to shift. Walter watched along with the new arrivals, as they saw lifeless, twig-like limbs flopping over the side of the truck. The arms seemed to be signalling a macabre farewell.

The French Jews in their winter coats saw it and their response was involuntary. They let out a wail, a thin cry of collective horror at the sight of scores of dead bodies piled up like so much discarded rubbish. The sound contained something else too: despair, for some surely understood what this grotesque spectacle augured for their own fate.

For a second, Walter thought this might be it. This might be the moment of mass hysteria, the trigger for uncontrolled panic, that he had been waiting for. These Jews from Paris, Marseille or Nice, or wherever they were from, might they now turn on their captors, demanding to know what the hell was happening here? Could the strongest even rush at the SS, perhaps overpowering one of them, maybe even grabbing a gun? In the melee that would doubtless follow, as the Nazis sought to re-establish control, somebody could make a run for it, escaping into the darkness. It could be one of these new arrivals; it could be one of the men of Kanada command. It could be Walter himself.

But then the truck made one more push, its engine groaning, its springs creaking, as it finally hauled itself over the tracks and on to the other side. It drove off, out of the pool of electric light and back into the night. It was gone. And with it went that noise of lamentation and shock. The wailing stopped and quiet fell once more.

It had lasted all of three or four seconds, and then it had vanished. For that briefest of interludes, the Jews on the platform had looked into the abyss. Walter watched them, exhausted after their journey and innocent of the depravity that, by now, was routine for him and his comrades, and saw how they steadily gathered themselves and regrouped. They acted as if the truck had been a trick of the light, a mirage that could not possibly exist, not in the world as they knew it. They concluded that it was their eyes, not their captors, that were telling lies.

So there was no rebellion on that or any other night. The French Jews who had stepped off the train lined up, as ordered. They followed the SS finger that sent them to the left or right. Those sent leftward marched without noise or fuss to the gas chambers where, within the hour, most would be dead.

Still, that wail, too brief though it was, gave Walter hope. It proved that, once the bubble of delusion was burst, people would respond, if only as a reflex.

He had drawn a conclusion that would become an article of faith, an unshakeable creed that would drive every decision he took next. He now understood that the difference between knowledge and ignorance, between truth and lies, was the difference between life and death.

It was clear to him from then on that the Jews destined for destruction could defy their fate here only if they knew of it, incontrovertibly and before it was too late. Somehow Walter had to get out of this place and tell the world what was happening. He did not know it yet, but he was about to meet the people who could help.

# 11

# Birkenau

THE MATCHMAKER WAS a louse. Specifically, the bearer of typhus. The cull of late August 1942 had brought only a temporary reprieve. Weeks later, it was back. The proof came in the wobbling, stumbling figures of prisoners once again doing their best to stand tall as they went before the hawk eye of Jakob Fries. Despite the pickings of the ramp available to his part of the Kanada detail, and the improved nutrition they brought, even Walter felt himself succumb to dizziness, his gait as unsteady as if he had helped himself to some of the contraband liquor that found its way into Auschwitz. The solution, he and his friend Josef decided, was to hide away for a couple of days, safely avoiding the inspections that might send them to the infirmary – where SS doctors conducted their own twice-weekly mini-selections, on Mondays and Thursdays, to weed out the unfit – and an early death.

Both of them reported themselves to one of the ambulance stations that, following the earlier typhus outbreak, were now dotted around the camp and which had the authority to give slave workers a day or two off. The boys thought they had done well, playing the system.

But it was an act of the most dangerous naivety. For Walter and Josef had inadvertently turned themselves in. They had done Fries's work for him. Walter only discovered that through one of those arbitrary acts of kindness that seemed to punctuate his life in those years. He had gone earlier to thank the orderly who had marked him down for a supposed day off. Now the man, a Polish prisoner, told him the truth: that he had registered Walter for the hospital where he would be lethally injected with phenol. In a gesture of generosity that made no rational sense, the man agreed to take Walter's name off the list.

Walter went to find Josef, to explain. But his old friend, a comrade since Majdanek and a fellow veteran of Buna and, earlier, the SS food store, would not listen. He was convinced that it was Walter who had been tricked, that it was safer to be on that list than off it. Josef was wrong, and when the time came he was led off with those branded as carriers of the dreaded typhus. Later Walter would learn that his friend did not die at the doctor's needle. At the last moment, he fought off the *Kapos* and made a dash for the fence, where he was shot. Doomed it may have been, but Josef Erdelyi had held true to the dream the pair had discussed right at the start: he had tried to escape.

There was little time for grieving, not when Walter could feel the typhus tightening its grip. He lay low for a while in Block 4, but there was only so long he could expect others to cover for him. He was too weak to work at the ramp, but was convinced there were places in Kanada itself he could hide away unnoticed. The challenge, given that he could barely walk, was getting there and back, past the ever-watchful Fries. But two comrades agreed to prop him up, taking an arm each and all but carrying him to Kanada, loosening their grip only for the few yards when they passed the *Oberscharführer* and Walter had to walk unaided. In his feverish, drained state, even those ten paces demanded deep strength; but he did it.

Once in Kanada, they led Walter into the warehouse where the clothes were sorted. This was the domain of the secret paramour and recipient of stolen love tokens for whom Walter had played courier. She remembered Walter's act of sacrifice and agreed to let him take refuge. The hiding place was ingenious: the young women lifted their sick, teenage fellow prisoner on to a lofty pile of old clothes, soft enough to serve as a hospital bed and so high he was safely out of view. There they brought him tablets to bring down his temperature and the odd glass of sugared lemonade.

For three days, he was ferried back and forth to that impromptu clinic. But it was not enough. Walter was not getting better. He weighed a mere forty-two kilograms, around ninety-three pounds or less than seven stone. The typhus, the flogging from Wiegleb, the surgery with minimal anaesthetic, they had all taken their toll. His adolescent vigour had deserted him: now he could barely move, let alone walk. It was obvious: he was dying.

The only hope, and it was slim, was medical treatment. That meant a return to round-the-clock rest in Block 4. Laco, the Slovak dentist who had got Walter and Josef into Kanada in the first place, the man who had acted as a human crutch walking Walter past Fries, found the right medicine. What's more, he arranged for a prisoner orderly from the infirmary to come to the barracks and inject it.

Like Walter and like Laco, he was a Slovak. His name was Josef Farber. The mere sound of his voice was such a blessed relief to Walter, after nights of sweat, delirium and hallucination that he did not think too much of the questions this seemingly old, grey-haired man – in fact, he was in his thirties – asked as he readied the needle. Walter submitted to the interview easily, chatting away, volunteering the story of how he came to be prisoner 44070: Majdanek, Nováky, the trip to Budapest, the night flight from Trnava, all of it. In a moment of supreme vulnerability, desperate perhaps to put himself in the hands of someone who might help, he dropped his guard altogether.

The doctor let slip the odd morsel about himself. He had been in Spain during the civil war, fighting with the International Brigades. He had once worked with the Hungarian socialists Walter mentioned.

Then Walter confessed his worry about his losing battle with typhus: that surely the patience of the deputy *Kapos* and Ernst Burger, the registrar of Block 4, was not infinite; they would not cover for him for ever. Farber sought to soothe his anxiety. The deputy *Kapos* were veterans of the anti-fascist fight in Spain too. As for Burger, he added, 'He's one of us.'

That remark had to pierce a haze of fever and illness before Walter understood it. Us? Who was 'us'? But finally it sank in and when it did, Walter felt an elation he had not known since he arrived in this desolate place. *Us*. It could only mean that there was a resistance organisation in Auschwitz, an underground. And by the use of that small, single word – *us* – had he not announced that eighteen-year-old Walter Rosenberg was in it?

Walter had not misread the signs. He had indeed just been recruited. Young as he was, his silence under the whip of Wiegleb had given him a reputation for resilience. This boy who had not talked even as the skin was flayed from his flesh, he could be trusted to withstand torture. For a putative member of the resistance, there was no more important credential.

Walter's status within the camp changed from that moment on. Now he enjoyed the protection of the underground, though it was hardly a single entity. All sorts of groups organised themselves clandestinely: it might be members of this or that Czech nationalist party or trade union, veterans of the same unit in Spain, or else fellow social democrats or communists. Walter was too young to have that kind of history, although the Austrian Marxists were impressed to learn of his connection to his Viennese cousin, Max: Walter's onetime rival for his grandfather's affections back in Nitra had gone on to become active in the Austrian communist party and his comrades remembered him. In any case, Walter was now seen by qualified medical personnel who administered legitimate drugs, taken from the hoard of stolen medicine that passed through Kanada, and given extra food rations to accelerate his recovery. It was all arranged by Farber and his comrades. There was no clearer mark of Walter's new, protected position than the fact that the deputy *Kapos* in Block 4 now looked out for him; if he needed the lavatory in the night, one would rise from his bunk and guide him there.

It made sense that the resistance was so deeply embedded in Block 4, home of the Kanada command. They had access to the currency essential to any functioning underground. The necessities and luxuries, the clothes and the cognac, that were in abundance in Kanada could be used to extract favours and ensure the blind eyes that were a prerequisite for any kind of secret network. The underground in Auschwitz could organise because they could 'organise'.

What's more, they exerted a powerful hold over those Nazis who were themselves drawn to Kanada and its riches. Walter had seen for himself the corruption of the SS, how tempted they were by money. All that cash stuffed into a trunk, bound for the Reichsbank? Not all of it made it to Berlin. Some of it tended to stick to the pockets of the Germans charged with its transfer. Prisoner members of the resistance witnessed those acts of petty theft, or learned of them, and then used that knowledge to blackmail their Nazi masters.

Which meant they had the means to restore Walter to health, finding a soft job for him in Kanada. A young man who had survived longer than most, fluent in both Czech and Slovak, with excellent German, Polish, Russian and a smattering of Hungarian to boot, was now an asset to be protected and cultivated. They arranged for him to sort spectacles, working his way through the piles of eyeglasses that had once defined the faces of thousands upon thousands of schoolteachers and tailors, bookbinders and watchmakers, radicals and loners, lawyers and mothers and poets and daughters who had been sent to their deaths in the gas chambers that stood no more than a couple of miles away.

He was deployed as soon as he was fit enough, tasked with pocketing medicines from the Kanada supply or carrying messages from one underground leader to another. Walter was delighted to do it. He did not mind that he was but a tiny cog in the machine of resistance. Every little act was a small step towards what was, surely, the underground's ultimate mission: an eventual revolt aimed at the destruction, or at least the sabotage, of the death factory.

The months passed, the autumn of 1942 turning to winter. Walter did his best to keep track of the transports rolling into Auschwitz, adding to his mental tally. Once the battles with Wiegleb and the typhus louse were over, he devoted himself less to mere survival and more to his survival's newly determined purpose: the gathering of information. That this was among Auschwitz's most precious commodities seemed obvious to him. He had only to look at how jealously the SS guarded it. So he set to work as a self-appointed researcher of the Auschwitz killing machine, taking every opportunity to expand his knowledge of the death plant that surrounded him. When the camp authorities looked for volunteers to work in Birkenau, Walter offered himself, so that he could take a closer look.

He was part of a Kanada unit put on a truck and sent to Birkenau to clear out a horses' stable stuffed, floor to ceiling, with the clothes of the dead. But that mattered less than the route there. It took them past a number of open fire pits, craters that were six yards wide, six yards long and six yards deep and that had been carved into the ground, and which warmed the air, even in midwinter. The prisoners had seen their glow from the main camp, but now Walter was close enough to feel their heat. He inched towards the edge of one pit and what he saw there would never leave him.

It was a sight that confirmed Auschwitz-Birkenau as the corner of earth where the human race had finally turned its perennial fantasies of hell into material reality. There, at the bottom of the smouldering pit, the flames now shrunk and spent, were human bones. Among them – not burned, but only charred – were the heads of children. Later he would learn that the head of a child contains too much water to burn easily. The bodies of their parents had been incinerated, but the children remained.

Walter committed the sight to memory. Perhaps it was the only way to carry that image once he had glimpsed it, to lock it away in a secure mental file of which he would be the eventual courier. If he had to be a spectator to horror, then he would make himself a witness. He would be a reporter.

Christmas came and went, the SS forcing their Jewish captives to learn and sing 'Stille Nacht' – 'Silent Night' – perhaps to remind the Germans of home. Those who did not sing it properly were murdered. In Birkenau, the SS put up a huge Christmas tree and on Christmas Eve they brought out a group of prisoners. For their own entertainment, they gave the men a pointless task, ordering them to gather up soil in their coats, shooting any man who collected too little. Then they stacked the corpses in a heap under the tree, piled up like festive gifts.

The new year brought a change, following a turf war between two of Auschwitz's big beasts: Wiegleb and Fries. The dispute was settled with a decision that Kanada be relocated. It would move to Birkenau.

On 15 January 1943 Walter and the others marched to their new barracks, noticing the contrast straight away. Where what Walter thought of as the Auschwitz mother camp was neat and organised, all paved pathways and red-brick buildings, Birkenau was a chaotic mess. Built on soggy marshland, it consisted of structures thrown together in wood, barely proofed against the elements.

If these structures seemed unfit for human habitation, that was because they were meant for animals. They were built from German army kits, flat-packs allowing for the rapid self-assembly of stables for military horses. The SS seemed to find it amusing to keep their prisoners that way. Sometimes, there would be straw on the floor, as if the Jews held within were livestock; there were iron rings on the walls, in case any of the animals needed to be tethered. One unit was meant to house no more than fifty-one horses, but the SS kept at least 400 Jews in each. The roof beams bore stencilled slogans: *Be Honest* or *Order is Holiness* or *Hygiene is Health*, the last exhortation especially cruel, given the insanitary conditions in which the inmates of Birkenau were held. Toilet facilities consisted of a long concrete slab, punctured with dozens of circular holes: defecation was to be en masse, privacy a memory. The washroom was one very long trough.

The killing programme in Birkenau was as ad hoc as its construction. While the SS waited for the streamlined, purpose-built facilities that would become Crematoria II, III, IV and V, they had to make do with the makeshift gas chambers formed out of that pair of converted farmhouses. When it came to the means of disposal of bodies – first burial, then incineration – the SS had no blueprint. As those flaming pits dug into the earth testified, in Auschwitz-Birkenau, a place that unlike Treblinka or Sobibor or Belzec was not designed for industrial-scale slaughter, the Nazis were improvising.

But if Birkenau was messier than the main camp on the outside, it was a harsher, crueller place on the inside too. When Walter put aside, for the sake of his calculations, the instant slaughter of the 'civilians' in the gas chambers, confining his numbers only to the prisoners, he could see that the death rate in Birkenau was faster and more furious than in Auschwitz. He had grown used to arbitrary killing, but in Birkenau murder was sport. *Kapos* might kick the head of a *Muselmann*, collapsed on the dirt, as if it were a stray football. Several had a competition, won by whichever *Kapo* was able to kill a prisoner with a single blow. If an inmate were too sick to work, a pair of *Kapos* would stretch their victim on the ground, place an iron bar across his neck and then – one, two, three – jump on each end. The neck would be broken, a life ended. All across the camp, in front of each barracks, there would be piles of stick-thin bodies, usually coated in mud. Birkenau reeked of rotting flesh.

Still, even in this mire, there was an underground and Walter arrived with a couple of names, along with an unwritten character reference from Farber. That led him to David Szmulewski, de facto head of the resistance in Birkenau. Another veteran of the International Brigades in Spain, Szmulewski was a Zionist and radical who had made his way to Palestine as an illegal immigrant, only to be chased out by the ruling British authorities. He deemed Walter of sufficient potential to merit introductions to the rest of the underground leadership. Before long, Walter was ushered into a world whose existence few inside or outside the topsy-turvy universe of Auschwitz would ever have imagined.

The resistance had used their leverage – the currency of bribery combined with the suasion of blackmail – to win posts for themselves that had previously gone only to the brutal green-triangle caste of ex-criminal *Kapos*. Slowly, the ranks of block elders and block registrars – those charged with keeping track of the inmates in each barracks, playing their part in the roll call that counted them out at dawn and counted them back in at night – were filling up with red-triangle political prisoners. For those lucky few – the overwhelming majority, some 80 per cent of them, Poles rather than Jews – the living conditions were, compared to the rest of the camp, positively luxurious.

To Walter, these men lived like aristocrats. They had their own rooms, narrow and bare, admittedly, but sectioned off from the rest of the barracks. They had access to real food, rather than the adulterated bread and not-quite-margarine or the thin, weak soup on which ordinary prisoners had to survive. These men – officially *Kapos*, secretly rebels – might gather in one of those small bedrooms to enjoy an evening meal of potatoes and margarine or a bowl of porridge, and high-level conversation. For Walter, the teenager from Trnava, it felt like a privilege just to sit and listen. His admiration for these men only deepened when he realised that they were, in fact, eating modestly, at least in comparison with the delicacies that were freely available to them via Kanada. They could have dined like the *Kapos* Walter had encountered in Auschwitz I, feasting on the finest fare of Europe. Instead they chose relative frugality, perhaps choking on the knowledge that outside those private rooms, close enough to breathe in the aroma, their fellow prisoners were starving.

Walter enjoyed his protected status. He liked the fact that the combination of his connections to the underground and his standing as an experienced prisoner earned him some wary respect from the green-triangle *Kapos*. When he was not at work – he had returned once more to the ramp – he could move around relatively freely.

And yet, glad though he was to have found shelter within Birkenau's prisoner elite, it was not straightforward. He was grateful to them for their protection; he admired their restraint. But a doubt about them took root and refused to wither.

Perhaps it was because of the job he was doing: he was seeing the Final Solution both intimately and at scale. Now that he lived in Birkenau, he was even closer to the process, which made his self-assigned task of collecting the data of the dead easier. He got to know some of the block registrars, the tellers and bookkeepers of death, against whose figures he could check his own. He had a good contact in the *Sonderkommando*, the special squad of prisoners charged with surely the worst job in Auschwitz, namely emptying out the gas chambers and disposing of the corpses: his friend Filip Müller was one of those who worked the ovens. Filip could work out how many bodies were to be burned in each shift by the amount of fuel that had been set aside for the task: when it came to fuel, the SS never over-supplied, preferring to provide exactly the quantity required and no more. Day by day, number by number, Walter Rosenberg was adding to his mental tally, a ledger that was no less comprehensive for not being written down.

But his new proximity to the killing gave Walter something else besides extra statistical detail. He was now a more direct witness to the journey of those new arrivals once they got off the train. He would see them herded towards the fake shower block; he would see with his own eyes the deception and its effects. He would see the mothers and their children quietly lining up to descend the steps that would take them underground, never to be glimpsed again, queuing politely for the Auschwitz butcher, as he saw it, all because they believed the lie they had been told.

That only entrenched his determination to get out and tell the world. For clearly the duty of any person who knew the horror of Birkenau was to stop it. He had assumed that that was the goal of the resistance, to bring production at the death factory to a halt. But now he began to wonder if he had got that wrong, if that was not their goal after all.

From what he could see, the underground was chiefly a kind of mutual self-help society, a fellowship dedicated to the welfare of its own members. In that goal, it was plainly successful. It used bribery and blackmail to powerful effect, ensuring those under its wing enjoyed better material conditions and leniency from the authorities when needed. To Walter, the resistance was part trade union, part anti-Nazi mafia.

What he could not see was much evidence of resisting, in the sense of striking a blow aimed at destroying or even slowing the killing machine. He wondered if he was being naive. Maybe there was a secret plan to which he was not privy. But even as time passed, there was still no sign of it.

To be sure, the underground had won improvements in daily life inside the Auschwitz concentration camp (as opposed to the death camp). Over the course of 1943, they succeeded in reducing the level of casual, quotidian violence against prisoners. The routine beatings, torture and murder of inmates: they all became rarer. Walter, the young would-be statistician, could see the shift in the data he was gathering in his own head. By his estimate, some 400 prisoners had been dying every day in Birkenau as 1942 turned into 1943. But by May 1943, the mortality rate had fallen drastically. For the underground, this was considered a great victory. Admittedly, the change in the weather had helped. But they had also succeeded in thinning the *Kapo* ranks of club-wielding criminal brutes, replacing them with German- or Austrian-born political prisoners who were not only recognised as fellow Aryans and therefore human beings by the SS, but also aspired to behave with dignity, even inside the inferno of Auschwitz. They wanted to humanise the prison camp and, judged by that narrow criterion, they were succeeding. But Walter could see, from his unending shifts on the ramp, that they were having next to no impact on what, to him, was the only issue that mattered: stopping or slowing the organised murder of the Jews of Europe.

Indeed, he came to believe that, for all its cunning and tirelessness, the underground was not hindering the Nazi project of mass slaughter but helping it, albeit indirectly and unintentionally. If only a thousand prisoners died in the camp, then only a thousand needed to be selected from among the new arrivals to take their place − which left more to be marched into the gas chambers. The better life was for the prisoners, the longer their life expectancy thanks to the ingenuity of the resistance, the fewer 'civilians' would be saved.

Besides, had Walter not already understood that order and calm was what the SS desired most, that it was, for them, an essential condition for the smooth running of their corpse factory? Granting a few privileges here and there, loosening the leash by which it held its inmates, was surely a small price for the Nazis to pay if, in return, their Auschwitz killing centre was buttressed by the presence of a settled, orderly concentration camp behind it.

He understood that Auschwitz was a special case. It was not like other concentration camps − Mauthausen, say, or Dachau − because Auschwitz doubled as a death camp. What might represent a noble policy for a resistance movement in those other places − a policy aimed at boosting the survival rate of the mostly political prisoners − served in Auschwitz only to oil and grease the machinery of mass annihilation. A teenager he might have been, but the victories of the underground, even those from which he directly felt the benefit, struck him as a bleak kind of success. He would have to do something more.

And yet, he knew it was impossible to act alone. It was only thanks to the underground that he was alive. Any hope of escape would remain a fantasy without them. He was about to learn that lesson anew − and to meet the man who would change his life.

# 12

## 'It Has Been Wonderful'

H$E$ HAD SPENT the best part of a year on the ramp, watching the Jews arrive, conscious that most would never be seen again. Now, in the summer of 1943, Walter gained access to yet more information on the inner workings of Auschwitz. It came thanks to a promotion, secured for him by the Birkenau underground and helped along by another wave of typhus.

A new surge of the disease prompted a transfer of prisoners to the previously unoccupied BII section of Birkenau, with Walter assigned to one sector of it, identified by the letter D: BIId. (These sectors were so large, they almost represented camps in their own right.) The change in arrangements, and the expected influx of new prisoners, created the need for extra assistants to the men who kept count: the registrars. Only recently had Jewish, rather than Polish, prisoners begun to fill such privileged posts and Walter benefited from the change. He would work under the registrar for the mortuary: Alfréd Wetzler.

Walter already knew of Fred. He remembered him from their shared hometown of Trnava, where Fred, who was six years older than he was, had seemed an impossibly glamorous figure: self-assured, bohemian, charming. Among the young, a six-year age gap is a chasm. Back in Slovakia, Fred had not so much as noticed Walter.

Which meant the first words the two ever exchanged were in the morgue at Birkenau. Walter was being shown around by Szmulewski, the underground leader, who was introducing his young recruit to the people he would need to know. Wetzler greeted Walter warmly, only too glad to trade memories of the town they had both left behind.

Even so, for Walter, the experience was unnerving, because this conversation took place in a wooden building stuffed with 300 or

400 dead bodies piled into neat rows of ten. Wetzler himself was unfazed, breaking off at one point to attend to his duties, which meant overseeing the transfer of corpses to a truck which had pulled up outside the building.

He was joined by four Polish prisoners for a process that had clearly become routine and swift. Before a body was flung out of the door and on to the back of the truck, one man would lift its arm and read off the number from the tattoo. As registrar, Wetzler would note it down. A second man would then prise open the mouth of the deceased, looking for gold teeth: if he saw one, he would yank it out with a pair of pliers, then toss the gold into a tin can at his side. Walter noted the clinking sound it made as it landed. These men were not expert dentists and they were rushed; sometimes a gold tooth would go into the can still attached to a fleshy chunk of gum. Then the other two would grab the corpse, two limbs each, and chuck it on to the back of the truck. All of this was done at speed, with Fred Wetzler as overseer.

And yet, macabre as the whole display had been on that first meeting, Walter found himself returning often. He and Fred would share a cup of coffee and talk of home and of all that was gone. Fred had lost three brothers in the *Sonderkommando*. Life expectancy for the 'special squad' was especially low, even by Auschwitz standards: the SS would periodically murder the entire unit, so that their knowledge would die with them. And yet, despite the presence of all that grief, Walter would go to Fred's little office whenever he could. It became a haven of sorts, even a hiding place. They were rarely disturbed. The SS tended to stay away from the morgue: they did not like the smell.

So Walter was delighted to work as Fred's assistant registrar. He regarded it as a step up. Walter thought he understood why the underground had placed him there too: this way he would have access to ever more valuable information, which of course he would relay back to his superiors even if he feared they were not yet doing anything sufficiently worthwhile with it. And yet his new boss, Fred Wetzler, understood the appointment very differently. He could see that Walter had been shaken by his months on the ramp, that he had come close to breaking. He suspected the underground had seen that too and had decided to remove their new asset from the front line of horror, for his own sake.

They were plainly happy with the results, because within six weeks they had arranged Walter's elevation to the rank of registrar in his own right. For the authorities, he was to keep track of the newly opened BIIa, the sector of Birkenau where new inmates would be quarantined; for the resistance, he would share all he knew and serve as a human link between this new sector and BIId, which otherwise operated as two distinct entities, each sealed off from the other. Walter would shuttle between the two, acting as courier.

That was the first clear benefit of this new job. As a clerk of the camp, Walter had a measure of free movement. So long as he looked purposeful, perhaps carrying a sheaf of papers, he could walk around the place without much risk of being challenged. Obviously that was helpful in his work for the underground, but it also made life much more bearable for him. True, the place in which he had now won the right to roam was a killing field, but his was better than the lot of the ordinary prisoner: confinement, surveillance and the permanent threat of physical violence.

Walter began to look less and less like a regular inmate too. He was fed rather than starved and he had returned to robust health. Always mindful of his appearance, he now had some discretion over his wardrobe. The zebra trousers could go, replaced by riding breeches and black boots, polished to a bright shine. His head was shaven, but he could cover it with a neat cap. Though he was still required to wear the regulation striped jacket, he had a bespoke version cut for him by one of the tailor inmates. Indeed, a hallmark of those in the upper reaches of the inmate hierarchy was a higher quality of prisoner garb: clothes without patches, proper shoes and, in what was an unofficial privilege granted to clerks such as Walter, a breast pocket sewn on to the outside of his striped shirt-cum-jacket.

But of all the advantages that came with his new role, the one that mattered most was his increased proximity to information. He was convinced that he saw the face of every new prisoner brought to the camp from 8 June 1943 onwards, because that was the day he began as the *Schreiber* of BIIa, the quarantine camp which was every new arrival's first stop. And although he was no longer on the ramp, he was still in a position to log the traffic heading to the gas chambers. It was a simple matter of location. BIIa was the sector closest to the main gate and, in the row of human stables that formed that sector, his own stable, number fifteen, was the second along, just forty or fifty yards away from that entrance and with a clear line of sight. If a convoy of trucks were carrying Jews to their deaths in Crematoria II and III, it went through that gate. It was quite a procession: an escort of motorcycle outriders, complete with a machine-gunner in each sidecar, just in case anyone got any ideas of jumping down from the truck. If, on the other hand, a convoy were heading to Crematoria IV and V, it would take the road that ran directly in front of Walter's barracks. In the daytime, he would simply count every vehicle as it went by, building up a tally based on the rate he had seen at the ramp: a hundred people per truck. At night, he would listen out for a new shipment of Jews, the whole barracks shaking as each vehicle trundled past. Walter had only to count the number of tremors to make his tally.

His job allowed him, within limits, to wander the camp and survey it. He had been granted a chance, all but unheard of among the inmate population, to glimpse the entire set-up and commit what he had seen to memory. Several times he took himself to the area between Crematoria IV and V, pretending that he had some business there, watching the people being taken into the gas chambers, then walking on. He filed away what he learned along with the numbers he was amassing in his head, adding new ones each day. And he no longer needed to rely on guesswork. His job required him to compile a daily report from the registration office, which meant constant access to first-hand information about every transport that reached Auschwitz, including the records kept by the chief registrar.

He may not have realised it yet, but thanks to a series of arbitrary events and lucky breaks, Walter Rosenberg had acquired an unusually comprehensive expertise in the workings of Auschwitz. He had lived or worked in the main camp, at Birkenau and at Buna: Auschwitz I, II and III. He had worked in the gravel pits, the DAW factory and in Kanada. He had been an intimate witness of the selection process that preceded the organised murder of hundreds of thousands.

He knew both the resistance and the *Kapo* class, and the overlap between them, from the inside. He knew the precise layout of the camp and believed he had a good idea as to how many had entered Auschwitz by train, and how many had left via the chimney. And he had committed it all to memory.

Throughout, he remained convinced that knowledge of this diabolical place and the terrors within was the only weapon that might thwart it. Once people knew their fate, their fate would be changed.

But that creed of Walter's was about to be jolted.

Even to an expert like Walter, Auschwitz-Birkenau remained a universe of mysteries. It contained black holes of the deepest darkness. This was a place where, thanks to the scarcity of latrines and a strict night-time curfew, regular prisoners were forced to choose between soiling themselves in their bunks, their faeces infecting the sores on their skin, or defecating in the same bowls from which they ate. This was a place where infanticide was commonplace. Childbirth was forbidden in Auschwitz, yet there were women who had passed through selection despite being in the early stages of pregnancy. Some would induce a miscarriage, but others carried their babies to term. That spelled death for both of them, because according to the Nazi principles of selection mothers of young children were a condemned category. Both mother and baby would be sent to the gas chambers within a week of the birth. The prisoner medics concluded they had only one option: in order to preserve the life of the mother, they had to end the life of the child. In Auschwitz, a newborn baby would know only a few moments of life before being poisoned. No record would ever be kept, the child's existence erased so that the bereaved mother could appear once more at roll call, apparently fit and ready for slave labour.

And yet through such inexplicable darkness came the odd beam of light, often no less inexplicable. One came in September 1943 with the arrival of a transport like no other. They were placed in the sector right next door to Walter's, BIIb, 5,000 Czech Jews, shipped to Auschwitz from the concentration camp-ghetto of Theresienstadt. Except they had undergone no selection to weed out those who were too young or too old or too sick. Families had been left intact:

mothers, fathers, children, all together. They were wearing their own clothes; their hair remained on their heads. They had been allowed to keep their own luggage.

Their journey had been smooth and they were assisted into their new quarters by SS officers who could not have been more solicitous, laughing and chatting, handing out fruit to the adults and sweets to the children, tousling the hair of those who held tight to their dolls and teddy bears.

Walter and the others looked on, open-mouthed in astonishment. What inversion of the Auschwitz laws of physics was this? How had so much life intruded into the kingdom of death?

The more the long-time prisoners found out, the more confused they became. It fell to the registrars to sign in these new arrivals, and Walter noticed one oddity straight away. He and Fred Wetzler had come to know the Auschwitz numbering system reflexively, able to pinpoint a prisoner's country of origin and date of entry with just a glance at the digits sewn on their shirt or inked on their arm. These ascended in an identifiable, ordered sequence. But the residents of the *Familienlager*, the family camp, were tattooed with a number that was entirely unrelated. Attached to each resident's registration record were the words: 'Special treatment after six months' quarantine'.

Quarantine was familiar enough. New prisoners were quarantined before entering camp life. But 'special treatment' meant only one thing. It was the SS euphemism for death by gas.

None of it made sense. Why keep these families alive only to kill them in six months? And why suspend the usual rules, why treat them so gently?

The confusion only deepened as Walter saw that this was no first-day trick, akin to the show of courtesy with which the SS liked, when time allowed, to greet transports en route to the gas chambers. No, the five-star service continued, day after day, week after week.

Of course, this was relative. Compared to normal life in the outside world, conditions in the family camp were sufficiently harsh that a fifth of those 5,000 inmates were dead within a few months of arrival. Still, besides the camp elder, who was a German green-triangle criminal *Kapo*, every other administrative post – whether as a block leader or the head of a work unit – was held by a Jew, usually a veteran of the Theresienstadt camp-ghetto. In contrast with the rest of Auschwitz, the Jews of BIIb were allowed to govern themselves.

And so Walter and his fellow inmates would look on in baffled awe as BIIb maintained a vibrant Jewish life, complete with music performances, drama productions and, above all, classes for the children. On one side of the fence were the inmates of BIIa, bald and thin in their uniform stripes, while on the other energetic youth leaders were instructing their charges in the glories of European history and culture, the battle of Thermopylae and the novels of Dostoevsky, reciting passages by heart from books they did not have. The *Familienlager* even had a choirmaster who taught the children to sing 'Ode to Joy', a hymn of praise to the brotherhood of man, singing it not a few hundred yards away from the crematoria that burned day and night, their chimneys turning Jews into ash.

For Walter, who turned nineteen four days after the arrival of the mysterious 5,000, his wonder was not confined to the strangeness of so much vitality in the midst of murder. His focus was earthier. He and the other men of BIIa could not but marvel at the sight of young women whose bodies were not emaciated like their own, but soft and full. They were so close too, separated by a mere wire.

Over-the-fence flirtations began; secret, if distanced, rendezvous were made. At first Walter could only look on. However much he had played the man of the world to the young Gerta Sidonová back in Trnava, far too experienced to be seen with a girl in a pom-pom hat, the truth is that he had left the town a boy and that is what he remained. Auschwitz had toughened him; it had educated him in the puzzles of the human soul. But it had also left him frozen in adolescence. He had been consumed with the business of staying alive and, when not warding off illness or death, the dream of escape. He knew nothing of sex or romance.

Nevertheless, and like many of the men of BIIa, he fell in love. Her name was Alicia Munk, and she was one of the youth workers over the fence. Three years older than Walter, tall and dark, she was, to him, unfathomably beautiful.

Slowly, they got to know each other, she telling of her life in a town north of Prague, he recounting the odyssey that had brought him here. They could not kiss; even their fingertips could not touch. The fence stayed between them. But in those conversations, which became daily, Walter felt his heart dissolve.

His work for the underground stepped up. For one thing, the presence of children in Auschwitz created new and unfamiliar needs, as the resistance tried to divert precious resources to the youngest. Demand increased in December 1943 when another 5,000 deportees from Theresienstadt arrived: once again, fathers and mothers, sons and daughters.

But hanging over all these efforts was the unbending fact written on every one of those registration records, some of which Walter himself had compiled: *Special treatment after six months' quarantine.* There was a deadline. The families that had arrived on 8 September 1943 were scheduled to die on 8 March 1944. And in matters such as these the SS tended to keep their word.

In March, with that deadline looming, there was a sudden change. BIIa was immediately emptied of regular prisoners, leaving just the likes of Walter: the permanent staff. In place of the evicted inmates, came the families from next door. Regardless of what the move portended, Walter could not help but be delighted. For among those Czech arrivals was Alicia Munk.

Until this moment, they had conducted their courtship across a boundary fence, the one that separated their two camps. But now even that short distance was gone. He could stand close enough to catch the scent of her. That evening they exchanged their first kiss. Walter felt embarrassed by his inexperience and gaucheness, but also filled with longing, for Alicia and for a future.

But 8 March was getting nearer. Walter was asked to take soundings, to see how many inside the family camp might be willing to revolt. Surely there would be many volunteers, given that they possessed what every other Auschwitz arrival had lacked: advance knowledge of what happened to Jews in this place. They could see the chimneys, they could smell the smoke. But few stepped forward.

The problem was, too many of the *Familienlager* inmates could not accept that the SS would murder the very children they had played with, whose names they knew. This was a problem Walter had not anticipated. These Jews had the information. The trouble was, they did not believe it.

It was on the eve of the dreaded day when, at last, Walter and Alicia spent a night together. They were in the small bedroom, partitioned off from the rest of the stables–cum–barracks, that, as a registrar, he could call his own. It was the first time he had ever had sex and he was hesitant, needing encouragement from Alicia. But together, in a place of relentless death, they clung to each other and insisted on life.

As 8 March dawned, the effort to organise some kind of resistance grew desperate. There was an attempt to recruit a leader for the family camp, someone who would set off an uprising that, yes, was doomed but which might just throw a wrench into the killing machine, perhaps even allowing a few dozen to escape into the forest. The chosen candidate, a much loved youth leader by the name of Fredy Hirsch, was approached, but he could not bear that the certain casualty of any attempt at insurrection would be the youngest children: they would not be able to fight, they would not be able to escape and fend for themselves. They would be left behind, to be butchered. Hirsch knew that those children would be gassed anyway, but he could not face it. He poisoned himself.

And so there was no uprising. The trucks arrived at the appointed hour. *Kapos* drafted in from elsewhere in Auschwitz wielded their sticks and clubs and forced the Jews of the family camp on to the vehicles. As the children screamed in terror, there was time for only the briefest farewell with Alicia. She whispered in Walter's ear that they would meet again one day.

'It'll be wonderful,' she said, before pausing. 'But if we don't . . .' She hesitated again. 'It has been wonderful.'

A moment later they were forced apart and she was pushed on to the convoy, which would make the journey of just a few hundred yards to the crematoria.

There was, at the last, a small attempt at physical resistance. When all doubt, and therefore hope, evaporated, when the Czech Jews had entered the gas chamber itself, and as others were still filing in, only then did some of the Jews of the family camp begin raging and cursing at their captors and rushing towards the door. Those who made it that far were instantly shot by SS men.

They had left it too late. Of the 5,000 Czech Jews who had arrived the previous September, only sixty-seven were kept out of the gas chambers, though that was hardly an act of mercy: among them were eleven pairs of twins preserved as subjects of medical experimentation.

Later, Walter would discover the truth of the *Familienlager*. It had existed for the same reason as the concentration camp-ghetto Theresienstadt itself: as a showpiece, a macabre Potemkin village that could be displayed before the inspectors of the International Red Cross, should they ever demand to come, as proof that rumours of the Nazi slaughter of Jews were untrue. (Ahead of such a hypothetical visit, it would not be hard to empty out the neighbouring sub-sections, to preserve the illusion.) The family camp, with its regular clothes for the adults and sweets for the children, was simply an elaborate extension of the same pattern of deception that characterised the entire Nazi endeavour to rid the world of Jews.

For Walter, first love had coincided with bereavement. That first night he had had with Alicia was their last together, and the last of her life.

But the heartbreak was accompanied by confusion. His faith had been firm that, once people knew that death awaited them, they would not walk quietly towards it. Now he understood that information alone was not enough. The inmates of the Czech family camp had had the information. They could see the crematoria with their own eyes; the chimneys were just a few hundred yards away. They had known that the Nazis were murdering the Jews they had brought to Auschwitz. The trouble was, they never believed this scheme applied to them.

The reason for their special status had been a mystery to them, as it had been to the other prisoners in Auschwitz, but special they believed they were. They had been certain that they would be exempt from the death sentence the SS were carrying out on their fellow Jews. Only when it was too late did they see that they had been entirely wrong.

Now, surely, the remaining Jews of the *Familienlager*, those who had been shipped to Auschwitz in December 1943, would be stripped of any delusions of specialness. They had to know that their death was a certainty, scheduled for six months to the day after they arrived. They had seen what had happened to the others, how they had been driven to the gas chambers, never to return. They knew they were going to die.

And yet life in the family camp went on as it had before. The musicians staged concerts, the amateur actors put on plays. The rival political factions kept debating the ideal future, even though the only certainty was that they had no future. Walter concluded that even incontrovertible knowledge of one's fate was not enough. If people were to act, there had to be a possibility, even a slim one, of escaping that fate. Otherwise it was easier to deny what was right in front of you than to confront the reality of your own imminent destruction. The surviving Czech Jews of the *Familienlager* knew they were doomed, but they were already prisoners in Auschwitz: what else could they do but live each day as best they could?

Even so, the Jews outside, the people of the world: they would be different. They would still have options for action so long as they did not board those trains, which they would not if they knew the fate that awaited them. They just had to be told. Walter would tell them – and he would do it soon. He would escape.

# PART III

The Escape

# 13

## Escape Was Lunacy

ESCAPE WAS LUNACY, escape was death. To attempt it was to commit suicide. Everyone knew that, even if they did not say it out loud. Calamity would surely rain down on whoever was reckless enough to utter the word and unfortunate enough to hear it.

The impossibility of escape had been taught to Walter Rosenberg early, within a week of his arrival in Auschwitz back at the start of July 1942. He and thousands of others had been forced to stand in silence and watch a public hanging, performed with full ceremony. The SS men had lined up with guns over their shoulders and marching drums strapped around their necks, while out in front stood two mobile gallows, wheeled into position, one for each condemned man.

The stars of the show were announced as two prisoners who had tried and failed to escape. Walter and the others had to watch as the men were brought out; a *Kapo* tied their ankles and thighs with rope, then placed a noose around each of their necks. One stood silent and impassive, while the other attempted to deliver a rousing speech, a final denunciation of their Nazi captors. No one heard a word he said, of course. The drums were there for a reason.

The *Kapo* turned a crank, a trapdoor opened and the first man dropped just a few inches: not enough to bring instant death. His body twisted and turned, first one way and then the other. It was not over quickly; the crowd was forced to watch a long, slow strangulation. Then the hangman moved to the second gallows, where the same sequence was acted out once more. Afterwards, the inmates were kept there a full hour, forbidden even to look away. They had to stand, in silence, staring at the two dead bodies twirling in the wind. They had notices pinned to their chests, written as if the words were spoken by the dead themselves: *Because we tried to escape . . .*

Walter understood that the Nazis wanted him and every other prisoner to conclude that escape was futile, that any attempt was doomed. But Walter drew a very different lesson, one that to him was obvious. The danger, he concluded, came not from trying to escape, but from trying and *failing*. From that day on, he had been determined to try – and to succeed.

The first step, he understood, was education. His schooling had been interrupted, but now he would become a student of escape. His primary texts would be the failures of others.

Small lessons came every day. He saw a political prisoner hang for the crime of wearing two shirts under his tunic, which the SS took to be preparation for an escape. Walter had made a similar mistake himself once, when those two pairs of socks had given him away. He made a mental note: no outward changes.

But the start of 1944 would teach a much deeper lesson. It came after he learned of the escape plan of one of the camp's larger-than-life characters: Fero Langer, the same man with whom Walter had briefly shared a prison cell in Nováky eighteen months earlier. Walter remembered him well: Langer had given him a hunk of salami for the journey that would end in Majdanek. 'Bullo' they called him in Birkenau, a one-man organising machine who had acquired a cash fortune in less than a year in the camp. Bullo had hatched a plot to achieve the same ambition nurtured by Walter: to get out and reveal the truth of Auschwitz to the world. What's more, and in violation of one of the cardinal rules of camp life, he talked about it. One afternoon, over a bowl of potatoes in Fred Wetzler's block, Walter sat quietly and listened as the Bull set it all out.

He would escape with fellow prisoners from Poland, Holland, Greece and France. That way, he calculated, their testimony would spread across the globe with no need for translation. Central to the scheme was the help of an SS man whom Fero had known as a schoolboy back in Slovakia, an ethnic German by the name of Dobrowolný. Fero said he trusted him like a brother. Indeed, it had been this Dobrowolný who first came up with the idea.

Langer's fellow Jews were sceptical, but Bullo insisted he was not relying on trust or human kindness: he had also promised the man a reward, in the form of food and valuables from Kanada, in addition to the diamonds, gold and dollar bills his rescuer would need to bribe assorted SS men. The plan was simple. Together with a second SS officer, Dobrowolný would march the polyglot quintet to the perimeter, then show the guard permits authorising the prisoners to engage in essential work outside the camp. From there, they would walk the three or four miles to where Dobrowolný would have parked a truck, bought especially for the purpose. They would then drive to the Slovak border and to freedom.

Sure enough, one day in January 1944 the escape siren sounded. The headcount had shown some prisoners to be missing. Walter imagined his old cellmate, now on the run in a hidden corner of Slovakia. But by six o'clock that same evening Fero Langer had returned to Auschwitz. Or rather his body had returned. He had been shot dead, his face ripped apart. Three of the failed runaways lay on the ground, while the other two had been placed on wooden stools, their bodies propped up by spades thrust into the dirt. Their clothes were soaked in blood and next to them a sign read: *Three cheers, we've come back again!* Prisoners returning from work could see this little tableau and, in case they failed to get the message, they could hear the voice of the *Lageraltester*, the camp leader, bellowing, 'That's how you will all end up if you try to escape.'

It turned out that Dobrowolný and his SS comrade had marched Langer and the others out, as planned, then urged them to run ahead to the supposed getaway vehicle before shooting them in the back. The SS men informed the camp authorities that they had success-fully shot inmates attempting an escape – but not before they had rifled through their pockets and claimed their reward. Fero never reached the truck, let alone the border. It was a reminder of a lesson Walter had already learned for himself, a lesson about trust.

Still, that episode did not stop those with resources plotting to break out. Walter had struck up an unlikely friendship with a block senior in the quarantine camp, a Polish-born Jew who had grown up in France, rising to become a captain in the French army, and who was now, aged thirty-three, a man of terrifying physical strength and menace. His name was Charles Unglick. Like Fero, he had built a network that included the *Sonderkommando*, who were sometimes able to pocket the valuables of those herded into the gas chamber. That, combined with his mafioso's power to intimidate, had made him an Auschwitz millionaire, with SS officers on the payroll. Of particular interest to Walter, who always liked to be well turned out, was Unglick's standing as one of Birkenau's sharpest dressers. Walter especially admired the older man's brown leather belt, which had been patterned with two criss-crossing lines that formed a kind of double helix. They had a joke between them: Charles would leave Walter that belt in his will.

Unglick was determined to use his position to escape and, like Bullo, he believed he had found an SS man who would help him. And not just any SS man, but an ethnic German who had been adopted and raised by a Jewish family in Romania and was now deployed in Auschwitz as a driver. To Walter's astonishment, this Nazi spoke to Unglick in Yiddish.

The plan called for the SS man to drive his truck into BIIa. Unglick would climb into the vehicle's vast toolbox and hide there. The Yiddish-speaking Nazi would lock it and, when challenged, would claim to have lost the key. They would drive away, and the German would be rewarded in diamonds and gold.

There was one more thing: Unglick liked Walter and suggested he join him in that toolbox. They would escape together, splitting Unglick's huge fortune between them.

Walter was wary. Trusting an SS officer was surely an elementary error; they had all seen what had happened to Bullo. And yet Unglick's confidence, his certainty, was hard to resist. Had Walter not dreamed of escape from the start? Was this not, at last, his chance?

He said yes and the two men drank a toast to liberty.

The truck would pull in and open up at 7 p.m. on 25 January 1944. At the appointed hour and at the appointed place, Unglick's barracks, Block 14, Walter stood and waited. But there was no sign of Unglick or the truck. The minutes kept passing. Walter paced around, trying to look as natural as he could. A friend approached, inviting him to share a bowl of soup with a fellow underground member. Walter felt compelled to accept: it would look too strange to say no. Looking over his shoulder, back at the meeting point, he slipped into Block 7. His mood was bleak: he had thrown away his shot at freedom.

Around 8 p.m., there was a commotion down by the gate. Soon enough, Walter saw it: the bloodstained corpse of Charles Unglick. It did not take long for the SS to sit the body on a stool, once again propped up with a pair of spades. They kept him that way for two full days, as yet another warning.

The Birkenau bush telegraph soon revealed what had happened. Unglick had been running late. He had looked for Walter everywhere, only reluctantly giving up. After that, it was a re-run of the death of Fero Langer. The SS Yiddish-speaker had parked up, as agreed, and had concealed Unglick, as agreed. Except he had driven not to the border but to an empty garage. There he unlocked the toolbox and shot his co-conspirator dead. It was a profitable evening's work. He had gained both Unglick's diamonds and gold and the esteem of his SS masters, who admired his courage in foiling yet another attempted getaway.

As for Walter, he was left numb by an hour that had included abject disappointment at missing his chance to break out, bereavement at the loss of a friend and a strange kind of relief. Had he not accepted that spontaneous invitation to share a bowl of soup, he would have kept his appointment with Unglick and shared his fate. Instead, he had narrowly escaped death.

Afterwards, and in keeping with what had become a custom in the camp, the prisoner elite, including some of Birkenau's most brutal *Kapos*, gathered to hand out the dead man's clothes to the living. Normally, this was done in order of seniority, but this time they made an exception: in honour of the friendship the pair had shared, Walter could take whatever he wanted. He asked only for the belt. On the inside he inscribed in ink Unglick's prisoner number and the place and date of his death: 'AU-BI' for Auschwitz-Birkenau, '25.1.1944'. It would remind him, again, of the importance of trusting only those who deserved to be trusted.

The masters of Auschwitz made the most of these failures, ensuring they were known, betting they would sap their captives of all hope. But the attempts kept coming. From the creation of the camp in 1940 until 1942, only fifty-five prisoners had broken free. In 1943, the number of successful escapes rose to 154. Except most of those were Polish non-Jewish prisoners, whose conditions in the camp were better and who, crucially, had the bulk of the jobs, whether in the hospitals, specialised work details or bureaucracy, that made escape more feasible. The rest were Soviet prisoners of war. As far as Walter could tell, no Jew had ever got out alive.

Yet his situation was less hopeless than most. For one thing, his job gave him the ability to move around relatively unimpeded. For another, he was in Birkenau, where the ratio of SS men to prisoners was one to sixty-four: that made it relatively unguarded compared to the mother camp, where there was one Nazi for every fourteen inmates.

Also, and this was not as simple as it might sound, he knew where he was. He had once been part of a twenty-strong group of prisoners that were marched into the nearest town of Oświęcim: a public relations stunt, Walter suspected, to show the locals that the prisoners were being well treated. From that trip, he knew that between the camp and the town flowed a minor river: the Soła. He could see mountains on the horizon and had identified those as the Beskyds.

That torn-off page from the children's atlas he had found back in Kanada had allowed him to orientate himself further. He had worked out, in those few stolen minutes in the latrine, that Oświęcim sat about fifty miles north of Slovakia's northern border. Better still, he could see that the Soła originated on that same border and it flowed in an almost straight line, south to north. That meant that to navigate from Auschwitz to Slovakia, all he had to do was follow the river against its current. That would get him to the border by the shortest possible route. He had even committed to memory the sequence of settlements he would have to pass to get there: Kęty, Saybusch (or Żywiec), Milówka, Rajcza, Sól. He was young, fit and smart, and he knew this hellhole inside out. If anyone had a chance, it was surely him. What's more, he soon had a new and urgent motive.

# 14

## Russian Lessons

ONE OF THE advantages of his role as barracks pen-pusher for
BIIa, the quarantine camp, of Birkenau was that he had a good
view of everything and everyone that came in and out. So when,
at 10 a.m. on 15 January 1944, a group of people stood on the road
that separated the men's and women's camps of Birkenau, it caught
Walter's eye. They were prisoners, but they stood out instantly. Their
clothes were better than most inmates', for one thing, and they were
carrying specialist equipment: tripods and theodolites, calibrated rods,
measuring instruments and the like. They looked like surveyors,
checking out a new construction site.

Walter approached the electrified fence that stood between him
and them and saw that the man in charge was familiar: a German
red-triangled political prisoner, a former trade unionist and anti-Nazi
by the name of Yup, short for Joseph. Walter remembered him from
when they had both been imprisoned in the main camp, in 1942. They
had formed a connection back then; perhaps Yup was impressed that
Walter had had his own brush with the socialist resistance during
that brief flit to Hungary.

'What a pleasant surprise,' Yup said, smiling broadly. 'Who'd have
thought it? You're alive! And looking well too.'

Across the barbed wire, Yup asked whether Walter was able to
'organise' a cigarette, and Walter obliged.

'So,' Walter said eventually. 'What's all this then?' He gestured
towards Yup's men. 'What are you doing here?'

Yup told Walter that what he was about to say was strictly confi-
dential. His voice dropped. 'We're building a new railway line.
Straight to the crematoria.'

Walter looked sceptical. 'A new line? But they've just repaired the old ramp.' He knew all too well about the work on the *Judenrampe*, its timber planks reinforced with concrete.

But Yup was adamant. He had overheard from the SS that Auschwitz was bracing itself for a huge new influx of Jews to be killed. The Jews of Hungary were coming soon, he said, about a million of them. The SS had determined that the current ramp simply could not cope with that kind of number, and certainly not quickly enough.

It was his experience on the ramp that made Walter instantly accept what Yup had told him as the truth. He knew better than most that if the SS wanted to kill on that scale and at that speed, they would have to change the current set-up. The big bottleneck in the system was the journey the victims had to make from the ramp to the gas chambers: a short but time-consuming truck ride for every hundred Jews. Extending the railway line for that one-and-a-quarter-mile stretch would make the process far more efficient.

And of course it would be the Jews of Hungary. They were the last ones left, the one major Jewish community of Europe not yet to have been pulled into the inferno. Walter had seen the Jews of France, Belgium, Holland, Poland, Czechoslovakia, Italy, Germany and Greece in Auschwitz. The Jews of Hungary had been conspicuous by their absence.

Confirmation came via the grapevine of the green-triangle *Kapos* and their chums in the SS's lower orders. Unglick had found that the SS duo assigned to the quarantine camp were both easily bought with liquor. They also became chattily indiscreet when drunk. That was how Walter learned that, having savoured Greek olives, French sardines and Dutch cheese, the SS was licking its lips for the arrival of 'Hungarian salami'.

And so by the early spring of 1944 there was a double urgency to Walter's determination to escape. Those 5,000 or so Czechs who had entered the family camp in the second wave, arriving on 20 December 1943, would be put to death exactly six months later on 20 June. That was beyond doubt; it was the hardest of deadlines. But now there was the prospect of an even more imminent, and much larger, slaughter: hundreds of thousands of Hungarian Jews would board trains for Auschwitz in a matter of weeks, trains that would take them to the very gates of the gas chambers.

Walter had his motive and now he acquired a mentor. After the Poles, the most successful escapees from Auschwitz were Soviet prisoners of war. Many thousands had been brought to the camp at the start, dying in the cold and dirt as they worked as slaves to build Birkenau. But there was another group, Walter estimated there were about a hundred of them, known to the Auschwitz veterans as the 'second-hand prisoners of war'. Captured in battle, they had been sent initially to regular PoW camps but then despatched to Auschwitz as punishment for bad behaviour, including attempted escape. Among them was one Dmitri Volkov.

Not for the first time, Walter had reason to be grateful for the Russian he had taught himself back in Trnava. It meant he could talk with the second-hand PoWs as he registered them, even those whose appearance was forbidding. To Walter, Volkov was a bear of a man from the land of the Cossacks, Zaporizhzhia in Ukraine. Enormous and with dark, deep-set eyes, and still in his Red Army uniform, he looked like someone to be approached with care.

But with time they got to know each other, eventually striking an unspoken bargain not dissimilar to the high-school deal that had seen Walter trade lessons in Slovak for tuition in High German. Volkov allowed Walter to practise his Russian. In return, the young pen-pusher handed over his allocation of bread and quasi-margarine, honouring a vow he had made to himself much earlier: that he would not take his official ration so long as he had access to food from elsewhere. He noticed that Volkov did not eat even that meagre portion, instead cutting it into quarters, to be shared with his comrades.

They began talking. Not, at first, about the camp, but about the great Russian literary masters Tolstoy and Dostoevsky, moving on to the Soviet writers Gorky, Ehrenburg and Blok. Eventually, Volkov began to lower his guard.

He revealed that he was no mere conscript but a captain in the Red Army. In making this admission, Volkov was taking a huge risk: it was Nazi practice to shoot all Soviet officers. But he had decided to trust Walter, and not only with that information. He also told him of his own experience of escape, for the captain had once broken out of the Nazi concentration camp of Sachsenhausen. As his teenage pupil listened, and over several days, Volkov proceeded to give Walter a crash course in escapology.

Some lessons were intensely practical. He told him what to carry and what not to carry. In the second category was money. Kanada might be overflowing with the stuff, but it was dangerous. If you had money, you would be tempted to buy food from a shop or a market, and that meant contact with people which was always to be avoided. Better to live off the land, stealing from fields and remote farms. Also not to be carried, at least when making the initial escape, was meat: the SS Alsatians would sniff it out immediately.

So: no money, no meat. As for what he would need, that category was larger, starting with a knife for hunting or self-defence, and a razor blade in case of imminent capture. That was a cardinal rule for Volkov: 'Don't let them take you alive.' Also: matches, to cook the food you had stolen. And salt: a man could live on salt and potatoes for months. A watch was essential, not least because it could double as a compass.

The tips kept coming. All movement was to be done at night; no walking in daylight. It was vital to be invisible. If they could see you, they could shoot you. Don't imagine you could run away; a bullet would always be faster.

Keep an eye on the time, hence the watch. Don't be looking for a place to sleep when dawn breaks; make sure you've found a hiding place while it's still dark.

But some of the advice belonged in the realm of psychology. Trust no one; share your plans with no one, including me. If your friends know nothing, they'll have nothing to reveal when they're tortured once you're gone. That advice fitted with what Walter already knew for himself: that there were others eager to give up your secrets. The Politische Abteilung, the Political Department of the SS, had built up quite a network of informers among the prisoners, always listening out for talk of escape and revolt. (They were recruited by a threat from the SS that, if they refused to betray their fellow prisoners, their relatives back home would be murdered.) You never knew who you were really talking to. Best to say little.

Volkov had more wisdom to impart. Have no fear, even of the Germans. In Auschwitz, in their uniforms and with their guns, they look invincible. But each one of them, on his own, is just as small and fragile as any other human being. 'I know they can die as quickly as anybody because I've killed enough of them.'

Above all: remember that the fight only starts when you've broken out of the camp. No euphoria, no elation. You cannot relax while you are on Nazi-ruled soil, not even for a second.

Walter did his best to take it all in, to remember it along with the mountain of numbers and dates that was piling ever higher in his mind. But there was one last bit of advice, for the escape itself.

The Nazis' tracker dogs were trained to detect even the faintest odour of human life. If there was a single bead of sweat on your brow, they would find you. There was only one thing that defeated them.

Tobacco, soaked in petrol and then dried. And not just any tobacco. It had to be Soviet tobacco. Volkov must have seen the gleam of scepticism in Walter's eye. 'I'm not being patriotic,' he said. 'I just know *machorka*. It's the only stuff that works.'

Volkov let Walter know that he had his own plans for escape and that he would not be sharing them with Walter or anyone else. He was happy to serve as the younger man's teacher. But he would not be his partner.

For that role, there could only ever be one person. Someone whom Walter trusted wholly and who trusted him, someone whom he had known before he was in this other, darker universe, someone who, for that very reason, had an existence in Walter's mind independent of Auschwitz: Fred Wetzler.

More than 600 Jewish men from Trnava had been sent to Auschwitz in 1942. By the spring of 1944, only two were still alive: Walter Rosenberg and Alfréd Wetzler. All the rest had either been swiftly murdered, like Fred's brothers, or suffered the slow death in which Auschwitz-Birkenau specialised, worn down by disease, starvation and arbitrary violence, a group that almost certainly included Fred's father. Fred and Walter had grown up with those 600 boys and men – as teachers and schoolmates, family friends and acquaintances, playground enemies and romantic rivals – and now every last one of them was gone. From the world they had both known, only Fred and Walter were left.

Despite the six years that separated them, that fact had sealed a bond of trust between them. Walter now regarded Fred as his closest friend. Their daily experiences were similar too. Fred had moved from the mortuary and was also now a registrar, a barracks pen-pusher, doing in the BIId sector of Birkenau II, the same job that Walter was doing in BIIa. Both had a close-up view of the slaughter and its consequences. For Fred, that was literally true: his office had a window through which he could look out on to the yard of Crematorium II, enclosed by electrified fences and surrounded by watchtowers. When Walter visited, sipping coffee at the table by that window, he would take in the clarity of the view for himself. He could note the athleticism with which one particular SS man would vault on to the roof of the gas chamber, getting into position to shake out the pellets of Zyklon B. From their distinct vantage points, both Walter and Fred were able to count the dead.

And perhaps their states of mind were similar too. Fred had already seen the toll the permanent stench of death was taking on his friend, the signs of anxiety and depression. The massacre of the thousands from the *Familienlager*, including Alicia, had clearly shaken Walter badly. Fred had endured his own shocks to the system, even beyond the loss of his father and brothers. In the summer of 1943, in a rare example of a transport *away* from Auschwitz, the SS had shipped a group of prisoners from Birkenau to Warsaw, to work on 'fortifications'. Those transports took away most of Wetzler's remaining Slovak friends. After they left, he felt lonely and alone. His mind turned more seriously to escape.

So the two men, bereft and bereaved, came together. In truth, they had whispered to each other of escape from the moment they had first come face to face in this place. Like Walter, Fred had been dreaming of breaking out from the start. There was an aborted scheme to crawl out through a sewer: he even did a test run. Another plan came to him when he worked at the morgue, back when the dead were taken to the town of Oświęcim for burning. Fred reckoned he could hide among the corpses as they were loaded on to a truck, then jump off while in transit. He had to abandon that plan when the SS started burning bodies inside the camp instead.

Walter, still mindful of the disciplines of the underground, sought the approval of his contact in the resistance leadership, David Szmulewski. It seemed obvious that an unauthorised breakout aimed at revealing the secrets of Auschwitz had less chance of success than one with the underground's backing. On 31 March 1944 Szmulewski gave Walter the leadership's answer. It came as a grave disappointment.

They had concluded that Walter's 'inexperience, personal volatility and impulsiveness', as well as some unspecified 'other factors', made him 'unreliable' for this mission. What's more, they thought it highly unlikely that the outside world would believe him. Nevertheless, Szmulewski offered the leadership's assurance that, though they would not help the planned escape, they would not stand in its way. For his own part, Szmulewski stressed that he was sorry about the 'higher decision', which Walter assumed had been taken by the command group in Auschwitz I rather than in Birkenau.

The underground leader then added a request. Should Walter and Fred fail, it was the underground's wish that they 'avoid interrogation'. If they did not, it would spell disaster for anyone who had spoken to either of them before the escape. *Avoid interrogation.* At that, Walter doubtless remembered Volkov and his recommended razor blade.

Walter was becoming impatient. The background din of construction, of cement mixers and the assembly of flat-pack huts, was now constant. Work on the three-track railway extension and the new platform it would require was going on without interruption. From his perch in the quarantine camp, Walter could see it take shape, hour by hour. He knew there was so little time. He had seen what had happened with that first transport of Czech Jews, how the truth had reached them too late, at the threshold of the gas chambers or, later still, once they were inside. He was determined that the Jews of Hungary would learn of their fate while they were still relatively free, while they could still act.

This had to be the moment, he was sure of it. All he needed now was a plan that could not fail.

# 15

## The Hideout

THE PREMISE OF the plan was daringly, even absurdly, simple. Auschwitz II, or Birkenau, consisted of an inner camp and an outer camp. The inner camp was where the prisoners were kept at night, penned in behind not one electrified, barbed-wire fence that would kill anyone who touched it but two, each one fifteen feet high. A would-be escapee would have to surmount both those high-voltage barriers in the full glare of the arc lights that swept back and forth through the night, illuminating the vista for the benefit of the SS men stationed in watchtowers, surveying the scene, their fingers forever on the triggers of automatic weapons.

In the daytime, the set-up changed. Now the inner ring of sentry posts was vacated, the SS manning instead the wider ring of tall, transportable wooden watchtowers that circled the outer camp, monitoring the terrain where prisoners undertook forced labour from first light until evening. The towers were placed at eighty-yard intervals, all the way along the four miles of outer perimeter. An apron of clear space, barren scrubland, lay just inside this fence, so that any prisoner who attempted to make a run for it would be spotted instantly and gunned down. Indeed, any prisoner who got within ten yards of the outer cordon would be shot without warning.

The security protocol never varied. The inner camp was guarded at night, the outer camp during the day. In the hours of darkness, there was no need to watch over the outer camp. After all, every last prisoner had been herded back inside the inner camp. There was no one in the outer camp.

Only one circumstance would make the SS deviate from that system. If an inmate was missing, presumed to have attempted an escape, the SS would keep up the outer ring of armed sentry posts while the area was searched. It would stay like that for seventy-two hours. Only then would the SS conclude that the escapee had got away, passing the baton to the SS men already scoping the terrain beyond Auschwitz. At that moment, the outer cordon would come down, the security perimeter shrinking back to the inner camp. The outer camp would be unguarded once more.

It was the only break in what was otherwise a watertight seal. If a prisoner could somehow hide in that outer area, waiting out those three days and nights after the alarm had been raised, even while the SS and their murderous dogs combed every inch of the terrain, he would emerge on that fourth night into an outer camp that was deserted and unwatched. He would have his chance to break free.

This, then, was the premise of the attempt that Walter would mount. He and Fred would inveigle their way into the outer camp. Once there, they would secrete themselves in a designated hiding place and wait for three days and nights. Only when it was clear that the SS had called off the search and the outer camp was restored to empty silence would they come out.

The groundwork had been done by four others, who had spotted that same all-important weak point in the security set-up. Three of them worked as delivery boys for the morgue: their task was to travel around the many sub-camps of Auschwitz-Birkenau, collecting corpses, before delivering them, on handcarts, to the mortuary in the main men's hospital. It meant they had the same relative freedom of movement as Fred and Walter.

It was while on their travels that they entered a new Auschwitz territory, a land fast becoming known as Mexico. The camp there was under construction: it was to be Birkenau III, ready to house the expected surge of Hungarian prisoners, and the inmates quartered in this unfinished site had been given no clothes at all. All they could do was wrap themselves in coloured blankets: to the long-time Auschwitz population, they looked like indigenous, 'Indian' Mexicans. Hence: Mexico.

The three corpse-carriers were in Mexico when they encountered a fourth, Mordka Cytryn, doubly condemned as both a Soviet prisoner of war and a Jew. He told of his determination to escape – and of the discovery he had made.

The place was part building site, part lumber yard. All over, and stacked in piles, were the panels that would be assembled into quick-build huts. But Cytryn had seen that in one spot there was a crater carved into the ground, perhaps a shell-hole, which the group rapidly resolved to line and cover with a combination of wooden planks and door frames. Before long, they had constructed an underground shelter that could hold four people and that was well camouflaged. Next, they kitted it out, starting with a few blankets. Then, no doubt at the prompting of the Russian among them, they scattered the surrounding ground with Soviet tobacco soaked in petrol.

The Red Army man was the guinea pig. On 29 February 1944, he climbed in. His three comrades, Alexander 'Sándor' Eisenbach, Getzel Abramowicz and Jacob Balaban, covered up the opening with extra boards and returned to camp. The trio listened out, waiting for the sirens at evening roll call that meant a prisoner was missing. Sure enough, the sounds came: Cytryn's absence had been noticed.

Out went the search teams: armed SS men, Alsatian dogs, all on the hunt for the Russian prisoner who had disappeared. The animals, their nostrils usually aquiver at the merest scent of a human, were led astray by the aroma of the petrol-soaked tobacco. It drove them away. And so Cytryn remained in his bunker, undiscovered.

After three days had safely passed, the others decided to risk it. Sick of carting around the flesh and bones of the dead, they would seize their chance of life. Eisenbach, Abramowicz and Balaban climbed into the hole.

That night, the roll call was again interrupted by that same piercing sound, more urgent this time as it announced that a further three men were missing. Back out went the SS search party: officers, *Kapos*, dogs, all under lights, scouring the entire area up to the ring of watchtowers that marked the outer perimeter. They came heart-stoppingly close. But once again, they found nothing.

It was day three, 5 March 1944, and the men were still in hiding in that cramped, covered hole in the ground. In one of several departures from the unwritten manual taught to Walter by Captain Volkov, they had confided the core part of their plan to a few trusted allies, Fred and Walter among them. Eisenbach, a fellow Slovak, had asked that Walter keep an eye on their secret hideout, that he warn them if they were in danger. And so, in the hours of safety, Walter would stroll over to the woodpile and, while appearing to study his paperwork, would whisper a word of greeting. A faint voice would answer back. It gave Walter great pleasure to tell the voice that the SS and their dogs had walked past the timbers a dozen times, but they had never taken so much as a proper look.

The four men remained still as afternoon became evening. They were waiting to hear the magic words, which finally echoed around the deserted camp once night had fallen: *Postenkette abziehen! Postenkette abziehen! Vacate the guard posts!*

The quartet waited a bit longer and only once they were absolutely sure they could hear no sound, that every last SS man had gone, did they push at the timbers that had been refashioned into a ceiling for their hideout. As quietly as they could, and one by one, they clambered out. Carefully, they replaced the planks so that they looked exactly as they had before: no more than a haphazard pile of wood. Then, in the pitch black, they stole into the night. Soon, they were out of Auschwitz.

Their initial destination was the town of Kęty. The Polish-speaker among them, Balaban, must have broken the captain's golden rule – avoid contact with other people at all costs – and with bad results, because he rapidly came to the conclusion that they could not expect any help from the surrounding population: they were on their own. They headed for the border with Slovakia.

But soon their luck ran out. Near the small town of Porąbka, they ran into a group of German foresters, who had only to see the shaved heads and tattooed arms of the four men to summon the police. It all happened too fast for the fugitives to fight back or to run; they had been caught entirely by surprise. Before they knew it, the Germans had them bound and chained, waiting for the authorities to arrive.

The next few minutes were crucial. The would-be escapees somehow found a way to dump the cash and valuables they had taken for the journey (a move that had been another inadvertent departure from the Volkov escape manual). They also got their story straight.

They were returned to Auschwitz, a full week after the sirens had first shrieked the news of their disappearance. Though they did not come back like Bullo or Unglick, as corpses, they were battered and bruised. The grinning SS men marched the group through the camp: captured slaves to be paraded as proof of the might of their masters.

Walter was watching, the despair rising. As a scholar of Auschwitz escapology, he had felt sure that this time they had cracked it, that they had finally hit upon a method that could not fail. He had wanted to believe they had found the one small point of weakness in the permanent Nazi chokehold over them. But he had been wrong. He did not know how or where or when, but these four men had failed. It would mean death for them and unending imprisonment for him and Fred: if this operation had been a success, they had planned to use that same bunker as their own escape hatch to freedom. That hope was now dashed.

One of the men, manacled as he was, caught Walter's eye. It was Eisenbach and, incredibly, he gave Walter the faintest hint of a wink. Walter took that to mean that they had not yet buckled; they had not given up the secret of the bunker. Still, they were on their way to the Auschwitz headquarters of the Gestapo, to be thoroughly searched and interrogated. After that they would face the notorious Block 11. Whatever secrets a man held, he did not hold them for long once he faced the torture of the punishment block.

During their questioning, they were escorted from Auschwitz to Birkenau where each was ordered to point out their hiding place. They did as they had agreed in those critical few moments after they had been seized by the German foresters: they all pointed to the same spot.

A few days later, on 17 March, a familiar tableau at Birkenau took shape once more. Thousands of inmates gathered, the SS drums struck up. The two mobile gallows were wheeled into position. The presiding SS Sturmbannführer gave the expected speech, warning that what the prisoners were about to witness would be their own fate should they ever be deluded enough to think they could break free. He invited them to gaze upon the six doomed men that stood before them, their wrists tied behind their backs: Cytryn, Eisenbach, Abramowicz and Balaban along with two others who had not made it nearly so far. Those two had not taken the precaution of ditching their valuables. Instead they had been found loaded with wealth: one version of the story said it was gold, another said it was diamonds concealed in a loaf of bread.

The crowd had to watch as the first of this pair, and then the second, was bent over the flogging block and subjected to fifty lashes. It took a full half-hour for each man to be flayed like that, the sound of leather against flesh ringing out in the silence, blow after blow. And when it was done, the drums rolled and the two ruined men were led up the steps to the place of execution. After that, the same performance that Walter had witnessed as a novice in this place nearly two years earlier: the hangman moving fast, rushing to get it done; the crash of the trapdoor; the terrible, twisting display.

Now it was the turn of Eisenbach and the others. First, came the flogging: thirty-five lashes for each of the four men who had escaped via the hiding place they had built in Mexico. And then . . .

Walter braced himself, but that was it. The four were marched back to Block 11, there to face God only knew what torments. Walter assumed his comrades would be spared no cruelty. He was sure they would be punished with a slow, tortured death.

Except that too turned out to be wrong. They were eventually released from the place known as a hell within Hell, sentenced to the hardest possible labour in the penal unit, isolated from the rest of the camp. They were meant to see no one there, but Walter had come to view Auschwitz's rules as surmountable. Using his registrar's unofficial licence to roam, he found his way there and to Eisenbach. The two did not make eye contact as he asked the older man the only question that counted.

'Do they know?'

Eisenbach was digging a ditch with his bare hands and he did not change his movement even slightly, grunting only 'No.'

He had not broken. Nor had the others. Partly because they were strong, even in the face of great pain. But also because they were clever. The tactic they had agreed in advance was to *seem* broken, to *appear* to crack under Gestapo pressure. When their interrogators had demanded to know how they had escaped, and where they had hidden, each one of them had, eventually, pointed to the same spot in Birkenau. But they had not pointed to the secret bunker. They had instead indicated a separate, pre-agreed but wholly bogus place of escape.

It meant the real escape hatch was still in place, intact and undiscovered. It was waiting for Fred Wetzler and Walter Rosenberg.

# 16

## Let My People Go

THEY SET THE date for Monday 3 April 1944. They had everything lined up. They had had both the advice of experts and the failure of others to guide them. They had no need to hide a change of clothes: as barracks bureaucrats, they were already allowed to dress close to the way they would need to on the outside. And they had supplemented what they had with strong boots, thick coats and first-rate trousers and jackets from Holland, all sourced via Kanada. They had the secret hideout, in the form of the still undisturbed hidden bunker of Mexico. They had the information they needed, all stored away in their heads. And they had the desperate urgency of men convinced they needed to sound the alarm not next week or next month but right now. They could see the three-track railway that was all but ready to receive the condemned of Hungary, to deliver them to the doors of the crematoria that would turn them into fire and ash.

Everything was set, the meeting time fixed for 2 p.m. Walter was ready. In his own eyes, he looked like a prosperous Dutch gentleman: tweed jacket, white woollen sweater, woollen riding breeches and high leather boots. He headed to the outer camp, as nonchalant as he could manage, acting the part of an Auschwitz official, out on his rounds.

He made it too, breezily telling the SS man on the gate that he needed to make a visit to the crematorium. In truth, his dearest hope was that today would be the last time he would ever see that place, where the burning of human bodies had become as routine as the smelting of steel in a metalworks, an unremarkable part of the industrial process. He was waved on his way.

Walter reached the outer camp and the woodpile. There he met

Bolek and Adamek, two Jews from Poland whom Fred and Walter had enlisted for the task ahead. The pair were in the *Planierung* commando: they worked in construction, charged with making the ground level. That gave them a comfortable alibi to be hanging around in Mexico near the hideout. True, involving them meant breaking one of the sacred Volkov rules, expanding the circle of trust. But Walter could see no other way.

The hour had come. The three of them were all set. But there was no sign of Fred.

The obvious decision followed. There was no time to linger; that would arouse suspicion. The three men drifted off in their different directions, as if there had never been a planned rendezvous, let alone one that had been missed. When they returned to the inner camp later that evening, Walter got word of the reason for Fred's no-show. Manning the exit from his part of the camp was an SS guard whom Fred knew to be especially vigilant: Fred had calculated that it was better to hang back than risk it. And so the four men – Walter, Fred and the two Poles – rescheduled. They would try again at the same time the next day.

Once again, Walter sailed through. So did Fred. But now one of the two Polish Jews failed to appear: apparently, his *Kapo* slavemaster had given him an extra task that meant he could not wander over to this part of Mexico.

Day three came, and with it the hope that it would be third time lucky. Walter made it, as did their two accomplices. But Fred was turned around at the *Blockführerstube*, the SS guard room, on the grounds that, of all things, his hair was too long. The mission had to be postponed again.

On the morning of Thursday 6 April, they were ready to make their fourth attempt. Except this time too the plan had to be aborted. The explanation was something neither Fred Wetzler nor Walter Rosenberg had ever allowed for, a story so unlikely that if they had not known of it first hand they would have dismissed it as a fantasy. It turned on love.

SS-Rottenführer Viktor Pestek was a strikingly handsome man. In his mid-twenties, he had something in common with the SS man who had tricked Bullo Langer: like him, he was a *Volksdeutsche*, an ethnic German, in his case originally from Romania. More unexpectedly, he also had something in common with Walter: as a *Blockführer* in the family camp, he had fallen in love with one of the young Jewish women imprisoned there. Her name was Renée Neumann, and Pestek was besotted.

He had resolved to save her from the gas chambers, which meant spiriting her away from Auschwitz. Renée had been adamant that she would not leave without her mother. That meant the SS man would have to find a safe house where he and the two women could wait out the war. Seemingly, that would require the help of anti-Nazis on the outside, people who would be prepared to lend a hand to two Jews in hiding. It was a wildly unlikely scheme, but Pestek had made up his mind to try.

Nor was he shy about his plan. He approached several prisoners, offering them a bizarre bargain. He would get them out and, in return, they would connect him with friends in the resistance.

He tried first to recruit Fred and then Walter, but neither was interested. Bullo's betrayal by his old schoolfriend had persuaded both that trusting an SS man was folly. But Siegfried Lederer, a forty-year-old Jew and block elder in the family camp, previously active in the Czech resistance, was not so wary. He said yes to Pestek's improbable offer, even after he heard what the plan entailed.

Which is how on 5 April 1944 Lederer came to be in a washroom putting on the uniform of an SS staff sergeant, down to the silver cord of the Special Service. He waited for the signal, a red light that would blink three times in the window of the SS guardhouse by the gate of the *Familienlager*. When it came, Lederer stepped out and got on the bicycle that, like the SS uniform, had been left for him, raising his right arm in a Heil Hitler salute as he rode right out of the gate of the camp. There to open the gate for him was his underling, SS-Rottenführer Pestek.

They carried on like that, Lederer soon discarding the bike and on foot, together with Pestek, breezing past cordons of guards, the password 'Inkwell' opening any and all barriers. By 8.30 p.m. the pair of them were on an express train bound for Prague.

When Lederer's absence was eventually noticed, and the sirens started shrieking in Auschwitz, the unlikely duo were far, far away. No SS man gave a second thought to the fact that Pestek was missing: he had signed himself off on official leave.

Lederer's friends in the resistance did not let him down. They met the two men at Prague station and led them to a hideout they had prepared in the woods. But Lederer did not hang around. He made his way back to the same Theresienstadt ghetto from where he had been deported four months earlier: he wanted to warn the Jews there of the truth of Auschwitz. Except the Nazi programme of deception had been so thorough, all but his closest friends refused to believe him.

It remained for Lederer to fulfil the second part of his bargain with the love-struck SS man, even more outlandish than the first.

Once again, Siegfried Lederer put on the uniform of an SS officer. In the intervening couple of months he had evidently been promoted. Now he was to play First Lieutenant Welker. At his side would be Second Lieutenant Hauser, the role taken by Viktor Pestek. They carried with them a perfectly forged warrant bearing both the Berlin letterhead of the Reich Security Main Office and the seal of the Prague Gestapo, authorising the pair to remove two women from the *Familienlager* of Birkenau for interrogation. They boarded an express train in Prague. Destination: Auschwitz.

The two men split up temporarily, so that Pestek could complete an errand, but they agreed to reconvene at Oświęcim railway station at noon the next day. The SS must have had a tip-off, because minutes before midday an SS flying squad on motorcycles arrived and promptly encircled the station buildings. When Pestek's train pulled in, they surrounded that too. The SS squad commander spotted Pestek, leaning out of a window from his carriage, and moved in. Seconds later, from his perch in the waiting room, Lederer watched as Pestek fought back, triggering a shootout. A hand grenade went off, scattering the SS men on the platform.

Seeing his moment, and still in his SS uniform, Lederer jumped out of the waiting room window and grabbed the first motorcycle he could find. He sped off, heading west. Within a couple of hours, he had abandoned the bike and was on a train back to Prague and from there to Theresienstadt, where he would hunker down and prepare a small group of comrades for resistance. Pestek was not so lucky. He was arrested, interrogated and shot before he could ever say goodbye to Renée Neumann.

The sounding of the sirens on 6 April, announcing Lederer's disappearance, prompted an immediate recalculation by Fred and Walter. It made no sense to attempt an escape when the SS were already in a state of high alert. Better to pause.

And so they waited until lunchtime on Friday 7 April. Once again Walter approached the gate, poised to tell the SS man standing sentry the same yarn about needing to visit the crematorium. The guard seemed suspicious, but Walter made it through. He headed towards the timber pile. He could see it. Would today be the day?

Then, without warning, Walter felt hands grab at him. They belonged to two SS-*Unterscharführer*s who had pounced, seemingly out of nowhere. His mind raced through the possibilities. How could these men possibly know what was afoot? Unless . . . had Walter and Fred been betrayed, their plan exposed before they had even taken the first steps towards implementing it?

Walter now looked hard at the two officers who had apprehended him. The trouble was, he did not recognise either of them. They were new. Which meant Walter could not make the kind of instant decision he, Fred and the other inmates had learned to make every moment of every day in Auschwitz and on which their survival depended. It was the same decision Fred had made three days earlier, on the day first slated for the escape: namely, whether this or that SS guard was not just cruel or vicious – that much was taken as read – but whether they were particularly sharp-eyed, vigilant and zealous or, alternatively, lazy and easily duped. Gazing at these two men who had grabbed him, their faces new and therefore blank, Walter had no clue.

The first sign either one of them gave him to go on was a sneer. 'What have we got here?' the man said, taking in Walter's elaborate get-up. Rosenberg's garb was familiar among the camp regulars, including the SS men who knew that the rules permitted a registrar to wear clothes of his own. But these men were not yet accustomed to the idiosyncrasies of Birkenau's permanent population.

Of course, mere sneers and taunts from the new SS men posed no threat. But that was not what worried Walter. His fear was that, now that he had caught their attention, the pair would make the next, obvious move and search him. And that would be a disaster.

Because, although Walter dressed like this – the riding breeches, the neatly tailored jacket, the high-end boots – every day, he had made a change. Hidden inside his shirt, pressed against his skin, was a watch. He was remembering Volkov's advice: timekeeping would be essential, for the first stage of the escape especially. If these two *Unterscharführers* began frisking him, if they merely patted him down, they would find the watch instantly. And that would give him away.

He imagined the scene that would follow. The crowd staring at the gallows, the noose placed around Walter's neck, as the presiding Nazi bellowed out the words: 'Why should a prisoner have a watch unless he was trying to get away?'

Walter was right to be fearful. The SS men did indeed begin to search him, starting with the contents of his coat pockets. They dug in and pulled out dozens of cigarettes, a hundred in all, by the handful. He had, in effect, been caught carrying currency. Would the SS men realise that this was a provision for escape?

The sweat began to bead on Walter's back. He did his best to stare straight ahead, to give nothing away. Out of the corner of his eye, he could see Bolek and Adamek walk by, en route to the 2 p.m. rendezvous that Walter now believed he would never make. In nearly two years, he had never been stopped like this. To have come so close only to be thwarted here, in this way, over some lousy cigarettes. Walter cursed the fates that were clearly bent on keeping him in Auschwitz until his last breath.

And then he felt it, the thwack of a cane on his shoulder, a firm, stinging blow, followed by another. One of the SS pair was thrashing him with a bamboo stick, abusing him as a 'dressed-up monkey' and a 'bastard'. Yet Walter felt not pain but relief. For though the SS man was beating him, he was not inflicting what would have been a far greater punishment: he was not searching him any further.

'Get going,' he said eventually. 'Get out of my sight.' Walter was incredulous. It made no sense. A moment earlier, this man had threatened to send him to Block 11, and if he had wanted to do that he could have: the hundred cigarettes alone would have been sufficient grounds.

Perhaps he and the rest of the SS were thrown by word of Lederer's escape, and the first rumours that one of their own officers had been involved. Or maybe it was sheer laziness. The *Unterscharführer* had said something about having 'better things to do' than frogmarching a lowly, if uppity, Jew across the camp. Easier to administer a beating and leave it there. Maybe it was as simple, and as random, as that: the man in the uniform could not be bothered to perform a chore that would have taken perhaps ten or fifteen minutes out of his day, but which would have cost Walter Rosenberg his life.

Given all he had seen, it was hardly a surprise to be saved by the whim of one of his captors. In a way, every Jew still breathing in Auschwitz–Birkenau had been saved the same way. From that initial flick of the finger on the selection ramp – to the left, to the right – through to the hundred moments of caprice that played out every day, from the *Kapo* deciding he could win a bet by killing someone else rather than you, on the spot with a single punch, to the doctor in the infirmary deciding whether you could stand on your own two feet or were too weak to be allowed to live, the difference between life and death often came down to a fickle split second, a decision that was not even a decision but rather an impulse, one that could just as easily have gone the other way.

Walter was free to go, and so he walked – as naturally and unhurriedly as he could, with a hint of authority, as if he were a foreman – towards the wooden hideaway. Just a few yards separated him from the place where it would all begin.

'You old swine, how are you?'

Immediately, Walter took off his cap and stood to attention. It was another SS-*Unterscharführer*, though this time the face was familiar. It was Otto Graf, one of the duo of enforcers Walter remembered from Kanada. These days Graf was at the sharp end, overseeing the *Sonderkommandos*, watching over the removal and incineration of the dead from the gas chambers.

'I've been working all bloody night,' Graf complained, anxious to chat. Walter tried not to look impatient. He had no watch he could look at, but he knew the 2 p.m. deadline was imminent. If he did not get away from Graf, the moment would pass and, after four aborted attempts, who knew if there would be another.

Graf offered him a smoke. 'Here, have a Greek cigarette.' Of course. The latest shipment of Jews, about a thousand of them, had come in from Athens a few days earlier. Walter made some excuse – he said Greek cigarettes aggravated his throat – and Graf moved off. At last, Walter could approach the hideout.

When he did, he saw the others were already there. Without a word, Bolek and Adamek gave the signal, a small nod of the head that said: *do it now*. They peeled back seven or eight layers of wood, exposed the opening, and Fred and Walter slipped in. Once inside, they heard the sound, above their heads, of planks being moved back into place and then, from one of their comrades, a whispered 'Bon voyage.' After that, nothing but silence and darkness.

It was 2 p.m. on 7 April 1944. Some of the SS men may have been in spiritual mood that day; perhaps they had been in church that morning, closing their eyes in prayer as they honoured the solemnity of Good Friday. But as Walter Rosenberg and Fred Wetzler lay still and silent in a hole in the ground, and as the daylight faded into evening, they did not know that this was also the night of the Seder, the start of the Jewish festival of Passover. On this night, the date shifting each year according to the lunar calendar, Jews were called to celebrate their liberty, to give thanks to a wise and mighty God for not forgetting his people, for rescuing them from an evil ruler and for delivering them from bondage. As Fred and Walter crouched in the dark, the instruction of ancient tradition was clear: this was the night Jews made their escape from slavery to freedom.

# 17

# Underground

THOSE WERE THE longest three days and nights of Walter's life. In that tiny hole, the hours lasted for weeks. Contracted by space, time seemed to expand.

When it was light outside, he would picture his fellow inmates just beyond the woodpile, a matter of yards away, working as slaves from dawn till dusk. He would listen out for the punctuation of the day, the midday break for what passed for lunch and, a few hours later, the rhythm of marching feet: the sound of prisoners ending their shift and returning to barracks. At that point, he and Fred would hear the orders barked at the men, by *Kapos* mostly, and the strains of martial music, the camp orchestra forced to strike up a tune to herald the return of the working units.

On that first night, the Friday, Walter imagined the roll call: the initial discovery of first one missing name and then another, followed by some head-scratching conversation between the *Kapos* and the block leaders, one of them eventually having to tell the men in uniform that two Jews were unaccounted for. That admission would almost certainly have brought them a beating.

He imagined the reaction of his comrades as word slowly spread of who had gone missing. He knew how they would have winced as for ten long minutes that awful, howling siren filled their ears, the sound that was always the cue for an extended roll call, forcing the prisoners to stand in formation for hours on end, shivering and exhausted, as they were counted and counted again. But he also knew how they would have delighted in the possibility that not just one but two of their fellow Jews had, at last, got away.

Questions sped through Walter's mind as the minutes ticked by.

What if the petrol-soaked tobacco eventually lost its scent? What if one of those who knew about this hiding place cracked? And why had Walter thought it a good idea to bring a watch with luminous hands, which meant that he and Fred could see just how glacially the minutes were passing?

That night, hunched in their hole in the ground, Walter and Fred heard a familiar sound: the heavy rumble of a convoy of trucks ferrying the condemned from the *Judenrampe* to the gas chambers. Their hideout was just a short distance north-east of Crematoria IV and V. The Jews were still arriving, still stumbling out of the trains that brought them here from all points across Europe, still standing to be assessed and selected, still climbing on board the vehicles that would carry them to their deaths.

Walter counted the trucks as they went past. Then, an hour or two later, he heard the clash of metal against metal, as the iron racks carrying corpse upon corpse were rattled into the ovens where they would be turned into smoke and ash. All the pair of them could do was listen, rigid and mute. (What they had heard was the incineration of 274 people: Jews from Belgium, thirty-six of them children under the age of twelve.)

The killing continued but so did the search when Saturday dawned, the sounds of it – boots, dogs, shouts – echoing and ricocheting around Mexico, sometimes reverberating against the uncompleted and as yet uninhabited wooden barracks, sometimes resonating directly above their heads.

When 5 p.m. on Monday finally came, the end of the working day signalled by the sound of the band playing another cheerful ditty, every note a taunt to the men who had been whipped and beaten into a day of brutal labour, there was a new worry. Now, Walter knew, there would be another roll call. If any other prisoner were missing, if anyone else had attempted an escape, he and Fred would be back to the beginning: the outer perimeter would stay manned for another three days. So they waited, desperate that there be no new siren. The hands on the watch crawled so slowly, it seemed time itself had stopped. But no alarm was sounded.

They looked up at the ceiling. It was so tempting, but Walter was firm: too risky. Not until 9 p.m., after fully eighty hours concealed in that small hole in the ground, did Walter and Fred decide it was safe to move.

Opening up their hideaway was harder than they had bargained for, and not only because of the weight of the boards, stacked above their heads. Those three days spent lying still had taken their toll. Their muscles had atrophied. The boards now seemed unnaturally heavy, shifting them all but impossible. Each shove brought a fierce, tingling pain. Their legs trembled; they seemed unable to support their own weight. Habit and caution – because there might still be a regular patrol passing nearby – made them want to do the work silently. Which made it harder still.

They looked at the bread and coffee they had set aside, safer to consume now. They were both painfully hungry and desperately thirsty. But when they attempted to take a sip, or eat even a little, both men found the same trouble: they were not able to swallow. It was as if their bodies had turned in on themselves, as if their innards had coiled up and closed.

And yet they could not afford to wait much longer. The night hours were all they had. Come dawn, and the start of another working day, the outer perimeter would be manned once more, the guns of the watchtowers locked and loaded. They had to get out now.

Working together, shoving in unison, they at last got one of the bottom boards to move. Eventually the rest followed and, with enormous effort, they pulled themselves up and out. Exhausted from the exertion and the three days' confinement, the two men allowed themselves a short moment to sit on the woodpile that had protected them and look out. They paused to take in the night sky. It was clear; the moon was shining.

They needed to get going, but first they put the boards back in their original position. Part of it was a determination to be thorough, to leave no clue for those who would be here the next morning. But part of it was the hope that this small concealed hole might serve as an escape hatch for someone else. Until that moment, there had not been a single known case of a Jew escaping from Auschwitz helped only by his fellow prisoners, evading capture and reaching freedom for good. Fred Wetzler and Walter Rosenberg were on course to become the first. They did not want to be the last.

They headed west, out of Mexico and towards the little birch wood that gave Birkenau its name. They advanced not on foot, but on their stomachs, inching along, commando style. No needless risks now. They did not get up until they had reached the trees, the same small forest that held the pits that had burned corpses day and night. Now they went into a careful, crouching run until they hit open ground, which sent them back on to their bellies. They could see so little.

They ran into a fresh obstacle. They could not be sure if it was a road or a frozen river. There was no snow on the ground and yet its surface was glistening in the moonlight. About eight yards wide, it seemed to extend far into the distance, both to the left and to the right. Yet it yielded no ripple or sound. Low to the ground, Walter stretched a hand to it, bracing for the cold.

But the touch surprised him. For this was no river but rather a ribbon of sand. Was it a minefield? Or was it more cunning than lethal, a stretch of sand laid down to record any attempt at a breakout, preserving the fugitives' footprints, revealing their direction of travel?

There was no way to walk around it; it was too long for that. There was only one option. Walter went first, treading gingerly. He tried to make himself light, a burglar striving not to wake the house. Finally, he reached the other side. He looked back at Fred, who then repeated the manoeuvre, taking care to place each foot in the print left by Walter. That way, they hoped to avoid any mines and, who knows, maybe confuse the chasing SS men who would inevitably follow.

Soon they were at the inner ditch that bounded the perimeter of the camp. They followed it, until it brought them at last to a fence.

It was not like the ones they had known from the inner camp. It did not have electric lights attached to each post; the wire was not electrified. Even so, the pair were taking no chances. They had fashioned in advance something that could function as a kind of clothes peg, protecting their hands as, working from the bottom, they lifted the wire above the ground. That made an opening big enough for each of them to crawl through.

Now they were on the other side of the fence. They would stay close to it, walking a near complete circuit around the camp. Before long, they passed the inner camp, the lights that marked its perimeter warm and glowing. If you did not know better, the sight could almost look cosy, given the barren bleakness all around. Except they did know better. For they could also see the chimneys of the crematoria, pumping out their greenish-blue, oil-refinery flames and their thick smoke of death. The pair took a last look, as clear as they had ever been that they never wanted to see this place again.

They kept on, walking as stealthily as they could, their limbs still stiff, slowed down by the marshy terrain. At about two o'clock in the morning, crossing open moorland, they reached a signpost with a warning to those coming in the opposite direction: *Attention! This is Auschwitz Concentration Camp. Anyone found on these lands will be shot without warning!*

It had taken them far too long, but they had at last reached the end of the vast 'zone of interest' that enveloped the camp. For a moment at least, they could congratulate themselves. The date was 10 April 1944 and they had broken out of Auschwitz.

# 18

## On the Run

SUNDAY 9 APRIL was no day of rest for the SS. Sturmbannführer Hartenstein, the man in charge of the units responsible for guarding the camp, had been notified by teleprinter at 8.33 p.m. on Friday that two prisoners were missing. But it was not until Sunday that he telegraphed word of Fred and Walter's escape to his superiors in Berlin. He addressed his cable to Gestapo headquarters, but copies were sent to all Gestapo units in the east, to all units of the SD, or Security Service, and to the Kripo, or Criminal Police, as well as to the Grepo, the border police and to SS administrative head office. In the flat, bureaucratic idiom of the Third Reich, telegram No. 2334/2344 told the story so far:

> To RSHA, Berlin, WC2, to the SS Administrative Office D, Oranienburg, to all commanders Eastern Gestapo criminal investigation police and border commands in reference to: Jews in preventive arrest. 1. Rosenberg, Walter Israel, born 11 Sept. 1924, at Topol'čany, arrived 30 June 1942, from RSHA. 2. Wetzler, Alfréd Israel, born 10 May 1918, at Trnava, arrived 13 April 1942, from RSHA: Rosenberg and Wetzler escaped 7 April 1944, from concentration camp AU II, Sections II A and II D. Immediate search unsuccessful. Request from you further search and in case of capture full report to concentration camp Auschwitz. Additional to RSHA: request from you transcripts on Rosenberg and Wetzler from official search leader. Additional to SS headquarters: information forwarded to the Reichsführer. Further report follows. Fault of any guard so far not determined. Concentration camp AU, Division II, 440709, 4/8/44 D4 (signed) Hartenstein, SS Major

As those words pulsed along the wires connecting Auschwitz to both Berlin and the eastern reaches of the Nazi empire, Fred and

Walter remained unmoving in their small, almost airless cavity inside Birkenau. They had no idea that the Reichsführer himself, Heinrich Himmler, had been told of their escape. They did not know that the camp authorities had all but given up hope of finding them, or that the SS major in charge of keeping Auschwitz's prisoners locked up had admitted yet another grave lapse on his watch and had, as yet, found no one to blame. *Fault of any guard so far not determined.* They did not know that their names − with the addition of 'Israel', which the Nazis bestowed on all Jewish males whose first names did not appear on their list of 185 identifiably Jewish names − would soon be pinned up on the bulletin board of every police station, however small, even in the remotest frontier town of occupied Europe.

For although the SS thought they had escaped, it would be many hours before Fred and Walter believed it for themselves.

They did not emerge from their hole in the ground until nine o'clock the following night. Even when they had wriggled under the fence of the camp, even when they had crossed the line marking the 'zone of interest' − an area of some fifteen square miles, taking in the swathe of land between the Vistula and Soła rivers and including dozens of Auschwitz sub-camps − they would hardly be able to breathe easy. The universe outside Auschwitz contained almost as many perils as were held within.

That was especially true for two Jewish escapees. From the day they arrived back in 1942, the two of them, like all Jewish prisoners of the camp, had been cut off from the world. They had no network of comrades they could contact. There was no resistance organisation waiting for them to emerge, armed with food or clothes or false papers or indeed arms. While non-Jewish prisoners in Auschwitz had been allowed to receive food parcels and the like, thereby retaining at least a connection to the rest of the human race, the Jews had been very deliberately isolated. Just nineteen and twenty-five years old, Walter and Fred were entirely on their own.

The way Walter saw it, they had been written off by the world the day they stopped being Alfréd Wetzler and Walter Rosenberg and became prisoners 29162 and 44070, if not the day they stepped on to those deportation trains. True, they had become people of standing in the Auschwitz inmate hierarchy, but all that was lost now.

The moment they crept out from under that fence they had entered a social vacuum. They knew no one; they had no one.

But that also meant no one had them. While Bolek, Adamek and one or two others knew the pair were plotting to escape, no one knew of their plans once out of the bunker and no one knew their route. The underground had refused to authorise official help, and so there was no risk of a comrade giving away that information under torture and no risk of a mole, one of the Political Department's informers, doing the same more freely. On this Fred and Walter had been fastidious: they had not even talked of their route to each other.

All they had agreed on was that they would head south, to Slovakia. It was relatively near, about fifty miles away, but its chief commendation was that it was the land of their birth, the one place where their accents would not mark them out as foreigners and so attract instant suspicion. They had no contacts here in Poland. In Slovakia, they had no idea who, if any, of their friends or family were still alive. But in the land of their birth they would at least know where to start.

To Slovakia, then. With no documents, no map and no compass, just that list of names in Walter's head, assembled from a torn page of a child's atlas: Kęty, Saybusch (or Żywiec), Milówka, Rajcza, Sól.

Walter was beginning to worry about dawn. They could not risk being out in the daylight, and yet obviously they needed to be further away from the camp. They could see the outline of a forest: if they could get there before daybreak, they would find a place to hide and rest.

But even as they kept on walking, the trees seemingly refused to get any nearer. At first light, they came out on to open ground: they were still so close to the camp that, to their alarm, they heard the Auschwitz gong announcing morning roll call. They were in a cornfield, exposed for all to see.

They took a look around and then, a heartbeat later, threw themselves to the ground. Perhaps 500 yards away were the distinctive grey-green uniforms of the SS. There were several of them, escorting a group of women prisoners.

Flat and on their fronts, Fred and Walter were breathing fast. Had they been seen? Would the SS men come over here and shoot them on the spot? Volkov's advice had been clear: no running. They would have to hold tight.

Eventually, one of the pair lifted his head, a periscope breaching the surface. There was no sign of the women or the SS. They had been lucky.

But they resolved not to reveal themselves again, not in the light of day. So they completed the rest of the trek to the forest like jungle warriors, advancing on their stomachs, rising to their feet only when they spotted a hollow or ditch, some of them filled with snow, in the hope that these dips in the ground might keep them hidden from view.

Finally, they were in among the thick fir trees. They rested a while; they might have dozed.

The quiet was broken by the sound of drums and song. The voices were young, belting out a chorus in healthy, hearty German. Fred and Walter hid themselves in the bushes, then heard the crunch of footsteps as SS men walked close by.

Eventually they peeked through the branches, only to see that they had run into a gathering of the Hitler Youth. Perhaps these young servants of the Reich were camping or going on an improving hike, rucksacks on their backs, getting to know the terrain of the new, expanded Fatherland. It would make sense in this part of Silesia, which had once been Polish but was now, following annexation, heavily Germanised, the original Polish population driven out of their homes, replaced by ethnic German settlers. Walter watched as these children, not thirty yards away and under a canopy of trees, ate their sandwiches. He reflected that their fathers were either the *Volksdeutsche* who had displaced the locals or the SS who had enslaved him and murdered his people.

The pair were paralysed, stuck in the bushes, not daring to move. Then, as if in answer to a prayer, rain began to fall. Gentle at first, no more than a shower, certainly not enough to deter the young believers of the Hitlerjugend. But soon the heavens opened and a torrent of rain sent Nazism's next generation scurrying for shelter.

It was too risky to linger. Breaking one of the Volkov rules against daytime travel, Fred and Walter marched on, grateful for their coats and caps against the cold, and for their boots as the ground turned to mud and bog.

Once they had found a sufficiently dense patch of bushes, they decided to catch up on the sleep that should have begun at dawn. It was 11 April.

They tried to get back on track, journeying after dark, stopping to drink from a stream when they crossed one, otherwise cleaving to the route, if not the banks, of the Soła. On their second night they lost the river and strayed too far west, edging dangerously close to the small village of Jawiszowice. Dangerous, because Jawischowitz, as the Nazis had renamed it, was one of the thirty-nine sub-camps of Auschwitz: an SS-operated coal mine where, around the time Fred and Walter approached, some 2,500 slaves laboured, most of them Jews. The fugitives had wandered into an all-too-familiar compound of barracks, barbed wire, electric lights and watchtowers. The sentry posts were empty for now, because it was night-time. But few knew better than Fred and Walter that daybreak would bring the day shift of armed SS guards.

They fought to ward off panic. But each route they took seemed to lead them back to another fence or guard tower. Morning was coming; they had to get away. But it was so hard to see. They were on unknown terrain in an unfamiliar country, with no guide and no equipment.

They saw a wood that at least looked to be outside the boundaries of the camp. They went inside, found a spot, ate a small portion of the bread and margarine they had had with them since they first went into the bunker, but which had to be rationed carefully, then broke off a few branches, covered themselves as best they could and hoped to sleep until dusk. To keep them both calm, or perhaps to allow their minds to float far away, Fred would talk in those closed, hidden hours of chess. He was the teacher, Walter his pupil, his voice soothing and reassuring until first one and then the other fell asleep.

That was the plan, at any rate. But as the sun grew brighter, it became clear that this was no secluded wooded grove. On the contrary, blinded by the darkness earlier, they had chosen to hide themselves in a public park. Its clientele were the new masters of the region, SS men with their wives and children, out for a stroll during the Easter holiday week. Fred and Walter had escaped an SS death camp only to walk into an SS playground.

They swiftly assessed the danger. Given where they were hiding, they determined that the chief threats were dogs, who might sniff them out, and children: all it would take was a misplaced ball to roll in their direction and they would be done for.

Sure enough, a little boy and a young girl came bounding by, giggling and playing, getting close, then wandering away, then coming back again. Walter's heart was thumping.

Suddenly they were there, right in front of them, the two, blue-eyed children gawping at Fred and Walter. A moment later, they were haring off to find their father who, Walter could see, wore the uniform of an SS-*Oberscharführer*, right down to his regulation pistol.

'Papa, Papa, come here,' the girl was saying. 'There are men in the bushes.'

The SS man approached. Reflexively, both Fred and Walter pulled out their knives.

The children's father came close enough that he was now staring directly into their eyes. They stared back. The silence seemed to last for long minutes. Finally, a look of comprehension, harsh in its judgement, spread across the face of the SS squad leader. Walter watched him shoo away his children and then consult his blonde wife, whose pursed lips left no doubt as to what her husband had just told her. The shocked family hurried away, scandalised that two men would bed down together so brazenly in a public park, and with children around too. They must have considered it an assault on the otherwise impeccable morals of the new Germany.

It was too risky to attempt to relocate. That would mean emerging from the bushes and getting noticed. Fred and Walter stayed where they were till nightfall, when the walking could begin again.

The trouble was, sticking to the path of the Soła was easier on the page of an atlas than in real life. They kept getting lost. There was comfort, for example, in seeing the lights of Bielsko, about twenty miles south of Auschwitz, because that confirmed they were roughly on the right track. The plan was always to avoid human contact, which meant steering around places rather than marching right into them. And yet, once the night grew late and the lights of Bielsko dimmed, Fred and Walter became disorientated. Soon, and very suddenly, they found themselves right inside the town. They were surrounded by streets and buildings and, therefore, hundreds of pairs of eyes, ready to spot them – and betray them.

They tried to go back the way they had come, to retreat once more into the anonymous countryside. But in their confusion and in the darkness they could not seem to do it. Wherever they turned, there was another building, and then another. It would only be a matter of time before they ran into men with guns, whether the SS or their Polish collaborators, it hardly made much difference.

For now, their prime opponent was the dawn. They could not risk being caught in this maze of Bielsko streets in the light of day. They had to get out.

They only half managed it. As the sun came up on Thursday 13 April, they had escaped the town but only as far as the nearby village of Pisarzowice. True, there were fewer people to spot them, but the pair were more visible now that it was morning. They would have to hide and that meant breaking one of Volkov's most solemn rules: they would have to make contact with a stranger.

But which one? There was no way of weighing up the options; this would have to be a decision taken at random. They would have to pick a front door and try it. If they got it wrong, and a newly installed *Volksdeutsche* answered, they would surely be done for. But even if they got lucky and a local Pole opened up, that could spell trouble too. The rules of the occupying power were clear: any Pole found harbouring, or even assisting, a Jew would be executed. Conversely, a Pole who found a Jew in hiding and gave them up would be rewarded for doing so: the going rate was a kilo of sugar or perhaps a bottle of vodka. So which house to pick? Make a mistake, and it could be fatal.

They decided to try a tumbledown peasant cottage where there were chickens outside and even a wandering goose. Rather than give a formal knock, Fred and Walter wandered round the back, picking their way through the animals. They saw there a woman clad in black, her head scarved, with a teenage daughter lurking anxiously behind.

It was not just Walter who had a knack for languages. Fred too was sufficiently adept in Polish that they both knew the right way to introduce themselves.

'Praise be the name of Jesus Christ,' the two Jews from Slovakia said.

'May His name be praised for ever, amen,' the woman said in reply.

She ushered them in, which was the first good sign. The second came when she said, 'I'm afraid my Russian is not very good.'

It was probably their accents that had given them away: she knew they were not Polish. But there would have been other signs too. They were wearing expensive, though now dirty, clothes and they were stopping at a random house in the middle of nowhere. It must have been obvious that they were on the run. That they were Soviet escapees from a prisoner-of-war camp was not a bad guess, and a convenient one for Fred and Walter. Better she think that than guess the truth.

She turned to her daughter, still mute, and signalled for her to bring something for these men to eat. Out came a breakfast of bread, potatoes and imitation coffee, which, after several days of foraging, counted as a banquet.

As they ate, she sketched out the current lie of the land. She confirmed that the villages of this area had indeed been heavily Germanised. If Walter and Fred saw people working in the fields, the chances were high that they were German civilians. They carried weapons, even when out farming, and they had the authority to shoot 'unidentifiable loiterers' on sight. The area was full of partisans, she said, and so the Germans were especially vigilant.

The remaining Poles in the region were now confined to houses further away from the roads and from the river, and therefore, thought Walter, away from their route to the border. Not that many would be too eager to help a pair of fugitives. Not only had the Nazi occupier made the granting of help to the wrong kind of strangers a capital crime for those directly found guilty of it, a perpetrator's entire family often paid the same price. The woman added that many Poles had already been killed for making the mistake of giving food or shelter to men who had posed as escapees, speaking Polish or Russian, but who were, in fact, German *agents provocateurs*.

It turned out that the woman had had two sons: one was dead and the other was himself a prisoner in a concentration camp. Perhaps that was why she took what she clearly understood was an enormous risk, allowing Fred and Walter to stay in her house until the early hours of the next morning.

They made themselves useful, chopping wood, taking a break for lunch of a bowl of potato soup followed by . . . potatoes. Once the work was done, they slept until the middle of the night, when Walter woke suddenly. He jumped up, startled. It was the woman, with a jug of coffee and a warning that if they were to cross open country and make it to the mountains unseen, they needed to leave right away. She wanted them to take some money, 'Just for luck.' It meant breaking another Volkov rule, but Walter found it impossible to say no.

Her advice proved sound. They travelled unchecked for three hours, reaching the mountains, capped with snow even in April, by dawn. They were still within reassuring distance of the Soła, trekking along the western banks of the river through a valley thick with trees. Only occasionally did they see a house and, when they did, the residents usually closed their doors and shuttered their windows if either Fred or Walter drew near. If, in a moment of rare necessity, the fugitives attempted conversation, the locals tended not to answer. Was it a refusal to help two Jews in their midst or, more simply, had the woman in Pisarzowice been right: the local population were terrified of an occupation that had made basic human kindness a fatal risk? Either way, it made the pair appreciate all the more those Poles who would glimpse them on their trek, then accidentally drop half a loaf of bread near their path.

On Sunday 16 April they emerged from the forest, but that brought a new fear. They had come out in the mountains overlooking Porąbka. Both Fred and Walter had been warned, separately, of the dangers of this place: a nearby dam made it enough of a military target that barrage balloons hovered like dumb sentries in the sky above, and it was teeming with German soldiers. Indeed, this was the spot where Eisenbach, Balaban and the others had run into those German foresters and where their own attempt at escape, a success until then, had come unstuck. And now Fred and Walter were eyeing the same barrage balloons, just as fat, grey and sullen as they had been warned to expect.

They would stick to the mountainside, its steep slopes carpeted in dense green forest, thereby avoiding the dam and the town. But it was tough going. They were getting tired; their legs were beginning to swell. There was snow on the ground, and in the dark they had to move gingerly. Every sound of a broken branch or dislodged stone brought dread. If it were one of them who crunched a twig underfoot, then they feared they had given themselves away; if the noise came from elsewhere, then it meant a stranger, or enemy, was close by.

After a few hours' rest in the daylight, evening approached and they readied themselves to set off once more. Except now, for the first time, they were to confront a threat which could not be swerved or outwitted. They were about to face a Nazi bullet.

# 19

# Crossing the Border

WALTER WAS LYING down, eyes closed, when he heard it. The crack of a rifle and the whizz of a bullet over his head. Instinct made both him and Fred leap to their feet, though whether that was wise, neither of them could know.

Now they could see it. A patrol of about a dozen German soldiers was on the next hill, about seventy yards away. They had dogs on leashes and they had guns, which they were aiming at the two of them. Perhaps these Wehrmacht men had seen the telegram, cabled by the SS major a week earlier, alerting every outpost of the Reich to the disappearance of two wanted prisoners of Auschwitz. Perhaps they had a description which Fred and Walter matched. Either way, they had seen enough to open fire.

The old Red Army captain had been adamant. You could never outrun a bullet. So never leave yourself in that position, never let your only hope be a request of your legs that the laws of physics would always refuse. But as Walter scrambled up the hillside, stumbling through the snow, hoping to make it to the top and then disappear down the slope on the other side, he had no use for Volkov's golden rules, almost all of which he had broken. Uniformed Germans had opened fire on them and with great accuracy. All they could do was run.

Fred was faster, spotting a boulder big enough to hide behind. He hurled himself into place and Walter was desperate to catch up and do the same. But he tripped, falling flat on his face. There was no way to get up now; he would be too slow, too easy a target. The air was crackling with gunfire, bullets clipping the rocks all around. To move, even a muscle, was to be shot dead. There was nothing he could do. He was paralysed with fear.

Seconds later he heard the order to cease fire. 'We've got him!' the commander told his men. They began to climb down the hillside, doubtless to identify their two kills. Walter leapt up and completed the journey he had tried to make before, flinging himself behind that rock.

Now Fred gave his own order, urging Walter to push on ahead. They made it to the brow of the hill and down the other side, but the Germans had not given up and their dogs were closing in.

The fugitives kept on running, setting their sights on a small wood halfway up the next hill. They could disappear in there, if only they could make it that far.

Except the only way to reach that next hill was to cross a wide stream at the bottom of the valley. The dogs were getting nearer. There was no choice. They simply had to plunge in.

The water was ice cold and moving fast. The opposite bank was so near, but the current was tugging at their clothes, pulling them under. Walter lost his footing and sank into the water, not once but twice. Immersed in the glacial liquid from head to toe, he felt the cold bite into his bones.

Somehow they made it to the other side, but that brought little respite. The ground was covered in snow so deep their legs sank into it. Soaked from the stream, they were in snow up to their waists. But they kept on, determined to make it to the trees. They looked over their shoulders to see that the soldiers were still giving chase, scrambling down the hillside towards the water.

Walter and Fred were in the wood now, running in a zigzag pattern, hoping to confuse their pursuers, running and running until one of them noticed the sound that they could not hear: there was no more barking, no more baying of dogs. Drained and drenched, they fell into a ditch. They lay as still as they could, shivering from the cold, listening for the sound of human tread. After a while they realised that in the scramble to escape their pursuers they had lost both their meagre provisions and their overcoats.

They kept on walking by night, resting by day. They were fighting hunger and the cold, trekking in thin clothes through forests still partially covered with snow. They would keep well away from any inhabited settlement now. Porąbka had been too narrow an escape; they dared not push their luck. From that moment on, they would avoid any path that looked too well worn, even if that made the available pickings of food slimmer. All they wanted was to get out of this country, where death and danger seemed to wait for them at every turn. Once across the border, they felt sure, things would become easier.

On Wednesday 19 April, fully ten days into their trek, they were in the hills overlooking the Polish town of Milówka: Walter remembered the name from that page in the atlas. By that measure, they were just two towns away from the border. Here and there, they could see the ashes and charred earth of past fires: perhaps, they thought, partisans were close by. They were in a field near a forest, avoiding people as usual, when they spotted a small herd of goats. Fred and Walter were doubtless assessing the animals' potential as food when, a second later, they saw the middle-aged woman who watched over them.

There was a silent stand-off, each party eyeballing the other, assessing the mutual threat they represented. She knew these gaunt, wild-eyed men were fugitives, that much was obvious; she equally knew, therefore, that if she offered them any help the Germans would kill her. And yet also in her eyes was the clear knowledge that if she did not help, these men might kill her themselves.

It lasted a good few seconds before Walter broke the stalemate. Given how careful they had been, given all Volkov had taught him about unnecessary risk and all the two of them had learned on that same subject, the words that came out of his mouth made no sense. 'We're heading for the Slovak border,' he said. 'Can you show us the way? We've escaped from a concentration camp. From Auschwitz.'

Why did he need to say that? Why identify themselves that way? Even if the pair did not know there was an international warrant out for their arrest, Walter would have known that, once prisoners had escaped from Auschwitz, the entire region would be on the lookout. So why take the risk of saying the word out loud?

Perhaps, he thought, it was because there was no point trying to hoodwink this woman. She was not going to be fooled by some tall tale; anyone could see who they were. Perhaps it was because her tatty clothes and worn hands did not look like those of a police agent. Maybe it was a gamble on human kindness, a bet that it still existed despite everything they had seen. It might have been all those things. But it also crossed Walter's mind that his mission, the reason he and Fred had broken out, was to tell the world outside Auschwitz of the camp and what happened within it or, failing that, at least to speak of Auschwitz's existence, and so far they had told no one. In that moment, some kind of small, absurd weight lifted from his shoulders. He had told one person. He had uttered the word out loud and beyond the perimeter. He had said it: Auschwitz.

The woman gestured towards her little goat-hut and beckoned them to go inside. She was still wary; she never stopped looking at their faces. And they were wary too; they suspected a trap. But they went inside. She gave them a piece of bread and the blanket she had with her, and told them to wait. She would send food immediately and, after that, some help.

They watched her go down the hill, eventually crossing a bridge about half a mile away. They eyed the bridge carefully. If she was planning on betraying them – either to the Nazi occupiers, to a local police unit or to a militia – then those men would first have to cross the bridge before they could reach Fred and Walter. That would give the two of them a head start. They would be able to see the enemy approaching and quickly disappear into the forest behind them. Not that they could be that quick: Walter's feet were now so swollen he could barely walk, let alone run. Thanks to all that trekking, and a diet of crumbs alone, he was hobbling like a man four times his age.

The minutes passed, too many of them. The old woman had said she would send food 'immediately'. Yet here they were, nearly two hours later, alone in a goat-hut, easy prey. Had it been a trick? Had she changed her mind? Or had she somehow collided with the authorities, which now made it impossible to help two men on the run?

There was movement down below, close to the bridge. They squinted to see who was approaching. The figure got nearer.

As he approached, they saw that climbing up the hill towards them was a young boy. He could not have been more than twelve. He was carrying a parcel, which he handed over. He looked terrified, as if he were about to burst into tears: hardly surprising, given the condition Fred and Walter were in, their faces unshaven, their feet bandaged and bleeding. A frightened little boy, and yet he was just a few years younger than Walter.

Inside the package was a generous helping of cooked potatoes and some meat. Fred and Walter devoured it, only realising as they ate how famished they truly were. They had been foraging on next to nothing since Porąbka, filling their empty bellies with water sipped from streams. The boy watched them. Then he said that his grandmother would return at nightfall.

Fred and Walter wondered if they should get out while they were ahead. The bridge would no longer function as a visual early-warning system once it was dark. If this woman was going to give them away, then tonight, once they had been lulled by the gift of a meal, would be the time to do it.

They considered it. Their scepticism was strong, but their need for help, and their hunger, were stronger. Besides, if the woman did return with armed men, their footsteps would at least be audible over that bridge: Fred and Walter would have time to melt back into the trees. They would wait.

Eventually evening came and, out of the twilight, the woman emerged. As she climbed up the hillside, a man was at her side. But he wore no uniform, just the shabby clothes of a country worker. They were close, far too close, when Fred and Walter saw that the man was carrying a gun.

Calculations of life and death, of capture and murder, were now becoming swift and instinctive for Walter Rosenberg and Fred Wetzler. Without needing to confer, both worked out that the probability that this man was there to kill them was low. If he was hostile, he most likely planned to march them at gunpoint into the arms of the Gestapo. That, they decided wordlessly, was a manageable risk: he was old, there were two of them and they had knives.

The woman handed them another parcel, while the man looked on without saying a word. It was a second meal, which they demolished as quickly as the first. In less than a minute, they had eaten it all. The man watched, and then began to laugh.

'You're from a concentration camp, all right,' he said, as he put away his pistol. Apparently, the depth of their hunger had convinced him. Until then, he had wondered if these two fugitives his friend had run into were, in fact, undercover agents of the Gestapo, despatched to trick and expose those locals who were helping the partisan resistance. Duly reassured that Fred and Walter were the genuine article, he told them to pack up and stay the night with him. The next night, he said, he would guide them across the border. With tears in her eyes, the woman said goodbye and wished them luck.

The man led them to his cottage in the valley, where they slept in real beds and where Walter at last had the chance to remove the boots that, thanks to the state of his feet, had become unbearable. Each foot was swollen so badly, he had to use his razor blade to slice the leather away. Their Polish host gave them both new boots, but the swelling made it impossible to wear them anywhere but slung over their shoulders. Walter made do with a pair of borrowed carpet slippers instead.

The next day, they stayed indoors, waiting for the old man to return. He fed them and then, once it was dark, they set off, having promised to do exactly what he told them. They headed back into the mountains by first crossing the railway tracks near Milówka. Without proper shoes, Walter struggled to keep up.

At one point, their guide signalled for them to stop. A German patrol passed through this area every ten minutes, he warned. They would hide, watch it pass, and then they would have a nine-minute interval to get clear. This, he explained, was the Nazis' great flaw: they stuck to routine so faithfully, their movements were predictable. Walter and Fred could nod to that: their entire escape plan had been predicated on it.

The three men concealed themselves in some bushes and watched as the Pole's observation came good. As if on cue, German soldiers marched by. If Walter and Fred had any last doubts over the wisdom of trusting this man, they fell away.

They took the occasional break, as the man went into the woods, returning with food: apparent confirmation that there were partisans nearby. As they ate, the man offered in an even voice his theory that the two of them were probably the fugitives who had escaped from the camp at Oświęcim on 7 April. He gestured towards their sleeves, under which were their tattooed numbers, as if to show that he too knew all about Auschwitz, perhaps even that he had been a prisoner there himself. They asked for his name, so that one day they might thank him. He said only that he was called Tadeusz. Of course. That was the unwritten rule: no names, no addresses, on either side. That way, if either they, or he, were captured and tortured by the Nazis, they would have nothing to reveal.

The trio pressed on, covering some eight miles in the darkness, until it was the morning of Friday 21 April. They had been together two days and now they had reached a clearing. The old man pointed at a forest, no more than fifty yards away, and said the words they had longed to hear: 'That's Slovakia.'

There was nothing to stop them. No fence, no border post. They could sprint over there right now, and they would be out of occupied Poland once and for all. But their guide had two more instructions. First, he said, the German patrols were as regular here as anywhere else, but the intervals were longer. Every three hours, one would pass. The only guarantee of safety was to hang back, hide in the trees, watch the patrol come and go and then make a run for it.

Once they had crossed the border, they were to head for the village of Skalité. There they were to look for house number 264, where they would find a man who could be trusted and who would give them food and clothes. They were to say that 'The living hillsman from Milówka' had sent them. And with that, his voice cracking slightly, 'Tadeusz' said goodbye.

Fred and Walter did as they were told. They watched the patrol pass, waited a moment or two and then headed up the dark hillside opposite. They had not been walking long, perhaps ten minutes, when they saw embedded in the ground the short, stubby stone posts – a 'P' on one side, an 'S' on the other – that marked the border between Poland and the land of their birth. They crossed in broad daylight, at nine o'clock in the morning.

Did they feel euphoric? They felt relieved. They were no longer in the same country as Auschwitz. But they could feel little joy. Though it was not occupied by the Nazis, Slovakia was still run by the Nazis' allies, the same home-grown fascists led by Father Jozef Tiso who had longed for and organised the expulsion of Fred and Walter, their families, their friends. This was still the country that had let that happen.

Every move they would make was fraught with risk. The Hlinka Guards had not gone away. Besides, they could not remain under cover of darkness here, even with the trusted friend Tadeusz had mentioned. They needed to make contact with the remnant Jews of Slovakia, those who had somehow evaded deportation and clung on, and that need would force them into the open.

And so they kept walking, through the woods along the hillside ridge, until they began the descent into the border village of Skalité, with its few, scattered houses, a gentle stream and an onion-domed church. The state of their clothes, ripped and torn now, and Walter in his tattered slippers, a pair of boots slung over his shoulder, announced them as strangers. The proximity of the Polish border filled in the rest.

They found the house, uttered the password – invoking 'The living hillsman of Milówka' – and were taken in by farmer Ondrej Čanecký. He told his guests to wash, while he gave each of them a change of clothes: peasant garb that would allow them to pass for locals. Over a meal, Fred and Walter explained that they needed to meet whatever semblance of a Jewish community they could find: they needed to get word to them, urgently. Čanecký replied that the doctor in Čadca was a Jew by the name of Pollack.

That name rang an instant bell. Back in Nováky, there had been a Dr Pollack scheduled to be on the same transport that took Walter to Majdanek. And yet his name had been removed from the list at the last moment. It turned out that the authorities made a sudden exception for Jewish physicians, bowing to pressure from the Slovak public, especially in rural areas, who overnight found they had no medical care. Tiso had not reckoned with the fact that, though Jews made up only a small portion of Slovakia's population, they accounted for a big share of the country's doctors. The president reprieved those Jewish medics who had not already been deported, despatching them to small towns and villages. Given all that, it was wholly believable that the same Dr Pollack was in Čadca. And if he was, then that was the obvious place to start. They needed to get to Čadca immediately. Fred and Walter looked at each other: they should leave right away.

Hold on, said Čanecký. If they were to travel the twenty-odd miles to Čadca the same way they had come here, by a night march through forests and woods, it would take them a full three days. But the farmer had a suggestion. Monday was market day in the town; he was planning to go there by train to sell his hogs. What if Fred and Walter hid in this cottage during the weekend, then re-emerged on Monday morning in their new peasant garb, posing as farmhands? If they stayed close to Čanecký and his pigs, helping him and chatting away in their native Slovak, the police and their informers would barely notice them, not least because the train to Čadca was controlled by Slovak gendarmes rather than Germans.

And so, on 24 April, Walter Rosenberg, the boy who had once worn his hair in *payos* and run errands for the local rabbi, found himself in a Slovak livestock market, herding a group of ten pigs and listening as the traders around him bantered with their customers, cheerfully rejecting a cash offer they deemed too low by asking whether the cheeky bidder was a Jew or a human being.

It worked though. Čanecký sold his pigs and no one paid any attention to his two young helpers. He even wanted to share some of the proceeds, but Walter and Fred said no. He had risked his life for their freedom; he had done enough.

The farmer's last good turn was to point the escapees in the direction of the doctor. His place of work was not what they were expecting or hoping for: Dr Pollack's clinic was inside the local army barracks. Guarding the door were two soldiers of Slovakia's pro-Nazi army. Since Walter was the one who knew Pollack, it would fall to him to walk past those men and pretend to be a patient. He girded himself and went in.

He found Pollack's room and, as soon as he was inside, he saw that, yes, this doctor was the same man he had known in Nováky. Except he was not alone. There was a female nurse at the doctor's side. Thinking on his feet, Walter said he had come about a 'gentleman's disease' and would prefer it if the woman were to step out.

Walter could see that Pollack did not recognise him. No wonder: Walter was dressed as a peasant and, only two weeks out of Birkenau, there was stubble on his head instead of hair.

So he explained who he was and where he and the doctor had first met. And then he spoke about Auschwitz. He did it as briefly as he could; still, Pollack paled and began to tremble. Walter understood why. He, Walter, was an emissary from the grave. He was the first of the 60,000 Jews who had been deported from Slovakia between March and October 1942 – half of them to Auschwitz – to have returned to the country. He was bringing the dread news that, of all those thousands, only sixty-seven Slovak Jewish men were still alive in Auschwitz, along with 400 Slovak Jewish women.

'Where are the rest?' Pollack asked.

'The rest are dead,' Walter replied.

He explained that they had not been 'resettled', as those who stayed behind had been told and desperately wanted to believe. They had been murdered.

Pollack himself had been spared back in the spring of 1942, along with his wife and his children. But his parents, his brothers and sisters and their families had all been deported. The doctor had heard nothing from his relatives since 1942. They and the rest of the deportees had disappeared, leaving only silence. And yet Walter's words still made the doctor shake. Because now he knew.

Collecting himself, Pollack asked what he could do. Now it was Walter's turn to ask the questions. Was anything left of the organised Jewish community of Slovakia? Did any groups still exist, anything approaching a leadership?

The doctor answered that the ÚŽ, the Ústredňa Židov, the Jewish Centre, or council, in Bratislava, still functioned. It was the only Jewish organisation the regime permitted, tasked now with

representing the 25,000 Jews like Pollack who had evaded deportation and lived on. But the ÚŽ had to work discreetly. The doctor
could arrange a contact immediately. He then handed over an
address where Walter and his friend could stay the night in Čadca:
they would be under the roof of a Mrs Beck, apparently a relative
of Leo Baeck, the eminent rabbi.

There was one last task to complete. They had been talking for
fifteen minutes; the nurse might get suspicious. Better if Walter
left with bandages on his feet, to explain what had kept them so
long (though the woman might have been mystified as to exactly
which 'gentleman's disease' affected that part of the anatomy).

The next morning, still disguised as peasants, the pair walked a careful
distance behind Dr Pollack as he led them to the railway station of
Čadca. He peeled away, and they boarded the train.

They were heading for the much larger town of Žilina. Their
only instruction was to be in the park in front of the railway station
at ten o'clock. By way of cover, Fred and Walter sat on a bench and
knocked back slivovitz. In their peasant shirts and with their heads
shaved, drinking early and in public, they could pass for new recruits
to the Slovak army. No one bothered them, until Erwin Steiner,
representative of the ÚŽ, approached. He nodded to indicate that
they should follow him, and they walked the seven or eight minutes
to the strikingly modern building on Hollého Street that stood as
a monument to the confidence of the community that had put it
up less than a decade earlier. It was the Jewish old people's home
of Žilina, though since 1940 it had found new purpose as the Žilina
branch of the Jewish council. Steiner led them straight down the
stairs to the basement.

They passed the boiler room and the laundry and went through
the last door off the corridor. Few people would come across them
here, in the bottom corner of the building. There were windows on
to the street, but the glass was opaque and at the level of any passing
pedestrians' feet. With luck, no one would know they were here.

There was some food – salami, eggs, salad – and water to drink.
Soon Steiner's wife, Ibolya, joined them: she would later act as
typist.

And so, there, in that building, Walter Rosenberg, with Fred Wetzler at his side and the bandages still on his feet, began to fulfil the dream that had sustained him through the agony of the previous two years. He began to reveal the truth of Auschwitz.

# PART IV

The Report

## 20

# In Black and White

THE CONVERSATION – part debrief, part interrogation – would last several days. As soon as he heard the men give the outline of their story, Steiner understood that this was bigger than him: the ÚŽ's leadership needed to hear this. He telephoned Bratislava to speak to Oskar Krasňanský, a chemical engineer by profession who was one of the council's most senior figures. Steiner urged him to come right away. Jews were not allowed to travel by train, but Krasňanský wangled a permit and was in Žilina later that same day. The head of the Jewish council, the fifty-year-old lawyer and writer Oskar Neumann, joined them twenty-four hours later.

For the officials, the first task was to establish that these two men were who they said they were. That was simple enough: Krasňanský had brought with him the records kept by the council of every transport that had left Slovakia, for what was then destination unknown. There was a card for every deportee, including their name and photograph. So when Fred and Walter gave the date and point of origin of the transports that had taken them away, the records backed them up.

More than that, Fred and Walter were also able to name several of the others who had been jammed into the cattle trucks with them, along with specific individuals who had arrived in Auschwitz on subsequent transports. Each time, the names and the dates tallied. And each time, the escapees were able to confirm the fate of the people on those lists: with next to no exceptions, they were naming the dead.

Krasňanský found these two young men credible right away. They were clearly in a terrible state. Their feet were misshapen and they were completely exhausted; he could see that they were undernourished, that they had eaten almost no food for weeks. He summoned a doctor and between them they decided that the men should stay here, in this basement room, to recover their strength. A couple of beds were brought down.

Yet, for all their physical weakness, Krasňanský was struck by the depth and sharpness of each man's memory. It was a thing of wonder. The engineer was determined to get their testimony on record and to ensure that it would be unimpeachable.

With that in mind, he decided to interview the two separately, getting each story down in detail and from the beginning, so that the evidence of one could not be said to have contaminated or influenced the other. In sessions lasting hours, Krasňanský asked questions, listened to the answers and wrote detailed shorthand notes. Whatever emotional reaction he had to what he was hearing – which was, after all, confirmation that his community had been methodically slaughtered – he hardly showed it. He kept on asking questions and scribbling down the answers.

Walter alternated between speaking very fast, as if in a torrent, and very slowly, deliberately, as if searching for the exact word. Before the formal, separate interviews, Fred saw how Walter strained to be strictly factual, like a witness in a courtroom, only for the emotional force of the events he was describing repeatedly to prove too much. The younger man could not help himself: he seemed to be reliving those events in the telling, every fibre of his tissue and every pore of his skin back in Auschwitz. After an hour, Walter was utterly drained. And yet he had barely got started.

For the separate interview, Krasňanský ushered him into a room which he locked. It was less a protection against interruption than a security measure, given that the Jewish old people's home of Žilina was now harbouring two fugitives from the SS, with a Gestapo warrant out for their arrest. (That was another reason to keep them in this building, day and night, for as long as two weeks: if they went out on the street looking like this, they would be noticed. People might start to talk.) Either way, Walter began the conversation by asking for a piece of paper and a pen.

He began to draw a map, the distances as close to scale as he could make them. First, he sketched the inner layout of the main

Staring straight ahead, into the future. The boy in the front row, second from the right, is Walter Rosenberg, posing for the class photo of 1936–7. Three years later, he would be gone from the school – expelled for being a Jew.

An outdoor prison where nothing grew. Majdanek, the concentration camp outside Lublin, Poland, where Walter was imprisoned for twelve days in June 1942.

Kanada was another country and another world. Walter's first job in the Auschwitz Eldorado was moving bags from the mountain of luggage, every item stolen from new arrivals.

The *Alte Judenrampe*, where Walter worked for ten months. He was among the first to see the doomed arrivals off the cattle trucks that had brought them to Auschwitz.

Auschwitz II or Birkenau, where Walter was an inmate from 15 January 1943. Four of the five gas chamber and crematorium complexes were in Birkenau.

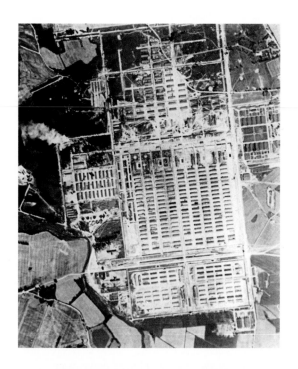

'Immediate search unsuccessful.' SS telegram received by the Gestapo on 9 April 1944, notifying them that Fred and Walter had escaped from Auschwitz. In fact, they were still hiding in the camp.

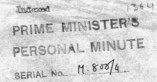

FOREIGN SECRETARY

Is there any reason to raise these matters at the Cabinet? You and I are in entire agreement. Get anything out of the Air Force you can and invoke me if necessary. Certainly appeal to Stalin. On no account have the slightest negotiations, direct or indirect, with the Huns. By all means bring it up if you wish to, but I do not think it is necessary.

W.S.C.

7.7.44.

'Get anything out of the Air Force you can.' Winston Churchill's note to Foreign Secretary Anthony Eden, sent soon after the prime minister had read a distilled version of the Vrba–Wetzler Report.

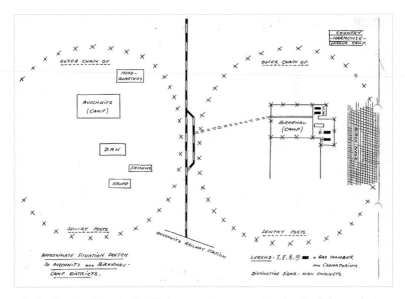

Rudi's sketch of Auschwitz-Birkenau, as it appeared in the English translation of the Vrba–Wetzler Report. When drawing maps, Rudi tended to put north at the bottom, a habit he picked up as a schoolboy.

Rudi was awarded the Czechoslovak Medal for Bravery, the Order of the Slovak National Insurrection (Second Class) and the Medal of Honour of Czechoslovak Partisans.

They called her Helena: they both thought she was the most gorgeous creature they had ever seen. Rudi, Gerta and baby Helena, Czechoslovakia, 1953.

They would always call him Tata. Zuza, Helena and Rudi in England.

What Rezső Kasztner would – and would not – do with the report would become one of the shaping events in Rudi's life. Kasztner testified during legal proceedings in Nuremberg in March 1948.

They were brothers now, bound by an experience only they shared. Rudi's partner in escape, Alfréd Wetzler, after the war.

He was a prosecutor's dream. Not only fluent in multiple languages, but with an exceptional body of memories to draw upon. Rudi at a war crimes trial, Frankfurt, West Germany, 1964.

'Why do you smile so often when you talk about this?' Lanzmann asked.
'What should I do?' Rudi replied. 'Should I cry?' Rudi interviewed for
the epic documentary *Shoah*.

A ride in a punt down the River Cam, one of his English grandchildren on
his lap, would uncork a broad smile. Rudi with Zuza's son, Jan, in the late 1980s.

camp, Auschwitz I. Then, and this was more complicated, he drew Birkenau or Auschwitz II, with its two sections, BI and BII, and multiple sub-sections, BIIa, BIIb, BIIc and so on. Between the two, he drew the *Judenrampe*, explaining what he had seen and done there. He showed where the behemoths of German industry – IG Farben, Siemens, Krupp and the others – had their factories, powered by slave labour. He showed where, at the far end of Birkenau, stood the machinery of mass murder: the four crematoria, each one combining a gas chamber and set of ovens.

For forty-eight hours, whether separately or together, Walter and Fred described it all: the transports, the ramp, the selection, during which those chosen to work were marched off while those chosen to die were ferried towards the gas. The tattoos for the living, the ovens for the dead. The two men rattled off the dates and estimated numbers of every batch of Jews that had arrived since the late spring of 1942 right up until the week they had made their escape. They spoke in particular detail about the fate of their fellow Slovak Jews and the Czech family camp. Walter admitted that the plight of the latter had been especially close to his heart, given the ties of language and background: perhaps he expected his questioners would feel the same way.

Krasňanský, often joined by Neumann, listened to it all, absorbing every word. Neumann was a lawyer by training and it often felt like a cross-examination as he pressed and pushed Walter and Fred on every aspect of their evidence. Neumann might name an old school-friend whom he knew to have been on a specific transport, say in September 1943, asking if the pair knew the fate of that group. They would give their answer, knowing it would be checked against what they had already said about that same transport nine or ten hours earlier. The officials of the Jewish council were looking for incon-sistencies, either within the testimony of Fred and Walter or between them. But they found none.

The tenor of the questioning irritated Walter. He could see that these men were interested in what they were hearing, that they were deeply engaged in it, but they were hardly brimming with human sympathy. They were officials, bureaucrats, in the business of seeking precision rather than showing compassion. Of course, Walter affected not to care – who wanted compassion from a bunch of fat Jewish lawyers and administrators anyway, he would say – but it needled him all the same.

Walter's resentment predated this encounter in Žilina. He had harboured a grudge against the Jewish council ever since that day in February 1942 when he had received his deportation summons, sealed with the stamp of the ÚŽ. No wonder they had had his name and photograph on file all this time, along with the records of the deportations and lists of names: *they* had been the ones to draw them up.

If he had asked the men across the table to defend themselves, doubtless they would have insisted that they had been forced into an impossible position. A Nazi edict in 1940 had banned every Jewish organisation in Slovakia, replacing them with this single Jewish council, the ÚŽ. The country's Jewish leaders had debated in a fever the moral rights and wrongs of taking part in such an entity. Some took Walter's view: that to serve in the ÚŽ was to do the devil's work for him and to bless it with the credibility of the Jewish community's own leaders. Others had feared that Jewish refusal would only mean that the fascist devil would perform that work himself and do it more brutally. At least if Jews were involved, there might be a chance to cushion or delay the blow that would soon come raining down on Jewish heads. In the argument that raged, it was the second group that had prevailed.

To Walter, that was not good enough: in his mind, anyone associated with the ÚŽ was a despicable enabler of Nazi rule. But there was something Walter did not know. There was a resistance cell within the ÚŽ, a secret council within the council known as the Working Group ready to go to extreme lengths to rescue as many Jews as it could. Among its key members were the very people Walter and Fred were talking to in Žilina, Neumann chief among them.

Walter knew nothing of that, just as he did not think too hard on what other options Jewish leaders might have had when confronted with a fascist Slovak government bent on deporting its Jewish minority, backed by a Nazi superpower. But he was in no mood to give his inquisitors the benefit of the doubt. It even annoyed him that these officials were reliant on the word of two young men who had risked bullets and starvation to make the trek across the border. Why, he wondered, had they not despatched one of their number to Auschwitz to see first hand the fate visited upon their fellow Slovak Jews who had been shipped out of the country? That seventy-five-odd mile journey was hard and perilous, to be sure; no one knew that better than him and Fred Wetzler. But they had just proved it was not impossible, and they had been two young men with no map, no money and their names on an international arrest warrant. Surely, Walter thought, Neumann and the others could have sent a single undercover operative with the right papers and the required resources. The Jewish council had heard rumours about what 'resettlement' really entailed: why had they not done more to discover the truth?

Walter and Fred kept talking nonetheless, answering every question that was put to them. Finally, Oskar Krasňanský took away the notes he had assembled, the words directly from the mouths of the two men, and, at rapid speed, with Mrs Steiner at the typewriter, merged the pair's accounts, distilling them into a single text. Written in Slovak, it ran to thirty-two, single-spaced pages. It included a series of professional drawings, setting out the ground plans for Auschwitz I and II and the basic layout of the crematoria buildings, rendered by an architect but based on Walter's rough sketches and the testimony he and Fred had provided. The opening page was a foreword written by Krasňanský, though his name did not appear. It explained that the report had been written by two young Slovak Jews 'whose names will not be disclosed . . . in the interest of their own safety'. It briefly set out the separate deportation history of both men, before declaring that the document would not tell of the men's entire experience but would include 'only what the one or both together underwent, heard or experienced at first hand. No individual impressions or judgements are recorded and nothing passed on from hear-say.'

Then came the crucial line, confirmation that Fred and Walter had passed the rigorous, forty-eight-hour oral examination to which they had been submitted: 'The declarations tally with all the trustworthy yet fragmentary reports hitherto received and the dates given with regard to transports to various camps agree with the official records. These statements can therefore be considered entirely credible.'

The report was written in a shifting first person plural: its first paragraphs referred to 'our' deportation from Sered' to Auschwitz; later it spoke of 'our' convoy from Nováky to Majdanek, without spelling out that the first experience belonged to one escapee, the second to the other. It then described the life of an Auschwitz prisoner and the topography of the camps: the initial journey by cattle truck, the shaving of heads and bodies, the tattooing of numbers, the colour-coded triangles that marked the different categories of prisoner, the barracks, the inner and outer chain of watchtowers, the roll call, the sign saying *Arbeit Macht Frei*, the slave factories, the hanging of attempted escapees, the starvation, the casual beatings, the twice-weekly selections at the infirmary, all of it.

Perhaps because the job of distillation was done by an engineer overseen by a lawyer, rather than by a journalist, the document was bald and spare, free of rhetorical fire. It gave the floor to facts rather than passion. And it did not declare its most shocking news at the top. On the contrary, the word 'gas' did not appear until page seven, and its core revelation – that all but a small number of Jewish deportees to Auschwitz were murdered on arrival – did not come till the following page. Even then, that horrific fact was delivered with no oratory or even emphasis; it was all but slipped out as an aside. It came after a list of transports that arrived in the spring of 1942, the last made up of 400 Jewish families from France:

This whole convoy consisted of about 1,600 individuals of whom approximately 200 girls and 400 men were admitted to the camp, while the remaining 1,000 persons (women, old people, children as well as men) were sent without further procedure from the railroad siding directly to the Birch forest, and there gassed and burned. From this moment on all Jewish convoys were dealt with in the same manner. Approximately 10% of the men and 5% of the women were allotted to the camps and the remaining members were immediately gassed.

From there, the report went on to list the transports, each one denoted, and committed to memory, by the numbers that were allocated to the handful selected from each for work:

38,400–39,200: 800 naturalized French Jews, the remainder of the convoy was – as previously described – gassed.

47,000–47,500: 500 Jews from Holland, the majority German emigrants. The rest of the convoy, about 2,500 persons, gassed.

48,300–48,620: 320 Jews from Slovakia. About 70 girls were transferred to the women's camp, the remainder, some 650 people, gassed.

It carried on in that vein, listing every transport or group of transports, until the prisoner numbers of those selected for work reached 174,000. Sometimes the entry would be terse and factual, offering no more than a place of origin and an estimate of the number of dead. But sometimes the report would offer additional information, even the names of individuals, usually fellow Slovak Jews, who had been selected for work from a particular transport. There were references to Esther Kahan from Bratislava, Miklós Engel from Žilina and Chaim Katz from Snina, 'now employed in the "mortuary" (his wife and 6 children were gassed)'. An entry for a transport of 2,000 French political prisoners, communists and others reported that among them was the younger brother of the former French prime minister Léon Blum: he was 'atrociously tortured, then gassed and burned'.

Not until page twelve did the report describe the mechanics of murder. Alongside a drawing presented as a 'rough ground plan', there was a description of the four crematoria then in operation at Birkenau in stark, strictly factual sentences:

A huge chimney rises from the furnace room around which are grouped nine furnaces, each having four openings. Each opening can take three normal corpses at once and after an hour and a half the bodies are completely burned. This corresponds to a daily capacity of about 2,000 bodies.

Referring to the diagram, the report took care not to leave out what, to Walter, was the heart of the matter: the centrality of deception in the Nazi method:

The unfortunate victims are brought into hall (b) where they are told to undress. To complete the fiction that they are going to bathe, each person receives a towel and a small piece of soap issued by two men clad in white coats.

All the key details were there: from the Zyklon B and how it was dropped through vents in the ceiling to the work of the *Sonderkommando* in removing the bodies. It detailed the typhus wave of August 1942 and the fate of the Czech family camp in March 1944. It explained that the 'internal administration' of Birkenau was carried out by a group of 'specially selected prisoners', with its own hierarchy of elders and block registrars, and identified the constituent sections that made up Birkenau II, from the quarantine camp BIIa to the Gypsy camp BIIe. It named the commandant as Rudolf Höss. Concise as it was, it sought to be comprehensive.

It concluded with a list, billed as a 'Careful estimate of the number of Jews gassed in Birkenau between April 1942 and April 1944 (according to countries of origin)':

| | | |
|---|---|---|
| Poland (shipped by trucks) | approximately | 300,000 |
| Poland (shipped by trains) | approximately | 600,000 |
| Holland | approximately | 100,000 |
| Greece | approximately | 45,000 |
| France | approximately | 150,000 |
| Belgium | approximately | 60,000 |
| Germany | approximately | 60,000 |
| Yugoslavia, Italy, Norway | approximately | 50,000 |
| Lithuania | approximately | 50,000 |
| Bohemia, Moravia, Austria | approximately | 30,000 |
| Slovakia | approximately | 30,000 |
| Various camps of foreign Jews in Poland | approximately | 300,000 |
| TOTAL | approximately | **1,765,000** |

Krasňanský showed the text to the two men whose words he had taken down verbatim and whose testimonies he had amalgamated. He wanted their approval to release it immediately. Walter read it quickly and could see its flaws. The change in first person perspective, from Fred to him, could confuse. And, given that the document was not intended solely for Slovak consumption, there was perhaps a disproportionate volume of detail on the fate of the Jews of Slovakia, down to the inclusion of those individual names.

But surely the biggest defect was contained in the words that were not there. The final text made no mention of the imminent catastrophe about which Fred and Walter had been so desperate to warn. It did not speak of the urgent threat to the Jews of Hungary.

They had certainly discussed it. In the presence of Neumann, president of the Jewish council, the pair had described the construction work they had seen in the camp and relayed the excited SS talk of 'Hungarian salami'. And yet in this document there was not a word about it. What was more, when the final text mentioned the planned extension of the camp, the area known as Mexico where Walter and Fred had hidden for three days and nights, there was no hint that this section, BIII in Nazi officialese, was apparently intended to contain a new influx of Hungarian prisoners. On the contrary, the report insisted that 'The purpose of this extensive planning is not known to us.'

Why would a document written by two Jews who had escaped for the purpose of alerting Hungary's Jews not even mention the specific threat to that community? Walter confronted Krasňanský: there had to be an explicit warning in the text. But Krasňanský was equally adamant: the credibility of the report depended on it being a record of murders that had already taken place. No prophecies, no forecasts, just the facts. Krasňanský was sticking to the promise he had spelled out in the foreword: this document would only be believed if it confined itself to what *had* happened, eliminating any intimation of what was to come. The talk of 'Hungarian salami', along with the words *Kapo* Yup had spoken to Walter, had apparently fallen foul of that standard, classified as speculation and hearsay and therefore deemed unfit for inclusion. Still, Krasňanský was at pains to reassure the escapees that what they had revealed about preparations for the mass murder of Hungarian Jewry would be passed on to the relevant authorities.

Walter had a decision to make. Of course he wanted the warning to Hungary's Jews to be loud and clear. Of course he would have preferred that the report be explicit on that point and much else. But that would have meant a delay. There simply was no time for a rewrite, for correcting errors or retyping pages, not when every day, every hour, counted. Better to get a flawed report out today than a perfect one tomorrow. Walter and Fred signed their approval.

But if Walter expected Krasňanský and Neumann to dash out of the door that instant, stuffing the report into the satchel of a messenger who would rush to Budapest as fast as a locomotive could take him, he was to be disappointed. The next day, Friday 28 April, the home for the elderly became the venue for a secret meeting of the Slovak Jewish leadership, with Neumann in the chair. They were in resistance mode, so the rules of illegal work applied: no names were to be used.

The two escapees were subjected to a final round of questioning from this group, called to defend the report like doctoral students summoned to defend a dissertation. One man, a lawyer, seemed incredulous that 'civilised Germany' was, in effect, executing people without due legal process. He returned to the point several times. Walter's patience reached its limit. He sprang out of his chair and began to shout.

*Back there, they are flinging people into the fire at this moment*, he said. *You need to do something. Immediately!*

Fred tried to restrain him, but it was no good. Walter started pointing at individuals around the table, including the lawyer, accusing them of just standing there, like pillars of salt.

*You, you, you – you'll all finish up in the gas unless something is done.*

Fred tried again to calm his young friend and eventually Walter's shoulders slumped and he sank back into his chair.

After that, Krasňanský readied the document for dissemination. He got to work on a translation of the text into a language that would be comprehensible to the greatest number of people: it certainly would not go very far in Slovak. Krasňanský decided it would be most effective if it were written in German.

Meanwhile, there was an equally practical matter to attend to. April was drawing to a close; the workers' festival of May Day was looming. That date tended to make the Slovak authorities anxious – they saw 1 May as a potential focus for anti-fascist activity – and so their habit had been to search the few remaining Jewish buildings, on the lookout for 'Judeo-Bolshevik agitators'. Fred and Walter could hide no longer in the pensioners' home in Žilina. The Working Group had arranged a safe house for them in the mountains, some fifty-five miles east of Žilina, in the town of Liptovský Svätý Mikuláš. Walter and Fred were given money to live on and, far more precious, false papers certifying them as pure Aryans of at least three generations standing. That status would give them complete freedom of movement around Slovakia. If they were on a train or in a restaurant that was raided by the police, there would be nothing to fear: these bogus documents were flawless.

Naturally, they were not in the name of Alfréd Wetzler or Walter Rosenberg. Those men were Jews and the subjects of an international arrest warrant. Instead, the papers verified the identity of two new men. Fred was to be 'Jozef Lánik', while Walter Rosenberg would be reborn as 'Rudolf Vrba'. For Fred, the move would prove temporary: he would revert back to his original name as soon as he could. But for his friend, this was a change for good.

Rudolf Vrba was not an entirely new creation. There had been an influential Czech Catholic priest of that name who had died five years earlier, having built a reputation as an energetic antisemite: he had proposed a set of measures to secure the exclusion of Jews from Bohemian life. But the new Rudi, as he was to become, was not bothered by that association, if he was aware of it at all. (Nor, apparently, was he much fazed by sharing his new first name with the commandant of Auschwitz.) All that mattered was to be free of what, to him, was the Germanic taint of 'Rosenberg'. He wanted to sever every connection with that supposedly 'civilised' nation. Walter Rosenberg was no more. From now on, and for the rest of his days, he would be Rudolf Vrba, with a name that was impeccably Czech, carrying no hint of German or, for that matter, Jew.

The two men, reborn as Jozef and Rudi, headed for the mountains. Meanwhile, the work of their lives, the Auschwitz Report, was about to embark on a journey of its own.

# Men of God

Producing the report had been a mammoth undertaking, involving mortal risk. Distributing it, ensuring it reached the right people, would prove almost as daunting a prospect. Krasňanský and the Working Group had decided they would despatch the document to contacts they had in Geneva, Istanbul and London, Jews mainly, who could be trusted to petition governments or brief officials. But a priority from the very start was getting word to Hungary.

There could be no doubt about the urgency. Just as Fred and Rudi were preparing to leave Žilina, the elderly woman who brought them food had reported with great distress that she had seen trains passing through town, filled with Hungarian Jews. 'Thousands of them,' she had sobbed. 'They're passing through Žilina in cattle trucks.'

Even if Krasňanský had excised all mention of the imminent danger to Hungary's Jews from the report – no prophecies, no forecasts, as he put it – he acted like a man who understood that time was running out. He arranged a rendezvous in Bratislava a matter of hours after the text had finally been signed off: on 28 April, he would personally hand the document to Rezső Kasztner, a journalist in his late thirties who had emerged as the de facto leader of Hungarian Jewry. What Kasztner would – and would not – do with the report would become one of the shaping events in the life of the newly minted Rudolf Vrba.

Hungary had hardly needed the arrival of an occupying German army in March 1944 to act against its Jewish population. The regent of the kingdom, Miklós Horthy, had made antisemitism a core part of his programme when he came to power immediately after the First World War; twenty years later he had passed a raft of laws restricting the lives of Jews without requiring a directive from Berlin. All of which meant that when a copy of the Auschwitz Report reached Budapest in late April 1944 or early May, finding its way into the hands of Hungary's anti-Nazi resistance movement, the immediate calculation was obvious: if Hungary's Jews faced the threat of mass murder, there was no point looking to Hungary's anti-Jewish government to protect them. Given that the government was collaborating with the Nazis, a different group of leaders was best placed to mount any kind of rescue effort: the men of God.

True, plenty of churchmen had happily endorsed the 1938–9 measures against the Jews. Still, the opposition had to work with what they had. And what they had was a handful of clerics of conscience.

First to get a copy of the report was Dr Géza Soós, a Calvinist activist who was of particular value to the resistance because he held a job, and a desk, in Hungary's Foreign Ministry. He contacted a young pastor friend, József Éliás, telling him he had something 'important' to discuss. They met in the café of the National Museum in Budapest, Soós vibrating with excitement as he explained that a document had reached him that very morning. It had been smuggled across the Slovak–Hungarian border. It was, said Soós, nothing short of a miracle. It was the work of two men who had escaped from Auschwitz.

He nodded to the empty chair that separated him and the pastor, gesturing for each of them to put their briefcases on it, side by side. As discreetly as he could, Soós slipped the report from his case into Éliás's. Then he explained what he needed. Most urgent was an accurate, clear translation of the document from German into Hungarian. Once they had that, they would need six typed copies. To be safe, those copies could not be made on office typewriters where Éliás worked, which was the Calvinist church's Good Shepherd Mission, dedicated to the spiritual wellbeing and protection of Hungary's 100,000 Christians of Jewish origin: Jews who had converted to Christianity. The copies had to be impossible to trace. Finally, and most importantly, Éliás was to get the report into the hands of five specific individuals, the five most senior figures in Hungarian Christianity. (The sixth copy would be for Soós himself.)

But there was a crucial condition: those five could not know from where or through whom they had received the document. 'Government officials must not learn that the report is in our hands,' Soós explained. The resistance's goal was to have the church leaders fully informed so that they would then 'exert pressure on the government to prevent the tragedy awaiting the Jews'.

Éliás returned to the office. There was no question of making the report public: clerics more senior than him had decided earlier that information they had picked up about mass killings of Jews was not to be shared lest it cause panic in Jewish circles and make any rescue effort impossible. So Éliás beckoned a young colleague into a small room where they would not be overheard. She was Mária Székely, a volunteer at the Mission fluent in several languages, and he asked her to read the text he pulled out of his briefcase, then tell him whether she would be able to translate it. A few hours later, and looking ill with shock, she said she would. She felt it was her duty.

She found that first read of the report agonising. She knew translating it would require absolute concentration so she took the text away to the attic room she rented from a family on Érmelléki Street, where she could work on it day and night for a week. She had heard the odd rumour, but now, laid before her, was the total and terrible reality set out in a dry text, apparently drained of feeling, as if, or so it seemed to her, the authors were presenting a recipe for the baking of bread. The language was not florid or colourful. She resolved to echo that same, spare register in her translation.

The drawings were a challenge. She had no talent for it, and after working for days on end her eyes were so tired, but with the help of tracing paper, she somehow pressed the illustrations into the purple carbon sheets she had threaded through her typewriter. Slowly, in that garret, the Hungarian edition of the Auschwitz Report began to take shape.

The work was laborious, the attic room stuffy. Székely had to go outside. She went down to the small, ground-floor terrace, clutching her papers and a dictionary. It was breezy and suddenly the wind snatched a page of the original German text, including a telltale drawing of Auschwitz. It flew against the wire garden fence where it got stuck. At that moment, an armed German soldier was walking on the other side of the boundary, on guard duty. Székely had forgotten that the Germans now occupied all the houses on Érmelléki Street.

She rushed towards the fence, but it was too late. The Nazi guard had got there first. He reached over and dislodged the piece of paper. He would only have to look at it to know that this document contained the secret of Auschwitz, that this woman and her associates had discovered it. Obviously she would be arrested, along with Éliás and anyone else involved. Worst, the Auschwitz Report would be stopped in its tracks.

Terrified, Székely braced herself for what was to come. But the soldier did not so much as look at the piece of paper. He handed it back to her with a polite smile. She took it, went back inside and, with the adrenaline of fear rushing through her veins, set about getting the job done.

Once the Hungarian text was complete, she gave the five copies to Éliás as requested, and headed to Géza Soós to give him the sixth plus the German original. Except his office was near the royal residence and security was tight. A guard checked her papers. If he had asked to go through the contents of her bag, she – and the report – would have been done for. But somehow she got through.

Now came the moment to put the document in the hands of those senior clerics. At first, the operation made great headway. The leading Protestant bishop responded immediately, writing to the prime minister on 17 May, urging the government to stop the deportations which were, he now knew thanks to the Auschwitz Report, the first step to mass slaughter. But in the same letter he threw away what could have been the church's most powerful weapon: he vowed that he would not make the plight of the Jews public.

Still, the big prize was landing the report in front of the Catholic cardinal, Archbishop Jusztinián Serédi, which the secret network of activists achieved by the middle of May 1944. Three concerned Christians, two priests and a journalist, asked for an audience. They would urge Serédi to act on what they all now knew.

The trio went to the castle in Buda that served as the cardinal's official residence, where they were received with full ceremony. Serédi entered and held out his finger. The men lowered themselves to their knees and kissed his ring. The cardinal sat down and signalled for them to begin.

They explained that the Protestant leadership was considering an edict denying communion to any official or worker who helped the Germans round up the Jews or detain members of the resistance. Perhaps the cardinal should issue a similar ruling in the name of Hungary's Catholics?

Serédi was silent for a long time. The air seemed to thicken as the delegation waited for his answer. Finally, he tore his biretta from his head and threw it to the ground.

'If the pope himself does not undertake anything against Hitler, what can I do?' he said. He cursed in exasperation: 'Hell!'

The cardinal picked his biretta off the floor and apologised for his loss of control. He wanted to help, but he could not. His hands were tied.

Later, at the beginning of June, the trio saw Serédi again, once more at the castle. By now, the danger to the Jews was not merely imminent; it was clear and present. The deportation trains had been rumbling out of Hungary in earnest since 15 May, more than a month after Fred and Rudi had made their escape. Their report had made plain what fate awaited those on board. The first transports had deported the Jews of the provinces, and now word had come that the Jews of Budapest would be next: the city was filling up with armed police fresh from the countryside. At least save the children, the trio pleaded. Take them under the protection of the church, so that they might be spirited to some neutral country, perhaps Switzerland or Sweden.

If I could do anything, I would, the cardinal said. But any plan we might come up with, the Germans would thwart.

At that moment, the sirens sounded. The city was under attack. The group rushed to the basement, where the archbishop sank to his knees and began to pray. He stayed like that, praying, until the air raid was over, two hours later. He might have used that time to thrash out a strategy with the other three or, failing that, to write a rousing public address to his flock, one that would have spelled out what the Nazis were about to do to their Jewish fellow Hungarians and demanded they rise up to prevent it. But the cardinal stayed on his knees.

Apparently, the Catholic church would not move unless the pope himself was moved. If only he or one of his aides could hear from Vrba and Wetzler directly, then, surely, Rome would act. In the middle of June, nearly two months after his escape from Auschwitz, Rudi would have precisely that chance.

It would come just as the report changed shape. For that document was about to grow stronger, fed by the only source that counted. Soon it would contain not only a prediction or warning of the fate of Hungarian Jewry but fresh, hard proof – and it would come from inside Auschwitz.

## 22

# What Can I Do?

WHEN THE SIRENS had sounded in Birkenau on 7 April 1944, signalling that a prisoner or prisoners had been missing from roll call and that there had been another attempted escape, the whispers started immediately. *Who could it be?*

It did not take long for word to spread. The fugitives were Walter Rosenberg and Alfréd Wetzler. That last name left one prisoner in particular flabbergasted. Czesław Mordowicz was a Polish Jew and a close friend of Wetzler's. They were both block registrars – Fred for Block 9, Czesław for Block 18 – and they used to meet and chat every day. Czesław had never picked up so much as the thought of escape from Fred, let alone a plan. Yet here he was, apparently gone. Mordowicz thought about how much his fellow record-keeper knew of Auschwitz and thrilled at the prospect that he might get away. *Finally*, Czesław said to himself, *the great secret of this cursed place will be uncovered before the world*.

Across the camp, the sound of the sirens, along with the names Wetzler and Rosenberg, brought silent rejoicing. Even though everyone knew that the escape of a Jew was next to impossible, that it had never once succeeded. And even though they knew that it would come at a price for those left behind.

At the evening roll call, Kommandant-Lagerführer SS-Untersturmführer Johann Schwarzhuber issued a new order: all Jewish registrars were suspended from their duties and would do hard labour, starting tomorrow. Schwarzhuber then summoned all the Jewish clerks to come to the front, where they were each given twenty-five lashes. The blows were administered by a special instrument, said to have been fashioned from the tails of bulls for extra hardness and elasticity. It cut through the flesh especially easily.

The SS were enraged by the 7 April escape. It was a humiliation. And they took out their frustration on their Jewish captives, inflicting punishment and pain on the slightest pretext. Any association with the escapees brought extra attention and suffering. Arnošt Rosin, for example, had been the elder at an earlier block of Wetzler's and was a fellow Slovak Jew: he was interrogated and tortured by SS men who assumed he must have been in on Fred and Walter's escape plan. Rosin insisted that he had had no inkling of it: in fact, he said, he was furious that the pair had not taken him with them. It was a recklessly brave thing to say, not least because it was only partly true: Rosin was one of the few people who did know of the planned escape. He had even helped the two of them prepare for it. But Fred and Walter had told him none of the details, so that he would have nothing to reveal under torture. Somehow Rosin's gambit worked. The Nazis did not kill him. Instead they beat him and sentenced him to hard labour, in the gravel pit.

Mordowicz had been given the same punishment, assigned to that same detail. During one shift, the two made a discovery. In a steep sidewall of the pit, there was a short, narrow passageway, one that had clearly been carved out as a hideaway by other would-be escapees. It had been filled in with broken stones, presumably by prisoners, perhaps to prevent it from collapsing. If the stones were removed, there was no reason it could not be used again. Over the next two weeks, when the coast was clear, the two men took turns, one acting as lookout at ground level, the other taking a spade and digging out the space. When it was done, it was like a double grave, with room enough for two people to lie still, side by side. Mordowicz stashed a can of water there, along with some bread and two pairs of over-alls, and waited for the right moment.

It came on 27 May 1944 when Mordowicz and Rosin repeated the trick pulled off by Rosenberg and Wetzler. They hid in the crawl space planning to wait three days and nights, though they would rely on turpentine rather than petrol-soaked tobacco to ward off the dogs, whose numbers had increased following the 7 April escape. But their hideout was not as well made as the one that had housed Fred and Walter. Gravel crumbled in, and the makeshift ventilation pipe did not work. They felt sure they would suffocate, if they were not buried alive. They could not hold out for seventy-two hours. Instead, after around half that time, they took the risk and emerged from the hole. Whether from lack of oxygen, lack of movement or the exertion required to clamber out, they both promptly fainted.

When they came round, they found a camp that was not focused on finding two missing Jewish prisoners but rather entirely preoccupied with the job of mass murder. Two transports had arrived that night packed with Hungarian Jews, and the SS was devoting its resources, including its dogs, to that task. As the SS corralled their victims just a few hundred yards away, Mordowicz and Rosin were able to creep off into the darkness. They crawled between the watchtowers, embarking on a journey that would see them swim across the Soła, climb on to the roof of a crowded passenger train, jumping off as it slowed on a bend, wade across the Černý Dunajec river, then trudge through a forest until they found a matchbox whose Slovak label confirmed they had at last crossed the border. It was 6 June 1944, the day of the D-Day landings.

They heard about that event from a peasant and, coupled with the euphoria of being back on what, for Rosin, was home soil, it led them to drop their guard. They went to toast what they assumed was their imminent freedom at a local watering hole and, before they knew it, they were under arrest: someone had reported two suspicious-looking men.

While they were held in a cell, a couple of local Jewish community activists had the wit to visit and slip a few dollars into their pockets. Now, rather than be exposed as Auschwitz escapees, the pair would be charged with the crime of smuggling, which entailed transfer to a different court. The pair were sent by train to Liptovský Svätý Mikuláš, which just happened to be the same small mountain town where Vrba and Wetzler were in hiding. When Mordowicz and Rosin pulled into the station, they were stunned to see Rudolf Vrba – still Walter Rosenberg in their eyes – on the platform. The men hugged. To Rosin, it felt like the most sincere embrace of his life.

After they had served eight days in jail, with Rudi in the unlikely role of prison visitor, it was the turn of Mordowicz and Rosin to sit down with Oskar Krasňanský and tell what they knew. Their testimony fell into two parts. First, they described the Auschwitz-Birkenau set-up, corroborating fully what Krasňanský had already heard from the first two escapees. But then the pair told of what they had witnessed in the camp after the others had got away, describing a death factory that had dramatically increased production.

They reported the transport that had come from Hungary on 10 May and the ones that had followed from 15 May onwards, arriving with such frequency that, they estimated, some 14,000 to 15,000 Jews were reaching Auschwitz daily. Of those, they reckoned only 10 per cent were registered as prisoners in the camp; the rest, they said, were immediately gassed and burned. They described the stream-lined efficiency of the operation, aided by the new ramp and the railway spur whose initial construction Vrba had seen a few months earlier. It now ran right through the middle of Birkenau, bringing deportees to the very threshold of the gas chambers.

Once again, Krasňanský took it all in, cross-checking and summarising their testimony to produce a seven-page addendum to the Vrba–Wetzler text, focused chiefly on the seven weeks that separated the first escape from the second. Now Krasňanský and the Working Group could speak of the Auschwitz Reports or Protocols in the plural, a set of papers documenting a newly intense slaughter in the present tense. The bloodbath was happening at this very hour. Krasňanský gave Mordowicz and Rosin money, fake papers and new names, and sent the new, updated document to his contacts – and out, he hoped, into the world.

Rudolf Vrba could find no peace. Yes, he was well fed. Yes, his feet had healed. Of course it was good to be with comrades who had travelled from the same distant planet he had. And it was a joy to taste normality again: to get a haircut, drink in a bar, meet women. But the news Mordowicz and Rosin had brought suggested his escape had been futile. He and Fred had got the word out, but it had done no good: twenty days had elapsed between their completion of the report and the arrival of the 15 May transport and in that time the future victims had clearly received no word of warning. The Jews of Hungary remained utterly ignorant of their imminent fate. They were boarding the trains that would take them to the doors of the crematoria, just as Rudi had feared they would.

During those three days and nights hidden in the woodpile, he had imagined that his revelations' impact would be instant, that the moment he and Fred told of the hell they had endured, word would spread and the imminent massacre of Hungarian Jewry would be averted. And yet, despite his escape, despite his raising the alarm, the Jews of Hungary were being murdered, at this very moment, even as he sipped beer in a Slovak tavern.

At last, in the middle of June, came the invitation he had been waiting for: a summons to tell someone with influence the truth about Auschwitz.

Early on, the Working Group had passed a copy of the report to Giuseppe Burzio, the papal apostolic delegate in Bratislava. He had passed it to the Vatican in late May, and in mid-June he could point to a result. Monsignor Mario Martilotti, a papal envoy in Switzerland, was on assignment in Bratislava and asked to meet the authors of the document. He insisted that the venue be discreet: he nominated the Piarist monastery of Svätý Jur, some twenty miles from Bratislava.

The distance was short, but the journey to Svätý Jur was perilous. For along that route was located the Gestapo headquarters for all of Slovakia as well as for the top brass of the country's military. Oskar Krasňanský decided it was too risky for all four escapees to travel together: it might attract the attention of police informers. Only Vrba and Mordowicz would go. Barely out of Auschwitz, they would have to pass under the noses of the Nazis and their Slovak collaborators. But they did not hesitate to say yes. The meeting was set for 20 June.

With Krasňanský at their side, the pair arrived at the elegantly maintained grounds of the monastery. After the desolation of Birkenau, here they were, a matter of weeks later, in the beauty of a cloistered garden. The men approached a gate, which was opened by a monk or priest – they could not be sure which – who apologised as he explained that the papal representative had been delayed, called into a meeting over lunch with no less than the president of Slovakia, the Catholic priest turned politician Dr Jozef Tiso. The official would not reach Svätý Jur for another two hours:

perhaps the gentlemen would like to meet another church representative instead?

Vrba and Mordowicz declined that offer. Indeed, the delay only
confirmed their desire to meet this man rather than any surrogate:
if he was deemed worthy of an audience with the Slovak head of
state, surely he would have the standing to make use of the information they were about to give him. He was the one to whom they
needed to tell their story. They would wait.

Nearly two and a half hours passed before they heard the sound
of a long, expensive limousine drawing up outside. It was a Skoda
with 'CD' on the plates: *Corps Diplomatique*. From the car emerged
a man in his thirties, one who struck both of the younger escapees
as handsome and youthful. Perhaps they had been expecting a stooped,
white-haired priest.

The man was ushered in, extending his hand to the two Jews as
soon as he saw them. They were taken to a room and began to talk.
They kept on for six hours straight, the words tumbling out as fast
as Vrba and Mordowicz could form them. Mostly they spoke in
German, with Mordowicz resorting to French when he saw incom-
prehension flit across Martilotti's face. The churchman had a copy
of the Auschwitz Report in his hand, but even so the escapees gave
him the whole picture, from beginning to end, how the Nazis had
devised a method to eliminate the Jews of Europe, how they were
doing it in a camp in Poland where, by Rudi's reckoning, close to
two million Jews had been murdered already.

Martilotti pressed them on the details, going through the report
methodically, line by line, yet another sceptical counsel cross-
examining his witness. He returned to a few points several times,
probing at an apparent contradiction here, a gap there, which only
added to the impression of a man who was not convinced. Mordowicz
began to sweat.

Twenty-four years old and therefore the adult of the fugitive pair,
he tried to present as sober and credible a front as he could, partly
to compensate for what he feared was the insufficiently grave
demeanour struck by nineteen-year-old Vrba. The Vatican diplomat
had given the men wine and Camel cigarettes, which they had never
seen before, and at one point he lit up a cigar, inviting them to join

him. Mordowicz declined the offer, anxious to let nothing slow their momentum. In fact, there was more to it than that. He wanted to show this representative of the pope that the matter at hand was so serious, what they had survived was so desperate, that there was no room for fripperies or pleasure of any kind. Of course they would not sit here smoking cigars, not when their fellow Jews were in the inferno no more than 200 miles away, being murdered in their thousands this very instant.

But Rudi took a cigar. What's more, he watched Martilotti and copied him, borrowing the cleric's little knife and clipping the end off his cigar, lighting it as Martilotti had lit it, then laughing at the ritual of it, the performance. Laughing, if you please. Smiling and laughing, while Auschwitz still existed. Mordowicz thought Vrba was being unforgivably childish, bafflingly so given the import of the moment.

It did not cross Mordowicz's mind that perhaps this was the teenage Vrba's way of staring horror in the face; or that it might be the bitter, cynical smile of one who had been robbed of any illusions about humanity. For many years to come, Rudolf Vrba would adopt the same seeming insouciance when describing the slaughter he had survived and witnessed, smiling as he recounted acts of unspeakable savagery, unnerving others the way he unnerved Mordowicz that day in the cloisters of Svätý Jur.

Mordowicz worried that Martilotti was unconvinced or, at the very least, unmoved by the testimony he was hearing first hand. He seemed oddly detached, never offering a judgement on the crimes the men were describing, only jotting down the occasional brief note or pausing to photograph the tattooed numbers on their arms. Perhaps the mass killing of Jews did not pierce the heart of a servant of the Catholic church. 'Monsignor, listen to me,' Mordowicz began. 'Not only Jews are being murdered there. Catholics are being murdered there also.'

He explained that Catholic priests, men just like Martilotti himself, were arriving at Auschwitz. Except they were not being killed like the Jews, herded into gas chambers. For one thing, they tended to come at night. For another, when they reached Auschwitz, they were already dead. 'Tens, maybe hundreds of trucks would come from different areas of Kraków, Katowice, Sosnowiec,' Mordowicz told Martilotti, and these trucks would be full of boxes. 'And in those boxes were the corpses of priests.' They had been shot. Their bodies were brought to the crematoria of Birkenau to be burned.

When the monsignor heard this, he put his hands to his head. This man who had been so methodical, urbane and smooth, now cried out in German, *Mein Gott! Mein Gott!* Vrba and Mordowicz watched as Martilotti fainted and fell to the floor, passed out cold.

When he came to, he asked through tears: 'What can I do?'

At last Mordowicz and Vrba knew they were believed. Rudi begged him: 'Sound the alarm,' he said, 'with all and any means.'

Mordowicz stressed that Martilotti had to hurry, that even during the hours they had sat in this room, talking, thousands more had been gassed, their corpses thrown into ovens. 'You have to do one thing,' Mordowicz said: take the report and leave Slovakia right away, perhaps for Switzerland. 'From there you send it to all the statesmen: to America, to England, to Sweden, to the International Red Cross. And, of course, to the pope.'

The priest looked at the two men. 'I promise you,' he said. 'I will do it.'

But if they hoped for an instant and public statement from the pontiff, one that would send the word 'Auschwitz' around the world, they were to be disappointed. There was nothing the next day or the day after that. On 27 June, one week after the priest had collapsed in grief – moved to that state, admittedly, by the deaths of his fellow Catholic priests rather than by the deaths of hundreds of thousands of Jews – four separate transports arrived in Auschwitz, all from Hungary. From Debrecen, 3,842 Jews. From Kecskemét, 2,642. From Nagyvárad, 2,819. From Békéscsaba, 3,118. They totalled close to 12,500 people, in a single day. Almost all of them were gassed on arrival.

# 23

## London Has Been Informed

NATURALLY, THE WORKING Group always hoped that the escapees' testimony would reach the Allied nations fighting the Third Reich. They had no clear idea how exactly it would get there; instead they cast the document upon the waters, hoping it would land on the right shore. The Auschwitz Report would be a message in a bottle.

One early copy fell into exactly the wrong hands. Oskar Krasňanský sent it to Jewish officials based in Istanbul through a courier who he had been assured was 'reliable'. But it never arrived. Krasňanský later concluded that the messenger had been a paid spy who took the report to Hungary, only to hand it to the Gestapo in Budapest.

Another copy, also originally destined for Istanbul, followed an especially circuitous path. A Jewish employee of the Turkish legation in Budapest passed it to the head of the city's Palestine office – representing those who were determined to turn that country into a refuge for Jews – who, keen to get the information to neutral Switzerland, passed it to a contact in the Romanian legation in Bern who, in turn, handed it to a businessman from Transylvania who had once been known as György Mandel but who had now, however improbably, become the unpaid first secretary of the consulate of El Salvador in Geneva, under the name of George Mantello.

The route was bizarre, but at last the report had found the right person. Mantello was a man ready to flout convention, and if necessary the law, if that's what it took to rescue Jews from the Nazis. And for him, the Auschwitz Report had a bleakly personal significance. As he read it, he knew that his own extended family in Hungary had already been deported. The words of Vrba and Wetzler, reinforced by Mordowicz and Rosin, confirmed that all of those relatives, some 200 people, were almost certainly dead. He resolved immediately to do what he could to spread the word.

Mantello's copy was a five-page summary in Hungarian, produced at an earlier stage of the report's convoluted journey by an orthodox rabbi in Slovakia, so he now enlisted the help of assorted students and expats to make immediate translations of this abridged version into Spanish, French, German and English. On 22 June 1944 he handed the document to a British journalist, Walter Garrett, who was in Zurich for the Exchange Telegraph news agency. Garrett saw the news value immediately, but he also recognised that, even in its pared down form, the Auschwitz Report was still too lengthy for easy newspaper consumption. He had his British–Hungarian secretary, one Blanche Lucas, produce a fresh translation and he then distilled the core points into four arresting press releases.

Garrett made a break from the reporters' unwritten code, which would forbid a journalist from receiving financial help from a source: doubtless for the sake of speed, he allowed Mantello to pay for those four texts to be sent to London by telegram, costly as that was. Still, despite that departure from traditional Fleet Street practice, and in welcome contrast with Krasňanský, Garrett understood the grammar of news. His telegram despatch, wired on the night of 23 June 1944, led with what was his most stunning revelation:

FOLLOWING DRAMATIC ACCOUNT ONE DARKEST CHAPTERS MODERN HISTORY REVEALING HOW ONE MILLION 715 THOUSAND JEWS PUT DEATH ANNIHILATION CAMP AUSCHWITZ BIRKENAU . . . REPORT COME EX TWO JEWS WHO ESCAPED BIRKENAU CORRECTNESS WHEREOF CONFIRMED . . . FROM THE BEGINNING JUNE 1943 NINETY PERCENT INCOMING JEWS GASSED DEATH STOP . . . THREE GAS–CHAMBERS FOUR CREMATORIUMS BIRKENAU–AUSCHWITZ STOP EACH CREMATORIUM . . . TWO THOUSAND CORPSE DAILY STOP GARRETT ADDS ABSOLUTE EXACTNESS ABOVE REPORT UNQUESTIONABLE . . . END

As soon as those words were humming along the telegraph cables to London, Garrett acted to ensure that his story – surely one of the scoops of the century – would get the widest possible distribution. The technology of 1944 allowed for few short cuts. And so, in the early hours of 24 June, Walter Garrett rode his bike through the streets of Zurich, pushing copies of his despatch by hand into the mailboxes of the city's newspapers. Attached was a covering letter of endorsement, supplied by Mantello, from a quartet of senior Swiss theologians and clerics, all apparently vouching for the gravity of the revelations. (In fact, none of the four had seen the report: in a typical Mantello flourish, he had put their names to the letter but had dispensed with the formality of asking their permission first.) And so the first newspaper story based on what would become known as the Vrba–Wetzler Report appeared in Switzerland's *Neue Zürcher Zeitung* later that same day.

Mantello's efforts had worked. Thanks to those 'two Jews who escaped Birkenau, correctness whereof confirmed', the word was out. Breaking the dam of censorship, the following eighteen days saw the publication in the Swiss press of no fewer than 383 articles laying bare the truth of the Auschwitz death camp, even if, by accidentally omitting the estimated 50,000 Lithuanian dead, Garrett had revised down Vrba–Wetzler's death toll. Put another way, between 24 June and 11 July more articles appeared about Auschwitz in the Swiss press than had been published about the wider Final Solution throughout the entire course of the war in *The Times*, *Daily Telegraph*, *Manchester Guardian* and the whole of the British popular press put together.

Churches held special masses and memorial services in Basel and Zurich; there were protests on the streets of Basel and Schaffhausen. On 3 July, the *New York Times* ran a story from its correspondent in Geneva, headlined 'Inquiry Confirms Nazi Death Camps', reporting the existence of two 'extermination camps' in Auschwitz and Birkenau, based on the evidence brought out by Fred and Rudi. Using Garrett's mistaken figure, it estimated that 'more than 1,715,000 Jewish refugees were put to death' in 'execution halls' by means of cyanide gas between 15 April 1942 and 15 April 1944.

What Vrba and Wetzler had dreamed of was becoming a reality. The truth of Auschwitz was at last emerging into the daylight.

It had come far too late for most of the Jews of Hungary. The deportations had begun in earnest in mid-May, becoming daily. By the time Garrett's story was published, more than two and a half months after Fred and Walter had climbed out of that hole in the ground, hundreds of thousands of Hungarian Jews were already dead.

Garrett and Mantello did not rely on the power of the press alone. Indeed, the reporter's first impulse on seeing the document Mantello put in front of him had been to insist that the sometime diplomat show it to the Allied governments that very day, even before Garrett had had a chance to publish a word. With the Vrba–Wetzler Report in hand, Mantello duly went to see the British military attaché, whose staff then contacted Garrett for confirmation that this unlikely representative of El Salvador was telling the truth. They told the journalist that they found the report 'shocking'.

The next day, 23 June 1944, Garrett himself had contacted Allen Dulles, the most senior US intelligence official in the neutral, and therefore crucial, country of Switzerland. Dulles ran the Swiss bureau of the Office of Strategic Services, then the lead US intelligence agency, and would go on to head the CIA. Garrett found Dulles stunned and shaken by the report. The American's response was unequivocal: 'We must intervene immediately,' he said, promising to cable the report to Washington right away.

Garrett would not rely on that promise. That evening, as he wired his story to London, and just before he got on his bike, he telegraphed versions not only to the world's press but also to the offices of Franklin Roosevelt, Winston Churchill, Anthony Eden and the Queen of Holland, as well as the Archbishop of Canterbury and the Cardinal Archbishop of New York.

And yet Garrett was not the first to feel the urge to share with the most powerful people in the world this new, comprehensive and detailed account of Auschwitz and to do so immediately. Others had made the same move, even via the same people. For all his apparent shock, Dulles had almost certainly seen the Auschwitz Report already.

In fact, the testimony of Vrba and Wetzler had travelled along multiple pathways, passed from hand to hand and across borders. One copy reached Jaromír Kopecký, clinging on in Geneva as the last diplomat of a country that no longer existed: Czechoslovakia. Armed with a radio transmitter and assisted by a courier able to bring secret messages from the resistance – her codename was 'Agenor' – Kopecký was a critical point of contact with the Czechoslovak government in exile, by then based in London.

On 10 June, 'Agenor' brought Kopecký the Auschwitz Report. Amid the horror, what leapt out was Vrba and Wetzler's account of the Czech family camp, and especially the second transport that had arrived at Auschwitz on 20 December 1943. The document said that those inmates were due to face 'special treatment' – death by gas – exactly six months later. Kopecký had only to look at the calendar to realise that was a matter of days away.

He spoke to the World Jewish Congress's man in Geneva, Gerhart Riegner, who was as appalled as he was. Together they contacted a British diplomat in Bern, Elizabeth Wiskemann, who was an expert on, and therefore, they hoped, especially sympathetic to, Czechoslovakia. Their telegram to her began, 'According report made by two Slovakian Jews who escaped from Birkenau . . .' They spelled out the imminent threat to the children and adults of the Czech family camp, stressed that 'Bratislava' should not be mentioned as the source, presumably to limit the risk of exposing Vrba and Wetzler, and made a very specific request: that the revelations made by those two Slovak escapees 'be broadcasted immediately through BBC and American radio in order to prevent at last moment this new massacre.'

Wiskemann did as she was asked and at speed, transmitting her message to London on 14 June. The next day, as requested, the BBC's services in Czech and Slovak broadcast a brief item on the looming threat to 4,000 Czech deportees imprisoned in Birkenau. The radio monitoring arm of the Reich Protector Office in Berlin noticed that broadcast. 'London has been informed,' it reported. The same office took note of the BBC transmission the following day, which warned that all those responsible for the murder of the Czech families would be brought to account, though without spelling out exactly how that would be done or by whom. The eavesdroppers of the Third Reich were not the only Germans to hear the item on the BBC. Listeners to the *News for Women* programme on the BBC's German service would also have heard it at noon on 16 June. Even in Auschwitz itself, via Kanada, there was the odd illicit radio set. And so the inmates of Auschwitz heard the BBC relay the Allies' warning to the SS not to go ahead with their plan to murder the children, women and men of the family camp.

But even before her cable had reached London, Wiskemann contacted Allen Dulles, the American spymaster in Switzerland. The two of them were often in touch, Dulles seeing the Englishwoman as a useful source of information which he tended to tease out of her with flowers, flirtatious notes and high-end meals prepared by his personal chef. 'I have just wired this,' she wrote, attaching the telegram with its summary of the Vrba–Wetzler Report. 'Could you also?' In other words, a full week before Garrett would register Dulles's apparent shock at reading the Auschwitz Report, seemingly for the first time, the American had, in fact, been given his own copy.

He did not do as Wiskemann had suggested and wire the news to his bosses in Washington, nor did he mark the document as extremely urgent. Instead, he passed the information to Roswell McClelland, the representative in Switzerland of a new US body, the War Refugee Board, with a cover-note that deployed a well-worn idiom of bureaucratic buck-passing: 'Seems more in your line.'

Whether he was moved by what he read, or simply stung into action by the publicity Mantello and Garrett had begun to generate, McClelland wrote a three-page memo, summarising the report, to John Pehle, the head of the WRB, on 24 June. He accepted that there was 'little doubt' that Vrba and Wetzler's word should be trusted, even if he did slightly downgrade their estimate of the dead to 'at least 1,500,000'. But, beyond that, McClelland was almost as lethargic as Dulles had been. He did not send the full text of the Auschwitz Report to Washington until 12 October, nearly four months after he had received it, and, even when he did, he wondered out loud if there was any point. 'I personally feel that the handling of such material as the enclosed reports cannot be considered as a positive contribution to real relief or rescue activities,' he wrote, in words that would have incensed Rudolf Vrba. Rudi had escaped because he believed that secrecy was the Nazis' most lethal weapon. Yet at his desk in Geneva a senior official of the US government was musing on whether shattering that secrecy was of any value.

On 1 November, McClelland's boss, John Pehle, decided that the

Vrba–Wetzler Report ought finally to be made public, with the full text given to the press. But even that ran into resistance. The head of the Office of War Information refused to authorise publication. He argued that no one would believe the report, that it would therefore destroy the credibility of any future information issued by the US government about the war. It took Pehle until the end of the month to overcome that opposition. Meanwhile, *Yank*, a US Army journal which had asked the WRB for material on Nazi war crimes for an upcoming feature, declined to use the copy of the Auschwitz Report it had been given. *Yank* found it 'too Semitic' and requested a 'less Jewish account'.

In fact, the words of Rudolf Vrba and Fred Wetzler would not be officially published in English and in full until a press conference in Washington on 25 November 1944, exactly seven months after the pair had completed their testimony to Krasňanský in that cramped room in Žilina. It had come so late that, on that same day, the Nazis had been hard at work demolishing Crematorium II and its gas chamber, after killing the last thirteen people who would be murdered on that spot on 25 November.

Still, the Auschwitz Report was never an end in itself; its goal was not merely its own publication. Those who wrote and distributed it hoped it would stir the conscience of the world, pushing the Allies to use their military might to halt the killing. Oskar Krasňanský had appended an afterword to the report, calling for the Allies to destroy the Auschwitz crematoria and the approach roads. Meanwhile, one of Krasňanský's colleagues in the Working Group, the orthodox rabbi Michael Dov Weissmandl – incidentally, the man who produced that five-page summary that reached Zurich – further pressed the case for military action. It fell to him to translate the report into Yiddish, but he also wrote a pair of coded telegrams, sent out on 16 and 24 May, which, brimming with desperation, spelled out what was needed.

Weissmandl intended for the telegrams, formally addressed to his counterpart in Switzerland, to be relayed to the United States, which they duly were. They reached a fellow orthodox leader, Jacob Rosenheim of New York, who in turn passed them on to the War Refugee Board. Their central message was a plea for the Allies to use their air power to ensure the 'prompt disturbance of all transports, military and deportation', and, specifically, to begin 'bombarding' the railway lines between Košice and Prešov, for that was the route along which Jews from eastern Hungary were shipped to their deaths in Auschwitz. The idea was simple to the point of crudity: to stop the Nazi killing machine, smash the conveyor belt.

Rosenheim had read the Vrba–Wetzler Report; he understood the urgency. 'The bombing has to be made at once,' he wrote. 'Every day of delay means a very heavy responsibility for the human lives at stake.'

The head of the WRB, John Pehle, took Rosenheim's proposal to the War Department, sitting down with Assistant Secretary of War John McCloy. But he did not bang the table demanding immediate action. On the contrary, Pehle confessed that he had 'several doubts', including whether air bombardment of the railway lines would have that much impact on the functioning of Auschwitz. Later that same day, he wrote a memo recording that he had 'made it very clear to Mr McCloy that I was not, at this point at least, requesting the War Department to take any action on this proposal other than to appropriately explore it.'

But that exploration was nugatory. The War Department did not undertake a study of whether bombing the railway lines was militarily feasible; no one looked for alternative means of halting, or even slowing, the transports. Instead, the operations division of the department's general staff came back to Pehle two days later to say that the bombing proposal was 'impracticable', adding the stock response: that the best hope for the victims of Nazism was that Nazism be defeated. The US military would not so much as look at any proposed operation that might require a 'diversion' from that effort. On 3 July, McCloy instructed his aide to 'kill' the idea.

And yet bombing Auschwitz or the train tracks that fed it would hardly have required a diversion at all. As it happened, American bombers were in the skies over Auschwitz a matter of weeks later. On 20 August, the 15th US Air Force unloaded more than thirteen hundred 500-pound bombs on Monowitz, the place Rudi had known as Buna when he worked there as a slave during his first few weeks in Auschwitz: that's how close the US bombers would come. To have struck the gas chambers and crematoria would have entailed diverting those aircraft all of five miles.

The bomber pilots would have known exactly where to direct their ordnance too. US reconnaissance planes flew over Auschwitz taking aerial photographs often in the spring and summer of 1944, including on 4 April, the day Walter and Fred made their second attempt at escape. The images were detailed and revealing. They showed everything the Vrba–Wetzler Report described – the barracks, the gas chambers, the crematoria, even a line of people being led from the railway track into the camp – if only someone had taken the time to look. But no one did. No one ever examined those pictures.

The Vrba–Wetzler Report never failed to shake those who actually read it. Once Pehle had seen the full version, he pleaded with McCloy to read it: 'No report of Nazi atrocities received by the board has quite caught the gruesome brutality of what is taking place in these camps as have these sober, factual accounts,' he wrote. Pehle's earlier equivocation vanished: now he urged an all-out aerial bombardment of the death camp. But McCloy did not budge.

In that, he perhaps took his lead from the president himself. It seems Roosevelt had discussed the rights and wrongs of bombing Auschwitz with McCloy, expressing his concern that it would simply see Jews killed by American bombs, leaving the US 'accused of participating in this horrible business'. Neither man seemed to consider that, for one thing, that logic did not apply to destroying the railway tracks to Auschwitz, rather than the camp itself or, for another, plenty of those calling for military intervention believed that any such deaths were a price worth paying, to stop the future killing of much greater numbers of Jews. Such thoughts apparently did not register. The inaction came from the very top.

When he planned his first escape, it was London the seventeen-year-old Walter Rosenberg dreamed of. When Rabbi Weissmandl wrote those coded messages pleading for action, they were bound for the US but it was the outstretched arm of the Royal Air Force he was hoping to summon. If the Americans refused to act to rescue the Jews from the Nazis, perhaps the British might.

The Vrba–Wetzler Report certainly made it to London. It reached Whitehall via multiple routes: Elizabeth Wiskemann had sent her urgent cable on 14 June, Walter Garrett had wired his version ten days later and on 27 June it arrived there again, this time distilled in the form of a memo drafted by a Jewish Agency official for the Zionist leadership in Jerusalem. 'Now we know exactly what happened, and where it has happened,' wrote the official, spelling out the report's significance. The intended addressees were Chaim Weizmann and Moshe Shertok, respectively the future president and prime minister of the state of Israel, but the note found its way to the Foreign Office and from there to the British prime minister. The testimony of the nineteen-year-old boy from Trnava was now in the hands of Winston Churchill.

The prime minister read the document, with its details of the mechanics of mass murder – the gas chambers disguised as shower rooms, the selections, the burning of corpses – and its appeal for bombs to take out the railway lines and the death camp itself, and scribbled a note to his foreign secretary, Anthony Eden. For a man then commanding a major imperial power engaged in a world war, Churchill's tone was oddly plaintive, even despairing: 'What can be done? What can be said?'

While the Auschwitz Report meandered slowly through the maze of US bureaucracy, in Britain it had reached the top rapidly and, seemingly, to great effect. Prompted in part by their own receipt of the report, Weizmann and Shertok headed for London where on 6 July they met Eden and pressed the demand that, among other Allied actions, 'the railway line leading from Budapest to Birkenau, and the death camp at Birkenau and other places, should be bombed.' Eden passed their request to Churchill, who responded on the morning of 7 July with a clarity and directness he had never displayed before. 'Is there any reason to raise these matters at the Cabinet? You and I are in entire agreement. Get anything out of the Air Force you can and invoke me if necessary.' Three months to the day since Walter and Fred climbed into their bunker, it seemed they had made the breakthrough. At that moment, the international distress signal they had sent out from that basement room in Žilina looked as if it was about to be answered.

And yet, master of Britain's destiny though he was, Churchill was apparently unable to ensure that his will would be done. Right away, Eden contacted Archibald Sinclair, the government minister in charge of the Royal Air Force, stressing that he was backed by 'the authority of the Prime Minister', asking about the feasibility of air strikes on Auschwitz. Sinclair rejected the idea. He replied that 'interrupting the railways' was 'out of our power' and that bombing the gas chambers themselves could only be done by day: the RAF could not do 'anything of the kind'. (The Allies stuck to a clear division of responsibility: the Americans bombed by day, the British by night.) Only the US Air Force would be capable of such raids, though even then such a mission would be 'costly and hazardous'. Eden did not follow up on the matter.

Perhaps Churchill and Eden were thwarted by their subordinates or frustrated by their US allies. Or maybe their determination to act was more apparent than sincere, the determination to be documented demanding action stronger than the urge for action itself. Either way, the Allies never did bomb Auschwitz (except once, and that was by accident). The Vrba–Wetzler Report had reached the very centre of Allied power and yet the inmates of Auschwitz would keep looking up at the sky, praying for a deliverance that would never come.

# 24

# Hungarian Salami

RUDI WOULD HAVE been as disappointed by the inaction of the Allies as any prisoner still in Auschwitz. Even so, the summoning of British and American bombs was never the chief motive for his escape. Of course he would have been delighted that his words had reached a British prime minister and a president of the United States, but neither Churchill nor Roosevelt was his prime intended audience. The people he wanted to warn were his fellow Jews.

When the report had been checked and completed, Rudi had pestered Krasňanský on this point, demanding to know if the document would get to Hungary immediately, so that Jews there would have the one precious commodity their counterparts in Slovakia, France, Holland, Belgium, Greece and Poland had all lacked: advance knowledge. If they knew what he, Fred and all those hundreds of thousands of others had not known, then surely they would not allow themselves to be loaded like cattle on to freight trains or, at the very least, they would not go quietly. They might use what tiny force they could muster, their fists if necessary. They might stampede or panic, turning every transit point into a scene of ungovernable mayhem. Some might try to escape in the chaos. Whatever form their reaction took, those who knew they were being shipped to their deaths would not make it easy for their killers. They would be deer, not lambs.

Within a day or two, Krasňanský reassured Rudi that he had fulfilled his mission, that the report was now in the hands of the Hungarian Jewish leadership, specifically Rezső Kasztner, whom Krasňanský described as 'the most important' of all of them. Kasztner had emerged as a key figure in the Va'ada, the mainly Zionist committee that, starting in early 1943, had led the effort to support and rescue Jewish refugees who had fled Poland and Slovakia to seek a haven in Hungary. On 28 April 1944, Krasňanský had personally handed Kasztner a copy of the document, in German, delayed only by the few hours it took him to make the journey from Žilina to Bratislava.

Kasztner returned to Budapest, where he read and reread Fred and Rudi's testimony. He did not sleep that night. The next day, 29 April, he presented the report to the members of the Jewish Council when they met at their headquarters on Sip Street, holding nothing back. And yet the men at that meeting did not rush out on to the streets or start hammering on doors, urging the Jews to save themselves. In fact, they said and did nothing. Part of it was incredulity. Samu Stern, the president of the council, had doubts whether the report could be believed: was it not more likely to be the product of the fertile imagination of two rash young men? If that was right, then it would be reckless to disseminate it: council members themselves would be arrested by the country's new masters, the Nazis whose occupation of Hungary was just six weeks old. They would be charged with spreading false information. The leaders resolved to do nothing that might spread alarm.

Less than a week later, there was another meeting. Kasztner went to see Carl Lutz, the Swiss vice-consul in Budapest, clutching a copy of the Auschwitz Report. They met in Lutz's official residence, a magnificent manor house in old Buda, in one of the lavish reception rooms. Surrounded by gold chandeliers, gilt-edged mirrors and epic paintings, Lutz read the testimony that Rudi and Fred had smuggled out of the darkness of Auschwitz. When he had finished, Lutz was shaking with rage and grief. Immediately, the pair got into Lutz's car and headed to an impromptu meeting with two other Jewish officials in Budapest. There, Ottó Komoly, titular head of the Hungarian Zionist Organisation, urged his colleagues to do precisely what Rudi and Fred would have wanted: to let the Jewish community know what they knew and begin organising a self-defence effort. But Kasztner said no.

Why did Kasztner, who just a year earlier had won admiration as a devoted rescuer of refugees fleeing persecution, keep his fellow Jews' imminent fate secret? The explanation lies, in part, with another secret. For within a fortnight of the start of the German occupation, Kasztner had been engaged in negotiations with the Nazis, specifically with the official now charged with solving 'the Jewish question' in Hungary: Adolf Eichmann.

The talks went through several variations, but their defining theme was a proposed swap: cash or goods in return for Jewish lives. In the first round, the Nazis demanded the colossal sum of two million US dollars; later the price would be 10,000 trucks for use on the eastern front. In return, the SS would spare the Jews of Hungary. Yes, such negotiations would mean supping with the devil, but there was at least one plausible reason to believe they might provide sustenance. For there seemed to be a precedent.

In Fred and Rudi's community of Slovakia, the Jewish leadership had opened up their own channel of communication with Eichmann's subordinate, Dieter Wisliceny, two years earlier. They rightly concluded that he was susceptible to bribery and they paid him at least $45,000 in two payments in August and September 1942. It appeared to get results: the deportations from Slovakia stopped, so that those Jews who had not been shipped off could carry on living in their own country, albeit under punishing restrictions. The leading lights of the Working Group believed it was that bribe that had made the difference.

It was a fateful error. In fact, the SS had halted the forced exit of the country's tiny Jewish community for its own reasons, not least alarm at a Slovak government request to visit the new 'Jewish settlements' in Poland, a visit that would have exposed the reality of Auschwitz. It was not the cash the Jews had handed Dieter Wisliceny that had halted the deportation trains. But the Jewish leaders did not know that, just as they did not yet know that the deportations from Slovakia had merely paused and would start up again in the autumn of 1944. In their ignorance, and convinced of their success, they hoped to scale up their efforts, devising a 'Europa plan' whereby much larger bribes to the Nazis would save the lives not only of Slovakia's Jews but of Jews across the continent.

In that spirit, they wrote to their counterparts in Hungary, assuring them that Wisliceny, now posted to Budapest, was a 'reliable' man with whom they could, and should, do business. Sure enough, Wisliceny emerged as the lead negotiator on the Nazi side in the talks with the Jewish leadership in Budapest that began on 5 April 1944, the same day it became compulsory for Hungarian Jews to wear the yellow star. Facing him across the table was Rezső Kasztner.

Almost immediately, Kasztner felt the change in his own status. As the designated representative of his community, but unlike the rest of his fellow Jews, he would now be eligible for permits to travel beyond Budapest, though he would have to ask first. Unlike the rest of his fellow Jews, he was allowed to keep his car and his telephone. And, unlike his fellow Jews, he would not have to wear a yellow star. Meanwhile, in Auschwitz, Fred and Walter were hiding inside a pile of wooden boards.

There were reasons to suspect from the start that the SS was not negotiating in good faith, that these talks were a trick, and the events of April only reinforced those suspicions. The Nazis were methodically rounding up Jews in the Hungarian provinces, confining them to ghettos which just so happened to be handily situated near railway junctions. Word came of an agreement reached by the rail networks of Hungary and Slovakia, allowing for the transportation of 150 trainloads of Jews from Hungary to Auschwitz via Slovakia. These looked like the actions of a regime determined to implement its deportation plan, not abandon it.

And then, at the end of the month, came the testimony of Vrba and Wetzler, confirming in black and white exactly what deportation to Auschwitz meant.

Kasztner grasped the implications of their report immediately. He asked for a meeting with his SS contact, Eichmann's deputy Hermann Krumey. Kasztner may even have shown the document to Eichmann himself, telling the architect of the Final Solution that he at last knew his secret: Eichmann's response was said to be a demand that the report be suppressed and its authors captured dead or alive. If the Vrba–Wetzler Report were made public, the talks would be off.

When Kasztner finally got his meeting with Krumey on 2 May, he confronted him about a train that had left a couple of days earlier from Kistarcsa, carrying 1,800 Jews, the first such transport out of

Hungary. Was that bound for Auschwitz, to the place Vrba and Wetzler had described?

No, Krumey insisted. Those Jews were being shipped to a camp in Waldsee, in Germany, where they would be used as farm labourers.

Kasztner knew the Nazi was lying. There was no camp in Waldsee. It was a Nazi fiction. Kasztner told him to stop playing games. That was the cue for the talk to get serious. Now they got down to business, hammering out an accord whose terms Krumey would classify as a 'Reich secret'.

Even so, the nature of the bargain would soon seem clear enough. The offer to spare all of Hungary's Jews receded; now the SS man held out a much smaller prize: exit permits for 600 Jews. That number rose to a thousand when Eichmann authorised the sparing of several hundred Jews from, tellingly, Kasztner's home town of Kolozsvár. The figure would rise again with the addition of nearly 200 'prominent' Jews from various ghettos around the country until eventually the number singled out for rescue would stand just short of 1,700. They would board a train – Kasztner's train, as it would become known – that would, ultimately, ferry them to Switzerland and to safety.

What the SS wanted in return was money – the Jewish rescue committee handed over $1,000 per head for every passenger on the Kasztner train, a total of $1,684,000 in cash and valuables – and, more precious still, a Jewish community that would be sufficiently pliant and passive to enable the deportations to proceed smoothly. Eichmann made clear that he did not want 'a second Warsaw', meaning no repeat in Hungary of the resistance the Nazis had met in that ghetto a year earlier. The Nazis wanted Kasztner's silence.

And they got it. Rezső Kasztner kept the Vrba–Wetzler Report to himself and the small leadership circle around him. He would issue no urgent warnings to his fellow Jews to stay away from the trains and resist deportation. He would not say that waiting for them at the other end were the ovens of Birkenau, that they should run for their lives or pick up whatever meagre weapons they could find. Instead, he would give Eichmann and the SS the one thing they deemed indispensable for their work, the one thing whose importance the teenage Walter Rosenberg had grasped as he stood on the

*Judenrampe* through those long days and nights: order and quiet. The Jews of Hungary would board those trains calmly, even obediently, because they never heard the word that Fred and Rudi had fought so hard to bring them. They remained in the dark. They were led into the charnel house blindfolded.

Worse than that, they were actively steered in the wrong direction by those they trusted. Kasztner kept the Auschwitz Report hidden away, but he did order the distribution of the notorious postcards which purported to offer greetings from those who had been supposedly 'resettled' in new homes. In fact, those messages were written under duress by new arrivals in Auschwitz hours before their deaths. Even when Kasztner's colleagues suspected that the cards were a trick to deceive the Jewish public and urged him not to pass them on, he ordered that a batch of around 500 such cards, brought to the Jewish Council by the Nazis, be delivered.

In late June, just as the Vrba–Wetzler Report was finally becoming public thanks to its circulation in Switzerland, Kasztner did something curious. He wrote to his own contacts in Switzerland, letting them know that thousands of postcards had arrived with a 'Waldsee' postmark, in which Jewish deportees reported that they were alive and well. This was nearly two months after Kasztner had had it confirmed from the SS that Waldsee was a fiction and from the Vrba–Wetzler Report that Auschwitz was a death factory. Eichmann himself had told Kasztner that the Jews were being gassed in Auschwitz. And yet on 24 June, the very day that the Swiss press began publishing information from the Auschwitz Report, Kasztner was spinning an opposing tale, contradicting the word of Fred and Rudi with bogus evidence that Hungary's deported Jews were safe. If the SS had ordered a misinformation campaign tailored to blunt the impact of the Vrba–Wetzler Report, it would scarcely have looked any different.

Whether Kasztner truly believed that his negotiations with the SS might eventually save the Jews of Hungary, or whether he did the Nazis' bidding solely to preserve the friends, relatives and 'prominents' he had handpicked for rescue – abandoning the many to save the few – the result was the same. While his talks with Eichmann went on, with his silence the apparent price, the Nazis conducted their largest and swiftest deportation operation. Starting on 15 May

1944 and over the course of fifty-six days, 437,402 Jews were transported from the Hungarian countryside, crammed into 147 trains. Almost all of them were gassed on arrival in Auschwitz.

Next in the Nazis' sights were the 200,000 Jews of Budapest.

Eventually the frustration got too much for Rudi and his fellow escapees. They knew so little of the journeys their report had made, the dead ends it had hit in Budapest, London and Washington, whether thanks to Hungarian cardinals, American presidents, British prime ministers or Jewish leaders. All they knew was that it was June 1944 and, even though Fred and Rudi had brought out their testimony in April, Mordowicz and Rosin had seen with their own eyes that Jews were being shipped from Hungary to Poland through Slovakia, en route to their deaths. What few nuggets of news they could pick up in the pro-Nazi papers suggested the deportations were continuing, even now, weeks after the second pair's escape.

Had the Slovak Jewish council and the Working Group within it not grasped the urgency of the situation? Did these people not understand what was happening? The four former inmates resolved that, if these supposed leaders could not do the job of spreading the word, they would do it themselves.

Rudi had already decided his best hope was to produce copies of the report in both Slovak and Hungarian, behind the back of the ÚŽ, and then somehow smuggle them across the border into Hungary. Now the four escapees could do that together. Except they were living illegally, on a modest ÚŽ stipend of 200 Slovak crowns per week: running a samizdat publishing operation would not be easy. And it certainly could not be done in the mountain hideaway of Liptovský Svätý Mikuláš.

The answer was to head to Bratislava, where lived an old Trnava friend who had evaded deportation two years earlier. His name was Josef Weiss and he was working now in the Office for Prevention of Venereal Diseases which, thanks to the sensitivity of the personal information it held, was very well protected, even from the police. It was the ideal clandestine publishing house, the perfect place to produce the copies they would need.

It was in Bratislava that Josef made an introduction that would change Rudi's life. Or rather a reintroduction. He mentioned that a mutual friend from Trnava was also in Bratislava, having spent much of the intervening two years in hiding in Hungary. Like Rudi, she was living on Aryan papers and under a false name – she was now Gerti Jurkovič – but Rudi would have remembered her as Gerta Sidonová. She was the girl in the pom-pom hat, the one young Walter had shooed away for looking too childish.

In that summer, 'Gerti' was just seventeen, working as a junior secretary for a house-removals company, a job Josef had arranged as part of his activities with a Zionist underground cell engaged in, among other things, forging identity documents for Jews. The group liked to place people in office jobs: that way they would have access to typewriters and other equipment that could prove useful.

Josef had mentioned Rudi's presence in Bratislava quite casually, but for Gerta it was thrilling news. So much time had passed, so much had happened, and yet she still carried a torch for the serious, brilliant, imaginative boy she had known in Trnava. They made a plan to meet that week, on a little pebble beach on the banks of the Danube.

Josef offered a word of warning. 'Walter has had some very bad experiences,' he said. He had been in a camp. He had changed.

'Be prepared to meet another man, not the one you know.'

If anything, that only made Gerta more excited to see him again.

She waited at the agreed spot. It felt like old times, back when they used to meet in Trnava: he was always late then too. But she did not mind. The sun was shining and she was in the shade of a weeping willow tree, the only sound the music of the moving river. It was so peaceful and perfect. And then, there he was.

He was coming down the path towards the beach and gave Gerta a wave. But while his mouth made a smile, his eyes took no part in it: they were filled with sadness, even despair. Josef was right. The Walter she had known was gone. This man was not much taller than the boy in Trnava, no more than five foot six inches, but he was stronger and squarer. Still, it was the eyes that struck her most. She had always liked the hint of mischief in Walter's eyes, but Rudi's were filled with sadness and something she had not expected: suspicion.

And yet his intelligence was undimmed; as they talked, the old smile would occasionally break through. And when it did, and when he held her hand, she thought she truly loved him, perhaps for ever.

Gerta stood up and embraced him, but his body stiffened. She suggested a swim. She hoped that might somehow narrow the distance between them.

But as he took off his shirt, she saw the five blue digits inked on his forearm: 44070. She blurted out the words: 'What have you been doing tattooing yourself?' A strange smile formed on Rudi's lips; it struck Gerta as not only sarcastic but cruel. Yet his eyes did not alter. 'Where did you think I was, in a sanatorium?' Gerta felt this man, this 'Rudi', had returned from wherever he had been filled with hate and, at this moment, that hate seemed to be directed at her.

There was a silence and then he put his arm around her shoulders and drew her close. He said he was sorry, but that she would understand once she knew what he had lived through these last two years.

And so there they sat, under a tree by the river, as Rudi told her, with great precision and little emotion, of the death camp he had been in from the last day of June 1942 until a few weeks earlier. He talked of transports and cattle trucks and Kanada and gas chambers and crematoria and his determination to tell the world the truth about Auschwitz. He saw the incredulity on her face. Don't worry, he said. Most people had reacted the same way, unable to believe what they were hearing.

He then reached into his bag and brought out a few sheets of paper: the Auschwitz Report. He explained that he wanted extra copies, so that he, Fred and the others could distribute them themselves. It was vital to get the word to Hungary. Gerta took the pages and, in the office where she worked, she would later do as she was asked. She did not know exactly what Rudi did with the copies she typed up: he was secretive, even with her.

Eventually, they left their shady spot on the beach, walking hand in hand, in silence. And yet that tension she had felt at the start, that distance between them, never fully disappeared. Eventually she would conclude that, somewhere in Auschwitz, the Walter she had known had lost the ability to trust anyone.

Every path the report had taken had seemed to end in a wall of solid brick, Rudi and Fred's testimony either suppressed or leading to no firm action. The escapees were doing what they could, hand-copying their own report, but the trains were still rolling out of the Hungarian countryside, still rolling into Auschwitz.

And yet, invisible to them, there was another route the report was following. Slowly, and by twists and turns, it was finding its way into the hands of the one person who might stop the deportation of the 200,000 Jews of Budapest: Miklós Horthy, regent of Hungary.

Its path began with Sándor Török, a journalist who had been interned by the Germans in May only to escape. It was Török who had taken one of the six copies of the Auschwitz Report to Cardinal Serédi, who, throwing his biretta to the ground, had sighed that he could do nothing unless the pope acted first. Now Török was given another addressee for the document. The Hungarian opposition had held back one of Mária Székely's copies, expressly for this purpose. They tasked Török with getting Fred and Rudi's evidence inside the royal residence. The conduit would be someone sympathetic to their aims, likely to be moved by the plight of the Jews and with the ear of the man in charge: the regent's daughter-in-law, the widow of his son István, who had served as Horthy's deputy. Her name was Countess Ilona Edelsheim Gyulai.

A small group of conspirators would gather often in her private rooms, piecing together what news she brought from the regent's circle with the fragments of information they could glean from the outside world. Török got himself an introduction to the countess, and became part of her secret circle. But access was not easy. The Nazis had located their headquarters right next to the residence. A German tank and a line of German guards stood directly across from the guards of the Hungarian court, staring right at them and watching everyone who came in and went out. And, however exalted her position, the countess could not speak freely. Török was to phone her each day, posing as a bookbinder by the name of Bardócz. He would ask the countess if she had any work for him. If she said yes, there was a bookbinding job to be done, that was the signal for him to make his way to the palace. Those meetings proved crucial. By the latter half of May 1944, the report had smuggled its way inside the royal walls.

Its pages filled the young widow with both compassion and shame, but another consideration pressed on her and her group. If the Allies won the war, what would they make of those eminent Hungarians who had enabled this Nazi slaughter, handing over several hundred thousand Jews to be murdered? The countess agreed to present the report to her father-in-law.

It seemed to work. The countess told Török that the regent had read the document and accepted all of it as the truth. There was now no doubt in the mind of Hungary's head of state regarding the fate of his country's Jews. He even discussed the report with one of his senior police commanders. 'These gangsters!' Horthy said of the SS. 'I read it and saw it in black and white – that they put children into gas chambers!'

And yet the deportations continued, the trains steaming towards Auschwitz throughout May and into June.

But now some of the other seeds planted by Rudi and his fellow escapees began to flower. Perhaps it was that meeting with Monsignor Martilotti in the monastery on 20 June that did it, prompting the young papal envoy to report back to Rome. Maybe it was the first reports in the Swiss press on 24 June, generated in part by Walter Garrett cycling around Zurich in the early hours, that provided the last crucial push. Either way, on 25 June Pope Pius XII sent a telegram to Admiral Horthy in Budapest. It read:

> We are being beseeched in various quarters to do everything in our power in order that, in this noble and chivalrous nation, the sufferings, already so heavy, endured by a large number of unfortunate people, because of their nationality or race, may not be extended and aggravated. As our Father's heart cannot remain insensitive to these pressing supplications by virtue of our ministry of charity which embraces all men, we address Your Highness personally, appealing to your noble sentiments in full confidence that you will do everything in your power that so many unfortunate people may be spared other afflictions and other sorrows.

The pope had not been able to utter the word 'Jews', or to make his plea public, but his meaning was clear enough. The American president, meanwhile, was not quite so squeamish. The very next day, 26 June, and just as the truth of Auschwitz was becoming ever more public thanks to the press coverage coming out of Switzerland, Roosevelt had his secretary of state deliver a message to Horthy:

> The United States demands to know whether the Hungarian authorities intend . . . to deport Jews to Poland or to any other place, or to employ any measures that would in the end result in their mass execution. Moreover, the United States wishes to remind the Hungarian authorities that all those responsible for carrying out those kind of injustices will be dealt with . . .

The pressure, unleashed by the publication of the Vrba–Wetzler Report, was unremitting. On 30 June, the king of Sweden, Gustav V, wrote to Horthy with a warning that, if the deportations did not stop, Hungary would become a 'pariah among other nations'. But it was that US warning, that war criminals would be held to account, that seemed to concentrate the regent's mind.

'I shall not tolerate this any further!' Horthy told a council of his ministers the day Roosevelt's message arrived. 'The deportation of the Jews of Budapest must cease!' Tellingly, that exhortation did not apply to the deportations outside Budapest. Those continued. The next day, 27 June, would see 12,421 Jews shipped to Auschwitz in four separate transports. The deportations would continue the next day and the next.

Despite his royal title, Horthy was not the master of his kingdom: issuing a command did not make it happen. There now ensued a power struggle inside the Hungarian government, as those bent on continuing to do the Nazis' bidding, collaborating in the effort to rid the country of its Jews, sought to resist the regent's edict. The security forces themselves were split: there was a tank division loyal to the regent, battalions of provincial gendarmes loyal to the Final Solution.

If Horthy was to prevail, he would have to move fast. Adolf Eichmann and his local fascist allies had drawn up a plan to ensnare the last major Jewish community still untouched by the hand of the

SS: the 200,000 Jews of Budapest who were the last Jews of Hungary – and, in effect, the last Jews of Europe.

This is how it would work. On 2 July, thousands of Hungarian armed police would gather in Budapest's Heroes Square on a pretext designed to arouse minimal suspicion: a flag ceremony to honour their comrades. Then, once the formalities were over, the gendarmes would quietly spend their three days of supposed leave making themselves familiar with the locations of the single-building mini-ghettos known as 'yellow-star houses', in particular working out how to block off potential escape routes for any Jews minded to flee. The trains carrying Budapest's Jews to the gas chambers were scheduled for departure on 10 July.

Except events did not run to plan. On 2 July, the 15th Air Force of the United States dropped 1,200 tons of bombs in or near Budapest, killing 136 people and destroying 370 buildings. The bombs' targets were, in fact, factories south of the capital, but that was not how it looked from inside Hungary's ruling circles. To them, it seemed as if Roosevelt was making good his threat to hold the Hungarian political leadership responsible for the slaughter of the country's Jews. Those at the top trembled at the prospect.

By 5 July, Horthy had installed a loyalist as the chief military commander in the capital and instructed him to take 'all measures necessary to prevent the deportation of the Budapest Jews'. That same night, he sent in the tanks. As the army moved in, the provincial police, there to round up Jews, were pushed out.

In the clash of wills, the regent had won. To be clear, his prime motive was self-preservation and the assertion of his own authority, rather than the saving of Jews. The deportation of the Jews of Hungary had not especially troubled him until that moment. Indeed, it would continue for the next three days, at the same intense pace as it had throughout May and June: there were five transports from the provinces on 9 July alone. There was one more on 20 July.

But the rest were stopped. One train bound for Auschwitz was even turned around and sent back, on Horthy's orders. Eichmann was livid: 'In all my long experience, such a thing has never happened to me before,' he raged. 'It cannot be tolerated!' Under Horthy, there would be no deportations from Budapest.

The Jews of the capital city were saved, for now. There were many explanations – starting with the shifting calculus of Hungarian politics, as Germany began to look like the losing side in the war – but a crucial role was played by a thirty-two-page document, written by two men, one of them a teenager, who had done what no Jews had ever done before and escaped from Auschwitz. They had crossed mountains and rivers, they had hidden and starved, they had defied death and the most vicious enemy the world had ever seen. Their word had been doubted, it had been ignored and it had been suppressed. But now, at last, it had made the breakthrough they had longed for. Rudolf Vrba and Fred Wetzler had saved 200,000 lives.

# PART V

The Shadow

# 25

## A Wedding with Guns

FEW OF THOSE saved ever knew who they had to thank, but there was one exception. She was very clear in her own mind that it was the information conveyed to her by Rudolf Vrba that had saved her life. She was the girl who had nurtured a childhood crush on him back in Trnava: Gerta Sidonová.

When Gerta and Rudi met in those summer weeks in June 1944, taking afternoon walks and swimming in the Danube, Slovakia felt like a haven compared to neighbouring Hungary where, Rudi had told her, the Jews were now being shipped to the gas chambers of Auschwitz at a rate of 12,000 each day. In Slovakia, the deportations had stopped in the autumn of 1942.

Gerta had moved to Hungary and back to Slovakia again in the intervening years, shifting to whichever of the two countries was not murdering Jews at the time. And so she and her parents had fled to Hungary in 1942, only for she and her mother to return to Slovakia soon after the Nazis marched into Budapest. Her father did not make the journey with them. Trusting in authority, he had turned himself in to the Hungarian police and was never seen again.

Gerta had only been back in Bratislava a few weeks when she saw Rudi, and when he gave her what amounted to her own private version of the Auschwitz Report, describing what he had witnessed, even handing her the pages of the text for retyping. That information proved critical.

In late August 1944, the Nazis invaded Slovakia and soon took direct charge of what they still called the Jewish question. Before long, the round-ups and deportations that had stopped two years earlier had resumed, the trains heading once more to Auschwitz. There was no refuge to be found by crossing the border back into

Hungary. By the autumn Horthy had been toppled; power now lay in the hands of Hungary's own Nazi party, the Arrow Cross, who once again set about the swift and brutal mass murder of Jews, deploying death squads and working with Adolf Eichmann to restart deportations, either in slave labour details or to death camps, killing tens of thousands. One way or another, the Nazi dragnet was still pulling in Jews across the continent, and now it was back in the place where it had all started: Slovakia.

Gerta and her mother had impeccably forged Aryan papers and held out for a while. But one night in November 1944 there came the knock on the door: 'Open up, this is the Gestapo.'

They were detained and interrogated at the Gestapo's Bratislava headquarters for a week. Gerta was in no doubt that they had to try to escape: the alternative was Auschwitz which she was convinced, thanks to Rudi, meant near-certain death. But her mother could not accept what she was hearing. She told Gerta, 'Escape on your own.' And so, when the chance came, Gerta took it alone. She jumped out of a window of the Gestapo building and ran and ran.

The decision haunted her. Even if she had won her blessing to do it, Gerta had abandoned her mother. She had only done it because she was certain what staying in the hands of the Gestapo would mean, knowledge she had been given by Rudi.

She could not tell him, because he had long left Bratislava. Following the Nazi invasion, the Slovak resistance was now engaged in a national uprising and Rudi was determined to be part of it. He headed to western Slovakia, where a Sergeant Milan Uher was leading a group of partisans, and there took an oath, pledging his allegiance to the Czechoslovak government in exile in London and vowing to fight until victory over the Germans or death.

Training was rudimentary and brief. Within twenty-four hours, Rudi had a gun in his hand and a mission. Some 700 SS men had taken over a school building in Stará Turá, charged with wiping out resistance in the area. Uher's men would launch a pre-emptive strike.

And so Rudolf Vrba, only just out of his teens having turned twenty that September, found himself in the dead of night inching towards a schoolhouse in the Slovak countryside, until Uher finally gave the order to rush the building. They hurled grenades at its windows and eventually burst through the door to spray the room with bullets.

Rudi saw at least two of his comrades fall beside him, but that did not dilute the euphoria that coursed through him. He found himself laughing with the joy of it; he was weeping with happiness. He heard the screams of the SS men inside that building, he heard them die, and it delighted him. Volkov, the Soviet prisoner of war, had been right. The Germans were not superhuman, they were not invincible: they died like anyone else.

Rudi fought in at least nine more battles against SS units and took part in several raids on German artillery posts, in the destruction of railway bridges and in the sabotage of Nazi supply lines. At one point he and his comrades, ordered to stay behind enemy lines to disrupt the Germans' communications and harass them by all available means, found themselves isolated. Partisan headquarters in the Soviet Union had to parachute in a new commander from the Red Army, who was soon killed in action. Uher returned, now promoted to captain, but he too was killed in action. By the time the Soviets entered Slovakia in April 1945, Rudi's unit was severely depleted. But he was still standing.

Those who remained took on one last operation and were then sent to a military hospital to recuperate. Rudi assumed he would be returning to the front and to combat, but, while his body recovered its strength, word came that the war was over: Hitler was dead, the Nazis had surrendered. He was now a veteran of the Second Stalin Partisan Brigade and, as such, Rudi was awarded the Czechoslovak Medal for Bravery, the Order of the Slovak National Insurrection (Second Class) and the Medal of Honour of Czechoslovak Partisans – as well as membership of the communist party.

Only three years had passed since Rudi had climbed into that taxi, dreaming of his first escape. But he did not stop to take stock of what he had seen and what he had endured. He was in a hurry. He got himself discharged and, without pause for breath, he was soon back in Bratislava, thirsty for the elixir that had been snatched from his lips when he was barely fifteen years old: knowledge.

By May he was enrolled in a special school for military veterans, allowing them to catch up on the studies they had missed thanks to the war. In five months he made up at least three years of ground, passing the exam that secured him a place to study at the Czech Technical University in Prague, in the department of chemical technology. Not many years earlier, he had been forbidden so much as to read a chemistry textbook, sharing a hidden copy with his friend Erwin. Now Erwin was dead and he was about to study for a degree in the subject.

He had not hesitated in his choice. True, he had seen where technological progress could lead; he knew what science and scientists were capable of. From the chemistry of Zyklon B to the precision engineering of the crematoria, Auschwitz and the industrialisation of mass murder had been a monument to advanced technology: it operated at a speed and on a scale made possible only by the efficiency of science. And yet Rudolf Vrba, who had lost his faith in God as a child and in whom talk of 'faith in one's fellow man' prompted an ironic smile, never lost his belief in the purity of the scientific ideal. He regarded the fraternity of scholars as his one, unshakeable affiliation.

As for where he would study, it had to be Prague, rather than Bratislava. Events had played out differently there. It had taken a German occupation for the Czechs to deport their Jews; the Slovaks had organised their transports early and eagerly, paying for the privilege, with no need for external, Nazi prompting. Prague felt the right place to make a fresh start.

It must have seemed as if the darkness had finally lifted, that the worst was over. And for many years that would be true. But what Rudi did not know in the bright dawn of 1945 was that the event he would come to describe as the greatest catastrophe of his life was not behind him, but ahead and in the future.

The decision to move to Prague was not Rudi's alone. He had his own student lodgings and he was immersed in his studies, shuttling between his digs, the library and the lab, but there was someone else in his life. Two people to be precise.

While so many of his peers had seen their entire families wiped out, Rudi had returned to Trnava in the summer of 1944 to make an unexpected discovery. His mother was still alive and well. She was married to a man, one of three husbands she would have in the course of her life, who two years earlier had been deemed essential to the Slovak economy, thereby enabling her to evade that first round of deportations.

Rudi could not simply knock on her front door. There was still an international warrant out for his arrest; it was too risky. Instead he had engineered a reunion at the home of a friend in Trnava. He sat and watched as his mother walked in. She scoped the room, looking right past him. He had changed so much. It was the friend who finally pointed in Rudi's direction: 'There he is.'

Ilona Rosenberg embraced her son, wiped a tear from her cheek, then swiftly scolded him for disappearing for two years without so much as a letter home. Rudi explained where he had been, skipping the bloodiest details, and she listened without asking too many questions. He thought she sensed in him a reluctance to say more, and if she did, she was not wrong.

But her husband had a different reaction. Back in 1942, he and Ilona were not yet married. His exemption had allowed him to nominate a single relative to be spared from deportation: he could choose either his sister or Ilona, if she became his wife. He chose Ilona, and so the two were married. His sister was deported.

Now, thanks to Rudi, he knew what that decision of his two years earlier had meant. He was so devastated that when the deportations resumed a few months after Rudi's return, in September 1944, he quietly lined up to board one of the trains. He wanted to share the fate of his sister; he gave himself up to it. Rudi described it as suicide by deportation. Eventually Ilona herself would be deported. She was not shipped to Auschwitz, but to Theresienstadt in what she still thought of as her home country – and she, like her son, survived.

The other person of influence was the woman whose life Rudi had saved. Gerta Sidonová and Rudi were now an item, she a medical student in Prague, both of them rushing through an accelerated version of the education they had been denied. They would meet in his undergraduate room and make awkward, faltering love. They were free; they could have been together every night if they had wanted to be. But they were not. For Gerta at least, there was something missing. She wondered if it was her fault. Rudi would say that she lacked both passion and experience, but she wondered if she simply did not love him enough. Whatever the reason, their lovemaking lacked the tenderness, the gentleness, she craved. Instead she felt it carried a trace of violence. Maybe if they were married, that problem would disappear.

In the summers, they would take holidays but not always together. In that first vacation, in the summer of 1946, Rudi went back to Bratislava to join up with Wetzler, Mordowicz and Rosin: they were a band of brothers now, bound by an experience next to no one else shared. They were among the tiny handful of Jews who had broken out of Auschwitz.

Many survivors of that camp, and of the event that would gradually become known as the Holocaust, would vow never to set foot in Poland again. For them, that country would forever be associated with the mass murder of their fellow Jews; they could not bear to tread on soil they imagined to be drenched in blood. Others managed it, but only after an interval of many decades. Yet Rudi went back cheerfully and within just four years of his escape. What's more, he boarded a train to get there. In the summer of 1948, he and Gerta travelled to Poland on holiday.

They were part of a group of students. Voluntarily, they gathered at Prague station and headed east, steaming towards the country where Rudi had been enslaved and where Rudi and Gerta's fellow Jews had been murdered in their millions. They reached Kraków and then Warsaw, walking around a city of rubble and ruins. A student guide pointed out the sights. 'This was the ghetto,' he said at one point, 'where the Warsaw Jews were killed by the Germans during their uprising. The only good thing Hitler did.'

The group stood in silence. Gerta feared Rudi would attack the guide. But Rudi kept silent and the group headed away. Both of them badly wanted to be back in Prague.

The years went by, Rudi and Gerta walking along the riverbank, pausing at their favourite stop, a little island under the Charles Bridge called Kampa, sitting on a bench they considered their own. One late Sunday afternoon, over tea and cake, Rudi asked Gerta to marry him. It was what Rudi's mother, known to her future daughter-in-law as Ilonka, had been urging for ages: she believed Gerta was smart and good-looking and, besides, she was an orphan. It was Rudi's duty to marry her. Their friends were just as enthusiastic. Everyone considered them the perfect couple: clever, attractive, strong. If the pair harboured misgivings, they kept them quiet, hoping they would be dissolved in the fizz of wedding champagne.

The couple married on 16 April 1949, not in synagogue but in Bratislava's town hall, the vows in Slovak rather than Hebrew. The bride wore dark navy rather than white. Whatever hold tradition might once have exerted was gone.

The night before the wedding, Gerta had slept badly. She was worried that she was making a mistake. The ceremony, and the party afterwards in Ilonka's flat, did not help. The alcohol flowed, Rudi got drunk and tried to kiss the bride's best friend, Inge. The band of Auschwitz brothers was in attendance – Fred Wetzler was a witness to the marriage, Arnošt Rosin was best man – but that only made things worse. Czesław Mordowicz had brought a couple of guns, which the men were taking apart and reassembling. Gerta found it distressing.

Still, marriage, not the wedding, was the thing. Soon they would have their own home. In newly communist Czechoslovakia, it was not easy to get a flat but Rudi's status as a former partisan put him at the front of the queue. He was allocated a one-bedroom apartment in the Dejvice neighbourhood of Prague, close to the castle and the city centre. Perhaps now their new lives could begin.

They immersed themselves in their work, Rudi completing his degree in organic chemistry and signing on for a PhD that would see him specialise in the emerging field of biochemistry of the brain. Gerta, meanwhile, graduated from medical school and moved on to studying the physiology of the nervous system. Their labs were near to each other and to their flat. They should have been happy.

And yet the gap that existed between Rudi and his wife remained. The boy who had grown up in Trnava had become a very different man. Sometimes Gerta would come home and find him drinking vodka alone. Or he would get possessive and fly into a jealous rage. Once they were on a tram heading home from a production of *The*

*Cherry Orchard.* Gerta smiled as she showed her ticket to the conductor. Rudi started shouting: 'You're flirting with the conductor, you slut.' The rest of the passengers could hear, but she said nothing. When an injury to her arm necessitated physiotherapy, Rudi accused his wife of having a lesbian affair with the therapist.

The paranoia was not only directed at her. He would complain that his colleagues in the lab were trying to sabotage him. 'They hid all the scissors, so I couldn't cut the filter paper to the right size and do my experiment,' he would say. There was an explanation, obvious and ready: Auschwitz had left him that way, stripping him of all trust. And yet Gerta wondered if it might not be the other way around: that it was not that Rudi had become paranoid because he survived Auschwitz, but rather that he had survived Auschwitz in part because by then he had already learned to be paranoid, trusting almost no one. Maybe the behaviour she was witnessing was not the effect of Rudi's survival, but its cause.

Whatever the explanation, and though to Gerta he remained the handsome, sharp heroic man who had saved her life, Rudi was hard to live with. Marriage had not eased that, nor had sharing a home together. Perhaps children would make the difference. And so, on 26 May 1952, a baby girl arrived: they called her Helena, partly in deference to Rudi's mother, and partly because they both thought she was the most gorgeous creature they had ever seen, her thick black hair and beauty making her a match for Helen of Troy. When Rudi held Helena for the first time, he told his wife that all the pain he had endured in Auschwitz had been worth it, just to know the joy of this moment. He had never guessed he could be so happy. Two years later, on 3 May 1954, another daughter arrived. She had delicate white skin and fluffy blonde hair. They named her Zuzana, but she was always Zuzka or Zuza.

They were a family now, with stimulating professional lives and a relatively privileged position in the society taking shape around them. And yet things were not right. Rudi and Gerta would clash, even over apparently trivial things. In 1954, nearly a decade after the war's end, food was still heavily rationed in Czechoslovakia. Children were entitled to an extra allocation of two eggs a week, along with some sugar and butter. Gerta put those rations aside, so that she could surprise the girls with a breakfast treat of pancakes. When the chosen morning arrived, Gerta looked for the ingredients, but the eggs had vanished. Just as he had done during those toddler raids on the family henhouse, Rudi had taken them. Gerta was furious with him for that. Only many years later did it strike her that Auschwitz had taught its inmates that if there was food available, you took it.

The two argued when they were together and spent more time apart. At night Rudi would go out drinking with his friends, coming home long after his wife and daughters were asleep. When he got back in the early hours, he would not tiptoe in but fling the door open, wake up the children and expect them to start playing with him. When he flagged an hour or so later, he left it to Gerta to resettle the girls and get them back to sleep, and to deal with their tired crankiness the next morning.

He was also having multiple affairs. Some of them were just sex. But even when he fell in love with another woman, he was adamant that he would not leave his wife – because of Helena and Zuza.

Eventually, it became too much for Gerta. She said she wanted a divorce: their home was tense and unhappy and it was not a good environment for the girls. Rudi would not hear of it. He loved his children and they loved him back. Gerta accepted that was true. They would try a separation, though with the housing shortage being what it was, they would have to separate within the same small apartment. She and the girls would live in the bedroom, Rudi would have use of the living room.

That too did not work out. One night, Gerta heard the front door open and two drunken voices. Rudi had brought a woman back to the flat. The pair went into the living room where they proceeded to have sex on the sofa, loud enough to wake the children. That night Gerta resolved that separation was not enough. She wanted a divorce. In time, Rudi agreed – on condition that Gerta paid the legal fees, he kept the flat and she and the girls moved out.

That hardly reduced the acrimony. In March 1956, Gerta was on board a plane heading to Paris for a conference, a rare chance to glimpse life on the other side of the Iron Curtain. Moments before take-off, an agent of the SNB, the Czech secret intelligence service, appeared at the door of the aircraft and escorted her off. He explained that the agency had received information suggesting she was about to defect to the west, along with her children. Only when the agent was persuaded that she had no such intention did he reveal who had denounced her: it was Rudolf Vrba.

Was this paranoia on her ex-husband's part? Later Gerta would conclude that it was more likely a desire for revenge. Rudi was still angry that his wife had left him.

Each levelled grave accusations against the other, which later they would deny ever making. In Rudi's recollection, Gerta had threatened to tell the authorities about friends of his who had criticised the communist regime and, worse, she had argued in court that divorce was necessary because Rudi was 'not able to guarantee a socialist education' for their children. Gerta would later insist she had done nothing of the kind. But she would also become forgiving, of both Rudi and her younger self. They were so young. And, she would come to understand, they were badly damaged. Both her parents had been murdered by the Nazis; he had spent two years inside the murder machine.

In post-war Czechoslovakia, politics barged into the most intimate corners of a life. But in the professional realm its elbows were especially sharp. His spell as a partisan had made Rudi initially sympathetic to the communist project. He remembered that, when others had been accommodating themselves to fascism, it was socialists who had been determined to resist and who had helped him in his first, doomed effort at escape. In the immediate afterglow of the victory against Nazism, he could even succumb to idealism about a new future of equality and brotherhood. That did not last long.

In 1947, he noticed that he was being followed. When he got back to his flat, he saw that his things had been interfered with. He spoke to friends, and discovered that some men had been sniffing around, asking questions about him. Rudi was determined to track down the man responsible for this unannounced investigation and eventually he found him. But all the official would say is that he 'wished to help'.

It would not be until February 1948, when the communists seized complete control of the Czechoslovak government, that Rudi understood. A poster had gone up at the university, and Rudi's name was on it. He had been named as a 'non-political' member of the action committee that would now rule the institution. It was the first he had heard of it, but it explained why the men had been snooping around a year earlier: the communists had been checking Rudi out, to determine whether he was acceptable. Clearly, he had passed the test. Soon they asked him to fill in as chair of the action committee, leaving no doubt that it would be dangerous to refuse.

A few weeks later, he was told there were too many 'unworthy' students at the university. He was to work through the student roll, removing 'bourgeois' elements and active anti-communists, while retaining party members and those of working-class backgrounds. He refused. It would be discrimination, he said, at odds with the entire ethos of a scholarly institution. The committee told him that, if he did as he was asked, he would be committing no 'moral offence'. He could say he was simply obeying 'higher orders'. Rudi replied that that was the excuse used by the Nazis. He would not do it.

The committee asked for his resignation and a public confession of his 'failures'. He gave them what they wanted and retreated into his studies, gaining his doctorate in 1951. But when his grant ran out the following year, he learned the price of his political disgrace. He could not get a research job anywhere. He ended up as a chemist on the night shift in a penicillin factory. He was Dr Vrba now, but earning a technician's wage.

When eventually he found a way out – offered a place in a friend's lab to explore brain biochemistry – it came with a strict condition: he would have to work in the basement and remain as inconspicuous as possible.

That was wise advice even beyond the lab. The climate had become much colder in Prague, with the authorities cracking down on those who did not fit the new socialist paradise. Friends of Rudi's had disappeared overnight, never to be seen again. A queasy feeling of déjà vu struck in 1952, when Rudolf Slánský and thirteen other senior officials of the Czechoslovak communist party were arrested and charged with ideological deviation. They were accused of straying into 'Titoism and Zionism'. Ten of them, including Slánský, were Jews. Eleven, including Slánský, were hanged.

Rudi was dispirited by this turn of events, but hardly shocked. In all the time he had lived in Prague after the war, no one had ever so much as asked him about Auschwitz. He could not decide if that was because the topic was taboo, or if it was simply of no interest to those around him, but the result was the same. Rudi went along to the annual Auschwitz commemorative evening organised by the Union of Anti-fascist Fighters in Prague, but even there nobody mentioned the fate of the Jews. He heard plenty about the heroism of the Czech communists and the suffering of other Czechs who had resisted the Nazis. But about the Jews, not a word. Not even about the Czech children of the family camp, gassed with their parents. Some of them had died singing the Czech national anthem, but their country did not want to know.

For four years, Rudi worked in that basement and in time it brought a professional breakthrough. A senior scientist at Moscow University noticed a paper he had written and, before long, that stamp of implicit Soviet approval meant Rudi was moved out of the cellar and into a well-appointed lab, his status as a non-person revoked. But he was living under a regime whose antisemitism was now naked and undeniable. His marriage was over. And he was lonely. He could not turn to his escape partner, because he and Fred Wetzler had lost touch, their friendship souring once Fred married. Etela Wetzlerová had been a prisoner in Auschwitz. But instead of that common experience cementing a connection between Fred's bride and his escape partner, it made Rudi suspicious: what, he could not help but wonder, had Etela done in that camp to buy her survival? Had she been a *Kapo*?

Rudolf Vrba, whose greatest hunger had been for freedom, did not feel like a free man in the Prague of the 1950s. And so, once again, his mind turned to escape.

# 26

# A New Nation, a New England

HE HAD LEARNED in Auschwitz that escape was a science whose disciplines could not be rushed. They required time and patient study. If he was to break out of communist Czechoslovakia, he would have to get it right first time. If he tried and failed, he would make his situation much worse.

Once again, it was his job that made the difference. The interest his scientific paper had sparked in Moscow led to publication in the USSR's pre-eminent journal in the field: *Progress of Modern Soviet Biology*. He was the first Czechoslovak biologist to have won such recognition. His reward came in the form of a passport and the right to attend conferences or give lectures abroad. In the next couple of years, he travelled to Denmark, Ukraine and Russia – and came back each time. One of those scientific gatherings, in 1954, was in Poland. The hosts organised a bus tour to Auschwitz. Ten years after his escape, Rudi climbed on board the bus and went to take a look. As his colleagues moved around the site, full of questions, Rudi did not let on that he had been there before. What would have been the use? As far as Rudi was concerned, no one who had not experienced it could understand it.

In 1958, an invitation arrived to attend back-to-back conferences in Strasbourg and Vienna. Once again, he applied for permission. He would follow the usual drill. If he received official consent, he would travel to the airport where his passport, which was kept at the Ministry of Science, would be handed to him, allowing him to make an authorised exit. Since he had travelled to the west before without incident, the permission came through. Everything was going to plan.

Except Rudi was not the teenager Walter Rosenberg had been.

In Auschwitz, he had had no one to look out for but himself; he had had nothing to lose but his own life. Now, though, he had two children whom he loved. They were no longer living under the same roof, but they often stayed in Rudi's apartment. They kept some of their toys there. Somehow he could not bear to imagine his children being parted from their playthings for ever.

And so, perhaps a week before he was due to leave for Strasbourg, he visited his ex-wife. He said he was going to teach in the Soviet Union for a year and wanted to drop off the girls' toys. Gerta took them from him, but she was suspicious. She asked around and learned that while he had made no mention to friends or colleagues of a Moscow sabbatical, Rudi had been invited to the Fourth International Congress of Biochemistry in Vienna. The gathering was scheduled to last for only a few days, which meant there was no reason for Rudi to have returned the children's things. Unless he was not planning on coming back.

Rudi did not know it, but Gerta had also been dreaming of escape. She had met and fallen in love with a British scientist, Sidney Hilton, who was a regular visitor to Prague. But if she was the ex-wife of a defector to the west, Gerta would come under intense state scrutiny: she would never be able to leave. She and her daughters would be trapped. Yet she had learned from the master, her former husband. She now plotted an escape of her own.

She too had a scientific conference to attend, this one in Poland. With a visa that included permission to return to Czechoslovakia via any country in Europe, she devised an elaborate, and audacious, plan. She would go to the meeting in Poland, steal back, undetected and on foot, into Czechoslovakia via the Krkonoše Mountains, return to Prague, scoop up Helena and Zuzka, then aged just six and four, before making the same mountain trek, on foot and still undetected, with the children back into Poland. From there, and by forging the required documentation for the girls with her own hand, the three would fly to Copenhagen – and to freedom.

Which is how it came to be that Rudi and Gerta, the childhood sweethearts from Trnava, tore through the Iron Curtain to start a new life on the very same day. They had not co-ordinated it. On the contrary, each would later say they were prompted to act by fear that the other would get away first. But, as fate would have it, while his infant daughters and ex-wife were scrambling up Mount Sněžka in the mist and rain, before making a slippery, six-hour hike downhill to reach Poland, Rudi entered Vienna airport. On that day, the Vrbas became a family troupe of escape artists. For when Rudi bought a ticket, it was not for a short flight back home to Prague. He was heading instead to a country not much older than his children. His destination was Israel.

This was no journey of Zionist homecoming. For Rudi, it was more pragmatic than that: he had chosen Israel chiefly as a gateway to the west, a country outside the communist bloc where he could be guaranteed entry. As a Jew under the law of return, Israeli citizenship would be automatic.

Within six weeks of his arrival in Israel, he was offered a position in the United States. He was thrilled and applied for a visa right away. But he did not get it. The US authorities of 1958 were not well disposed to former members of the Czechoslovak communist party, whatever explanation they might offer. Rudi got a post instead in the biochemistry department of the Veterinary Research Institute, an arm of Israel's Ministry of Agriculture, in Beit Dagan, a small, unglamorous town south of Tel Aviv.

Rudi did not take to Israel. Partly he found it too clannish. The country's rhetoric talked of Jewish unity, but the reality he saw were groups of people clustered in tribes: German Jews over here, Hungarian Jews over there. He had no great desire to be defined once more by the category of Slovak Jew. Nor was he much moved by the romance of a perennially persecuted nation at last capable of defending itself. As far as he was concerned, he had already defended himself.

But there was something more painful. He looked around this new state and, often in high places, he saw the very individuals he believed had failed the historic test that had confronted them all less than fifteen years earlier. Among them were the Slovak Jewish leaders – the likes of Krasňanský and Neumann – who he believed had failed twice over: first by making the Nazi deportations possible through drawing up the very lists that had sent Rudi to Auschwitz, and then, after Fred and Rudi had escaped, failing to spread word of their report when it still might have saved more lives. These men were now comfortable and settled in a new land. They were alive when so many others were dead.

The wartime behaviour of those Jewish leaders was a radioactive issue in the Israel that Rudolf Vrba had just landed in. In August 1952, Malkiel Gruenwald, a pamphleteer in the cause of right-wing 'Revisionist' Zionism, had published a denunciation of the man who now styled himself as Israel Rudolf Kasztner. Gruenwald was an elderly Hungarian Jew who had lost fifty-two of his relatives to the Nazis and he pointed the finger at Kasztner, now an official of the state, a spokesman for the Ministry of Commerce and Industry and a would-be member of Israel's parliament for the ruling Mapai party. Gruenwald's philippic accused Kasztner of collaborating with the Nazis to save his own skin, along with a handpicked group of nearly 1,700 others, at the expense of hundreds of thousands of Jewish lives.

Because Kasztner was a government official, this was no private matter. The attorney general of the young state sued Gruenwald for criminal libel. The trial lasted a year, attracting huge interest from both press and public, domestic and foreign, as it became clear that, in truth, it was Kasztner, not Gruenwald, who was in the dock. Was he a dogged rescuer who had used every wile and ruse to save 1,684 Jews from the gas chambers? Or had he helped smooth the Nazis' path to murdering the Jews of Hungary, rewarded with the right to smuggle out his own friends and family along with a few chosen notables? Did he believe that by negotiating with the Nazis he was buying time for Hungary's Jews? Or did he understand that, on the contrary, he was buying time for the SS to murder them? A libel trial in Jerusalem had become the forum for the infant Israel to wrestle with what the German-Jewish political theorist Hannah Arendt would later call the 'darkest chapter in the whole dark story': the role Jewish leaders such as Kasztner were accused of playing in the destruction of their own people.

Running through the proceedings were variations on the same, pivotal question: what did Kasztner know and when, exactly, did he know it? And in that argument, the report written by Fred Wetzler and Rudolf Vrba was central. Gruenwald's lawyer accused Kasztner of keeping the Vrba–Wetzler Report from those who needed to see it. He said that the 'VIP train' for Kasztner's relatives and friends was the Nazis' reward for his silence.

A turning point came on 25 February 1954 with the courtroom revelation that Kasztner had been a helpful contact for the SS not only when the Nazis had a knife at the throat of the Jews – when the desperation of the times might indeed have called for desperate measures – but after the war too. When he could no longer claim that he was trying to save Jews by negotiating with the SS, Kasztner had acted as a character witness for some of Eichmann's most vicious henchmen. He had travelled to Nuremberg in 1947 and had vouched in writing for SS-Standartenführer Kurt Becher, the man charged with the looting of Jewish-owned economic assets in Hungary, saving him from prosecution as a war criminal. Later it would emerge that Kasztner had produced similar testimonials for several senior SS officials he had dealt with, including Becher's commanding officer, Obergruppenführer Hans Jüttner, as well as the two men with whom he struck his eventual bargain: Obersturmbannführer Hermann Krumey and Hauptsturmführer Dieter Wisliceny. Kasztner had even stayed in touch with the SS men's families. He had written to Krumey's wife offering to send 'food packages'. Perhaps Kasztner's motivation was less compassion for Nazis in need than a blackmailed man's fear of exposure.

The trial was only narrowly a contest of two Hungarian Jews, Kasztner versus Gruenwald. It was also a battle between Israel's ruling Labour party and the rightist, Revisionist opposition. It was a clash too between a new Israel that imagined itself fearless and strong in the face of all enemies, and what it saw as the Jewish past, a diaspora of weaklings that had let itself be led into the gas chambers like sheep to the slaughter and whose leaders had tried to cut a deal rather than fight back. To his defenders, Kasztner was a convenient vessel into which the new state could pour all its rage and its shame. 'They need someone to blame,' Kasztner's lover, Hansi Brand, told him during the trial.

On 22 June 1955 the judge delivered his ruling, and it was damning. He concluded that the one-time leader of Hungarian Jewry was guilty of 'collaboration in the fullest sense of the word', that he had 'sold his soul to the devil', making a diabolical bargain in which the lives of most of Hungary's Jews were traded for a privileged few. Central to his crime was his failure to share knowledge. Thanks to the words of Vrba and Wetzler, Kasztner had known the destination of those trains; he knew what Auschwitz meant. But he had kept that knowledge to himself. He had not urged his fellow Jews to resist or escape. On the contrary, he had denied them the essential spur to such action: the facts that spelled out their fate.

The judgment shook Israeli society, triggering a political crisis that would eventually bring down the government. The attorney general appealed against the judge's decision, so that a case that touched on the most neuralgic spot in the psyche of an ancient people and a new state – probing how its leaders had handled the threat of murderous eradication – would now move to its highest court.

Kasztner worked on the appeal, eking out a living in the cramped office of *Új Kelet*, the same small, Hungarian-language newspaper that had operated in pre-war Kolozsvár and was now reborn in Tel Aviv. It was after a night shift there in March 1957 that he parked his car and noticed two young men approach, with a third loitering behind. One of the men asked if he was 'Dr Kasztner'. When he said that he was, the man held out a gun and pulled the trigger. But it misfired. Kasztner bolted out of the car, shoving the gunman aside, only for the assailant to shoot again, twice. Kasztner collapsed on the street, the blood draining from him. He was rushed to hospital where he died from his wounds nearly a fortnight later.

The following January, the five-judge panel of the Supreme Court delivered what was now a posthumous decision. They ruled in Kasztner's favour by four to one. They held that it was unjust to judge a man with knowledge that was only available in hindsight. They accepted that Kasztner had in good faith believed that he was engaged in an effort to save the many, rather than just the few, even if that belief proved fatally misguided. The presiding judge said: 'Judge not thy neighbour until thou art in his place.'

This, then, was the country Rudolf Vrba had entered as a new citizen, a country torn apart by a case in which his own actions had played a critical part. The Supreme Court was keen to smooth over that divide, to soothe the pain. The new Israel wanted the Nazi destruction of the Jews to be in the past, the province of historians. Except for Rudolf Vrba, still in his early thirties, the past was not dead. It was not even past.

He stayed in Israel for little more than eighteen months. Once he learned that his children and his ex-wife were in England, he applied for a visa and work permit and made plans to head there. And so, as the 1960s got under way, Rudi finally achieved the goal that had inspired, but eluded, the teenage Walter Rosenberg nearly two decades earlier: he arrived in London.

He had almost no money, but early on he had a stroke of luck. He met again the woman who had once rewarded him with cake for pretending to be her child with a treacherous lover. Now living in London, she lent him enough money to furnish his flat. All these years later, in England rather than provincial Slovakia, she was still what his mother would have called a 'kept woman'.

His job was in the neuropsychiatric research unit of the Medical Research Council, based in Carshalton in Surrey. Now he had a chance to build on the work he had been doing in Prague and that had got him noticed in Moscow. For several years, he had been focused on understanding the details contained in the mystery of how cells maintain themselves, how they interact with other cells, how they respond to the demands of neighbouring cells, how they find, absorb and consume energy, how they repair, how they divide and, importantly, how they die. That last question mattered especially. In Rudi's work, death was inescapable because death was an indispensable part of all biological life. Even the healthy life of a complex animal depended on a process of death by selection. That was the term of art: *selection*. Later biologists would refer to the phenomenon as apoptosis, or even programmed cell death.

Did Rudi detect a reminder of his past life as he peered at a microscope slide or checked cell culture dishes on the outskirts of south London? The research he had begun in Prague and now continued in Carshalton was concerned chiefly with what happened to cell tissue when the host creature was subjected to stress: what exertion, for instance, did to the brain or the heart, and how the cell metabolised glucose and oxygen to do all that was required of it. In his papers for the scientific journal *Nature*, which were appearing with some regularity now, Rudi described the experiments he had performed, using what were at the time standard laboratory practices, with rats as his captives and himself as their captor. For one study, he had divided the animals into two groups of six and forced them to swim for four and a half hours. Then, after 'cessation of swimming, the rats were thrown into liquid air and frozen in vivo. The frozen brains were taken out, homogenized at low temperature by crushing into fine powder . . .' For another, 'the animals were killed by decapitation, and the blood (1 ml.) was immediately collected . . . Brain (whole, except for cerebellum), heart, liver and a sample of the gastrocnemius muscle were rapidly removed and frozen in liquid nitrogen . . .' By 1964, he was working with mice, injecting them before killing them at fifteen-minute intervals, once more dropping them into liquid nitrogen. Each time, he was asking the same question, one that he had himself faced long before he ever set foot in a laboratory: what happens to a living creature when confronted with extreme, mortal stress?

From the start, Rudi was aware that he was but one part of an international effort that had preceded, and would outlive, his own career. Under way was a global campaign to understand the cell and how it works that involved evolutionary biologists, embryologists, biochemists, geneticists, pharmacists, chemists, engineers and physicists, a campaign that would span both the earth and the century. Just as he had been when he fought under Captain Uher, Rudolf Vrba was but one foot soldier.

And yet England was not only the site of a laboratory. It was home to his children. Gerta and the girls were now living in London suburbia, in Kenton, with Sidney Hilton as husband and stepfather. But, even if they were no longer under the same roof, Rudi and Gerta still managed to provoke each other – and to make things complicated.

For one thing, Rudi started seeing Sidney's ex-wife Beth. Sometimes he would visit her home in Highgate, sometimes they would stay at his place in Sutton and, at weekends, they might have the children with them. Back in Prague Rudi would infuriate Gerta by playing with his daughters in the middle of the night. Now, in London, he was in the habit of having the girls with him for the weekend, but forgetting to take them home on Sunday evening. They would wake up on Monday morning in Surrey, when they needed to be back at school in Kenton.

Rudi found Gerta no less enraging. Immediately after his arrival in England, he had gone to see his children, a reunion after eighteen months apart. The way he told it, he turned up unannounced at the house to find the girls playing in the garden. He went up to the fence and the younger child eyed him nervously. Eight-year-old Helena spoke first. 'Zuza, that's Tata,' she said, using the Czech word for Daddy that Rudi and his daughters would always hold on to. The little girl looked at her father and said, 'They told me you were dead.' Rudi could not forgive that easily.

The former couple drove each other to distraction. Rudi accused Gerta and Sidney of trying to have him deported from Britain, and of once hiding Helena from him, refusing to say where she was. Gerta insisted that her ex-husband was consumed with paranoia.

Eventually Gerta decided that, yet again, she needed to resort to the law. She went to a firm of family solicitors, Theodore Goddard, where she sat across from a woman famed as one of London's most distinguished matrimonial lawyers. Her name was Blanche Lucas. Gerta began to fill in some of the background, mentioning her ex-husband's extraordinary past. As she spoke, Lucas seemed to be remembering something. Finally she made the connection. Twenty years earlier, while working in Zurich as a secretary for British journalist Walter Garrett, she had produced the English translation of the Vrba–Wetzler Report, a distilled version of which had been wired around the globe. And now she would act against one of that report's two authors, successfully as it turned out: Gerta won total legal custody over the children, with Rudi granted only limited visitation rights.

One way or another, Auschwitz was never far away. Rudi had not been in England long when, for perhaps the first time, the death

THE SHADOW

camp became a subject of public conversation. Adolf Eichmann had been snatched off the streets of Argentina in May 1960 and was on trial in Jerusalem eleven months later. After fifteen years of incurious silence, the world was suddenly interested in the Nazis' murder of the Jews. A friend suggested Rudi should approach a British newspaper and tell his story.

The result was a five-part series that ran Monday to Friday in the *Daily Herald* on the eve of the trial, with the first instalment headlined, not wholly accurately: 'I STOPPED EICHMANN KILLING 600,000 MORE JEWS'. TV and radio appearances followed, as the articles, each one a thousand words long and written with reporter Alan Bestic, saw a lift in the *Herald*'s daily sale. As a gesture of gratitude, the paper handed Rudi a cheque: it equalled his annual salary as a scientist.

Soon that led to a book. The prompt was a conversation between Rudi and his Sutton milkman. The man had read the *Herald* series and confessed that he did not like it. He believed Dr Vrba was spreading lies about the Germans and that it was not right. Of course, the man knew that Hitler was a menace: he himself had lost a leg fighting in the war. But the stories Rudi had told in the paper could not possibly be true. The Jews were clever people, the milkman said: it beggared belief to imagine they would take their children by the hand and board trains that would deliver them to the gas chambers. Such a thing was inconceivable. Rudi understood then that he would have to do much more to explain how the Nazis had pulled off perhaps the greatest crime in human history.

Over eighteen days in August 1963, he sat down again with Bestic, this time telling the whole story as fast as the reporter's shorthand could get it down. The result was *I Cannot Forgive*, published that same year. The assumption – of the publishers, and perhaps of the readers – was that the object of that title sentence was Adolf Hitler and the Nazis: it was they whom Rudolf Vrba could not forgive. But his ex-wife Gerta harboured a different thought. She had seen how the more time passed and the more Rudi learned of the events of wartime, the angrier he became, his fury directed especially at those who had failed to pass on the word that he and Fred Wetzler had smuggled out of Auschwitz. Gerta looked at the book written by her ex-husband and reckoned that high on the list among those whom he would never forgive was Rezső Kasztner.

The Eichmann trial saw some of that anger erupt. It happened in the courtroom in Jerusalem, where Hungarian survivors of the deportations interrupted the testimony of a former member of the Budapest Jewish Council, screaming at him in Hungarian and Yiddish from the public gallery. But it reached Britain too. Rudi had wanted to testify at the Eichmann trial. One of the judges voted in favour, the same judge who in 1955 had condemned Kasztner for selling 'his soul to the devil'. But the other two said no. Rudi had to make do with giving a sworn deposition at the Israeli embassy in London. Still, when Hannah Arendt, who had covered the trial for the *New Yorker*, published some of her conclusions in London's *Observer* newspaper, Rudi had a chance to weigh in. On the letters page, he defended Arendt from an Israeli scholar who had been appalled by the writer's focus on the role of the Jewish councils or *Judenräte*. Rudi described how he and Fred had escaped, compiled their detailed report and got it into the right hands, motivated by the desire to warn the Jews of Hungary that they would be next. 'Did the *Judenrat* in Hungary tell their Jews what was awaiting them? No, they remained silent and for this silence some of their leaders – for instance, Dr R. Kasztner – bartered their own lives and the lives of 1,684 other "prominent" Jews directly from Eichmann.'

The outlines of a possible life in England were taking shape. He was starting to develop a profile; his work was fulfilling and, even if he no longer had a wife, he was at least living in the same country as his two daughters. And then, bit by bit, things fell apart.

Whatever the legal position, the conflict with Gerta over the children had not eased. In 1964, access to Helena and Zuza became harder still when his ex-wife and her husband were relocated to the University of Birmingham. Things deteriorated professionally too. His manager at the institute in Carshalton had always been supportive but, in a re-run of the episode in Prague, Rudi became convinced that his boss was stealing his ideas. Instead of thrashing it out with the man directly, Rudi complained to the supervisory body, the Medical Research Council. It was only going to end one way, and

Rudi was told his contract would not be renewed. Gerta always believed it was his paranoia that had kept him alive in Auschwitz. Now it had ruined him.

And yet Rudolf Vrba had not lost his talent for finding a way out. If he reached a dead end, he simply took another route.

# 27

# Canada

I~N THE LATE~ summer of 1967 he moved countries yet again, and for the last time. He still could not get a visa to live in the US, thanks to his past membership of the Czech communist party. But now that long-lapsed affiliation proved useful. A visiting scholar in Carshalton knew of a pharmacology department in Vancouver run by a couple of American communists who had fled north to escape McCarthyism. Rudi's colleague made contact with the pair, letting them know of a Czech comrade, similarly barred from the US over his party card, for whom they might provide a haven. Moved by the spirit of international Marxist solidarity, they opened their door – unaware that Rudolf Vrba was now a strident anti-communist. He was appointed as an associate professor in the faculty of medicine at the University of British Columbia in Vancouver, on the far west coast of Canada. He had made it to the land of impossible plenty that he and his fellow prisoners in the clearing *Kommando* had once imagined. He was forty-three years old and about as far away from Auschwitz as it was possible to be.

He settled into his department with an additional post as an associate of the Medical Research Council of Canada. He continued publishing papers – 'Molecular Weights and Metabolism of Rat Brain Proteins' appeared in 1970 – and soon there was to be some stability in his personal life too.

It came thanks to the fulfilment of an ambition that had been thwarted more than a decade earlier. In 1973, just a year after he was granted citizenship of Canada – the fifth state of which he had been a citizen – he was appointed to a two-year visiting lectureship at Harvard Medical School, alongside a research fellowship working on cancer markers in the gastroenterology department at Massachusetts

General Hospital in Boston. Perhaps it was the sponsorship of an elite institution such as Harvard that made the difference, but the US authorities were now prepared to look past his brief history as a communist. True, what with the money he was sending to his mother in Bratislava and his daughters in England, he barely had a penny to his name. But he would finally be in the US.

He had not been in Boston long when he saw her. It was at a party: everyone was talking about Nixon and Watergate, he was coming up to fifty, she was twenty-four. Her name was Robin Lipson and the instant she saw him, she thought he looked adorable. She was pretty striking herself. The youngest person in the room, she was working as a truck driver for L'eggs pantyhose. The company's first gimmick was that their tights came packed into a little plastic egg, but their second was distribution via a fleet of female drivers, dressed in skimpy outfits. Robin was one of those. She was just two years older than Rudi's daughter Helena. He was older than her mother and only a year younger than her father. Nevertheless, she and Rudi hit it off right away.

Their first date was a night at the opera. They went to see *War and Peace*. Soon afterwards they took a trip to Walden Pond, the spot beloved of Thoreau and Emerson. The pair sat on a rock, not saying much while Rudi brooded on a scientific puzzle that had eluded him in the lab. Suddenly he looked at Robin and said, 'Oh yeah. I got it.' She was enchanted.

On 13 September 1975 they were married – once they had persuaded a Boston judge that divorce papers issued by the Czechoslovak Socialist Republic were valid. Slowly the agitation and restlessness began to recede; Rudi seemed to mellow. Back in Prague, he had policed Gerta's behaviour, wanting to know where she went and whom she saw, as well as insisting that she fulfil what he regarded as her wifely responsibilities in the home. But in Vancouver, Rudi accepted his young wife's independence. He was happy for Robin to work – she eventually became a hugely successful real estate agent and the main breadwinner, so that for the first time in his adult life he did not have to worry about paying the monthly rent – leaving him to run the household, even to do the cooking that he had once seen as exclusively woman's work. He specialised in dishes from the old country: goulash, chicken paprikash, schnitzel.

When his first wife heard word of her former husband's new life, she would marvel at the change in him. She put the transformation down to Robin. It was clear to Gerta now that this was what Rudi had needed: a woman from a different generation and a different continent, entirely outside the orbit of planet Auschwitz.

Rudi told Robin that he found the subject of Auschwitz 'boring', just as he told colleagues that he spent no more than one half of 1 per cent of his time on the Holocaust: he did not like to talk about it if he could avoid it, he said. To learn his life story, Robin had to read his memoir in the Boston Public Library. (She looked up 'Rudolf Vrba' and there were two books under that name. The first was by a vehement Czech nationalist and it had been published in 1898.) She found *I Cannot Forgive* and read it in two sittings.

Of course, she had seen the tattoo on his arm early on, so she knew he was an Auschwitz survivor. But she had not wanted to probe further: she had been raised to believe that it was bad form, insensitive, to ask those who had come from the Holocaust about their experience. Rudi himself had never mentioned that he had written an autobiography: it was a mutual acquaintance who told her she had to read it. Outside, in the library's courtyard Robin chain-smoked her way through those two sittings and once she was done, she felt guilty, as if she had invaded this striking man's privacy.

And yet, even in Vancouver, where Canada ends and the Pacific Ocean begins, a place regularly anointed as the most habitable city in the world, Auschwitz would intrude. Robin and Rudi might be out walking, and if she struggled to keep up he would upbraid her with mock irritation: 'What are you, a *Muselmann*?' It was in jest, but Robin picked up the message all the same: Don't be weak; the weak don't survive.

Or they might meet people at a party or faculty event. Rudi would make an instant assessment of what fate this or that person would have met in the camp. 'Oh, they would die right away,' he might say. 'They wouldn't make it. Oh, and that one would be a *Kapo* . . .'

Or there was his wardrobe, his fondness for safari suits, often in khaki – a reminder of the soldier he had been – and the bespoke tailoring adjustment he made to almost all his clothes. He would have multiple pockets added, always with zips. That way he would have no need to carry a bag. It was another Auschwitz lesson: anything of value was best kept on your body.

That place was never far away. On a sweltering July day in New York in 1978, Rudi was in a restaurant when he noticed that his waiter, wearing short sleeves, had a tattooed number on his arm. Instantly, Rudi told the man that he must have been a Jew from Będzin, Poland who had arrived in Auschwitz in the summer of 1943. The astonished waiter confirmed that Rudi was right in every particular. For Rudi had memorised the details of each and every transport and that knowledge, seared into his memory so that he might smuggle it out of Auschwitz, had never left him.

To his young wife, Rudi was parentally gentle and sweet, calling her his 'Robchek'. His tread was soft when he walked and he grinned easily. But his temper was fierce. Once provoked, especially if he felt Robin had behaved unkindly or unjustly, he could be harsh and biting. He would run rings around her in arguments, until, by the end, she was confused and found herself apologising, even when he was in the wrong. He was a skilled debater, and she was, in her own estimation, young and simple. He would argue her into submission, including on the most delicate of questions.

They never had children, chiefly because he talked her out of it, to the point of intimidation. In their conversations on the topic, his objections steamrollered over her wishes. He was adamant that he wanted no more. He told Robin that he had survived the war in part because he had no children. He saw now that the presence of Helena and Zuza in his life had made him vulnerable. It had weakened him; he felt too much. He could not risk becoming weaker still.

And, for all his protestations of boredom with the subject and despite the 5,000 miles that separated Vancouver from Auschwitz, he could not keep away from it. The pattern had been set a few years earlier when, prompted by the *Daily Herald* series, the office of the public prosecutor in Frankfurt had got in touch, asking Rudi to help in the preparations for the upcoming trial of a dozen or so SS men who had served at Auschwitz. Rudi travelled to Germany in 1962, long before many, perhaps most, Holocaust survivors felt able to set foot in the country. So began a relationship with the German prosecuting authorities that would stretch over many decades, with Rudi repeatedly called as a witness in the trials of Nazi war criminals. He was a prosecutor's dream. Not only was he fluent in multiple languages, but he also had an exceptional body of memories to draw upon with an unusually panoramic perspective on the camp. The Nazis had taken great pains to ensure next to no one glimpsed the entire process of mass murder from beginning to end. Admittedly, Rudi had never been in the *Sonderkommando*, he had never worked inside the crematoria, but he had seen for himself almost every other stage of the sequence that led to that final moment.

And so he testified in the trials of, among others, Hermann Krumey and Otto Hunsche, henchmen to Adolf Eichmann in Budapest. In the course of one of those trials, Rudi's relations with the presiding judge grew testy. Several times, the judge interrupted his testimony to correct his grammar. Eventually, Rudi had had enough. He declared that if his German was not intelligible on account of his incorrect use of the 'German version of the *conjunctivum cum accusativo*', then the court was welcome to bring in a Slovak–German translator and they could start again. After that, Rudi reckoned the judge cooled down a bit. In the event, in August 1969, once the trials and subsequent appeals were finally over, Hunsche was sentenced to twelve years' imprisonment and Krumey to life.

Sometimes Rudi was not merely a witness, but the initiator of legal proceedings. That pattern too was set a few years earlier. After the war, Rudi had received an extraordinary job offer. The Auschwitz sub-camp known as Buna had become a major industrial centre, just as Himmler dreamed it would, though now under the management of the Polish state rather than the SS. Rudi was invited to take up a post there as an industrial chemist. Though he had travelled to both Poland and Germany, where many of his peers feared to tread, that was too much, even for him. He could not forget the blood that had been shed to build that place. Indeed, far from forgetting, Rudi joined a group of fellow survivors who in 1961 sued the German conglomerate IG Farben, then still trading despite its documented exploitation of slave labour. Rudi and the others demanded backpay for their work constructing the site. A West German court awarded each of them 2,500 Deutschmarks, equivalent at the time to $625, but it issued no demand that the company compensate the families of the slaves who had lost their lives. For IG Farben, the judgment was a great bargain. As Rudi would put it, the corporation had got 90 per cent of the labour they had used for only 'the pennies they paid' the Auschwitz camp commandant Rudolf Höss.

In 1963, Rudi set in train proceedings of a different sort, this time against the last SS man he ever spoke to in Auschwitz and one of the brutal trio that oversaw Kanada. Rudi had heard that SS-Unterscharführer Otto Graf was alive and well and, just like the young Adolf Hitler, working as a house painter in Vienna. So unafraid of justice was he, that Graf had seen no need even to change his name. The post-war Austrian desire to hold Nazis to account was not urgent, and it took until 1971, by which time Rudi was in Vancouver, for Graf finally to be arrested and tried on thirty criminal charges. Once again, Rudolf Vrba testified for the prosecution, both as a victim of the accused and, in effect, as an expert witness. Graf was found guilty, but on a charge that had exceeded the statute of limitations.

The prosecution of Graf's comrade, the man Rudi and the others had known as 'König', the King of Kanada, looked to have made similarly little headway. It arose out of the Auschwitz trials that took place in Frankfurt in the mid-1960s, but did not reach a courtroom until 1987. The central charge against Ernst-August König was that in 1943 and 1944 he had been involved in the gassing of more than 21,000 inmates of the so-called Gypsy camp, BIIe, which was just a short walk away from Rudi's sector of Birkenau, BIIa. The charges had been brought against König by a group representing Sinti and Roma people in Germany and they summoned three Auschwitz survivors from Canada to support their case. One of them was Rudolf Vrba.

But when Rudi reached the courthouse in Siegen he saw instantly that the man in the dock was not the vicious overseer he had known in the storehouse of stolen goods of the dead. As he put it, the accused had 'killed untold numbers of Gypsies but he wasn't the Kanada König of the SS'. The man in the dock, a retired forester who referred to himself as an 'angel of Auschwitz', swearing that he had never hurt a soul, was sentenced in 1991 to life imprisonment for killing three Sinti prisoners with his own hands and for aiding in two mass gassings that killed 3,258 others.

And yet the Kanada König who had brutalised the lives of Rudi and the other slaves of the clearing *Kommando* would not evade the justice system entirely. The trial of his apparent namesake ensnared him too, and in a remarkable way.

One day in court, the prosecution called as a witness against Ernst-August König a man who had become an admired opera singer in the latter's hometown of Essen. His name was Heinrich-Johannes Kühnemann. Rudi had only to see him take the oath to know that this Kühnemann, happily pointing the finger at the accused, was in fact the König of Kanada. He had been so certain that justice would never find him, he had been prepared to walk into a war crimes trial and testify for the prosecution. He told the court that he had been a guard at Auschwitz, but one who had had nothing to do with killing. On the contrary, he said, he had been popular with the inmates. The judge warned him that he did not have to testify, but Kühnemann was adamant: he had nothing to hide. He did not count on the presence of Rudolf Vrba, the man who had committed to his extraordinary memory every building, every transport and every face he saw in Auschwitz.

Kühnemann was tried in the regional court of Duisberg from 1991 to 1993, with Rudi once again summoned to the witness box. But the SS man would not serve time in jail, or even receive a sentence. The trial was stopped in 1993 on medical grounds: the tormentor of Kanada was too sick.

Rudi was on the other side of the world. He had a young wife to whom he had insisted that he found the subject of Auschwitz a bore. And yet Auschwitz would not let him go. As the decades went by, his scientific work slowed down. In those years in Prague and Carshalton, he had been prolific, publishing twenty-three full papers in scholarly journals in little more than fifteen years. In Vancouver, he would write just eight more in three decades. Appointed as an associate professor in 1967, he was never promoted. He held that same rank until his retirement.

But his war against the old enemy never flagged, even if he waged it now from his office in British Columbia. He was in touch with the Viennese Nazi hunter Simon Wiesenthal, especially about those war criminals who had made it to Canada, among them Josef Nemsila, a former officer of Slovakia's fascist Hlinka Guard who died before he could be tried for commanding a unit that had deported Jews to Auschwitz and killed Slovak civilians. Rudi and Wiesenthal were in touch too about Mikulás Polhora-Pomfy, whom Wiesenthal believed had been the commander of Rudi's first place of detention, the transit camp at Nováky.

One target Rudi pursued with particular intensity was Joseph Kirschbaum, who had entered Canada in the 1960s despite his past service as secretary general of the Hlinka People's Party. Happily living in Toronto, where he worked as an historian and leading light in the Canadian Slovak League, Kirschbaum had been one of the officials who met Adolf Eichmann in Bratislava in November 1938 to discuss solving Slovakia's 'Jewish problem'. Rudi tracked both his wartime record in Europe and his new life in North America, gathering enough material to fill four thick files.

In Auschwitz, Rudi had understood, perhaps more swiftly than others, that an essential part of the Nazis' method, one that made the process of mass murder possible, was their denial that they were engaged in any such activity. Deception was integral to the operation: the lie that Jews were not being killed at all but merely resettled helped the killing proceed. At the heart of the crime, from the start, was a confidence trick.

In the decades after the war, Rudi came to realise that the denial had not stopped. It just presented itself differently. He had seen it in a mild form in communist Czechoslovakia, where it was taboo to mention that the Nazis had singled out Jews for elimination or even that Czech Jewish children had been murdered in gas chambers. But now, in Vancouver, he saw it florid and unabashed.

He had already been in contact with everyone from Alexander Solzhenitsyn to the Office of Special Investigations of the US Justice Department in the 1970s to discuss the burgeoning phenomenon of

Holocaust denial. He kept tabs on Robert Faurisson in France, Wilhelm Stäglich in Germany and Arthur Butz in the US, but his most direct encounter was with the German-born Ernst Zündel, who had made his home in Toronto. In 1985, Zündel was tried under the criminal code for spreading false news by publishing a tract called *Did Six Million Really Die?* Though Zündel was in the dock, in reality it was the truth of the Holocaust that was on trial. Rudolf Vrba would be one of the central witnesses.

He was questioned for hour after hour. With the exception of his memoir, those several days in a Toronto courtroom represented the fullest chance Rudi would ever get to bear witness to what he had seen and what he had done. He was given the floor to describe in detail his spell in Buna, the typhus outbreak, his work in Kanada and on the *Judenrampe*, the selections, the barracks and the roll calls, as well as his escape and the report he co-wrote. 'I escaped and warned the world,' he told the court.

Once again, the atmosphere was testy. Rudi's antagonist this time was not the judge but the lawyer for the accused, Doug Christie. His approach was to poke and probe Rudi's account, starting with his autobiography: if he could prove that this text, authored by a vocal Auschwitz survivor, was unreliable, well, then surely the Holocaust itself could no longer be regarded as the truth. Christie pressed and pressed at what he thought were inconsistencies in the narrative. He was sceptical about the escape. Once out of the woodpile, could it really be true that Fred and Rudi had navigated their way out of the camp, just like that?

'That's right,' said Rudi.

'Without a compass.'

'That's right.'

'In the dark.'

'That's right.'

'Over territory you had never been.'

'That's right.'

When under fire, in that courtroom or elsewhere, Rudi often resorted to sarcasm. Christie challenged Vrba on his conviction that, since he had seen thousands enter the gas chambers, they had all been killed. How could he be so sure? 'A quarter million people go in and I never saw one civilian come out,' Rudi replied. 'So it is possible that they are still there, or that there is a tunnel and they are now in China; otherwise they were gassed.' If Christie got the geography or timeline of Auschwitz wrong, Rudi would pounce. 'You would help me if you would do your homework,' he told him, a college professor admonishing a dull student.

There were setbacks. Rudi had to admit that his 1963 memoir had allowed itself some 'artistic' licence, that it was more akin to a court reporter's sketch than a photograph, more a set of recollections than a work of scholarly, footnoted history. Perhaps he was too proud to suggest what was surely obvious to any reader of the book: that while the story was faithfully Rudi's, the prose was the work of Alan Bestic, a supremely skilled Fleet Street journalist of the old school.

Overall though, Rudi kept remarkably controlled. He was a commanding presence in the courtroom, repeatedly leaving the witness box to stand at an overhead projector, pointer in hand, as he guided the jury around diagrams and sketches he had made of the death camp. His recall was exceptional and consistent. When urged to return to the topic in hand by the judge, he was unfailingly polite and, just as often, charming. For Rudi was doing what he had itched to do when he was a teenager. He was standing up and telling the world the truth of Auschwitz.

At the trial's end, Zündel was pronounced guilty.

# 28

# I Know a Way Out

SOME OF THE foremost chroniclers of the Holocaust sought out Rudi, understanding that he was perhaps uniquely well placed to testify to the modus operandi of Auschwitz-Birkenau. He became a cherished source of Martin Gilbert, the official biographer of Winston Churchill, whose 1981 book *Auschwitz and the Allies* had the Vrba–Wetzler Report at last revealing to Washington and London the true function of the death factory, triggering the fateful debate in both capitals over the rights and wrongs of bombing the railway tracks that led to the camp. In the previous decade, Rudi was interviewed for two acclaimed, though very different, documentaries. First came the British-made television series *The World at War*, which devoted one episode to the Nazis' attempted annihilation of the Jews and in which Rudi gave off a brooding, movie-star charisma. Next came *Shoah*, the nine-and-a-half-hour epic by Claude Lanzmann. The French director interviewed Rudi for nearly four hours in November 1978 – though the film would not be released for another seven years – much of it outdoors, on the streets of New York, with Rudi in a tan-leather overcoat. On screen, Vrba is, once again, a striking presence. With his thick dark hair and heavy eyebrows, he could pass for Al Pacino in *Scarface*. In one sequence, Lanzmann asks Vrba about the mechanics of Auschwitz, how the Jews were unloaded off the trains and on to the trucks that would take them to the gas chambers. In a central European accent unaltered by a decade in North America, Rudi gives detailed, evocative answers. But he also makes what for him was always the crucial point: 'The whole murder machinery could work on one principle: that the people came to Auschwitz and didn't know where they were going and for what purpose. The new arrivals were supposed to be kept orderly and, without panic, marching into the gas chambers.'

A few years after the release of *Shoah*, the Canadian Broadcasting Corporation asked Rudi to return to Auschwitz to be filmed for a new documentary. It was 1990, the Berlin Wall had come down, Poland was opening up, but Auschwitz was not yet the well-tended museum and memorial site it would become. Birkenau in particular was all but unsecured; it looked like an abandoned wasteland.

Rudi, Robin, the director and a Polish crew had completed a day's filming, including an unauthorised shoot in Birkenau, when they realised that someone had shut the gates. They were locked into Birkenau. Everyone involved was terrified by the very idea of it, but one man kept calm. With no irony, Rudi said, 'Don't worry. I know another way out.'

Throughout these years, whether corresponding with historians or speaking to documentary filmmakers, Vrba was always at pains to mention his fellow escapee, Alfréd Wetzler. But the distance between them had grown since the initial cooling over Fred's marriage to an Auschwitz survivor.

Politics played a part. Rudi found it astonishing that his old friend could still live in a totalitarian system. He took Fred's continuing presence in Czechoslovakia to be a form of implicit approval for oppressive communism. He wanted to help him; he even sent money when he could. But the way Rudi saw it, if Fred Wetzler truly loathed life there, he had an option: he could escape. He had done it before.

The Iron Curtain that separated them seemed to have another effect too. Their recollections of the extraordinary deed they had performed together began to diverge. Fred had not set down his story directly, but rather in the form of a novel published under a pseudonym, the same false name he had been given when Walter become Rudolf Vrba: Jozef Lánik. The book was called *Čo Dante Nevidel* ('What Dante Didn't See') and in it Rudi is recast as Val, a young man who is full of courage, but also hot-headed, even heedless of the consequences of his actions. Fred also gave a couple of interviews, with scholars rather than filmmakers, and it's through those that the gap in the accounts of the two escapees became most visible.

The former comrades disagreed over details large and small, but the most significant dispute centred, perhaps predictably, on who deserved the credit for devising their scheme. Fred Wetzler felt he had not been given his due, a sentiment echoed to this day by the remnant Jewish community of Slovakia, those who, like him, stayed put. (Some of them like to refer to the 'Wetzler–Vrba Report', to give Fred what they believe is the appropriate seniority.) 'I feel sad about the fact that most of the people turn to Vrba to get essential as well as minor details about our escape,' he wrote to one historian in 1984. 'I have never tried to benefit either from the escape or from my participation in the resistance. They live in the west,' he added, referring to Rudi and other former Auschwitz inmates. 'They have profited and still profit from the past and put on paper whatever they can. Vrba's book aroused much outrage among certain prisoners, because he posed as an initiator and leader of the escape. Well, in the west they might believe it.' Their fellow Auschwitz escapee Arnošt Rosin shared some of Fred's anger towards Rudi. 'Vrba writes in his book as though he took Wetzler with him like a suitcase, not as a partner,' he told a fellow survivor.

And yet, in truth, Fred and Rudi were two men fighting over scraps. Neither of them was famous. Rudi had featured in a handful of documentaries, but considering the feat they had achieved together, they were hardly well known. Even in Israel, the nation that stops once a year to pause and remember the Shoah in silence, Vrba and Wetzler were barely recalled at all. Their story was not taught in schools and Rudi's memoir was not translated into Hebrew until 1998, and only then thanks to a tireless campaign fought by the Haifa academic Ruth Linn. Even at Yad Vashem, the country's official Holocaust archive, museum and memorial in Jerusalem, the Auschwitz Report was filed away without the names of its authors. When historians referred to the report, they tended to speak of 'two young escapees' or 'two Slovak escapees' as if the identities of the men who had performed this remarkable deed were incidental.

What might explain this relative lack of recognition? It certainly did not help Wetzler that he was out of sight of western writers and historians and, therefore, mostly out of mind. As for Rudi, while he was accessible, and a model interviewee, he was not an easy sell in Israel or in the mainstream Jewish diaspora. Those audiences would have thrilled to hear the story of his escape and his mission to tell the world of Auschwitz, but he never left it at that. He would not serve up a morally comfortable narrative in which the only villains were the Nazis. Instead he always insisted on hitting out at Kasztner and the Hungarian Jewish leadership, as well as the Jewish council in Slovakia. He faulted them for failing to pass on his report and, in the Slovak case, for compiling the lists that had put him on a deportation train in the first place.

What made Rudi a more awkward witness still was his tendency to refer to the Jews whom he blamed as 'Zionists'. As it happened, Rudolf Vrba was a supporter of Israel and rooted for it: he believed that the existence of the state of Israel was a good thing for Jews and for the world. But he could not contain his anger against those Zionists who he felt had betrayed the Jewish people, starting with Kasztner and, in his view, the early Israeli leaders who had stood by him.

It was quite true that Kasztner was a Zionist, as were some of the Working Group who took down Fred and Rudi's account in Žilina and whom Rudi castigated for failing immediately to inform the remaining Jews of Slovakia. But so too were several of the heroes in the men's story. George Mantello, the unlikely envoy for El Salvador who helped get the report to the world's press, was a Zionist. So was Moshe Krausz, the head of the Palestine office in the Hungarian capital who passed on the copy that eventually reached Mantello and who later played a pivotal role alongside Raoul Wallenberg in the 'protective passport' scheme that saved tens of thousands of Budapest Jews. Rudi's fellow escapee Arnošt Rosin was a Zionist, as was Josef Weiss, the friend who helped make samizdat copies of the report in Bratislava. It was also the case that several of those who were deceived, misinformed or betrayed by Kasztner were the Hungarian leader's comrades in Zionism. Meanwhile, some of those Jews who, in Rudi's estimation, made selfish or immoral choices were either non- or anti-Zionists. Rudi was hugely critical of Fülöp Freudiger, for example, a Jewish leader who, like Kasztner, negotiated his own exit from Hungary. He was an orthodox Jew with no ties to Zionism. In other words, the Zionist movement, like every other, produced both saints and sinners while under the Nazi jackboot. The human responses to the horror of the Third Reich were varied and seldom ran on ideological lines.

Nevertheless, Rudi tended to use the word 'Zionism' sweepingly, as shorthand for those Jews in authority who he believed had done him, and Jews like him, wrong. He never advanced a substantial argument for why Zionist ideology might have led the likes of Kasztner to act the way they did, beyond a hinted suggestion that Zionism was prepared to sacrifice the mass of European Jewry in order to salvage a remnant that would then establish a Jewish state in Palestine. It would have been hard to make such an argument, given that plenty of Zionists had stretched every sinew to thwart the Nazis and save Jewish lives, most notably the young Zionists who led the armed resistance in the Warsaw and Vilna ghettos and elsewhere. But given how toxic a case Kasztner's became, seized upon decades later by the most unbending anti-Zionists in Europe and the US as evidence of the supposedly inherent evils of Jewish nationalism, handing a platform to Rudolf Vrba may have come to seem like a risk.

Nor was Rudi much minded to soften his message to make it more palatable. On the contrary, he often used venomous language. In private correspondence, he alleged that one widely admired leader of the Slovak Working Group, a woman who was eventually murdered in Auschwitz, 'participated in treason and conspiracy against the unfortunate Jewish victims. This she did in the service of the Nazis, possibly in cooperation with the Nazi-dominated Zionist and rabbinical clique.' He speculated that Kasztner, like Hitler, believed in 'a master race'. An otherwise sympathetic student interviewer for the *Harvard Crimson* in 1974 concluded that Rudi not only harboured a 'deep bitterness' but was 'anti-Zionist, anti-communist, and even somewhat anti-Semitic, particularly with respect to American Jews'.

The problem was sharpest in Israel. When Ruth Linn sought to twin the belated publication of Rudi's memoirs in Hebrew with the award of an honorary doctorate at Haifa University, she encountered trenchant opposition. At the conference ahead of the award ceremony, with Rudi in attendance preparing to be honoured, one scholar read out a letter of protest. Several historians wrote to the Israeli press, praising the heroism of the 1944 escape but setting out their misgivings about Vrba (as well as suggesting that if garlands were being handed out, then Fred Wetzler's contribution should be recognised too). Some of Vrba's antagonists were motivated by the belief that there was still a case to make for Kasztner's defence. Others, especially Israeli historians of Slovak Jewish origin, took exception to Rudi's attacks on the Jewish leadership in Bratislava, which they believed had done all it could in the face of a morally hideous predicament.

Rudi's best-known critic was the doyen of Israeli Holocaust historians, Yehuda Bauer. Though he would later describe Vrba as 'a genuine hero of the Holocaust', Bauer also found him 'arrogant' and believed Rudi's 'deep hatred for the Jewish leadership, Zionism, etc.' coloured his judgement. He strongly objected to Rudi's insistence, maintained over many decades, that the leadership in Budapest could have made all the difference if they had only passed on what they knew to the ordinary Jews in the Hungarian provinces who, being uninformed, climbed aboard trains that took them to their deaths. Bauer's view was that those Jews in the Hungarian countryside were not uninformed: even without sight of the Vrba–Wetzler Report, there were enough fragments of information around, including via soldiers returning from the front, for them to have worked out that deportation meant death. The problem, he argued, was not inadequate publication of information so much as inadequate absorption of it. Hungary's Jews had not internalised the information they had received in such a way that it became converted into *knowledge*. They had not turned it into a conviction that might be a spur to action.

Rudi did not reject that quasi-philosophical argument about the nature of knowledge on theoretical grounds. He simply believed that in this particular case it rested on a flawed factual premise: in his view, the Jews of Hungary had simply not had enough information to go on. They had been denied the facts.

Rudi got his honorary doctorate and the belated translation of his memoirs. But those many years in which Israel's pre-eminent scholars kept their distance took their toll. They played a part in preventing him from entering the pantheon of revered survivors of the Holocaust. He corresponded with the Nobel laureate Elie Wiesel, and in *The World at War* TV documentary his contribution appeared straight after a clip of Primo Levi. But he did not have their fame. Some of that is because they were writers and he was not. But some of it is down to something subtler. Rudolf Vrba refused to conform to what the world expects of a Holocaust survivor.

You can see it in the Lanzmann film, *Shoah*. The other speakers look like old men, bent and broken by experience. They speak in soft voices, as if awed by what they have witnessed. But Rudi is tanned, fit and vigorous. His voice is loud and confident. He seems a generation younger than all the others; it is hard to believe he had lived through the same events thirty-five years earlier. He deploys sardonic, sarcastic humour. And he smiles, as if amused by the lunatic absurdity of what he is describing, even when speaking about the unspeakable. Lanzmann, as interviewer, remarks upon it. 'Why do you smile so often when you talk about this?' he asks. 'What should I do?' Rudi says in reply. 'Should I cry?'

Rudi knew that he was refusing to fit what he called 'the survivor clichés manufactured for the taste of a certain type of public': he would offer no uplifting aphorisms, reassuring his audience that, ultimately, human beings were good. He was unforgiving and he was angry. The result was to make Rudolf Vrba, for the best part of three decades, a peripheral figure even in the small world of Holocaust remembrance in Vancouver.

His message was awkward and he was a discomfiting messenger. For years, he had nothing to do with collective Jewish life in the city that had become his home, and not only because he had severed all ties with religious practice and almost never set foot inside a synagogue. He also carried an automatic suspicion of those in charge. At a ceremony to commemorate the Warsaw Ghetto uprising, he lambasted the Vancouver Jewish community so vehemently, those present wondered if he was speaking about them or the wartime leaders in Budapest that he felt had betrayed him.

When the organisers of an annual symposium on the Holocaust for high-school students, held at Rudi's own university, put together a panel of survivors, they did not invite Rudi. They did not trust him to speak to 500 sixteen- and seventeen-year-olds without serving up the familiar brew of 'accusations and rage'. The way the organisers saw it, the other survivors could be relied on to tell their stories without any political comment; they would not use their talks as a means to assuage their anger. Those in charge could not say the same about Rudolf Vrba.

And yet Rudi would turn up at the symposium all the same. He would stand outside the lecture hall – dapper in leather coat and fedora, a feather in its band – peeking in, watching the proceedings from a distance. He would linger for a while, and then quietly leave. And he did that year after year.

It meant that many of those who worked closely with Rudolf Vrba did not know the central fact of his life. One of his colleagues became very upset after chancing upon Rudi in *Shoah* when the film was screened on Canadian television. He asked if all the terrible things Vrba had described in the film were true. 'I don't know,' Rudi said, adding acidly, 'I was only an actor reciting my lines.'

He was guarded about discussing his past, and highly selective about those with whom he would do it. Once a conversation on the topic had begun, there was no guarantee it would be easy. When discussing the Holocaust, Rudi would often let loose a torrent of words, a monologue that brooked no interruption, repeatedly returning to the same theme: the betrayal committed by Kasztner and those who had failed to spread the word. Colleagues found that Rudi could be abrasive, aggressive and arrogant and, when on his territory, insistent on being in charge. When talking, he might grab your arm, intensifying the point he was making. Some speculated that Rudolf Vrba had never been promoted above the rank of associate professor not because his field of research was no longer at the cutting edge, but because his behaviour could be insufferably difficult. Others wondered if Rudi was shy or even anxious. They noted how he steered clear of big gatherings, that he did not seem to socialise much, that while he had colleagues he seemed to have few close friends.

Yet others saw a very different man. Despite all that he had witnessed and all that he had endured, Rudolf Vrba had not lost the lust for life, and adventure, that had marked him out as a young teenager. Even when he had next to no money in his pocket, he thought life was to be enjoyed. Leaving London for Vancouver in 1967, he did not take a plane but sailed across the Atlantic to Montreal, then travelled by train from one end of Canada to the other, just for the fun of it.

He loved travel and restaurants, coffee shops and hotels, exploring a new city and an occasional three-hour lunch in the faculty club, and derived an almost childlike pleasure from things others might take for granted: international phone calls, radio and television, anti-biotics and painkillers, French wine and Scotch whisky. A ride in a punt down the River Cam, one of his English grandchildren on his lap and a cigarette in his hand, would uncork a broad smile. During a rainstorm, Rudi might look out of the window and exult in his good fortune. 'Ah, isn't that beautiful?' he would say. 'And we're inside' – the voice of a man who had known nakedness in the bitterest Polish winter.

He could be vain about his appearance. He had always liked to look his best and so he might change clothes several times in the course of a single day, even when there was no one around to impress but his own family.

His sense of humour could be goofy. He liked practical jokes. Thanks to his accent and his looks, he could hoodwink strangers into believing he was anything he wanted them to believe. He once told a gaggle of attractive women surrounding him on a cruise ship that he was from Iran, a cousin of a Persian prince: they were intrigued. In Vienna, a German man, on hearing Rudi was from Canada, assumed he must have been indigenous, an 'Indian'. Rudi played along and, asked how he came to have such good German, explained that the tradition of his tribe was that the firstborn son of a chief, like him, would always learn the language of Goethe. The German thought that was a most admir-able custom.

Those whom he allowed in saw that Rudolf Vrba had not been defeated by life. On the contrary, he savoured it. And yet his resilience would soon be tested once more, by the event that Rudi considered the worst experience he ever endured. It did not take place in Auschwitz nor in the 1940s. It happened on the other side of the world.

# 29

## Flowers of Emptiness

FOR MOST OF their lives, Rudolf Vrba had been a long-distance father to his daughters, Helena and Zuza. He would see them on trips to England, or on return visits to Vancouver, but most of the relationship was conducted via holiday postcards, letters and the occasional phone call. They would write to him – *Dear Tata, GRRREAT!! to hear you are coming over* – and he would write back, encouraging them in their studies or dispensing fatherly advice. Once Helena reached her mid-twenties, the relationship with Rudi hit a rough patch. The letters became more infrequent until, for a three-year period, they stopped altogether. Rudi had a string of grievances: Helena had not thanked him for a birthday present, merely banking the cheque he had sent 'as if I were a rich and foolish American uncle'; she had stayed in closer touch with Gillian, an ex-girlfriend of Rudi's, than she had with him; he had been the last to know that Helena had qualified as a doctor, apparently because he was not 'considered worthy' of being informed. For her part, Helena had become a strong feminist and regarded her father as an unabashed male chauvinist. Rudi suspected that his elder daughter had absorbed much of the hostility her mother still harboured towards him.

Things turned especially sour in 1979, when Helena, whose physical resemblance to Rudi was by then uncanny, announced her intention to pursue her interest in tropical health research by relocating to Papua New Guinea to study malaria. Rudi was adamantly opposed to the move. His '6th sense' told him it would be trouble and he conveyed his worry to his daughter directly and graphically. He was a little drunk when he wrote to tell her: 'This is not a good idea, you're not a strong enough person. You're going to come back in a box.'

Helena ignored his advice and headed to the Pacific anyway. She worked in a clinic in the tiny village of Yagaum, and soon fell in love with a colleague, Jim. The trouble was, Jim had a wife back in Australia. In the first days of May 1982, Helena wrote to her sister Zuza, telling her that Jim was about to return home: 'Right now I'm oscillating between ultra-low and euphoric (? why), by Sunday afternoon I expect to reach a pretty stable rock bottom.' In fact, by 2 p.m. on Sunday 9 May 1982, less than a fortnight away from her thirtieth birthday, Helena Vrbova was dead.

The death certificate recorded the cause as 'Suspected self-poisoning with drugs'. She had taken an overdose of the anti-malarial medication chloroquine. Near her body they found a bottle of wine, a third of which had been drunk, and a note. In pale-blue ink, on a lined piece of A4 paper and spaced out like a poem, it was addressed to Jim. 'Even strong things break,' Helena had written. 'I've been grappling with it for some time – hear my fear and cries of despair . . . I'm not afraid now, only afraid of failing.' There was a book by her side. It was called *Flowers of Emptiness*.

Rudi was quite clear that 'Helena's death was the worst experience in my life.' Yes, he explained in a letter to his surviving daughter, whom he would address as Zuzinka, he had faced death, starvation and torture in Auschwitz and, yes, he had witnessed the murder of more than a million people. But the suicide of his firstborn child hit him harder. Because now he was 'facing a horrible catastrophe without any possibility to fight back'. Even against the Nazis, he did not feel as powerless as he felt at that moment.

He plunged into a terrible despair. There would be what he called 'crying fits' every day. He found it hard to work and he slept and slept. He would send Zuza long, sometimes rambling letters – one ran to forty-two pages – asking himself the same questions over and over again. Why had Helena done it? Was he somehow to blame? And why had Helena all but severed ties with him in the preceding three years? 'What did I do wrong?' he wrote. 'Should I have given Helena more from my strength, resilience and love of life? The question nags at me.'

He wondered if he should never have confessed his fears about her decision to head to the Pacific three years earlier. But he could not help himself. 'When I was in Auschwitz, I had the "illogical" but clearly perceived <u>premonition</u> that I will come out of there alive and I shall have the privilege to do damage to the worst enemy of mankind, to the Nazis,' he wrote to Zuza. 'I had a <u>premonition</u> that Helena's fate is to die in Papua New Guinea, and I cried out loudly at that time.'

He lashed out in all directions. Sometimes at the authorities in Papua New Guinea, sometimes at his ex-wife Gerta – whom he accused of stealing Helena's letters and papers and spinning 'a web of shit' – sometimes at Zuza, who he believed was exhibiting a 'pathological sentimentality' by holding on to Helena's things. And sometimes he would lambast Helena herself, for being nearly as 'unscrupulous' as her mother, as he put it, and for dropping him 'like an old rag'.

He tried to regain control over his emotions by using the equipment that had served him so well in the past: reason and a scientific mind. Just as he had once made himself a student of escape, so now he would make himself expert in the field of suicide. He bombarded Zuza with research papers from scholarly journals, as he examined the case of Helena in the light of the academic literature. It seemed to boil down to the same key question: was it free will that made a person take their own life, or the biochemistry of their brain? He did a line-by-line textual analysis of the suicide note, running to several pages. He came across research that showed higher suicide rates among those with roots in the former Austro-Hungarian empire and among those qualified in medicine. Since Helena, born in Prague, belonged in both those categories, he wondered if his daughter had been doubly doomed.

At times he doubted that it had been a suicide at all. The coroner had delivered an open verdict and Rudi – and Gerta, for that matter – thought there were some loose ends. Rudi wanted the note found by Helena's body to be submitted for handwriting analysis, just to be sure the words were hers. And he was frustrated that the post-mortem samples were lost, which meant there was no chance of having a pathologist in London establish the cause of death. He asked Zuza to look back through Helena's letters, searching for 'hidden clues'. He also spotted what he regarded as 'irregularities' in Helena's bank statements. 'Did she have any particular enemies in PNG?' he asked her former colleagues in Papua New Guinea.

Perhaps others would have been less questioning of that verdict, especially in light of a fact that had been withheld from Rudi until now: Helena had made a suicide attempt, or something close to it, more than a decade earlier. Aged sixteen, she had cut her wrists. An older man was involved and it happened in, of all places, Germany. But no one had told Rudi, which only added to his fury.

Still, Rudolf Vrba struggled to accept as the truth what others regarded as obvious. Two elements of his past created an additional dread of what it would mean to conclude that his daughter had taken her own life. The most obvious was Auschwitz.

'Now what's going to happen', he told his wife, 'is they're going to say, "Because her father was a Holocaust survivor, that's why she committed suicide."' He did not want Helena to be seen as a delayed victim of the Nazis, Hitler reaching into the second generation. He thought it was a nonsense.

But there might have been another, even earlier fear at work. At least two Vrba relatives told Robin that Rudi's father had not died of a viral infection, as he had always been led to believe. Elias Rosenberg had, they said, killed himself, driven to despair by an economic depression that saw him lose his sawmill. It would make a cruel kind of sense of a remark a group of local villagers had called out to the infant Walter as he headed home on that fateful day and which he had never forgotten: 'Hey, Jew! Your father's risen from the dead,' they had said. Did that mean Elias had seemingly survived a failed suicide attempt when the neighbours taunted his son, only to die a few hours later? Rudi refused to believe it.

Perhaps he shrank from both those explanations because they would have made him somehow responsible for the fate of his daughter, if not through his experience then through his genes. He wanted nothing to do with the nihilism that suicide represented, and which clashed with his own determination to live life and live it fully. He described suicide as a 'ricocheting bullet': it did not take only one life, but hit anybody who was close.

For month after month, year after year, he turned it over and over. It obsessed him. He told himself that he put on a good front. He felt sure colleagues had no idea what he was going through. But it would not have taken much to guess. When he was tasked with interviewing would-be medical students for admission to the University of British Columbia, the subject he chose to grill them on was suicide. One applicant was reduced to tears.

His daughter's death shook what had been core convictions. Rudi had broken from religion as a child, but now he was invoking 'my Creator', whose 'incredible mercy . . . brought me out of a hell where many better ones than I perished in a horrible death', and writing that he had received a 'message' that Helena had been summoned by a 'Higher Call'. He told Zuza that he was praying and said that they both needed to return to normality because their pain and grief was disturbing Helena's 'soul'.

The usually matter-of-fact scientist, the man who had catalogued mass murder in the coolly detached language of the statistician, could now not bring himself even to use the vocabulary of death. He would speak instead of Helena's 'departure'. As he entered his sixties, everything that had once seemed solid was melting.

And yet he was not beaten. In 1990, eight years after Helena's death and following the fall of communism, Rudi returned at last to the land of his birth. He was not sure how safe it was – he covered up his Auschwitz tattoo with a plaster, just in case – but he could walk around the streets and neighbourhoods that had once been home. During one of those walks, he seemed to have a moment of clarity. Robin and Rudi were about to discuss the perennial topic yet again, the same circular conversation – did she or did she not commit suicide? – when he suddenly stepped out of the circle. He stopped the discussion, just like that. He did not want to do it any more. Finally, thought Robin, the healing had begun.

Not for the first time in his life, Rudolf Vrba had been knocked to the ground, felled by a blow that would have destroyed many, if not most, others. And, not for the first time, he had found the strength to get back up again. He had survived – and he wanted to live.

# 30

## Too Many to Count

THE 1980s AND 1990s brought slightly more recognition than Rudi had had before, whether from his appearance in *Shoah* or in the witness box at the Zündel trial or the gradual thawing in relations with those who had previously kept a chilly distance. Haifa University awarded him that honorary doctorate in 1998; a year earlier the Vancouver Jewish community invited him to be the guest speaker at a major event to remember Kristallnacht, the 'night of broken glass' in November 1938 when Nazis and their supporters ran riot, smashing the shop windows of Jewish-owned businesses and torching hundreds of synagogues. Rudi spoke about what, for him, was a shamefully neglected aspect of Nazism's war on the Jews: its function as a money-earner, stealing from the Jews everything they owned – their cash, their property, the hair on their heads, the gold in their teeth.

There was satisfaction to be drawn from that invitation and others, but it was still clear that the unimaginable achievement Rudi and his old friend from Trnava had pulled off was only faintly recognised. In 1988, Fred Wetzler had died in Bratislava, 'bitter, drunk and forgotten', as Vrba's Israeli defender Ruth Linn put it. In his last years, Fred worked in a local library. Occasionally, a reader might pick up *Čo Dante Nevidel* by 'Jozef Lánik', marvelling at the heroism of the story within. The librarian would never let on that Lánik was him, that it was he who had escaped from Auschwitz.

Now it was Rudi alone who carried the memory of their mission. The escape had been predicated on three assumptions. First came the belief that the outside world had no knowledge of the horrors of the Final Solution, that Planet Auschwitz was in a permanent state of eclipse, with those who lived on earth always in the dark. Second was the related conviction that, since the only reason the Allies had not acted to halt the killing was their ignorance of it, the instant they knew of the slaughter they would surely move to end it. Third, and most important for Rudi especially, was an iron faith that once Jews themselves understood what Auschwitz meant, they would refuse to board the deportation trains and, by that refusal, they would gum up the Nazi machinery of death that had, until then, been lubricated by deception and secrecy.

In the last decades of his life, all three of those certainties would be shaken.

To be sure, Rudi never found reason to waver in his view that one part of the outside world – the Jews – knew nothing of Auschwitz. Rudi had seen that for himself. Talking to the new arrivals who were selected for slave labour as he registered them in the quarantine camp, he never once met a prisoner who knew anything about the gas chambers of Auschwitz before their train pulled in. And that position was repeatedly confirmed in the post-war years. Yehuda Bauer might argue that 'Large numbers of Hungarian Jews were aware of the mass murder in Poland,' that they had picked up the essential facts from rumour or reports, but Elie Wiesel spoke for many survivors, and for many more victims, when he wrote plainly, 'We had no inkling of what awaited us at Auschwitz.' The name of the place did not 'stir any memories or evoke any fear'. Wiesel was one of those Hungarian Jews kept forever uninformed, even after Fred and Rudi escaped and wrote their report. As Wiesel put it, 'Nobody cared enough to tell us: Don't go.'

So Rudi saw nothing to shift his conviction that the Jews of Europe did not know what the Nazis had in store for them. But as the years went by, he would discover that the rest of the world was not nearly as ignorant as he and Fred had assumed when they held their breath in that hole in the ground.

Of course, the Nazi ambition to rid the world of Jews was scarcely a secret. The front-page headline of the *Los Angeles Examiner* on 23 November 1938, a fortnight after Kristallnacht, had proclaimed: 'Nazis Warn World Jews Will Be Wiped Out Unless Evacuated by Democracies'. Adolf Hitler himself had all but announced it on 30 January 1942 when he declared that 'the result of this war will be the complete annihilation of the Jews', repeating a threat he had made in almost identical terms exactly three years earlier. Throughout 1942, the Allies saw and heard enough evidence to know that this was no mere aspiration. By December of that year, as Rudi and the other prisoners were forced to sing 'Stille Nacht' to their SS captors, the Polish government in exile had published an address to the embryonic United Nations titled, 'The Mass Extermination of Jews in German-Occupied Poland'.

The most powerful Allied leaders had received direct, eyewitness testimony of the Nazis' war on the Jews. By 1943 both Anthony Eden and Franklin Roosevelt had sat with Jan Karski, a non-Jewish Pole of aristocratic bearing who had gone undercover into the Warsaw Ghetto (twice) as well as into the Izbica transit camp, and whose reports had formed the basis for that address to the UN. Karski described mass shootings, as well as the loading of Jews on to goods trucks which were then sent to 'special camps at Treblinka, Belzec and Sobibor', purportedly for the sake of resettlement. 'Once there, the so-called "settlers" are mass murdered,' Karski wrote. In December 1942, Eden took to the floor of the House of Commons to read a declaration agreed by all twelve Allied nations, condemning the 'bestial policy of cold-blooded extermination' pursued by the Nazis, one that had now been confirmed by 'numerous reports'. Members of parliament stood in silence to show their support. Soon afterwards, in 1943, the Vatican learned that the toll of Jewish victims of the Nazis was running into the millions: Rome had been kept informed by its apostolic nuncio in Istanbul, Monsignor Angelo Roncalli, the future Pope John XXIII.

All of this Rudi would discover in the decades after the war, much of it set out by Martin Gilbert in *Auschwitz and the Allies*, for which Rudi had been a key interviewee. Gilbert laid bare the fact that London, Washington and others did, after all, know about the Nazi attempt to eliminate the Jews of Europe, even if they had only sketchy knowledge of Auschwitz, that 'unknown destination' in the east. But Gilbert went further, taking apart the second of the beliefs that had driven Fred and Rudi to escape: the notion that, once the Allies were informed of the Nazi slaughter of the Jews, they would act.

Naturally, Rudi was fully aware of the Allied failure to bomb Auschwitz or the railway tracks that led to the camp, even after he and Fred had smuggled out their report. But, thanks to Gilbert, Rudi began to understand what lay behind that inaction, and to see how wrong he had been to believe that it was only a lack of information that had stayed the Allies' hand. Gilbert showed there were political and military considerations, of course, but part of the explanation was 'scepticism and disbelief . . . and even prejudice'. The latter fed the former. 'Familiar stuff,' read one Colonial Office memo, written in London on 7 December 1942, responding to reports of mass killing: 'The Jews have spoilt their case by laying it on too thick for years past.' The full text of the Vrba–Wetzler Report had itself elicited a similar response at the Foreign Office. 'Although a usual Jewish exaggeration is to be taken into account,' wrote Ian Henderson on 26 August 1944, 'these statements are dreadful.' Less than a fortnight later, a colleague in the same department would write, 'In my opinion a disproportionate amount of the time of the Office is wasted on dealing with these wailing Jews.' The nineteen-year-old Walter Rosenberg had not bargained on any of that.

As the twentieth century ended and the new century began, and as the archives opened up, there was to be another blow to what had been the driving faith of Fred and Rudi. In Gilbert's account, whatever else was known about the wider Final Solution, Auschwitz itself had remained the 'unknown destination' or, almost as vague, 'somewhere in the east', closed with a watertight seal: no knowledge had seeped out. That was certainly true of the Jews shipped to the camp, who knew nothing, and of the global public, whether in Switzerland, Britain, the US or beyond, who had barely heard the word 'Auschwitz' until Fred and Rudi's report surfaced in the newspapers in late June 1944.

But new research published some two decades after Gilbert's book showed that, in the governing circles of London and Washington, the veil of ignorance was much thinner. Word of Auschwitz and its function had been reaching Polish exile groups since 1942, brought out via members of the Polish underground, including non-Jewish prisoners who had managed to escape from the camp: the likes of Stanisław Jaster, who in June 1942 smuggled out an account that referred to the killing of Jews, or the resistance fighter Witold Pilecki, who had sent out information mentioning the murder of Jews before his escape in April 1943. What's more, that word had reached those with the power to make decisions.

Admittedly, the Polish government in exile, headquartered in London, did not do much to publicise what it knew. That was partly because of the influence of hardline nationalists who preferred to play down Jewish suffering, and partly because the exiled Poles took their cue from a British government which chose to push the Nazi slaughter of the Jews to the margins of its propaganda effort, lest it diminish public support for the war. (Whitehall wanted Britons to be in no doubt that they were fighting the war for their own sakes, not to save Jewish lives.) What appeared publicly of this Polish intelligence tended to be piecemeal and fragmentary. Even in their raw, unpublished form, the Polish accounts did not match the scope, detail or depth of the Vrba–Wetzler Report. They did not carry the same weight and none had anything like the impact. Nevertheless, they did exist and perhaps as many as thirty-five of them reached the west ahead of Fred and Rudi's testimony; some of their findings occasionally made it into the newspapers. And yet the officials and others who were informed about Auschwitz did not act on what they knew, usually for the same reasons that Gilbert had already identified: the focus on other wartime goals, an impatience with the Jews, often shaped by bigotry, and a scepticism that such horrors could really be happening at all. When Churchill wrote to his deputy to ask, 'What can be done? What can be said?' it is at least conceivable that he was expressing not speechless horror, but rather a politician's practical need for advice now that what was once secret knowledge was becoming public.

Late in life, then, Rudi had to confront the fact that his younger self had been wrong to believe that the Allies did not know, and wrong to believe that they would come to the rescue of the Jews if they had. But he could cling to one last conviction: that if the Jews of Hungary had only known what he and Fred knew and had written down in their report, then they would have refused to go to their deaths.

Rudi held fast to that belief, and yet in his later years that too would be challenged. Several historians argued that, even if Rezső Kasztner and the others had not sat on the Vrba–Wetzler Report, it would have made little difference. Resistance would have been impossible given the absence of Jewish men of fighting age, the lack of weapons, a flat landscape that allowed few places to hide and a local population that was either indifferent or hostile to its Jewish neighbours. Rudi had an answer to all of that. Jews did not need to organise a formal resistance to thwart or slow the Nazi operation: even a chaotic, panicked refusal to go, a stampede on the railway platform, would have been enough. It would have forced the Nazis to hunt deer rather than sheep.

But there was one objection which struck with greater force, partly because of its source. Not long after the release of *Shoah*, Rudi met a man who had seen him in the Lanzmann film and who travelled to Vancouver all the way from his home in Sweden to thank him personally. This man believed Rudolf Vrba had saved his life. His name was Georg Klein. More than forty years earlier he had been György Klein, working as a junior secretary for the Jewish Council in Budapest.

A turning point had come in late May or early June 1944, when Klein's boss, a rabbi member of the *Judenrat*, had told him of a 'highly secret document' that the council had received. It was a report written by young Slovak Jews who had escaped from one of the annihilation camps in Poland. The rabbi would show it to György, on condition that his young aide tell no one but his closest friends and family what it contained. He then handed György a copy, in Hungarian and on carbon paper, of the Vrba–Wetzler Report.

As he read it, Klein felt a mixture of nausea and intellectual satisfaction. The former because he now knew the fate of his grandmother and uncles who had been deported, and the latter because he knew that what he was reading was the truth. 'The dry, factual, nearly scientific language, the dates, the numbers, the maps and the logic of the narrative,' Klein would write later, 'it made sense. Nothing else made sense.'

Klein went immediately to see his uncle, a rheumatologist whose practice was just across the street. Klein, who was still a teenager, told him what he had read. His uncle's reaction astonished him. The older man became so angry, he came close to hitting his nephew. 'His face got red; he shook his head and raised his voice.' How could György believe such nonsense? It was unthinkable, impossible.

György visited other relatives and friends, passing on what he had read in the Auschwitz Report. Soon a pattern emerged. Those who were young believed it and began to make plans to evade the deportations. But the middle aged, those who, like his uncle, had dependants, careers and property – those who had much to lose – refused to believe what they were hearing. The idea of abandoning all they had, of going underground, of living on false papers or making for the border in the dead of night – the very idea of it seemed to prevent them from believing. György himself only finally made his escape when he was taken to a railway station and could see the cattle trucks waiting for him. He remembered the words he had read on those sheets of carbon paper and, even at the risk of being shot, he made a run for it.

More than four decades later, Klein was sitting in the faculty club of the University of British Columbia with his unknowing saviour. Georg told Rudi that he, Georg, was proof that, even if the Vrba–Wetzler Report had been distributed as Rudi had wanted, it would not have brought the result he craved. Of the dozen or so middle-aged people Klein had warned, not one had believed him.

The two men argued the point back and forth. Rudi insisted that Georg had been disbelieved because he was young: it would have been different if the Auschwitz Report had been circulated by the trusted Jewish leadership. Georg countered that those who were not young would never have taken action, no matter who had given the warning. They were used to obeying the law. To disobey meant exposing their children, in the critical moment on the railway platform, to the certainty of being gunned down. No parent would risk that, even if they had been told that death awaited them at the end of the line. 'Denial was the most natural escape.'

Round and round they went. Rudi never retreated from his view that those Jews who boarded the trains at least had the right to make an informed decision, a right they were denied by those who kept them in darkness, those who hid the evidence he had given everything to reveal. Georg stuck to his position that very few would have acted any differently, even if their right to know had been honoured.

As it happened, the argument made by Georg Klein was not

wholly new to Rudi. He had had reason before to contemplate this difficult but stubborn fact: that human beings find it almost impossible to conceive of their own death.

After all, one of Rudi's fellow Auschwitz escapees had encountered this phenomenon directly and within months of his escape. In a desperate turn of events, Czesław Mordowicz was caught by the Gestapo in late 1944 and put on a transport that would send him back to Auschwitz. Inside the cattle truck, he told his fellow deportees that he knew what awaited them. 'Listen,' he pleaded, 'you are going to your death.' Czesław urged the people jammed into the wagon to join him and jump off the moving train. They refused. Instead they began shouting, banging on the doors and calling the German guards. They attacked Mordowicz and beat him so badly, he was all but incapacitated. He never did leap off that train, but ended up back in Birkenau. All because he had given a warning that the warned could not believe and did not want to hear.

Even among the prisoners inside Auschwitz, where the air was choked with the smoke of incinerating human flesh, there were those who refused to believe what they could see and smell. A former slave to Josef Mengele described how prisoners who knew only too well what happened in the gas chambers repressed that knowledge when the hour came to line up for their own execution. Even the young Walter Rosenberg had done it, when he first handled the suitcases and clothes of the dead in Kanada, pushing out of his mind his 'vague suspicions' about the owners of those stolen goods and their fate.

A horror is especially hard to comprehend if no one has ever witnessed anything like it before. When Jan Karski, the undercover operative, visited Washington to brief President Roosevelt on the Nazis' assault upon the Jews, he also met Supreme Court justice Felix Frankfurter. Karski told the judge what he had seen in Poland. Frankfurter listened for twenty minutes before finally saying, 'I do not believe you.' A diplomat in the room began to defend Karski's credibility, prompting the judge to explain himself. 'I did not say that he is lying. I said that I don't believe him. These are different things. My mind and my heart are made in such a way that I cannot accept it. No. No. No.'

After the war, Hannah Arendt admitted that when she read the *New York Times* despatch from Geneva, revealing the key facts of the Vrba–Wetzler Report, she and her husband 'didn't believe it'. Her husband thought it 'could not be true because killing civilians did not make any military sense'.

Walter's escape had been built on his initial conviction that facts could save lives, that information would be the weapon with which he would thwart the Nazi plan to eliminate the Jews. Witnessing the fate of the Czech family camp, and its residents' immovable faith, despite the evidence all around them, that they would somehow be spared, had led him to understand a more complicated truth: that information is necessary, to be sure, but it is never sufficient. Information must also be *believed*, especially when it comes to mortal threats. On this, if nothing else, he and Yehuda Bauer might eventually have found common ground: only when information is combined with belief does it become knowledge. And only knowledge leads to action.

The French-Jewish philosopher Raymond Aron would say, when asked about the Holocaust, 'I knew, but I didn't believe it. And because I didn't believe it, I didn't know.'

All this Rudolf Vrba understood, and yet he was not ground down by it. He discussed it with Georg Klein during those few days they spent together in Vancouver, the pair of them taking long walks in Stanley Park, Klein staying as a guest in Robin and Rudi's home, where he astonished the couple with his 5 a.m. starts. The dialogue between the two men continued: not long afterwards, this time in Paris, they would share a long lunch that turned into dinner with two fellow scientists. Nothing in what Klein said broke Rudi's spirit.

Klein marvelled at it, amazed that, despite all he had endured, Rudi was able to live life, encouraging students one moment or making small talk with waiters the next. Faced with such irrecoverable losses – of his people, of his daughter – a man might be expected either to go into denial or depression. But Rudi had done neither. Instead, he was doing something much harder and more admirable. He was carrying the losses he had endured, and living all the same.

Indeed, he loved life and was hungry for more of it. In May 2005, he called Robert Krell, a leader of the Vancouver Jewish community and a professor in the university medical school. Rudi had regarded Krell warily at first – he was a Jewish community leader, after all – but that resistance had steadily broken down. Krell was a Dutch Jew born in 1940, who had spent his first years in hiding. Eventually the hidden child and the Auschwitz escapee became friends. And now Rudi was on the phone. 'Robert, I need to talk to you.'

Rudi told Krell that he had had bladder cancer for about ten years: he had not mentioned it until then. Other than his wife, Rudi had hardly told anyone; his daughter Zuza had no idea. The last check-up had shown that the cancer had penetrated to a deeper layer.

But Rudi was not calling Robert for gloomy talk of an imminent end. Rather, he did not like the way his urologist was dealing with him and he wondered if Robert could have a word. Krell promptly called the doctor and explained something of his patient's history. Given where Rudolf Vrba had been, he would have good reason to view medical personnel with suspicion.

Surgery followed, removing Rudi's entire bladder and some other tissue and the outlook was hopeful. The tumour appeared to have gone and Rudi looked closer to seventy than a man approaching eighty-two. He had studied the survival rates for bladder cancer, as he had studied everything else about the disease, and he would joke that if he could reach the age of ninety-two, he would be content. It would fall short of the record set by his once seemingly indestructible mother who had died in 1991 at the age of ninety-six, but it would do. He was not ready to let go; he wanted to live.

Except that his cancer cells had learned from their host: they had escaped. They had broken out from the bladder and formed metastases in his legs. Rudi's doctors now switched their focus away from treatment and towards the alleviation of pain. He had suffered enough pain in his life; Krell told him there was no need to endure any more.

Friends were adamant that it had not needed to be this way. They believed that if Rudi had put himself in the hands of specialist doctors earlier, rather than trying to research and organise his own treatment, his cancer could have been cured. But Rudi had always been determined that one should never show weakness – *What are you, a Muselmann?* – that he should never seem vulnerable, to Robin, to himself, to the world. That very determination proved his greatest vulnerability.

His health went into a steady decline. But that period also brought a comfort he had not known for many decades. For the first time since the 1950s, he saw his daughter every day. Zuza, by then an editor of children's books in London, dropped everything to be at her father's side in Vancouver in his final months. Sometimes they would talk philosophy; sometimes they would talk of Helena, his firstborn. Their relationship had not always been smooth, but those last months were tender between them. Ever the scientist, Rudi said that he loved Zuza 'on a cellular level': that was how deep it went. She was his only living child, and he was her Tata.

Rudolf Vrba died at 7.25 p.m. on 27 March 2006. In the weeks before his death, Rudi had been reluctant to discuss funeral arrangements. 'He was in denial,' his wife would say later, 'and I kept up the denial.' He did not want to know.

Vrba was buried in the Boundary Bay cemetery in the small town of Tsawwassen, on the Canadian–US border. There was only one eulogy, from Dr Stephan Horny, a nephew of Rudi's who lived in Montreal. There were not enough Jewish men present to make a *minyan*, the traditional quorum, and in a departure from Jewish practice the ceremony was on a Saturday, the sabbath. But Robin's father said *kaddish*, the prayer of mourning. Nine months later there was a memorial event in Vancouver. About forty people turned up.

In life, Rudi was glad whenever his attempt to alert the world to the reality of Auschwitz was recognised, but he would hardly have expected a hero's send-off. He did not consider himself a hero, if a hero is defined by success in his chosen mission. Perhaps Rudolf Vrba saw himself instead in the tradition of the Jewish prophet, who comes to deliver a warning, only to grieve when that warning is not heeded.

During that long talk when they first met, a conversation that lasted ten hours, Georg Klein asked Rudi why he was still so angry about all that had not happened in Hungary, rather than feeling proud of all that *had* happened, thanks to his escape. 'Should you not be satisfied that you managed to save two hundred thousand?'

No, Vrba was not satisfied. Like many of the best-known rescuers of the period, he thought less about those he had saved than about all those he had not saved.

But Georg Klein did not see it the same way. He knew that he owed his life to what Fred and Rudi had done all those years earlier. He had gone on to become an eminent scientist, one who made breakthroughs in the study of tumours leading to great advances in immunotherapy against cancer, advances that would soon help many millions. None of that would have been possible without Rudi. Klein had had three children and seven grandchildren, who between them would go on to have twelve children of their own. None of those lives would have been possible without Rudi. None of those children would be alive today if it were not for Rudi.

Jewish tradition says that to save one life is to save the whole world. By their report, Fred and Rudi saved 200,000 Budapest Jews from immediate deportation to Auschwitz. Some would die a few months later at the hands of the Arrow Cross, but many more would not. And each one of those lives, and the lives of their descendants, would not have been possible without Rudolf Vrba.

Fifty years before Walter Rosenberg was born, and no more than a hundred miles away, a boy came into the world by the name of Erik Weisz. He was a Hungarian Jew, the son of a rabbi, and within a few years he had moved to the United States. There he began a career on the stage, first on the trapeze, then performing magic tricks and finally as an escape artist. He called himself Harry Houdini.

Rosenberg too was an escape artist. He escaped from Auschwitz, from his past, even from his own name. He escaped his home country, his adopted country and the country after that. He escaped and escaped and escaped – but he could never fully break free from the horror he had witnessed and which he had laid bare before the world.

When he lived in England in the 1960s, driving into central London from his home in Sutton, all he could see when he passed the belching chimneys of Battersea Power Station were the crematoria of Birkenau. When he was handled roughly by an X-ray technician in Vancouver, he thought the medic had something of 'the SS' about him. When his cancer spread inoperably, he sighed to a friend, 'the Gestapo has finally gotten to me.'

His life was defined by what he had endured as a teenager. But he was not crushed by it. When his daughter Zuza turned forty-four, he sent her birthday wishes reminding her that forty-four was his 'lucky number'. In parenthesis, and by way of explanation, he set down '44070', the Auschwitz number that had been tattooed on his arm, with the emphasis on the first two digits. He did not consider that number a curse; he believed it had brought him great fortune. After all, he had survived and he had escaped. 'I hope it will bring you luck too,' he told his daughter.

Rudolf Vrba was an escape artist whose achievement ranks among the very greatest of the century. By escaping from Auschwitz, he did what no Jew had ever done before – and then he told the world what he had seen. And though he never escaped Auschwitz's shadow, he lived a life in full, as a man in full. He became a scientist and a scholar, a husband, a father and a grandfather. He had helped the world, and history, know the truth of the Holocaust. And, thanks to him, tens of thousands of others went on to live lives that were long and rich, as did their children and grandchildren and great-grandchildren – so many, even he could not count them all.

# Postscript to the Paperback Edition

# Postscript to the Paperback Edition

THERE WERE TIMES writing this book when it felt as if I were plunging deep into history, mining the archives for documents written nearly a century ago, reconstructing events involving people long dead. But when the book was published, and in the weeks and months that followed, there came repeated reminders that this was a story that lived on, including in the memories of those very much alive.

Even before the book was in any shop or on any shelf, an email arrived from a reader who had seen some advance publicity. His name was Chris Arden:

> Back in 1961/2 I became a junior technician at the Neuropsychiatric Research Unit at Carshalton Beeches. It was my first appointment after finishing my A levels. It was at that institute that I met Rudi Vrba. He worked in another dept of the institute. I can attest to this very private man's amazing memory. I was talking to him about a biochemical problem and he told me I would find reference to that subject in a particular journal: he gave me the date of publication, the page number and paragraph – all from memory.

I later met Chris and he told me that, of course, Rudi's citation had turned out to be flawlessly accurate. What made his email especially gratifying was that this reminiscence had been wholly unprompted: the promotion of the book had made no mention of Vrba's astonishing memory, or the feat of mind that had enabled him to record, without pen or paper, the details of every transport of Jews whose arrival in Auschwitz he had witnessed. I knew that there were some historians who had doubted whether such an act of memorisation was even possible. Now, unbidden, came fresh corroboration that Vrba was blessed with an almost freakishly good memory, one that was not confined to the data of death he had collected between 1942 and 1944. Indeed, a British teenage scientist had been so struck by this talent, he had remembered it even sixty years later.

Chris Arden told me two more things about the Dr Vrba he had met in Carshalton, both of which also served to confirm what I had either known or guessed. 'I didn't realise that he had been in Auschwitz,' he wrote, 'as he never talked about the camp.' And this: 'I suspect as a foreigner he was not accepted in the scientific establishment in the early '60s.'

That correspondence was just the beginning. As I toured the country, speaking to audiences in almost every corner of the British Isles and then travelling to North America and beyond, I kept running into people who had known Rudi – some intimately. These were people who had carried with them their encounters with this remarkable man, as if waiting for the day when the wider world would recognise the scale of what he and Alfréd Wetzler had achieved, when someone would, at last, want to hear more about him. Now, with the publication of *The Escape Artist*, they stepped forward.

I was contacted by Jane Bennett, who introduced herself as the daughter of Beth, the woman who had been married to Sidney Hilton before Hilton left her for Gerta Vrbová – the same Beth who, however improbably, had dated Rudi.

Jane had memories of 'a lovely, modest man'. She remembered sitting at the kitchen table, riveted, as she read Rudi's Auschwitz story in the pages of the *Daily Herald* on the eve of the trial of Adolf Eichmann. And there, across the table from her as she read, sat Rudi.

According to Jane, Beth was one of the first people Rudi ever knew in England. He had come to the country chiefly to be reunited with his children, but he had no idea where Helena, Zuza and his ex-wife Gerta lived. His only clue was that Gerta was now married to Sidney Hilton. But how to find them? Rudi knew that the woman Sidney had cast aside was, like Sidney, a physiologist. So he worked his way through academic directories and associations until he finally tracked down Beth Hilton. They met at a railway station, probably Victoria, and, impressed by her looks, Rudi's first, incredulous words to Beth, referring to her ex-husband, were: 'He left *you* for *her*?'

They were soon a couple, Rudi a presence in the home Beth shared with Jane and her younger sister. It was Rudi's side of the acrimonious family story they heard: Jane remembered Rudi's distress that, when he sent gifts to his two daughters, his presents would be returned, unopened. The way they saw it, it was Gerta who had wrecked things, by depriving a good man of access to his children.

And yet, sympathetic as she was, Beth could not give Rudi all he wanted. He longed for a wife and he asked Beth to marry him. The result would have been a blended family of unusual symmetry: in effect, the Hiltons and the Vrbas would have swapped spouses. But Beth said no. Her daughters believed it was because she was simply not up for what would have been a third marriage. Even so, and hurt though he must have been, Rudi did not slam the door on Beth. On the contrary, the pair 'remained close friends' right until Beth's death in 2003.

You have only to look at pictures from the period to see that Rudi would have cut a dashing figure in 1960s London. And so perhaps it's no surprise that, more than once, after I had given a talk about this book, I would be approached by a woman from the audience, there to tell me that she or someone she knew had a romantic memory of Rudi during his England period. On a bright evening in Henley-on-Thames, it was an elegant lady with a Home Counties' accent who joined the signing queue to let me know that her sister had once dated the charming man from Czechoslovakia – and that she had found him rather charming herself. On a rainy afternoon in Golders Green, I was to hear of a connection that was far more direct.

I was speaking at the Holocaust Survivors Centre, a remarkable place that provides a safe harbour for the small, shrinking number of people who endured the events recounted in this book first hand. It had been a daunting prospect – to speak of the Shoah to those who had survived it – but the audience could not have been warmer. They all listened intently, though I noticed that one woman paid particular attention throughout.

Afterwards, she told me her name was Olga Steward, though everyone called her Olinka. She was now eighty-seven and living in London, but she had been born, like Rudi, in Slovakia, only coming to England in 1964. She became friends with the Hungarian émigré journalist and humourist, George Mikes, and it was at his home in Putney that she met Rudi. By then, Rudi had already made the move to Vancouver, but at the end of each academic year he would come back to London to spend the long university vacation near his daughters. Olinka and Rudi started seeing each other, through one summer and then the next.

She knew something of the world he had fled; she had even known Rudi's mother, Ilonka, back in the old country. She had survived the war years alternating between 'semi-hiding' and 'deep hiding' in central Slovakia, including an extended spell living below ground, in a potato cellar in the countryside. But she and Rudi said nothing of that past. 'The word "Auschwitz", I don't think the word was spoken once,' she told me. She owned a copy of his memoir, then a relatively recent publication – though, decades later, she couldn't be sure if Rudi or someone else had given it to her – but she couldn't read it. It upset her too much.

The pair were comfortable with each other; they could chat away in Slovak, about books, about his career, about the land of their birth. And when he went back to Canada, they would exchange occasional letters. One day, Olinka opened an envelope from Rudi – and there, in writing, was a proposal of marriage.

'I decided I wanted to see him in his own environment,' Olinka told me, some fifty-five years later. 'I was only seeing him in holiday conditions,' on those summer trips back to London. And so she headed to Vancouver.

'I knew in twenty-four hours it was not right,' she said. 'He was not fun – he was too heavy – and I was looking for something a little bit lighter: going out, dancing.' He drank more than she expected: he would go to bed with a bottle of wine. And he was 'very bitter' towards his ex-wife, Gerta. In this telling, he had returned to Prague one day only to find Gerta and the girls had upped and left. 'He was devastated.' He had followed his children to England, but England had not treated him well. He resented the country anyway, because England had failed to act on the report he had written with Fred Wetzler.

All this helped Olinka reach her decision. She told Rudi her answer was no. But, once again, he did not fly into a rage with the woman who had spurned his offer. He did not put her on the first flight back to London. On the contrary, the couple had a wonderful fortnight in Vancouver, lunching in the faculty club, swimming in the ocean. 'He did his best to entertain me.'

They went out a few times with a Polish couple, but they did not socialise much with Rudi's university colleagues. Olinka sensed Rudi, still new in Canada, was happier around Europeans. Once the two weeks had passed, she took her leave of a man she still remembered as simultaneously handsome and strange-looking, with his 'black hair and black eyes'.

In almost all cases, those who told me they had met Rudi were, naturally enough, of a ripe age. There was one exception, and she approached me with exceptional testimony. Other than Gerta, she was the only person I ever spoke to who had met both Rudolf Vrba and Alfréd Wetzler in person. Not much older than me, her name was Dr Bea Lewkowicz, an oral historian and social anthropologist. She worked with the Association of Jewish Refugees and led their effort to build an archive of testimony, the stories of refugees told in their own words. But her connection with Fred and Rudi was not professional. It was personal.

Bea had grown up in Germany as the child of two Holocaust survivors. Her mother, Gertrud, was from the Slovak town of Piešt'any but had spent much of the war as a Jewish teenager in hiding in Žilina. Gertrud had been in Žilina in the fateful weeks of April 1944.

She had just turned fifteen, though she looked younger. She was small and boyish, in contrast with her older sister, who was eighteen, beautiful and tended to attract attention. The family thought it safer to keep the older girl out of sight, so it fell to Gertrud to run errands, even to act as a secret courier. So it was that one day her uncle Armin – who, as the manager of a distillery in the town, had been deemed of sufficient economic importance to be exempt from deportation – came to her with a vital job.

He told her there were two men in the basement of the old people's home who needed to eat. She was handed a set of metal containers, stacked like Indian tiffin boxes, and headed for Hollého Street. She went down the stairs, opened the door, and saw Fred and Rudi. She had no idea who they were, where they had fled from or what they had witnessed. But she heard their reaction to seeing her. 'They really couldn't believe it,' Gertrud's daughter Bea told me. 'They looked at each other and said, "Wow! There are still children alive. There is a child still here."'

They had spent the best part of the previous two years in Auschwitz, where children were murdered on arrival and where new lives were snuffed out as soon as they began. They had lived in a world where the Jewish young were not allowed to exist: those in the Czech family camp had lived on borrowed time, which had run out. And yet here, in front of them, less than ninety miles away from Auschwitz, was a living, breathing Jewish child.

Gertrud took food to Fred and Rudi only once, but that was not the last time she saw them. The Slovak Jewish community was small to begin with, but in the post-war era it was little more than a huddle: everyone knew everyone else. Inevitably then, in Prague in the 1950s, the now adult Gertrud ran into Rudi and his wife Gerta. Gertrud was studying medicine and dentistry, while they were taking the first steps in their own scientific careers. Did Gertrud and Rudi discuss that first encounter in the basement, when Rudi had been out of Auschwitz little more than a fortnight? Maybe not. 'They were not thinking of the past,' Bea said. 'They were thinking of the future.'

Gertrud and Rudi stayed in touch in the decades that followed, even after she had left Czechoslovakia for Germany. They met up once in France, and on a family visit to Vancouver. Bea was only nine or ten, but Rudi left as strong an impression on her as he did on everyone else. He was glamorous, with a glamorous young wife. He spoke well; he wore 'a dapper white linen suit' and a hat. Bea was struck by his *joie de vivre*. 'That's what I remember,' she told me: the sheer zest for life of this man who had seen so much death.

The connection with Fred Wetzler was even closer and more enduring: they became family. Etela, the survivor of Auschwitz who married Fred, was a cousin of Gertrud's. When the Wetzlers had a child, Gertrud was their babysitter. When Gertrud got married in 1964 in Piešt'any, Fred acted as witness.

In January 1988, Bea, then aged twenty-three, visited Bratislava and stayed with the Wetzlers for a week. She remembered the contrast:

she had seen Rudi in fine French cafés or by the ocean in Vancouver, while Fred was in a wintry Bratislava, with its Stalin-era high-rise concrete blocks. Everywhere was cold and 'everything was grey'.

She liked her hosts. Etela was 'fun and loud and talked a lot', and the flat was constantly alive with conversation: Fred's wife was a language teacher and students were constantly coming in and out. The apartment was clouded in smoke: the Wetzlers were rarely without a cigarette. Fred was quieter than 'Eta', softly spoken; he struck the young Bea as a 'gentle soul'. And he had, she said, 'a wonderful, lovely face'.

Bea picked up a lot in that week. She learned that Fred had been 'excluded' by the ruling communist party. Unlikely as it may sound, the party accused him of spying for the Vatican: a charge apparently linked to the fact that the Vrba–Wetzler report had reached representatives of Pope Pius. The suspicion that Fred was an agent of the Catholic church was grounds enough for the authorities to cut the pension owed to him as a veteran of the partisan resistance – and to remove him from his job as a journalist. Which is why he worked in a local library.

The memory of the past hung as heavily as the smoke in that apartment. Bea kept a diary and she wrote: 'They still live in the world of Auschwitz . . . The concentration camp is part of daily life. The television is on in the background, but Fred is talking about his escape. Eta is talking about the *Kapos*.' Even chit-chat about acquaintances would soon turn back to that place. 'This one was in the camp, this one wasn't in the camp,' Bea recalled. 'It was very, very, very present.'

On 8 February, a couple of weeks after Bea had returned home, she recorded in her diary that Fred Wetzler had died. She wrote that she was grateful to have had time with him. When she and I spoke, she wanted to challenge the account of Fred having died 'bitter, drunk and forgotten'. In the week she had spent in Bratislava, she had seen no evidence of alcoholism. She did not deny there was bitterness. And there was no denying that, then at least, he had been all but forgotten.

Often when I spoke about this story, people assumed that I had been guided by the children of Rudi and Fred. But one of the tragedies both men shared was that their children did not live long. I never met Helena or Zuza, but I did meet people who had known them both and it was clear they had left a deep mark. A friend of the sisters, Robin Dance, wrote to me of the Helena he remembered from the late 1970s, when she was sharing a house in a Sussex village with friends of his. He could see her still, 'highly intelligent and well-educated, outward going and resilient – a beautiful woman, with her mass of thick curly hair, sparkling eyes and unrestrained smile.'

He painted a picture of Helena zipping around the English countryside in her old Hillman Imp and of Zuza the day he first met her, when she appeared at the cottage for a weekend party: 'wearing a light summer frock, cut just above the knee, and leather mountain boots.' The boots puzzled him, until he discovered that, like him, Zuza was a keen mountaineer: she had come to the party on her way home from the Alps.

There were memories of music from Helena's record player, albums by Joan Armatrading and Fleetwood Mac, as well as a summer of swims in the nearby river, home-baked bread and exhilarating motorcycle rides to and from Brighton. He remembered his admiration when Helena announced her move to Papua New Guinea: here was a woman driven by altruism, a desire to help those less fortunate than herself. Robin Dance also wondered if the boldness, this courage of Helena's, was inherited in part from her father.

He told me of his incredulity when he learned of his friend's death in May 1982, and of the funeral in London where he saw Rudi, 'sombre and composed'. He told me that Zuza never accepted that her sister had taken her own life; post-mortem documents had gone missing that left, in Zuza's mind, 'eternal doubt'. For his own part, Robin recalled that he had received a letter from Helena less than a fortnight before her death that, while it spoke of her loneliness, was looking to the future. 'See you in September,' were her parting words. For him, Helena's passing was surrounded by 'mystery and tragedy'.

That phrase lingered, for it seemed to fit not only the death of Helena but the life of her father. Rudi remained a mystery even to those who thought they knew him. I received a message from a woman in Canada who told me that her father, a biochemist colleague of Rudi's in the 1970s, had been astonished to come across the story told in this book as 'he knew nothing about it'. She wrote: 'The biochemistry community in Canada at that time was quite small . . . Dad was shocked he didn't know this story, even third hand.'

Rudolf Vrba had witnessed and endured such intense tragedy, but he was sparing in how, and to whom, he talked about it. Perhaps now his experience will be talked about more, with a new generation discovering that, although his story is from the past, it is not of the past – that there are timeless lessons to be drawn from his singular life. About the necessity of truth. About the insufficiency of mere information: how facts alone are not enough, because people must also believe them. About the defences human beings will build, the lengths they will go to, rather than contemplate the possibility of their own destruction. As Esther Gilbert, widow of the eminent historian Martin Gilbert, put it in a letter to me written a couple of months after this book was first published: 'Rudi is still teaching all of us.'

Jonathan Freedland
London, February 2023

# Acknowledgements

A book like this would be impossible without the kindness of others. First thanks go to Robin Vrba, who over many patient hours let me into the life she had shared with Rudi, digging out yellowing papers and faded photographs, answering an endless stream of questions and mining a rich store of memories. No less generous was Rudolf Vrba's first wife and childhood sweetheart, Gerta Vrbová, who sat with me in the final weeks of her life recalling a world that had long vanished – eventually handing me a suitcase packed with her ex-husband's letters, many of which touched on unimaginably painful experiences. I am also grateful to Gerta's daughter Caroline, her son Peter and grandson Jack, as well as to Rudi's friends and colleagues in Vancouver – among them, Chris Friedrichs, Robert Krell and Joseph Ragaz – for sharing their own recollections of this extraordinary man.

A legion of scholars were generous with their expertise, starting with Nikola Zimring who steered me through several of the most elusive aspects of the Vrba–Wetzler story. Yehuda Bauer, Paul Bogdanor, Ruth Linn, Deborah Lipstadt and Nikolaus Wachsmann, as well as a former member of the Hungarian underground, David Gur, all helped enormously, as did Peter Klein, son of Georg, and Richard Bestic, son of Alan. Tim Radford agreed to serve as interpreter of Rudi's scientific writings and did it with his trademark clarity. I want to offer particular thanks to Karen Pollock of the Holocaust Educational Trust. She and the organisation she heads do invaluable work and she gave me one lead in particular which proved essential as I set out on this journey. A portion of the proceeds of this book will be going to the trust.

Beyond those conversations with historians and the guidance of

Rudi's family and colleagues, this book is based on testimonies from survivors of the Holocaust, documents recording the events of that period and, above all, the words of Rudolf Vrba himself. He left behind not only a memoir, but also a copious personal archive of letters and writings, all held at the Franklin D. Roosevelt Presidential Library in New York. I'd like to thank Kirsten Carter and her team for their help in making that archive accessible, even in the age of Covid.

Thanks are due to Szymon Kowalski and Teresa Wontor-Cichy of the Auschwitz-Birkenau State Museum for answering so many of my questions, as well as to the team at Yad Vashem in Jerusalem and to Allen Packwood of the Churchill Archives Centre in Cambridge. I am grateful to Gordon Brown for making that latter connection and indeed for his encouragement of this project.

I am indebted to Marcelina Tomza-Michalska for acting as my guide and interpreter in Poland and to Jarka Šimonová for playing the same role in Slovakia. Further thanks go to Peter Švec, for fielding my enquiries as we walked a stretch of the annual Vrba–Wetzler march, retracing the escape route, a commemoration that exists thanks in part to the inspiration of Rudi's late daughter Zuza.

At John Murray, I could not have been in better hands than those of my editor Joe Zigmond: he and Jocasta Hamilton have managed to be simultaneously enthusiastic and wise, backed by the meticulous care and professionalism of Caroline Westmore and by the copy-editing vigilance of Peter James. In the US, thanks go to the reassuringly shrewd Sara Nelson and Kris Dahl. Whether in London or New York, all of them grasped the significance of this story when they had little to go on but my conviction that it needed to be told.

The Curtis Brown team went far beyond the call of duty, with Viola Hayden proving an especially canny reader while Kate Cooper and Nadia Mokdad have worked wonders taking this story to the wider world. Out in front, as always, has been Jonny Geller – not only the best agent any writer could ask for, but a true and loyal friend over four decades. It was a walk in the woods with him that set this book in motion: it would not have happened without him.

Once again, I am glad to thank Jonathan Cummings for his

exhaustive (and no doubt exhausting) work researching this project, chasing down every last detail. He plunged deep into the history with me, at my side as we burrowed into the archives, trudged through the forests of Slovakia and walked among ghosts in Auschwitz. I am deeply grateful.

Finally, I say thank you to my wife Sarah and my sons Jacob and Sam. This subject is not a light one to carry around. That I have been able to do so is down to their patience, their humour and their love. I appreciate them more with each passing year.

Jonathan Freedland
London, March 2022

# Picture Credits

Alamy Stock Photo: 7 below/Keystone Press. Auschwitz–Birkenau State Museum Archive: 3 above/photo Stanislaw Kolowca 1945, 3 below, 4, 7 centre right. © bpk Bildagentur: 7 above left. FDR Presidential Library & Museum: 5 below. Courtesy of Caroline Hilton: 6 centre right. National Archives, Kew, UK: 5 above/PREM 4/51/10. Private Collection courtesy of Hans Citroen: 2 below. Sovfoto/Universal Images Group/Shutterstock: 1 below. United States Holocaust Memorial Museum, courtesy of Yad Vashem: 2 above/Public Domain, 8 above/Created by Claude Lanzmann during the filming of *Shoah* used by permission of United States Holocaust Memorial Museum and Yad Vashem – The Holocaust Martyrs' and Heroes' Remembrance Authority, Jerusalem. Courtesy of Robin Vrba: 1 above, 6 above left and below, 8 below.

# Notes

## Abbreviations

| | |
|---|---|
| APMAB: | Archiwum Państwowego Muzeum Auschwitz-Birkenau (Archives of the Auschwitz-Birkenau State Museum), Oświęcim |
| CZA: | Central Zionist Archives, Jerusalem |
| FDRPL: | Franklin D. Roosevelt Presidential Library, Hyde Park, New York |
| JTA: | Jewish Telegraphic Agency |
| NA: | Národní archiv, Prague |
| USHMM: | United States Holocaust Memorial Museum, Washington, DC |
| YVA: | Yad Vashem Archive, Jerusalem |

## Prologue

1 **'Bon voyage'**: Wetzler, *Escape*, p. 108.
1 **sprinkled**: Wetzler, 1963 testimony, p. 37.
1 **phosphorescent**: Wetzler, *Escape*, p. 111.
2 **take his hand and squeeze it**: Ibid., p. 108.
2 **would not let themselves be interrogated**: Ibid.
2 **side by side**: Wetzler, 1963 testimony, p. 38.
2 **at last the waiting was over**: Vrba, *I Escaped*, p. 271.
2 **strip of flannel**: Wetzler, *Escape*, p. 124.
3 **200 of them**: Gilbert, *Auschwitz*, p. 196.
3 **search every ridge**: Wetzler, *Escape*, p. 125.
4 **their panting audible**: Ibid., p. 124.
4 **the SS and their henchmen**: Wetzler, *Escape*, pp. 134–5.
5 **'Stupid bastards!'**: Vrba, *I Escaped*, p. 274.
5 **several pounds of bread**: Vrba, 'Preparations', p. 247.
5 **margarine**: Wetzler, 1963 testimony, p. 36.

5 **bottle filled with cold coffee**: Ibid., p. 38.

5 **frosty morning mist**: Wetzler, *Escape*, p. 134.

5 **feeling in his fingers**: Ibid., p. 130.

5 **'They can't have got away'**: Vrba, *I Escaped*, p. 275.

6 **'They've got them! C'mon . . . Hurry'**: Ibid.

7 **a sharp pain**: Wetzler, *Escape*, p. 139.

7 **they hugged each other**: Ibid.

7 **'we'd have been trapped'**: Vrba, *I Escaped*, p. 277.

## Chapter 1: Star

11 **example to be followed**: Author correspondence with Robin Vrba.

12 **run an errand**: Vrba, Lanzmann interview, p. 71.

13 **bolt of lightning**: Author correspondence with Robin Vrba.

13 **Walter chose none**: Vrba, *World at War*, part I, p. 4.

14 **unreliable, untrustworthy**: Kubátová and Láníček, *Imagination*, p. 22.

15 **flat fields of ripe corn**: Vrbová, *Trust*, p. 11.

15 **set fire to both synagogues**: JTA, '2 Synagogues Burned in Slovakia', 14 December 1938.

15 **'Jews out, Czechs out'**: Vrbová, *Trust*, p. 14.

16 **inorganic and organic chemistry**: Vrba, *I Escaped*, p. 55.

16 **a personal tutor**: Author interview with Robin Vrba, 22 October 2021.

16 **hat with pom-poms**: Vrbová, *Trust*, p. 21.

16 **a bulletin board**: Vogel, USHMM interview, p. 2.

17 **keep his butcher shop alive**: Vrbová, *Trust*, p. 21.

17 **It was open season**: Spira, 'Memories of Youth', p. 43.

18 **'The strictest laws against Jews are Slovakia's'**: The front page of government propaganda paper *L'udové noviny* (People's Newspaper), 21 September 1941. The headline read: 'Already sent the Jews packing: the strictest racial laws against Jews are Slovak'.

18 **six inches across**: Vrba, *World at War*, part I, p. 2.

18 **daily humiliation and exclusion**: Vrbová, *Trust*, p. 17.

18 **the socialists**: Author correspondence with Robin Vrba.

19 **twenty-five kilograms**: Vrba, *World at War*, part I, p. 12.

19 **follow later**: Vrba, Lanzmann interview, p. 2.

20 **any future resistance**: Vrba, *I Escaped*, p. 4.

20 **stupid instruction**: Vrba, Lanzmann interview, p. 2.

20 **leaving his mother**: Vrba, *World at War*, part I, p. 12.

20 **'green cheese'**: Vrba, *I Escaped*, p. 1.

20 **locksmith**: Author interview with Robin Vrba, 16 November 2020.

21 **'where we got you'**: Vrba, *I Escaped*, p. 1.

21 **'take a taxi'**: Ibid., p. 5.


## Chapter 2: Five Hundred Reichsmarks

23 **a box of matches**: Vrba, *I Escaped*, p. 6.

26 **'dirty, bloody Yid'**: Ibid., p. 17.

26 **huge barracks**: Ibid., p. 19.

27 **pea soup and potatoes**: Frieder, *Souls*, p. 105.

27 **'bloody troublemaker'**: Vrba, *I Escaped*, p. 20.

28 **pathetically inadequate**: Ibid., p. 21.


## Chapter 3: Deported

31 **'dead duck'**: Vrba, *I Escaped*, p. 34.

32 **hit one of the adults**: Vrba, *World at War*, part I, p. 20.

33 **three years earlier**: Vrba, *I Escaped*, p. 45.

34 **you never knew how long**: Vrba, *World at War*, part I, p. 28.

34 **'you bastards'**: Vrba, *I Escaped*, p. 45.

35 **'between fifteen and fifty'**: *Vrba–Wetzler Report*, p. 21.

36 **a long trek ahead of them**: Ibid.


## Chapter 4: Majdanek

38 **'Anything in the pocket?'**: Vrba, *I Escaped*, p. 52.

40 **scavenging for food**: Ibid., p. 56.

41 **raised their arms in greeting**: Ibid., p. 60.

42 **up to a thousand people**: State Museum at Majdanek, 'Living Conditions', https://www.majdanek.eu/en/history/living_conditions/13

42 **empty their bowels**: Cesarani, *Final Solution*, p. 659.

43 **shot the rabbi dead**: *Vrba–Wetzler Report*, p. 23.

43 **artificial fat of the worst quality**: Ibid., p. 22.

43 **enormous physical effort**: Fackler, 'Music', p. 2.

44  **'in a few days'**: Vrba, *I Escaped*, p. 64.
45  **'Go there and you'll die'**: Ibid., p. 65.
45  **'You'll be sorry'**: Ibid., p. 67.
47  **primitive wooden shacks**: *Vrba–Wetzler Report*, p. 24.

## Chapter 5: We Were Slaves

51  **highly disciplined dogs**: *The World at War*, Thames TV, Episode 20, 'Genocide', 27 March 1974.
51  **secret was being guarded**: Vrba, *I Escaped*, p. 73.
52  **skin and bone**: Vrba, Testimony, p. 1333.
52  **special stipple**: Wetzler, 1963 testimony, p. 26.
52  **fainted**: *Vrba–Wetzler Report*, p. 1.
52  **'old number'**: Langbein, *People*, pp. 70–1.
53  **star formed from two triangles**: Długoborski and Piper, *Auschwitz*, vol. II, p. 17.
53  **non-men**: Levi, *If This Is a Man*, p. 103.
53  **feign vitality**: Langbein, *People*, p. 120.
54  **'They're today's harvest'**: Vrba, *I Escaped*, p. 81.
54  **'they knew too much'**: Ibid., p. 82.
54  **first transfer was to Buna**: *Vrba–Wetzler Report*, p. 24.
55  **'worked in your lives'**: Vrba, *I Escaped*, p. 112.
55  **the higher storeys**: Ibid., p. 94.
55  **one hundred prisoners**: Vrba, Testimony, p. 1247.
55  **other for the *Kapo***: Vrba, *I Escaped*, p. 113.
56  **nothing to eat or drink**: Vrba, Testimony, p. 1248.
56  **metal pipe**: Rothman, USHMM interview, p. 14.
57  **exhaustion and starvation**: Greif, *We Wept*, p. 368 n. 24.
57  **either potato or turnip**: *Vrba–Wetzler Report*, p. 24.
57  **There were no spoons**: Vrba, Testimony, p. 1248.
58  **the tainted source**: Ibid.
58  **'attempted to escape'**: *Vrba–Wetzler Report*, p. 24.
58  **'Run for the hat'**: Vrba, Testimony, p. 1250.
58  **on their shoulders**: Ibid., p. 1252.
59  **five and ten corpses**: Ibid., p. 1251.
59  **five on the other**: Ibid., pp. 1330–1.
59  **how many were alive**: Ibid., p. 1332.
60  **in the women's camp**: Ibid., p. 1253.
60  **rapidly became swollen**: Itzkowitz, USHMM interview, p. 14.

61   **mastered the pain**: *Vrba–Wetzler Report*, p. 25.

61   **to paint them**: Ibid.

61   **shot several Jews for sabotage**: Ibid.

62   **twenty yards back**: Vrba, Testimony, pp. 1254–5.

62   **run for his life**: Vrba, *I Escaped*, p. 130.

63   **500 lives a month**: Bacon, *Saving Lives*, p. 47.

63   **recover from typhus**: Langbein, *People*, p. 204.

63   **They would kill the sick**: Bacon, *Saving Lives*, p. 47.

63   **a total of 746 prisoners**: Ibid.

64   **'What the hell are you doing here?'**: Vrba, *I Escaped*, p. 131.

64   **'You're lucky, boys'**: Ibid., p. 132.

64   **Their hair was shorn**: *Vrba–Wetzler Report*, p. 2.


## Chapter 6: Kanada


67   **six large barracks**: Greif, *We Wept*, p. 338 n. 45.

67   **more than two acres**: Vrba, Testimony, p. 1306.

68   **any hidden valuables**: Greif, *We Wept*, p. 338.

68   **running a careful finger**: Hart, *I Am Alive*, pp. 69–70.

68   **twenty women**: Vrba, Lanzmann interview, p. 28.

69   **eat and survive**: Vrba, *I Escaped*, p. 43.

70   **vague suspicions**: Ibid., p. 145.

71   **swallowed up by the night**: Levi, *If This Is a Man*, p. 21.


## Chapter 7: The Final Solution


74   **sent to Auschwitz-Birkenau**: Cesarani, *Final Solution*, p. 522.

74   **haphazard integration**: Ibid., p. 520.

75   **some 600,000 Jews**: Wachsmann, *KL*, p. 292.

76   **It acquired that function gradually**: Author interview with Nikolaus Wachsmann, 28 May 2021.

76   **not discreet enough**: Długoborski and Piper, *Auschwitz*, vol. III, p. 121.

76   **burning corpses**: Ibid.

76   **served as a morgue**: Ibid., p. 122.

77   **great bellowing sound**: Ibid., p. 129.

77   **tatty clothes**: Ibid.

77   **'You will now bathe'**: Ibid., p. 131.

79 **violent banging and knocking**: Müller, *Eyewitness*, pp. 31–9.

79 **motorbike was doing laps**: Długoborski and Piper, *Auschwitz*, vol. III, p. 131.

79 **heavy coughing**: Wachsmann, *KL*, p. 301.

80 **some 60,000 people**: Ibid., p. 304.

80 **Auschwitz was 190,000**: Ibid., p. 307.

80 **trees and shrubs**: Auschwitz-Birkenau State Museum, 'The Death of Silent Witnesses to History', http://www.auschwitz.org/en/museum/news/the-death-of-silent-witnesses-to-history,466.html

81 **according to their combustibility**: Müller, *Eyewitness*, p. 98.

## Chapter 8: Big Business

84 **back to the Old Reich**: Cesarani, *Final Solution*, p. 653.

84 **went hand in hand**: Doležal, *Cesty Božím*, pp. 111–12.

85 **regular Auschwitz fashion**: Vogel, USHMM interview, p. 5.

85 **troops on the front line**: Holocaust Education & Archive Research Team, 'The Holocaust: Economic Exploitation'.

85 **fountain pens**: Cesarani, *Final Solution*, p. 653.

86 **with his boot**: Vrba, Lanzmann interview, p. 26.

86 **twenty suitcases**: Cesarani, *Final Solution*, p. 654.

86 **German factories**: *Der Spiegel*, 'Schaeffler'.

86 **delayed-action bombs**: Nyiszli, *Auschwitz*, p. 87.

86 **women's hair**: Ryback, 'Evidence of Evil', p. 68.

87 **'dentists' paused to vomit**: Wachsmann, *KL*, p. 314.

87 **six tons of dental gold**: Cesarani, *Final Solution*, p. 654.

87 **326 million Reichsmarks**: The estimate was made by SS Grüppenführer and Lieutenant General of Police Odilo Globocnik. His figures show a haul of RM100 million, with a note that material equivalent to 50 per cent of the assets listed was still warehoused and yet to be processed, which would add an additional RM50 million to the yield. There were a further 1,000 wagons of textiles valued at RM13 million. That would take the total to RM163 million. But Globocnik was insistent that he had relied on 'minimum values' and his tally was very likely to be an underestimate: 'the total value is most likely twice as much', he wrote. In which case, RM326 million is probably a more reliable figure. See: Office of United States Chief of Counsel for Prosecution of Axis Criminality, *Nazi Conspiracy and Aggression*, Supplement A, p. 752.

88 **splash of water**: Testimony of Kitty Hart in Langbein, *People*, p. 140.

89 **champagne traded for quinine**: Testimony of Manca Svalbova and Krystyna Zywulska in ibid., p. 141.

89 **printed on one side**: Vrba, Testimony, pp. 1438–9.

89 **an act of spite**: Vrba, Lanzmann interview, p. 27.

90 **ripped out the page**: Vrba, 'Preparations', p. 246.

92 **Wiegleb**: A sharp-eyed editor of the Danish translation of Vrba's memoirs noted that the SS man Vrba had referred to as Wiglep, and who was named as Wyklef in the Vrba–Wetzler Report was, 'presumably, Richard Wiegleb, who is known from a number of other lists of SS personnel in Auschwitz'. Vrba, *Flugten fra Auschwitz*, p. 162 n. 3. See also Strzelecki, 'Plunder', p. 251.

92 **forty-seven blows**: Vrba, *I Escaped*, pp. 152–4; Vrba, Testimony, pp. 1436–7.

93 **The operation**: An Auschwitz record shows that the surgeon was a Polish prisoner, one Dr Władysław Dering. He would become the subject of a notorious London libel trial in 1964, after Leon Uris named him in his bestselling novel *Exodus* as one of several doctors who had performed medical experiments in Auschwitz. Among the many charges against Dering, which the court found true in substance, was the claim that he had undertaken operations in the camp without sufficient anaesthesia. The case was dramatised by Uris in the novel *QB VII*. APMAB, Ibid.

93 **a week later**: The 'book of the block' for Block 4, which is one of the few to survive, is held at the Auschwitz Museum. It records that Walter Rosenberg was released from the infirmary on 5 October 1942 and deemed fit for work. APMAB, Labour Department, vol. 7, pp. 77–8.

93 **hospital registrar**: Vrba, *I Escaped*, p. 163.

## Chapter 9: The Ramp

94 **ten months straight**: Vrba, Lanzmann interview, p. 7.

95 **a dozen miles away**: Wachsmann, *KL*, p. 309.

95 *Rollkommando*: Vrba, Testimony, p. 1269.

95 **told to get ready**: Vrba, Lanzmann interview, p. 16.

95 **twelve or thirteen minutes**: Author interview with Teresa Wontor-Cichy, 6 August 2021.

95 **fifty cattle trucks**: Vrba, Testimony, p. 1271.

95 **the dining car**: Ibid., p. 1273.

96   **gangster elite**: Vrba, Lanzmann interview, p. 9.

96   **white gloves**: Vrba, Testimony, p. 1274.

96   *Alles raus!*: Ibid., p. 1275.

97   **wolf down its contents**: Vrba, *I Escaped*, p. 166.

97   **Halva and olives**: Vrba, 'Preparations', p. 241.

97   **Ladino**: Vrba, Lanzmann interview, p. 23.

97   **any deviation**: Vrba, Testimony, p. 1284.

98   **the dead from the dying**: Vrba, Lanzmann interview, p. 15.

98   **marched off first**: Vrba, Testimony, p. 1282.

98   **corporal of the sanitation service**: Ibid., p. 1277.

98   **good-looking women**: Ibid., p. 1278.

99   **crook of his walking stick**: Ibid., p. 1277.

99   **the camp's resources**: Wachsmann, *KL*, p. 311.

100   **nervousness and depression**: Wetzler, 1963 testimony, p. 35.

101   **different show**: Vrba, Lanzmann interview, p. 12.

102   **load them** : Vrba, Testimony, pp. 1304–5.

102   **flower beds**: Ibid., p. 1548.

102   **'What is your trade?'**: Długoborski and Piper, *Auschwitz*, vol. III, p. 130.

102   **'Afterwards you won't have to waste time'**: Greif, *We Wept*, p. 228.

102   **'coffee and something to eat'**: Wachsmann, *KL*, p. 318.

102   **shoes of murdered children**: Doležal, *Cesty Božím*, p. 112.

102   **Crematorium II**: Author interview with Teresa Wontor-Cichy, 6 August 2021.

102   **artificial odorant:** Borkin, *I.G. Farben*, p. 123.

103   **'Which gangster said this to you?'**: Vrba, Testimony, p. 1279.

104   **'Silence, everybody!'**: Vrba, *I Escaped*, p. 165.

106   **easier to slaughter lambs**: Vrba, Lanzmann interview, p. 4; Doležal, *Cesty Božím*, p. 109.

## Chapter 10: The Memory Man

107   **'Just leave everything'**: Vrba, *World at War*, part I, p. 40.

108   **beyond the outer perimeters**: Vrba, Testimony, p. 1271; Vrba, *I Escaped*, p. 255.

109   **everything was permissible**: The phrase, a version of which is usually attributed to Dostoevsky, was used by Rudolf Vrba in conversation with Robert Krell. See Krell, *Sounds from Silence*, p. 260.

109 **making a dog of her young son**: Aderet, 'The Mystery of the Jewish Boy Who Was Forced to Be Mengele's "Dog"'.

109 **that prisoner was dying**: Langbein, *People*, p. 97.

109 **it could be eaten raw**: Ibid., p. 98.

109 **around that man's neck**: Vrba, Lanzmann interview, p. 5.

109 **all this murder around him**: Ibid., p. 6.

110 **torture block**: Vrba, Testimony, p. 1316.

110 **justify his own survival**: Vrba, Lanzmann interview, p. 6.

111 **child's memory game**: Vrba to Martin Gilbert, 12 August 1980, FDRPL, Vrba collection, box 2.

111 **between 27400 and 28600**: *Vrba–Wetzler Report*, p. 8.

111 **'civilians'**: Vrba, Lanzmann interview, pp. 6–7; Vrba, Testimony, p. 1529.

112 **He was able to step inside**: Vrba, Testimony, pp. 1475–6.

112 **smooth process of destruction**: Vrba, Lanzmann interview, p. 5.

113 **bodies on board**: Ibid., p. 21.

114 **a mirage**: Ibid.


## Chapter 11: Birkenau


117 **forty-two kilograms:** Vrba, Lanzmann interview, p. 37.

118 **'He's one of us'**: Vrba, *I Escaped*, p. 182.

119 **withstand torture**: Vrba, Lanzmann interview, p. 37.

119 **social democrats or communists**: Vrba, Testimony, p. 1343.

119 **his comrades remembered**: Author correspondence with Robin Vrba.

120 **clear out a horses' stable**: Vrba, Testimony, pp. 1314–15.

120 **six yards wide**: Ibid., p. 1316.

121 **the heads of children**: Ibid., p. 1315.

121 **sing it properly**: Ibid., pp. 1455–6.

121 **festive gifts**: Auschwitz-Birkenau State Museum, 'Christmas Eve in Auschwitz as Recalled by Polish Prisoners', http://www.auschwitz. org/en/museum/news/christmas-eve-in-auschwitz-as-recalled-by-polish-prisoners,47.html

121 **15 January 1943**: Vrba, Testimony, p. 1246.

122 **fifty-one horses**: Information display at Auschwitz-Birkenau State Museum.

122 **with a single blow:** Vrba, *I Escaped*, p. 203.

122 **iron bar:** Ibid., p. 199.

123 **80 per cent of them, Poles**: Kulka, 'Attempts', p. 295.

123 **lived like aristocrats**: Vrba, *I Escaped*, p. 200.

123 **adulterated bread**: Cesarani, *Final Solution*, p. 527.

124 **fellow prisoners were starving**: Vrba, *I Escaped*, p. 201.

124 **queuing politely for the Auschwitz butcher**: Ibid., p. 200.

125 **anti-Nazi mafia**: Vrba, Lanzmann interview, p. 38.

125 **some 400 prisoners**: Ibid., p. 39.

126 **orderly concentration camp**: Ibid., p. 40.

126 **machinery of mass annihilation**: Ibid., p. 43.

## Chapter 12: 'It Has Been Wonderful'

127 **Only recently**: Kulka, 'Attempts', p. 295.

128 **300 or 400 dead bodies**: Vrba, Testimony, p. 1321.

128 **lost three brothers**: Ibid.

129 **a breast pocket**: Langbein, *People*, p. 71.

130 **every new arrival's first stop**: Vrba, Testimony, p. 1357.

130 **forty or fifty yards away**: Ibid., p. 1348.

130 **the whole barracks shaking**: Ibid., pp. 1348–9.

130 **watching the people**: Ibid., pp. 1472–3.

130 **first-hand information**: Deposition by Rudolf Vrba for submission at the trial of Adolf Eichmann, 16 July 1961, FDRPL, Vrba collection, box 10; Gilbert, *Auschwitz*, p. 194.

130 **the chief registrar**: Vrba, *I Escaped*, p. 202.

131 **soiling themselves**: Cesarani, *Final Solution*, p. 528.

131 **defecating in the same bowls**: Ibid., p. 660.

133 **'Ode to Joy'**: Interview with Otto Dov Kulka in Freedland, 'Every One', *Guardian*, 7 March 2014.

133 **Alicia Munk**: In Rudolf's memoir, which tends to use anglicised versions of names, she is 'Alice'. Gerta Vrbová told the author that her name was, in fact, Alicia.

134 **the permanent staff**: Vrba, *I Escaped*, p. 216.

135 **'It has been wonderful'**: Ibid., p. 227.

136 **rushing towards the door**: Müller, *Eyewitness*, p. 109.

136 **only sixty-seven**: Gilbert, *Auschwitz*, p. 235 n. 1.

136 **eleven pairs of twins**: *Vrba–Wetzler Report*, p. 16.

## Chapter 13: Escape Was Lunacy

142 **wearing two shirts**: Vrba, Testimony, p. 1441.

142 **came up with the idea**: Kulka, 'Attempts', p. 297.

143 *Three cheers, we've come back again!*: Müller, *Eyewitness*, pp. 55–6.

143 **'if you try to escape'**: Kulka, 'Attempts', p. 298.

143 **aged thirty-three**: Vrba, 'Preparations', p. 243.

144 **brown leather belt**: Vrba, *I Escaped*, p. 248.

145 **a pair of spades**: Ibid., p. 252.

145 **in order of seniority**: Ibid.

145 **inscribed in ink**: Rudolf Vrba gave the belt to the Imperial War Museum, London, in 1999. It is catalogued as item EPH 2722.

146 **escape more feasible**: Kulka, 'Attempts', p. 295.

146 **one Nazi for every fourteen inmates**: Ibid.

146 **public relations stunt**: Vrba to Martin Gilbert, 12 August 1980, FDRPL, Vrba collection, box 2.

146 **the Beskyds**: Vrba, Testimony, p. 1319.

146 **sequence of settlements**: Vrba, 'Preparations', p. 246.

## Chapter 14: Russian Lessons

147 **15 January 1944**: Vrba, 'Preparations', p. 246.

147 **'What a pleasant surprise'**: Ibid., pp. 238–9.

148 **'Hungarian salami'**: Ibid., p. 240.

150 **crash course in escapology**: Vrba, *I Escaped*, p. 238.

150 **'Don't let them take you alive'**: Ibid., p. 239.

150 **network of informers**: Vrba, 'Preparations', p. 245.

150 **would be murdered**: Vrba, Testimony, p. 1345.

151 **'I've killed enough of them'**: Vrba, *I Escaped*, p. 238.

151 **soaked in petrol and then dried**: Ibid., p. 239.

151 **who trusted him**: Author interview with Gerta Vrbová, 15 June 2020.

151 **only two were still alive**: Vrba, 'Preparations', p. 244.

152 **his closest friend**: Vrba, Testimony, p. 1321.

152 **the BIId sector of Birkenau II**: Kulka, 'Five Escapes', p. 205.

152 **yard of Crematorium II**: Vrba, Testimony, pp. 1327–8.

152 **he felt lonely**: Wetzler, 1963 testimony, p. 35.

152 **whispered to each other of escape**: Vrba, Testimony, p. 1321.

152 **through a sewer**: Wetzler, 1963 testimony, p. 35.

153 **'inexperience, personal volatility and impulsiveness'**: Gilbert, *Auschwitz*, p. 193.

153 **hour by hour**: Ibid., p. 194.

153 **they were still free**: Ibid., p. 193.

## Chapter 15: The Hideout

154 **without warning**: Kulka, 'Attempts', p. 296.

155 **Hence: Mexico**: Müller, *Eyewitness*, p. 179.

155 **doubly condemned**: Kulka, 'Attempts', p. 299.

156 **door frames**: Wetzler, 1963 testimony, p. 36.

156 **Alexander 'Sándor' Eisenbach**: Kulka, 'Attempts', p. 299. Some sources give 'Mendel' as Eisenbach's first name, refer to Getzel Abramowicz as 'Gecel', or as 'Abraham Gotzel', and have Mordka Cytryn as 'Mordecai'.

157 **a dozen times**: Vrba, *I Escaped*, p. 262.

158 **searched and interrogated**: Kulka, 'Attempts', p. 299.

159 **gold, another said it was diamonds**: Gold, according to ibid.; diamonds, according to Vrba, *I Escaped*, p. 263.

160 **wholly bogus place of escape**: Kulka, 'Attempts', p. 299.

## Chapter 16: Let My People Go

161 **in their heads**: see the note for 'details large and small' in Chapter 28.

161 **prosperous Dutch gentleman**: Vrba, *I Escaped*, p. 267.

161 **high leather boots**: Vrba, 'Preparations', p. 248.

162 **Bolek and Adamek**: Wetzler, 1963 testimony, p. 37.

162 **his hair was too long**: Ibid.

163 **Lederer stepped out and got on the bicycle**: Kulka, 'Five Escapes', p. 201.

163 **the password 'Inkwell'**: Ibid., p. 202.

165 **comrades for resistance**: Siegfried Lederer saw out the war fighting with anti-Nazi partisans, and lived in Czechoslovakia until his death on 5 April 1972, twenty-eight years to the day after he walked out of Auschwitz. He died in obscurity, unheralded for both his extraordinary escape and his attempt to warn the Jews of Theresienstadt.

165 **'What have we got here?'**: Vrba, *I Escaped*, p. 267.

166  **prisoner have a watch**: Ibid.

167  **a foreman**: Vrba, Testimony, p. 1365.

167  **'You old swine, how are you?'**: Vrba, *I Escaped*, p. 269.

168  **'Here, have a Greek cigarette'**: Ibid.

168  **come in from Athens**: 'On April 1st, 1944, a transport of Greek Jews arrived. 200 of them came to the camp and the rest, approximately 1500, were gassed immediately.' Report of a prisoner who escaped from Auschwitz, 28 July 1944, CZA A314/18.

168  **seven or eight layers**: Vrba, Testimony, p. 1366.

168  **'Bon voyage'**: Wetzler, *Escape*, p. 108.

168  **It was 2 p.m.**: Vrba, Testimony, p. 1368.

168  **the night of the Seder**: Doležal, *Cesty Božím*, p. 109. Vrba told his interviewer that he did not know 7 April 1944 had been Seder night until exactly fifty years later, when he gave a lecture to mark the anniversary of his escape.

# Chapter 17: Underground

169  **martial music**: Wetzler, *Escape*, p. 114.

170  **short distance north-east**: The precise location of the hiding place in BIII, or Mexico, is not clear. In one account, Vrba placed it '300 meters [*sic*] east from Crematorium V' (see Vrba, 'Preparations', p. 246). But given other details in Vrba and Wetzler's testimony, it is likely that that distance was somewhat greater, putting the hideout in the far north-eastern corner of Mexico.

170  **rattled into the ovens**: Vrba, *I Escaped*, p. 274.

170  **Jews from Belgium**: Czech, *Auschwitz Chronicle*, p. 607.

170  **another cheerful ditty**: Wetzler, *Escape*, p. 135.

171  **fierce, tingling pain**: Ibid., p. 144.

171  **the moon was shining**: Wetzler, 1963 testimony, p. 38.

171  **single known case**: According to the Auschwitz Memorial and Museum, there was a small number of attempted escapes by Jewish prisoners between November 1942 and April 1944. The outcome of most of those cases is unknown, but one came to a particularly bleak end: in December 1943, a Jewish agent of the Gestapo succeeded in getting out, only to be shot dead by his escape partner, a Polish prisoner who was, like him, a Gestapo agent.

172  **no snow on the ground**: Wetzler, *Escape*, p. 145.

172  **glistening in the moonlight**: Vrba, Testimony, p. 1370.

172  **each foot in the print**: Ibid.

172  **kind of clothes peg**: Wetzler, 1963 testimony, p. 38.

173  **see the chimneys**: Ibid., p. 39.

173  **oil-refinery flames**: Vrba, Testimony, p. 1374.

173  **never wanted to see this place again**: Vrba, *I Escaped*, p. 278.

173  **marshy terrain**: Vrba, Testimony, p. 1370.

173  **two o'clock in the morning**: Wetzler, 1963 testimony, p. 39.


## Chapter 18: On the Run

174  **notified by teleprinter**: Kárný, 'Report', p. 553.

174  **flat, bureaucratic idiom**: Telegram reproduced in Kulka, 'Five Escapes', p. 205.

175  **identifiably Jewish names**: The August 1938 Second Implementation Ordinance of the Law on Changing First and Family Names also listed ninety-one female names. See Nick, *Personal Names, Hitler and the Holocaust*, p. 65.

176  **social vacuum**: Vrba, 'Preparations', p. 245.

176  **not even talked of their route**: Ibid.

176  **no documents, no map and no compass**: Gilbert, *Auschwitz*, p. 196.

176  **heard the Auschwitz gong**: Wetzler, 1963 testimony, p. 39.

177  **SS men walked close by**: Ibid.

177  **ethnic German settlers**: Vrba, 'Preparations', p. 247.

178  **drink from a stream**: Ibid.

178  **electric lights and watchtowers**: Wetzler, 1963 testimony, p. 39.

178  **chess**: Vrba, *I Escaped*, p. 280.

179  **'Papa, Papa'**: Ibid.

180  **kilo of sugar**: Flaws, *Polish Complicity*, pp. 62–3.

181  **'Praise be the name'**: Vrba, *I Escaped*, p. 285.

181  **shoot 'unidentifiable loiterers'**: Vrba, 'Preparations', p. 247; Gilbert, *Auschwitz*, p. 196.

182  **German *agents provocateurs***: Vrba, 'Preparations', p. 247.

182  **shuttered their windows**: Ibid., p. 248.

182  **half a loaf of bread**: Ibid.

182  **barrage balloons**: Wetzler, 1963 testimony, p. 39.

183  **fat, grey and sullen**: Vrba, *I Escaped*, p. 287.

183  **broken branch or dislodged stone**: Wetzler, 1963 testimony, p. 39.

## Chapter 19: Crossing the Border

184 **German soldiers**: Vrba, 'Preparations', p. 248.

184 **Uniformed Germans**: Wetzler, 1963 testimony, p. 39.

185 **'We've got him!'**: Vrba, *I Escaped*, p. 288.

185 **their overcoats**: Vrba, 'Preparations', p. 248.

186 **past fires**: Wetzler, 1963 testimony, p. 39.

186 **'From Auschwitz'**: Vrba, *I Escaped*, p. 289.

187 **worn hands**: Wetzler, 1963 testimony, p. 40.

187 **little goat-hut**: Vrba, 'Preparations', p. 248.

187 **the blanket she had with her**: Wetzler, 1963 testimony, p. 40.

188 **burst into tears**: Ibid.

188 **carrying a gun**: Vrba, *I Escaped*, p. 291.

189 **'You're from a concentration camp'**: Ibid.

189 **tears in her eyes**: Wetzler, 1963 testimony, p. 40.

189 **new boots**: Ibid., p. 41.

189 **crossing the railway tracks**: Ibid., p. 40.

190 **Tadeusz**: Ibid. Rudolf Vrba's memoir gives no name for their guide to the Slovak border and no indication that he was a veteran of Auschwitz.

190 **'That's Slovakia'**: Vrba, *I Escaped*, p. 293.

190 **house number 264**: Wetzler, 1963 testimony, p. 40.

190 **'The living hillsman from Milówka'**: Wetzler, *Escape*, p. 179.

192 **a Jew or a human being**: Vrba, *I Escaped*, p. 295.

193 **Pollack paled**: Vrba, Lanzmann interview, p. 53.

193 **began to tremble**: Vrba to Martin Gilbert, 30 July 1980, FDRPL, Vrba collection, box 2.

193 **'The rest are dead'**: Vrba, Lanzmann interview, p. 53.

194 **relative of Leo Baeck**: Vrba, 'Preparations', p. 251.

194 **bandages on his feet**: Vrba to Martin Gilbert, 30 July 1980, FDRPL, Vrba collection, box 2.

194 **the railway station**: Vrba, Lanzmann interview, p. 54.

194 **salami, eggs, salad**: Wetzler, *Escape*, p. 192.

194 **act as typist**: Vrba, 'Preparations', p. 251.

## Chapter 20: In Black and White

199 **Krasňanský wangled a permit**: Gilbert, *Auschwitz*, p. 203.

199 **twenty-four hours later**: Vrba, 'Preparations', p. 251.

199 **name and photograph**: Vrba, Lanzmann interview, p. 56.

199    **completely exhausted**: Karmil/Krasňanský, Kulka interview, p. 4.

200    **a thing of wonder**: Krasňanský, 'Declaration', p. 1.

200    **every pore of his skin**: Wetzler, *Escape*, p. 193.

200    **locked**: Vrba, 'Preparations', p. 251; Krasňanský, 'Declaration', p. 1.

200    **two weeks**: Karmil/Krasňanský, Kulka interview, p. 3.

201    **close to his heart**: Vrba, 'Preparations', p. 251.

201    **cross-examination**: Gilbert, *Auschwitz*, p. 203.

201    **looking for inconsistencies**: Wetzler, *Escape*, p. 201.

201    **bureaucrats**: Steiner, Lanzmann interview, pp. 79–81.

202    **fat Jewish lawyers and administrators**: Vrba, Lanzmann interview, p. 59.

202    **debated in a fever**: Fatran, 'Working Group', p. 165.

203    **Why, he wondered**: Vrba, Lanzmann interview, p. 57.

203    **rumours**: *Vrba–Wetzler Report*, foreword by Oskar Krasňanský, n.p.

203    **from the mouths**: Krasňanský, 'Declaration', p. 1.

203    **an architect**: Kulka, 'Five Escapes', p. 207.

206    **TOTAL approximately 1,765,000**: Most scholars tend to rely on the calculation made by Franciszek Piper, former director of the research institute at the Auschwitz Memorial and Museum, who concluded that at least 1.1 million people were murdered at Auschwitz-Birkenau, close to a million of them Jews.

207    **the presence of Neumann**: Neumann, *Im Schatten*, pp. 178–82.

207    **No prophecies, no forecasts**: Vrba, 'Preparations', p. 263.

207    **deemed unfit for inclusion**: Miroslav Kárný is sceptical about this explanation for the absence in the report of any explicit mention of the imminent threat to Hungarian Jewry, noting that the report refers to an apparent rumour about the expected arrival of 'large transports of Greek Jews'. If rumours about one community were included, asks Kárný, why not another? To which an obvious answer is that Fred and Walter had already seen for themselves the arrival of Greek Jews: indeed, they had been the subject of Walter's very last conversation with an SS man in the camp. Krasňanský may well have believed that talk of Greek Jews did not therefore belong in the category of speculation and so could be included, while the danger to Hungary's Jews could not. Further evidence that Fred and Walter warned of Auschwitz preparations for the mass murder of Hungarian Jewry comes in the form of a letter from two Slovak Jewish leaders spelling out precisely that danger. It was sent on 22 May 1944: after Vrba and Wetzler had told their story in Žilina but, crucially, *before* the escape of Mordowicz and Rosin. The information behind that warning could only have

come from Fred and Rudi. Kárný, 'Report', p. 560; Vrba to Randolph
L. Braham, 17 January 1994, FDRPL, Vrba collection, box 1.

208 **secret meeting**: Vrba, 'Preparations', pp. 254–5.

208 **'civilised Germany'**: Ibid., p. 255.

208 **began to shout**: Wetzler, *Escape*, p. 205.

208 **'Judeo-Bolshevik agitators'**: Vrba, 'Preparations', p. 255.

209 **Czech Catholic priest**: Trencsényi, Janowski, Baár, Falina and
Kopeček, *History*, vol. 1, p. 552.

209 **Germanic taint**: Vrba, Testimony, p. 1377.

## Chapter 21: Men of God

210 **'They're passing through Žilina in cattle trucks'**: Vrba, *I Escaped*,
p. 302.

211 **'important' to discuss**: Baron, *Stopping*, p. 181.

211 **Christians of Jewish origin**: Baron, 'Myth', p. 187.

212 **panic in Jewish circles**: Baron, *Stopping*, p. 184.

212 **She felt it was her duty**: Ibid., p. 195.

212 **agonising**: Ibid., p. 191.

212 **total and terrible reality**: Ibid.

213 **the plight of the Jews**: Baron, 'Myth', p. 188.

214 **denying communion**: Baron, *Stopping*, pp. 209–10.

214 **'Hell!'**: Ibid.

## Chapter 22: What Can I Do?

216 **flabbergasted**: Mordowicz, USHMM interview, p. 24.

216 **silent rejoicing**: Ibid., p. 26.

217 **he was furious**: Rosin, Kulka interview, p. 8.

217 **reveal under torture**: Vrba to Martin Gilbert, 30 July 1980, FDRPL,
Vrba collection, box 3.

217 **steep sidewall**: Mordowicz, USHMM interview, p. 29.

217 **bread and two pairs of overalls**: Ibid.

217 **turpentine**: Ibid., p. 32.

217 **whose numbers had increased**: Ibid., p. 28.

218 **found a matchbox**: Kulka, 'Five Escapes', p. 208.

218 **most sincere embrace**: Rosin, Kulka interview, p. 21.

218 **prison visitor**: Zimring, 'Tale', p. 381.

219 **get a haircut, drink in a bar, meet women**: Vrba, *I Escaped*, pp. 305–6.

219 **twenty days**: Vrba to John S. Conway, 2 July 1976, FDRPL, Vrba collection, box 1, p. 4.

220 **police informers**: Ibid., p. 14.

220 **over lunch**: Krasňanský, 'Declaration', p. 3.

221 **Mordowicz began to sweat**: Mordowicz, USHMM interview, p. 50.

221 **wine and Camel cigarettes**: Kulka, 'Five Escapes', p. 210.

222 **only jotting down**: Ibid.

222 **'Monsignor, listen to me'**: Mordowicz, USHMM interview, p. 50.

223 **'all and any means'**: Vrba to John S. Conway, 2 July 1976, FDRPL, Vrba collection, box 1, p. 15.

223 **'You have to do one thing'**: Mordowicz, USHMM interview, p. 51.

223 **in a single day**: 'Death Trains in 1944: The Kassa List'.

## Chapter 23: London Has Been Informed

224 **hand it to the Gestapo**: Interview with Krasňanský, 22 December 1980, in Gilbert, *Auschwitz*, p. 203.

224 **unpaid first secretary**: Kranzler, *Mantello*, p. xxii.

225 **Spanish, French, German and English**: Ibid., p. 91.

225 **four arresting press releases**: Ibid., p. 98.

225 **telegram despatch**: Baron, *Stopping*, p. 18.

226 **mailboxes of the city's newspapers**: Rings, *Advokaten*, p. 144.

226 **none of the four**: Kranzler, *Mantello*, pp. 208–9.

226 **later that same day**: Bogdanor, *Kasztner's Crime*, p. 187.

226 **383 articles**: Fleming, *Auschwitz*, p. 233.

226 **revised down**: Rings, *Advokaten*, pp. 140–6.

226 **more articles appeared about Auschwitz**: Fleming, *Auschwitz*, p. 233.

226 **special masses**: Tibori Szabó, 'Auschwitz Reports', p. 113.

226 **Basel and Schaffhausen**: Zimring, 'Men', p. 81.

226 **correspondent in Geneva**: Daniel T. Brigham, 'Inquiry Confirms Nazi Death Camps', *New York Times*, 3 July 1944.

227 **'shocking'**: Interview with Garrett in Rings, *Advokaten*, p. 144.

228 **'broadcasted immediately'**: Gilbert, *Auschwitz*, p. 233.

228 **in Czech and Slovak**: Records on the broadcasting of London and Moscow radios, Central Archives, Prague, SUA4, URP. Cart. 1170, cited in Kárný, 'Report', p. 559.

228 **'London has been informed'**: Świebocki, *London*, p. 56.

228 *News for Women*: Fleming, *Auschwitz*, Appendix I, line 46.

229 **inmates of Auschwitz heard the BBC**: The episode was recalled by Erich Kulka in conversation with Gerhart Riegner, who discussed it in an April 1995 interview with Martin Gilbert at the World Jewish Congress in Geneva. Baron, *Stopping*, p. 15 n. 32.

229 **flowers, flirtatious notes**: Waller, *Disciples*, p. 136; Baron, *Stopping*, p. 16.

229 **'Could you also?'**: Gilbert, *Auschwitz*, p. 233.

229 **'Seems more in your line'**: Ibid.

229 **'at least 1,500,000'**: Winik, 'Darkness', p. 68.

229 **'a positive contribution'**: FDRPL, Records of the Department of State Relating to the Problems of Relief and Refugees (War Refugee Board), Miscellaneous Documents and Reports re Extermination Camps for Jews in Poland (1), box 69; Baron, *Stopping*, p. 21.

230 **'less Jewish account'**: Kárný, 'Report', p. 563.

230 **last thirteen people**: Ibid., p. 564.

230 **the Auschwitz crematoria**: Kulka, 'Five Escapes', p. 207.

230 **Jacob Rosenheim**: Gilbert, *Auschwitz*, p. 236.

231 **'lives at stake'**: Winik, 'Darkness', p. 67.

231 **'explore it'**: Wyman, *America and the Holocaust*, vol. XII, p. 104; Baron, *Stopping*, p. 20.

231 **a 'diversion' from that effort**: Gilbert, *Auschwitz*, p. 238.

231 **'kill' the idea**: Baron, 'Myth', p. 24.

231 **thirteen hundred 500-pound bombs**: Winik, 'Darkness', p. 69.

232 **No one ever examined those pictures**: Ibid., p. 70.

232 **the gruesome brutality**: Ibid., p. 75.

232 **'participating in this horrible business'**: Ibid., p. 77.

233 **'Now we know exactly what happened'**: Martin Gilbert, 'Could Britain Have Done More to Stop the Horrors of Auschwitz?', *The Times*, 27 January 2005.

233 **found its way to the Foreign Office**: Fleming, *Auschwitz*, p. 235.

233 **'railway line leading from Budapest to Birkenau'**: Gilbert, *Auschwitz*, p. 269.

233 **he had never displayed before**: The judgement is that of Sir Martin Gilbert, official biographer of Churchill. In a 1993 lecture, he declared: 'I have never seen a minute of Churchill's giving that sort of immediate authority to carry out a request.' Gilbert, 'Churchill and the Holocaust', https://winstonchurchill.org/the-life-of-churchill/war-leader/churchill-and-the-holocaust-the-possible-and-impossible/

233 **'invoke me if necessary'**: Fleming, *Auschwitz*, p. 249.

234 **'out of our power'**: Gilbert, *Auschwitz*, p. 285.

234 **'costly and hazardous'**: Ibid.

234 **more apparent than sincere**: This is the case advanced by Michael Fleming in *Auschwitz*, p. 250. He suggests that both Churchill and Eden were anxious above all *to be seen* to be acting to save Jewish lives, including by posterity. Martin Gilbert maintained the opposite view: that Churchill was in earnest in his desire to help Europe's Jews.

234 **by accident**: Gilbert, *Auschwitz*, p. 315. It happened on 13 September 1944 when a US air raid on Monowitz went slightly astray, hitting both Auschwitz I and Birkenau. In the main camp, fifteen SS men and twenty-three Jews were killed; in Birkenau the bombs damaged the railway sidings leading to the crematoria.

234 **would keep looking up at the sky**: Winik, 'Darkness', p. 70.

## Chapter 24: Hungarian Salami

235 **'the most important'**: Vrba, *I Escaped*, p. 293.

235 **led the effort to support**: Braham, 'Hungary', p. 40.

236 **in German**: Tibori Szabó, 'Auschwitz Reports', p. 102.

236 **He did not sleep that night**: Porter, *Kasztner's Train*, p. 134.

236 **headquarters on Sip Street**: Tibori Szabó, 'Auschwitz Reports', p. 103.

236 **two rash young men**: Ibid., p. 104.

236 **spread alarm**: Personal correspondence with Professor Zoltán Tibori Szabó, 1 November 2021.

236 **shaking with rage and grief**: Porter, *Kasztner's Train*, p. 136.

236 **Kasztner said no**: Tibori Szabó, 'Auschwitz Reports', p. 105.

237 **$45,000**: Fatran, 'Working Group', p. 171.

237 **for its own reasons**: Braham: 'Hungary', p. 40.

237 **'Europa plan'**: Fatran, 'Working Group', pp. 173–7.

237 **'reliable' man**: Braham, 'Hungary', p. 43.

238 **began on 5 April 1944**: Reichenthal, 'Reappraisal', p. 223.

238 **wear the yellow star**: Braham, *Politics of Genocide*, vol. 2, p. 939.

238 **he would not have to wear a yellow star**: Reichenthal, 'Reappraisal', p. 223.

238 **agreement reached by the rail networks**: Ibid., p. 224.

238 **knew his secret**: Rudolf Vrba believed that. See the epilogue to *I Escaped*, p. 320. The claim is also made in Tschuy, *Dangerous Diplomacy*, pp. 83–4, and echoed by Tibori Szabó, 'Auschwitz Reports', p. 105.

But documentary evidence that Kasztner showed Eichmann the report is elusive.

239 **stop playing games**: Reichenthal, 'Reappraisal', p. 225.

239 **sparing of several hundred Jews**: Kasztner, *Kasztner Report*, p. 158.

239 **nearly 200 'prominent' Jews**: Braham, *Politics of Genocide*, vol. 2, p. 955.

239 **$1,684,000 in cash and valuables**: Bogdanor, *Kasztner's Crime*, p. 191.

239 **'a second Warsaw'**: Kasztner, *Kasztner Report*, p. 129.

240 **500 such cards**: Reichenthal, 'Reappraisal', p. 234.

240 **Eichmann himself**: Kasztner, *Kasztner Report*, p. 145.

240 **bogus evidence**: Reichenthal, 'Reappraisal', p. 235.

241 **over the course of fifty-six days**: Stark, *Hungarian Jews*, pp. 21–31. There is conflicting information regarding the number of Jews deported from Hungary. According to a report by Gendarme Colonel László Ferenczy, the number was 434,351. Reich plenipotentiary in Hungary Edmund Veesenmayer cited 437,402.

241 **nuggets of news**: Vrba, 'Preparations', p. 256.

241 **grasped the urgency**: Kulka interview with Wetzler, 1964, YVA P.25/21/3, p. 5.

241 **200 Slovak crowns**: Vrba, 'Preparations', p. 261.

241 **Office for Prevention of Venereal Diseases**: Ibid., p. 256.

242 **Gerti Jurkovič**: Vrbová, *Trust*, pp. 79–80.

242 **serious, brilliant, imaginative boy**: Author interview with Gerta Vrbová, 30 June 2020.

242 **'very bad experiences'**: Vrbová, *Trust*, p. 85.

243 **perhaps for ever**: Ibid., p. 86.

243 **body stiffened**: Ibid., p. 88.

243 **'What have you been doing?'**: Author interview with Gerta Vrbová, 15 June 2020.

243 **'Where did you think I was?'**: Ibid.

244 **to trust anyone**: Vrbová, *Trust*, p. 92.

244 **tasked Török**: Interview with József Eliás in Baron, *Stopping*, p. 187.

244 **staring right at them**: Interview with Sándor Török in ibid., p. 205.

245 **make his way to the palace**: Ibid., p. 70.

245 **compassion and shame**: Ibid., p. 208.

245 **accepted all of it as the truth**: Ibid.

245 **'These gangsters!'**: The words were spoken by Horthy to the commander-in-chief of the provincial police, Gábor Faragho. Quoted in ibid., p. 74.

245  **report back to Rome**: Kulka, 'Five Escapes', p. 215. Kulka suggests it was the confirmation secured in the monastery that led the Vatican to act.

245  **telegram to Admiral Horthy**: Fleming, *Auschwitz*, p. 233.

246  **make his plea public**: Kulka, 'Five Escapes', p. 215.

246  **a message to Horthy**: Baron, *Stopping*, p. 75.

246  **'The deportation of the Jews of Budapest must cease!'**: Braham, *Politics of Genocide*, vol. 2, p. 873.

246  **12,421 Jews**: 'Death Trains in 1944: The Kassa List'.

246  **provincial gendarmes**: Baron, *Stopping*, pp. 80–2.

247  **departure on 10 July**: Braham, *Politics of Genocide*, vol. 2, p. 879.

247  **1,200 tons of bombs**: Baron, *Stopping*, p. 84. For more on the change of heart by the Hungarian leadership, see Gilbert, *Auschwitz*, p. 266.

247  **'all measures necessary'**: Office of Strategic Services report cited in ibid., p. 94.

247  **provincial police**: Ibid., p. 105.

247  **self-preservation**: Ibid., p. 42.

247  **'It cannot be tolerated!'**: Lévai (ed.), *Eichmann in Hungary*, p. 126.

## Chapter 25: A Wedding with Guns

252  **'this is the Gestapo'**: Vrbová, *Trust*, p. 94.

252  **'Escape on your own'**: Ibid., p. 115.

252  **fight until victory**: Vrba, 'Affidavit'.

253  **weeping with happiness**: Vrba, *I Escaped*, p. 315.

253  **sabotage of Nazi supply lines**: Vrba, 'Affidavit', p. 5.

253  **membership of the communist party**: Ibid., p. 6; Vrba, Testimony, p. 1518.

254  **his one, unshakeable affiliation**: Vrba, Testimony, p. 1386.

254  **rather than Bratislava**: Vrbová, *Betrayed*, p. 31.

254  **digs, the library and the lab**: Vrba, 'Affidavit', p. 7.

255  **'There he is'**: Vrba, *I Escaped*, p. 307.

255  **she was not wrong**: Ibid., p. 308.

255  **suicide by deportation**: Author interview with Robin Vrba, 16 November 2020.

256  **something missing**: Vrbová, *Betrayed*, p. 71.

256  **did not love him enough**: Ibid., p. 49.

256  **trace of violence**: Ibid., p. 71.

256 **join up with Wetzler**: Ibid., p. 59.

256 **only good thing Hitler did**: Ibid., p. 66.

256 **Kampa**: Ibid., p. 69.

257 **duty to marry her**: Author interview with Robin Vrba, 16 November 2020.

257 **dark navy rather than white**: Vrbová, *Betrayed*, p. 74.

257 **Gerta found it distressing**: Ibid., p. 75.

257 **vodka**: Ibid., p. 87.

258 **she said nothing**: Ibid., p. 88.

258 **'hid all the scissors'**: Ibid.

258 **already learned to be paranoid**: Author interview with Gerta Vrbová, 15 June 2020.

258 **Helen of Troy**: Vrbová, *Betrayed*, p. 105.

258 **fluffy blonde hair**: Ibid.

259 **the eggs had vanished**: Ibid., p. 114.

259 **multiple affairs**: Author interview with Robin Vrba, 30 November 2020.

260 **who had denounced her**: Vrbová, *Betrayed*, pp. 122–4.

260 **revenge**: Author interview with Gerta Vrbová, 28 July 2020.

260 **'not able to guarantee a socialist education'**: Vrba, 'Affidavit', p. 13.

260 **nothing of the kind**: Author interview with Gerta Vrbová, 15 September 2020.

260 **they were badly damaged**: Vrbová, *Betrayed*, p. 12.

260 **'wished to help'**: Vrba, 'Affidavit', p. 7.

261 **dangerous to refuse**: Ibid., p. 9.

262 **nobody mentioned the fate of the Jews**: Vrba, *I Escaped*, pp. xi–xii.

262 **Czech national anthem**: Kulka, *Landscapes*, p. 110.

262 **made Rudi suspicious**: Author interview with Gerta Vrbová, 15 June 2020.

## Chapter 26: A New Nation, a New England

263 **could understand it**: Klein, 'Confronting', p. 278.

265 **six-hour hike**: Vrbová, *Betrayed*, pp. 192–203.

265 **clustered in tribes**: Author interview with Gerta Vrbová, 30 June 2020.

265 **he had already defended himself**: Ibid.

266 **August 1952**: Segev, *The Seventh Million*, p. 257.

266 **'darkest chapter in the whole dark story'**: Arendt, *Eichmann in Jerusalem*, p. 117.

267 **reward for his silence**: Porter, *Kasztner's Train*, p. 331.

267 **travelled to Nuremberg in 1947**: Reichenthal, 'Reappraisal', p. 241.

267 **'food packages'**: Ibid., p. 249.

267 **fear of exposure**: Ibid., p. 251.

267 **'They need someone to blame'**: Porter, *Kasztner's Train*, p. 343.

268 **'collaboration in the fullest sense of the word'**: Harry Gilroy, 'Quisling Charge Stirs All Israel', *New York Times*, 3 July 1955.

268 **reborn in Tel Aviv**: Porter, *Kasztner's Train*, p. 313.

268 **the blood draining from him**: Ibid., pp. 354–5.

268 **'Judge not thy neighbour'**: Justice Shimon Agranat was quoting the ancient scholar Rabbi Hillel. See Klein, *Pietà*, p. 130.

270 **thrown into liquid air**: Vrba, Bachelard and Krawczynski, 'Interrelationship'.

270 **'the animals were killed by decapitation'**: Ibid.

270 **dropping them into liquid nitrogen**: Vrba, 'Utilization'.

271 **'They told me you were dead'**: Author interview with Robin Vrba, 30 November 2020.

271 **trying to have him deported**: Ibid.

271 **distinguished matrimonial lawyers**: Obituary for Blanche Lucas, *The Times*, 21 July 1994.

271 **total legal custody**: Author interview with Gerta Vrbová, 28 July 2020.

271 **limited visitation rights**: Vrba to Zuza Vrbová, 14 June 1983, p. 13, shared with the author by Gerta Vrbová.

272 **Jews were clever people**: Vrba, *I Escaped*, pp. xvi–xvii.

273 **he would never forgive**: Author interview with Gerta Vrbová, 30 June 2020.

273 **screaming at him**: Arendt, *Eichmann in Jerusalem*, p. 124.

273 **sworn deposition at the Israeli embassy**: Linn, *Escaping Auschwitz*, p. 13.

273 **'bartered their own lives'**: Rudolf Vrba, Letter to the Editor, *Observer*, 22 September 1963.

273 **access to Helena and Zuza**: Vrbová, *Betrayed*, p. 254.

## Chapter 27: Canada

276 **he looked adorable**: Author interview with Robin Vrba, 16 November 2020.

276 **monthly rent**: Vrba to Zuza Vrbová, 14 February 1983, p. 9, shared with the author by Gerta Vrbová.

276 **run the household**: Author interview with Gerta Vrbová, 15 September 2020.

277 **one half of 1 per cent**: Author interview with Chris Friedrichs, 13 December 2020.

277 **invaded this striking man's privacy**: Author interview with Robin Vrba, 16 November 2020.

277 **'What are you, a *Muselmann*?'**: Author interview with Robin Vrba, 30 November 2020.

277 **'that one would be a *Kapo* . . .'**: Author interview with Robin Vrba, 16 November 2020.

278 **The astonished waiter**: Vrba to Martin Gilbert, 12 August 1980, FDRPL, Vrba collection, box 2.

278 **young and simple**: Author interview with Robin Vrba, 16 November 2020.

278 **It had weakened him**: Author interview with Robin Vrba, 30 November 2020.

279 **German prosecuting authorities**: Vrba, *I Escaped*, p. xviii.

279 **cooled down a bit**: Vrba to Benno Müller-Hill, 25 June 1997, FDRPL, Vrba collection, box 4.

280 **'the pennies they paid'**: Vrba, *I Escaped*, p. 128n.

280 **statute of limitations**: Fulbrook, *Legacies*, p. 301. See also Kuretsidis-Haider, 'Österreichische KZ-Prozesse: Eine Übersicht', p. 20.

281 **'the Kanada König of the SS'**: 'Life Sentence Given to Ex-Nazi for Killing Gypsies at Auschwitz', *JTA Daily News Bulletin*, 29 January 1991.

281 **Kühnemann was adamant:** Recalling the trial, Rudi told an interviewer, 'The judge warned him that he did not have to testify, but he said he had nothing to hide.' Doležal, *Cesty Božím*, p. 112.

281 **trial was stopped**: Vrba, *I Escaped*, p. 140n.

282 **commanding a unit**: Purves, *War Criminals*, F.2.b.

282 **solving Slovakia's 'Jewish problem'**: FDRPL, Vrba collection, box 12; see also 'Kirschbaum, Slovakia's Aide of Eichmann in Toronto, Is Charged with War Crimes', *Canadian Jewish News*, 27 July 1962, p. 1.

283 **'I escaped and warned the world'**: Vrba, Testimony, p. 1542.

284 **'otherwise they were gassed'**: Ibid., p. 1528.

284 **a dull student**: Ibid., p. 1461.

284 **'artistic' licence**: Ibid., pp. 1389–90.

284 **was pronounced guilty**: That 1985 verdict was overturned on a legal technicality, prompting a second trial in 1988 where Zündel was again found guilty. He was finally acquitted by the Supreme Court of Canada in 1992 on the grounds that the false-news law was an unreasonable limit on free expression. See https://scc-csc.lexum.com/scc-csc/scc-csc/en/item/904/index.do

## Chapter 28: I Know a Way Out

286 **'without panic'**: Lanzmann, *Shoah: An Oral History*, p. 123.

286 **'I know another way out'**: Author interview with Robin Vrba, 2 February 2021.

286 **sent money**: Author interview with Robin Vrba, 22 October 2021. Getting money to communist Czechoslovakia was not easy. It had to go via Switzerland and be converted into so-called Tuzex vouchers.

287 **details large and small**: One of the starkest disputes between Vrba and Wetzler was over the question of whether they had escaped Auschwitz with documentary evidence. In his novel-cum-memoir, Wetzler had the pair attempting to take out two tubes stuffed with lists of transports, sketches, even a label from a Zyklon B canister, evidence gathered with the help of several other prisoners. In this telling, one of the tubes was lost during the skirmish at Porąbka. Vrba was adamant that nothing of the sort had happened or could have happened. Any prisoner found in possession of a pencil or paper would have been punished for conspiracy. See Vrba, Testimony, p. 1353.

Both accounts have their defenders, but one crucial fact counts heavily towards Vrba's version. When he spoke after the war of his role in taking down the Vrba–Wetzler Report, Oskar Krasňanský went out of his way to praise the escapees' 'wonderful memory'. He made no mention of any documentary proof. Had the two men presented documentation, Krasňanský would surely have mentioned it, not least in his foreword to the Auschwitz Report. But he never did. The episode with the New York waiter, recounted on p. 278, suggests Krasňanský was hardly overstating Vrba's powers of recall.

287 **deserved the credit**: In Wetzler's telling, the idea of an escape to inform the world originated with the communist-led underground inside Auschwitz. Fred was tasked with gathering as much information as he could, which he was to deliver into the hands of the mainly communist resistance fighters in Slovakia. As for his choice of escape partner, Wetzler held that that too was a decision taken by the underground leadership: they picked Walter for the mission, doubtless because they thought it required a brave fellow Slovak whom Fred knew and trusted.

Rudi rejected that account entirely. He insisted that, on the contrary, the decision to escape and tell the world was a mutual one taken by him and Fred, the last two male survivors of Trnava, and by nobody else. To be sure, he conceded in his memoir, 'Long before I thought of the idea, the underground had been concentrating on the problem of exposing Auschwitz, revealing its secrets and warning Europe's Jews of what deportation really meant,' waiting only for 'the right plan, the right moment and the right man' (Vrba, *I Escaped*, p. 256).

But when Walter had approached them with his scheme for escape, the resistance leaders had rejected him for all the reasons Szmulewski had given at the time: that he was too impetuous, too inexperienced and too young to be believed. As a result, and although they got crucial help from individuals – whether from *Sonderkommando* Filip Müller giving them the details of the gassing process, or the two Polish Jews, Adamek and Bolek, who covered over the hideout once Fred and Walter had dropped inside – this, Walter was adamant, was their own initiative. That was especially true of the specific mission of warning the Jews of Hungary which, Rudi stressed, was 'dictated exclusively by my conscience', and certainly not by 'a mythical committee in Auschwitz or elsewhere' (Vrba, 'Preparations', pp. 255–6). Proof that there was no plan for Fred and Rudi to hand their information to communist partisans in Slovakia comes from the fact that the pair did no such thing.

As for why Fred might tell such a different story to Rudi's, one explanation swiftly suggested itself. Rudi composed his memoir in Britain; he spoke to historians and others once settled in Canada. He could speak freely. Fred Wetzler was in a Soviet satellite state where expression was sharply restricted. Rudi had seen for himself that it was not politic in the socialist republic of Czechoslovakia to mention that the Nazis' prime victims had been Jews. Besides, Rudolf Vrba had defected to the west, turning himself instantly into a non-person in his home country: it would have been risky for Fred to have praised him as an equal comrade in an act of anti-fascist valour. Was it perhaps safer in communist Czechoslovakia to cast a group of communist prisoners as the heroes of the story? (See also, Zimring, 'Men', p. 43.)

287 **'I feel sad'**: Wetzler letter to Kárný, 19 November 1984, NA, Kárný collection, box 10; Zimring, 'Men', p. 43.

287 **'like a suitcase'**: Rosin, Kulka interview, p. 8.

287 **names of its authors; 'two young escapees'; 'two Slovak escapees'**: Linn, 'Rudolf Vrba', p. 179.

288 **rooted for it**: Author interview with Robin Vrba, 16 November 2020.

288 **the unlikely envoy**: Zimring, 'Men', p. 76.

288 **Rudi's fellow escapee**: Rosin was a member of Hashomer Hatza'ir. See 'Ernie Meyer: A Sole Survivor', *Jerusalem Post*, 30 April 1992.

288 **betrayed by Kasztner**: See, for example, the case of the Zionist paratroopers, in Bogdanor, *Kasztner's Crime*, pp. 159–76.

289 **to salvage a remnant**: Eric M. Breindel, 'A Survivor of the Holocaust', *Harvard Crimson*, 2 May 1974, FDRPL, Vrba collection, box 1.

289 **the most unbending anti-Zionists**: Perhaps the definitive example of an anti-Zionist treatment of the Kasztner case is the play *Perdition* (1987) by Jim Allen.

289 **'participated in treason and conspiracy'**: Vrba to Joan Campion, 8 August 1979, FDRPL, Vrba collection, box 1. Vrba was referring to Gisi Fleischmann.

289 **'somewhat anti-Semitic'**: Breindel, 'A Survivor of the Holocaust'.

290 **Several historians**: Gila Fatran and four other historians, 'For the Sake of Historical Justice', Letter to the Editor, *Yediot Aharonot*, 2 June 1998; Yehoshua Jelinek, 'A Hero Who Has Become Controversial', Letter to the Editor, *Haaretz*, 21 June 1998.

290 **'a genuine hero of the Holocaust'**: Yehuda Bauer, Letter to the Editor, *Jewish Journal*, 28 October 2004.

290 **'arrogant'**: Author interview with Gerta Vrbová, 15 September 2020. Vrbová met Bauer and was shocked that the historian used that word to describe her former husband.

290 **'deep hatred'**: Yehuda Bauer to John S. Conway, 23 May 1985, FDRPL, Vrba collection, box 1.

291 *The World at War*: *The World at War*, Episode 20, 'Genocide', Thames TV, 27 March 1974.

291 **'Should I cry?'**: Vrba, Lanzmann interview, p. 100.

291 **'survivor clichés'**: Vrba to Rex Bloomstein, 20 July 1981, FDRPL, Vrba collection, box 1.

292 **had betrayed him**: Krell, *Sounds from Silence*, p. 256.

292 **'accusations and rage'**: Author interview with Robert Krell, 31 December 2020.

292 **dapper in leather coat**: Krell, *Sounds from Silence*, p. 266.

292 **'an actor reciting my lines'**: Klein, 'Confronting', p. 279.

292 **monologue that brooked no interruption**: Ibid.

293 **travelled by train**: Author interview with Robin Vrba, 22 October 2021.

293 **three-hour lunch**: Author interview with Robert Krell, 31 December 2020.

293 **French wine and Scotch whisky**: In a letter to his daughter, Rudi listed those aspects of modern life at which he still marvelled. Vrba to Zuza Vrbová, 18 June 1982, p. 1, shared with the author by Gerta Vrbová.

293 **the firstborn son of a chief**: Author interview with Robin Vrba, 16 November 2020.

## Chapter 29: Flowers of Emptiness

295 **'a rich and foolish American uncle'**: Vrba to Helena Vrbová, 13 February 1980, p. 3, shared with the author by Gerta Vrbová.

295 **in closer touch with Gillian**: Author interview with Gerta Vrbová, 12 July 2020.

295 **'considered worthy'**: Vrba to Zuza Vrbová, 14 February 1983, p. 18, shared with the author by Gerta Vrbová.

295 **male chauvinist**: Author interview with Gerta Vrbová, 15 September 2020.

295 **to study malaria**: Vrbová, *Betrayed*, pp. 11–12.

295 **'6th sense'**: Vrba to Helena Vrbová, 13 February 1980, p. 4, shared with the author by Gerta Vrbová.

296 **'in a box'**: Author interview with Robin Vrba, 16 November 2020.

296 **'stable rock bottom'**: Helena Vrbová to Zuza Vrbová, May 1982, shared with the author by Gerta Vrbová.

296 **a third of which had been drunk**: Vrba to Dr Peter F. Heywood, Papua New Guinea Institute of Medical Research, 9 March 1984, shared with the author by Gerta Vrbová.

296 **'Even strong things break'**: The last note from Helena Vrbová,

written on 9 May 1982, shared with the author by Gerta Vrbová.

296   **'the worst experience in my life'**: Vrba to Zuza Vrbová, 28 April 1983, p. 5, shared with the author by Gerta Vrbová.

296   **'crying fits'**: Vrba to Zuza Vrbová, 14 February 1983, p. 38, shared with the author by Gerta Vrbová.

296   **'What did I do wrong?'**: Ibid., p. 10.

297   **'I had a premonition'**: Vrba to Zuza Vrbová, 18 July 1982, p. 7, shared with the author by Gerta Vrbová.

297   **'pathological sentimentality'**: Vrba to Zuza Vrbová, 28 January 1984, p. 2, shared with the author by Gerta Vrbová.

298   **'Did she have any particular enemies in PNG?'**: Vrba to Dr Peter F. Heywood, Papua New Guinea Institute of Medical Research, 9 March 1984, shared with the author by Gerta Vrbová.

298   **'why she committed suicide'**: Author interview with Robin Vrba, 30 November 2020.

298   **lose his sawmill**: Ibid.

299   **'ricocheting bullet'**: Vrba to Zuza Vrbová, 28 April 1983, p. 6, shared with the author by Gerta Vrbová.

299   **Helena's 'soul'**: Vrba to Zuza Vrbová, 18 July 1982, pp. 6–8, shared with the author by Gerta Vrbová.

## Chapter 30: Too Many to Count

301   **'bitter, drunk and forgotten'**: Linn, 'Rudolf Vrba', p. 181.

301   **never let on that Laník was him**: The story was told to the author by Dr Martin Korčok, Head of the Sered' Holocaust Museum, Slovakia, 7 August 2021.

302   **never once met a prisoner**: Vrba, 'Preparations', p. 241.

302   **'Hungarian Jews were aware'**: Bauer, *Rethinking*, p. 236.

302   **'We had no inkling'**: Elie Wiesel, 'A Survivor Remembers Other Survivors of "*Shoah*"', *New York Times*, 3 November 1985, section 2, p. 1.

302   **'evoke any fear'**: Langbein, *People*, p. 117.

302   **'Nobody cared enough to tell us: Don't go'**: Nicholls, *Christian Antisemitism*, p. 236.

302   **'complete annihilation of the Jews'**: Gilbert, *Auschwitz*, p. 20.

303   **'so-called "settlers"'**: Ibid., p. 94.

303   **informed by its apostolic nuncio**: Porter, *Kasztner's Train*, pp. 182–3.

304  **'scepticism and disbelief . . . and even prejudice'**: Gilbert, *Auschwitz*, p. viii.

304  **'laying it on too thick'**: Ibid., p. 99.

304  **'usual Jewish exaggeration'**: Kárný, 'Report', p. 562.

304  **'these wailing Jews'**: Gilbert, *Auschwitz*, p. 312.

304  **the 'unknown destination'**: Martin Gilbert, 'Could Britain have done more to stop the horrors of Auschwitz?', *The Times*, 27 January 2005.

304  **new research**: See the work of Richard Breitman, Barbara Rogers and Michael Fleming among others.

304  **mentioning the murder of Jews**: Fleming, 'Elusiveness Narrative', pp. 3–4.

305  **margins of its propaganda effort**: Ibid., pp. 8–9.

305  **thirty-five of them**: Ibid.

306  **'Nothing else made sense'**: Klein, 'Confronting', pp. 260–1.

307  **waiting for him**: Ibid., p. 263.

307  **not one had believed him**: Ibid., p. 274.

307  **'the most natural escape'**: Ibid., p. 275.

308  **'you are going to your death'**: Mordowicz, USHMM interview, p. 73.

308  **repressed that knowledge**: Klein, 'Confronting', p. 274.

308  **'I did not say that he is lying'**: Karski, Lanzmann interview.

309  **'not make any military sense'**: Van Pelt, 'Veil', p. 121.

309  **'I didn't know'**: Claude Lanzmann quotes Aron at the start of his film on Jan Karski, *The Karski Report*, 2010.

309  **small talk with waiters**: Klein, 'Confronting', p. 278.

310  **'Robert, I need to talk to you'**: Krell, *Sounds from Silence*, p. 261.

311  **'on a cellular level'**: Gerta Vrbová, obituary of Zuza, *AJR Journal*, p. 15.

311  **'in denial'**: Author interview with Robin Vrba, 22 October 2021.

312  **'Should you not be satisfied'**: Klein, 'Confronting', pp. 274–5.

312  **Battersea Power Station**: Email to the author from Richard Bestic, son of Alan Bestic, 24 August 2020.

313  **something of 'the SS' about him**: Krell, *Sounds from Silence*, p. 263.

313  **'the Gestapo has finally gotten to me'**: Linn, 'Rudolf Vrba', p. 209.

313  **'lucky number'**: Vrba to Zuza Vrbová, 23 April 1998, p. 1, shared with the author by Gerta Vrbová.

313  **he told his daughter**: Zuza Vrbová died in 2013, aged fifty-nine.

# Bibliography

Aderet, Ofer, 'The Mystery of the Jewish Boy Who Was Forced to Be Mengele's "Dog"', *Haaretz*, 8 April 2021

Arendt, Hannah, *Eichmann in Jerusalem: A Report on the Banality of Evil*, revised and enlarged edition (London and New York: Penguin, 1994)

Bacon, Ewa K., *Saving Lives in Auschwitz: The Prisoners' Hospital in Buna-Monowitz* (West Lafayette, IN: Purdue University Press, 2017)

Baron, Frank, 'The "Myth" and Reality of Rescue from the Holocaust: The Karski–Koestler and Vrba–Wetzler Reports', *Yearbook of the Research Centre for German and Austrian Exile Studies* 2 (2000): 171–208

——, *Stopping the Trains to Auschwitz, Budapest, 1944* (Lawrence, KS: University of Kansas, 2020)

Bauer, Yehuda, *Rethinking the Holocaust* (New Haven, CT, and London: Yale University Press, 2001)

Bogdanor, Paul, *Kasztner's Crime* (London and New York: Routledge, 2017)

Borkin, Joseph, *The Crime and Punishment of I.G. Farben* (New York: Free Press, 1978)

Braham, Randolph L., *The Politics of Genocide: The Holocaust in Hungary*, 2 vols (New York: Columbia University Press, 1981)

——, 'Hungary: The Controversial Chapter of the Holocaust', in Randolph L. Braham and William J. Vanden Heuvel (eds), *The Auschwitz Reports and the Holocaust in Hungary* (New York: Rosenthal Institute for Holocaust Studies Graduate Center/City University of New York, 2011)

——, and Attila Pók (eds), *The Holocaust in Hungary: Fifty Years Later* (New York: Rosenthal Institute for Holocaust Studies, Graduate Center of the City University of New York/Columbia University Press, 1997)

——, and Bela Vago (eds), *The Holocaust in Hungary Forty Years Later* (Boulder, CO: Social Science Monographs, 1985)

——, and William J. Vanden Heuvel (eds), *The Auschwitz Reports and the Holocaust in Hungary* (New York: Rosenthal Institute for Holocaust Studies Graduate Center/City University of New York, 2011)

Brigham, Daniel T., 'Inquiry Confirms Nazi Death Camps', *New York Times*, 3 July 1944

Cesarani, David, *Final Solution: The Fate of the Jews, 1933–1949* (London: Macmillan, 2015)

Chandrinos, Iason, and Anna Maria Droumpouki, 'The German Occupation and the Holocaust in Greece: A Survey', in Giorgos Antoniou and A. Dirk Moses (eds), *The Holocaust in Greece* (Cambridge, Cambridge University Press, 2018)

Czech, Danuta, *Auschwitz Chronicle 1939–1945* (New York: Henry Holt, 1990)

'Death Trains in 1944: The Kassa List', http://degob.org/tables/kassa.html

'Did German Firm Schaeffler Process Hair from Auschwitz?', *Der Spiegel*, 2 March 2009, https://www.spiegel.de/international/germany/claim-by-polish-researcher-did-german-firm-schaeffler-process-hair-from-auschwitz-a-610786.html

Długoborski, Wacław, and Franciszek Piper (eds), *Auschwitz, 1940–1945: Central Issues in the History of the Camp*, trans. William R. Brand, 5 vols (Oświęcim: Auschwitz-Birkenau State Museum, 2000)

Doležal, Miloš, *Cesty Božím (Ne)Časem* (Prague: Karmelitánské nakladatelství, 2003)

Fackler, Guido, 'Music in Concentration Camps 1933–1945', *Music & Politics* I, no. 1 (Winter 2007)

Fatran, Gila, 'The "Working Group"', *Holocaust and Genocide Studies* 8, no. 2 (Fall 1994): 164–201

Flaws, Jacob, 'Bystanders, Blackmailers, and Perpetrators: Polish Complicity During the Holocaust' (MA thesis, Iowa State University, 2011)

Fleming, Michael, *Auschwitz, the Allies and Censorship of the Holocaust* (Cambridge and New York: Cambridge University Press, 2014)

———, 'The Reassertion of the Elusiveness Narrative: Auschwitz and Holocaust Knowledge', *Holocaust Studies* 26, no. 10 (2020): 1–21

Freedland, Jonathan, '"Every One of Us Had His or Her Own Story of Survival. But We Never Talked About It"', *Guardian*, 7 March 2014

Frieder, Emanuel, *To Deliver Their Souls: The Struggle of a Young Rabbi During the Holocaust* (New York: Holocaust Library, 1990)

Fulbrook, Mary, *Reckonings: Legacies of Nazi Persecution and the Quest for Justice* (Oxford: Oxford University Press, 2018)

Gilbert, Martin, *Auschwitz and the Allies* (London: Michael Joseph, 1981)

———, 'Churchill and the Holocaust: The Possible and Impossible', Lecture at US Holocaust Memorial Museum, Washington, 8 November 1993, https://winstonchurchill.org/the-life-of-churchill/war-leader/churchill-and-the-holocaust-the-possible-and-impossible/

Greif, Gideon, *We Wept Without Tears: Testimonies of the Jewish Sonderkommando from Auschwitz* (New Haven, CT, and London: Yale University Press, 2005)

Hart, Kitty, *I Am Alive*, revised edition (London: Corgi, 1974)

Holocaust Education & Archive Research Team, 'The Holocaust: Economic Exploitation', http://www.holocaustresearchproject.org/economics/index.html

Itzkowitz, Sam, Interview, United States Holocaust Memorial Museum, RG-50.050.0006, 3 March 1991

Karmil/Krasňanský, Interview by Erich Kulka, Oral History Division, Institute of Contemporary Jewry, Hebrew University of Jerusalem, no. 65 (1), 1964

Kárný, Miroslav, 'The Vrba and Wetzler Report', in Israel Gutman and Michael Berenbaum (eds), *Anatomy of the Auschwitz Death Camp* (Bloomington and Indianapolis, IN: Indiana University Press. Published in association with the United States Holocaust Memorial Museum, Washington, DC, 1994)

Karski, Jan, Interview by Claude Lanzmann for *Shoah*, United States Holocaust Memorial Museum, no. RG-60.5006, 1978

Kasztner, Rezső, *The Kasztner Report: The Report of the Budapest Jewish Rescue Committee, 1942–1945*, ed. László Karsai and Judit Molnár (Jerusalem: Yad Vashem, International Institute for Holocaust Research, 2013)

Klein, Georg, 'Confronting the Holocaust: An Eyewitness Account', in Randolph L. Braham and William J. Vanden Heuvel (eds), *The Auschwitz Reports and the Holocaust in Hungary* (New York: Rosenthal Institute for Holocaust Studies Graduate Center/City University of New York, 2011)

———, *Pietà*, trans. Theodore and Ingrid Friedmann (Cambridge, MA, and London: MIT Press, 1992)

Kranzler, David, *The Man Who Stopped the Trains to Auschwitz: George Mantello, El Salvador, and Switzerland's Finest Hour* (Syracuse, NY: Syracuse University Press, 2000)

Krasňanský, Oskar, 'Declaration Made Under Oath by Oscar Karmiel, Formerly Krasňanský, at the Israeli Consulate in Cologne, February 15, 1961': FDRPL, Vrba collection, box 16

Krell, Robert, *Sounds from Silence: Reflections of a Child Holocaust Survivor, Psychiatrist and Teacher* (Amsterdam: Amsterdam Publishers, 2021)

Kubátová, Hana, and Jan Láníček, *The Jew in Czech and Slovak Imagination, 1938–89: Antisemitism, the Holocaust, and Zionism* (Leiden and Boston, MA: Brill, 2018)

Kulka, Erich, 'Five Escapes from Auschwitz', in Yuri Suhl (ed.), *They Fought Back: The Story of the Jewish Resistance in Nazi Europe* (New York: Crown, 1967)

————, 'Attempts by Jewish Escapees to Stop Mass Extermination', *Jewish Social Studies* 47, no. 3/4 (Summer/Fall 1985): 295–306

Kulka, Otto Dov, *Landscapes of the Metropolis of Death: Reflections on Memory and Imagination*, trans. Ralph Mandel (London: Allen Lane, 2013)

Kuretsidis-Haider, Claudia 'Österreichische KZ-Prozesse: Eine Übersicht', *Juztiz und Erinnerung* 12, December 2006: 14–21

Langbein, Hermann, *People in Auschwitz* (Chapel Hill, NC, and London: University of North Carolina Press, 2004)

Lanzmann, Claude, *Shoah: An Oral History of the Holocaust: The Complete Text of the Film* (New York: Pantheon, 1985)

Lévai, Jenö (ed.), *Eichmann in Hungary: Documents* (Budapest: Pannonia Press, 1961)

Levi, Primo, *If This Is a Man*, trans. Stuart Woolf (London: Orion Press, 1959)

Linn, Ruth, 'Naked Victims, Dressed-up Memory: The Escape from Auschwitz and the Israeli Historiography', *Israel Studies Bulletin* 16, no. 2 (Spring 2001): 21–5

————, *Escaping Auschwitz: A Culture of Forgetting* (Ithaca, NY, and London: Cornell University Press, 2004)

————, 'Rudolf Vrba and the Auschwitz Reports: Conflicting Historical Interpretations', in Randolph L. Braham and William J. Vanden Heuvel (eds), *The Auschwitz Reports and the Holocaust in Hungary* (New York: Rosenthal Institute for Holocaust Studies Graduate Center/City University of New York, 2011)

Mordowicz, Czesław, Interview, United States Holocaust Memorial Museum, no. RG-50.030.0354, 1995–6

Müller, Filip, *Eyewitness Auschwitz: Three Years in the Gas Chambers* (New York: Stein & Day, 1979)

Neumann, Oskar, *Im Schatten des Todes: Ein Tatsachenbericht vom Schicksalskampf des slovakischen Judentums* (Tel Aviv: Olamenu, 1956)

Nicholls, William, *Christian Anti-Semitism: History of Hate*, new edition (Lanham, MD: Aronson, 1995)

Nick, I. M., *Personal Names, Hitler, and the Holocaust: A Socio-Onomastic Study of Genocide and Nazi Germany* (Lanham, MD: Lexington Books, 2019)

Nyiszli, Miklos, *Auschwitz: A Doctor's Eyewitness Account*, trans. Tibére Kremer and Richard Seaver (New York: Arcade, 2001)

Office of United States Chief of Counsel for Prosecution of Axis Criminality, *Nazi Conspiracy and Aggression* (a Collection of Documentary Evidence Prepared by the American and British Prosecuting Staffs), Supplement A (Washington, DC: United States Government Printing Office, 1947)

———, *Nazi Conspiracy and Aggression: Opinion and Judgment* (Washington, DC: United States Government Printing Office, 1947)

Porter, Anna, *Kasztner's Train: The True Story of an Unknown Hero of the Holocaust* (London: Constable, 2008)

Purves, Grant, *War Criminals: The Deschênes Commission* (Ottawa: Library of Parliament, Research Branch, 1998

Reichenthal, Eli, 'The Kasztner Affair: A Reappraisal', in Randolph L. Braham and William J. Vanden Heuvel (eds), *The Auschwitz Reports and the Holocaust in Hungary* (New York: Rosenthal Institute for Holocaust Studies Graduate Center/City University of New York, 2011)

Report of a prisoner who escaped from Auschwitz, 28 July 1944, CZA A314/18

Rings, Werner, *Advokaten des Feindes: Das Abenteuer der politischen Neutralität* (Vienna and Düsseldorf: Econ-Verlag, 1966)

Rosin, Arnošt, Interview with Erich Kulka, YVA P.25/22, 1965–6

Rothman, Marty, Interview, United States Holocaust Memorial Museum, no. RG-50.477.1255, 30 January 1986

Ryback, Timothy W., 'Evidence of Evil', *New Yorker*, 15 November 1993

Segev, Tom, *The Seventh Million: The Israelis and the Holocaust* (New York: Hill & Wang, 1993)

Spira, Karen, 'Memories of Youth: Slovak Jewish Holocaust Survivors and the Nováky Labor Camp' (MA thesis, Brandeis University, 2011)

Stark, Tamás, *Hungarian Jews During the Holocaust and After the Second World War, 1939–1949* (New York: Eastern European Monographs, Columbia University Press, 2000)

State Museum at Majdanek, https://www.majdanek.eu/en

Steiner, Andre, Interview by Claude Lanzmann for *Shoah*, United States Holocaust Memorial Museum, no. RG-60.5010, 1978

Strzelecki, Andrzej, 'The Plunder of Victims and Their Corpses', in Yisrael Gutman and Michael Berenbaum (eds), *Anatomy of the Auschwitz Death Camp* (Bloomington and Indianapolis, IN: Indiana University Press. Published in association with the United States Holocaust Memorial Museum, Washington, DC, 1994)

Świebocki, Henryk, *London Has Been Informed: Reports by Auschwitz Escapees* (Oświęcim: Auschwitz-Birkenau State Museum, 1997)

Tibori Szabó, Zoltán, 'The Auschwitz Reports: Who Got Them and When?' in Randolph L. Braham and William J. Vanden Heuvel (eds), *The Auschwitz Reports and the Holocaust in Hungary* (New York: Rosenthal Institute for Holocaust Studies Graduate Center/City University of New York, 2011)

Trencsényi, Balázs, Maciej Janowski, Monika Baár, Maria Falina and Michal

Kopeček, *A History of Modern Political Thought in East Central Europe* (Oxford: Oxford University Press, 2016)

Tschuy, Theo, *Dangerous Diplomacy: The Story of Carl Lutz, Rescuer of 62,000 Hungarian Jews* (Grand Rapids, MI, and Cambridge: William B. Eerdmans, 2000)

Van Pelt, Robert Jan, 'When the Veil Was Rent in Twain: Auschwitz, the Auschwitz Protocols, and the Shoah Testimony of Rudolf Vrba', in Randolph L. Braham and William J. Vanden Heuvel (eds), *The Auschwitz Reports and the Holocaust in Hungary* (New York: Rosenthal Institute for Holocaust Studies Graduate Center/City University of New York, 2011)

Vogel, Michael, Interview, United States Holocaust Memorial Museum, no. RG-50.030.0240, 14 July 1989

Vrba, Rudolf, 'A Source of Ammonia and Changes of Protein Structure in the Rat Brain During Physical Exertion', *Nature* 176 (1955): 117–18

———, 'Utilization of Glucose Carbon in Vivo in the Mouse', *Nature* 202 (1964): 247–9

———, 'Affidavit in Application for Naturalisation as a British Citizen, 10 January 1967', 1967

———, Interview for *The World at War*, United States Holocaust Memorial Museum, no. RG-50.148.0013, 1972

———, Interview by Claude Lanzmann for *Shoah*, United States Holocaust Memorial Museum, no. RG-60.5016, 1978

———, Testimony in Ontario District Court, Between Her Majesty the Queen and Ernst Zündel; before the Honourable Judge H. R. Locke and a Jury; Appearances, P. Griffiths for the Crown, D. Christie for the Accused; [in] the Courthouse, 361 University Ave., Toronto, Ontario, 7 January 1985

———, 'The Preparations for the Holocaust in Hungary: An Eyewitness Account', in Randolph L. Braham and Attila Pók (eds), *The Holocaust in Hungary: Fifty Years Later* (New York: Rosenthal Institute for Holocaust Studies, Graduate Center of the City University of New York/Columbia University Press, 1997)

———, *Flugten fra Auschwitz* (Copenhagen: People'sPress, 2016)

———, H. S. Bachelard and J. Krawczynski, 'Interrelationship between Glucose Utilization of Brain and Heart', *Nature* 197 (1963): 869–70

———, with Alan Bestic, *I Escaped from Auschwitz: The Shocking True Story of the World War II Hero Who Escaped the Nazis and Helped Save Over 200,000 Jews*, ed. Nikola Zimring and Robin Vrba (New York: Racehorse, 2020)

Vrba–Wetzler Report, FDRPL, Records of the War Refugee Board, box

7, folder: 'German Extermination Camps', http://www.fdrlibrary.marist. edu/_resources/images/hol/holo0522.pdf

Vrbová, Gerta, *Trust and Deceit: A Tale of Survival in Slovakia and Hungary, 1939–1945* (London: Vallentine Mitchell, 2006)

——, *Betrayed Generation: Shattered Hopes and Disillusion in Post-War Czechoslovakia* (Cambridge: Zuza Books, 2010)

——, Caroline Hilton and Peter Hilton, 'Zuza Jackson (née Vrbová), Born Prague 3 May 1954, Died Cambridge 17 September 2013', *AJR Journal*, 14, no. 4 (April 2014): 15

Wachsmann, Nikolaus, *KL: A History of the Nazi Concentration Camps* (London: Little, Brown, 2015)

Waller, Douglas C., *Disciples* (New York: Simon & Schuster, 2015)

Wetzler, Alfréd, 'Testimony of Alfréd Wetzler, 30 November 1963', APMAB, Collection of Testimonies, vol. 40, 1963, 24–49

——, *Escape from Hell: The True Story of the Auschwitz Protocol*, trans. Péter Várnai (New York: Berghahn Books, 2007)

Winik, Jay, *1944: FDR and the Year That Changed History* (New York: Simon & Schuster, 2015)

——, 'Darkness at Noon: FDR and the Holocaust', *World Affairs* 178, no. 4 (Winter 2016): 61–77

Wyman, David S. (ed.), *America and the Holocaust: A Thirteen-Volume Set Documenting the Editor's Book, The Abandonment of the Jews* (New York: Garland, 1991)

Zimring, Nikola, 'The Men Who Knew Too Much: Reflections on the Historiography of Rudolf Vrba and Alfréd Wetzler's Escape from Auschwitz-Birkenau and Their Attempt to Warn the World' (MA thesis, Tel Aviv University, 2018)

——, 'A Tale of Darkness: The Story of the Mordowicz–Rosin Report', in Rudolf Vrba, with Alan Bestic, *I Escaped from Auschwitz: The Shocking True Story of the World War II Hero Who Escaped the Nazis and Helped Save Over 200,000 Jews*, ed. Nikola Zimring and Robin Vrba (New York: Racehorse, 2020)

# Index

# Index